The Production of Subjectivity

Historical Materialism Book Series

The Historical Materialism Book Series is a major publishing initiative of the radical left. The capitalist crisis of the twenty-first century has been met by a resurgence of interest in critical Marxist theory. At the same time, the publishing institutions committed to Marxism have contracted markedly since the high point of the 1970s. The Historical Materialism Book Series is dedicated to addressing this situation by making available important works of Marxist theory. The aim of the series is to publish important theoretical contributions as the basis for vigorous intellectual debate and exchange on the left.

The peer-reviewed series publishes original monographs, translated texts, and reprints of classics across the bounds of academic disciplinary agendas and across the divisions of the left. The series is particularly concerned to encourage the internationalization of Marxist debate and aims to translate significant studies from beyond the English-speaking world.

For a full list of titles in the Historical Materialism Book Series available in paperback from Haymarket Books, visit: www.haymarketbooks.org/series_collections/1-historical-materialism.

The Production of Subjectivity

Marx and Philosophy

Jason Read

Haymarket Books
Chicago, IL

First published in 2022 by Brill Academic Publishers, The Netherlands
© 2022 Koninklijke Brill NV, Leiden, The Netherlands

Published in paperback in 2023 by
Haymarket Books
P.O. Box 180165
Chicago, IL 60618
773-583-7884
www.haymarketbooks.org

ISBN: 978-1-64259-922-0

Distributed to the trade in the US through Consortium Book Sales and
Distribution (www.cbsd.com) and internationally through Ingram
Publisher Services International (www.ingramcontent.com).

This book was published with the generous support of Lannan
Foundation, Wallace Action Fund, and the Marguerite Casey Foundation.

Special discounts are available for bulk purchases by organizations and
institutions. Please call 773-583-7884 or email info@haymarketbooks.org
for more information.

Cover art and design by David Mabb. Cover art is a detail of *Construct
70, J.H. Dearle for Morris & Co. Iris, / Stepanova, Optical*, paint on paper
(2019).

Printed in the United States.

Library of Congress Cataloging-in-Publication data is available.

Contents

PART 3
Between Marx and Spinoza: Philosophy and Ideology

PART 4
Returns of Philosophical Anthropology: New Subjections/New Transformations

Acknowledgements

A collection of essays spanning nearly twenty years owes more debts than it can possibly repay, but I would like to thank the following people for inviting me to present, and reading, or commenting on the essays collected here: Ted Stolze, Philip Armstrong, Yutaka Nagahara, Katja Diefenbach, Hasana Sharp, Jason Smith, Warren Montag, Sjoerd van Tunien, Daniel Smith, Filippo Del Lucchese, Constanin Boundas, Panagiotis Sortiris, Jeremy Gilbert, Timothy Murphy, Bojana Cvejic, Cindy Zeiher, Dhruv Jain, and Fredric Jameson.

I would like to thank Joelle Glidden for help with editing and formatting the essays, and for being a supportive reader.

Finally, I would like to thank the editorial board at Historical Materialism for their work in bringing this, and many other texts, to light.

Earlier versions of the chapters of this book were published as follows:

Chapter 1 'Primitive Accumulation: The Aleatory Foundation of Capitalism', was previously published in *Rethinking Marxism*, 14, 2 (2002): 24–50.

Chapter 2, 'The Present as Pre-History: Adorno and Balibar on the Transformation of Labor' was previously published in *International Studies in Philosophy* 37, 2 (2005): 49–65.

Chapter 3, 'The Althusser Effect: Philosophy, History, and Temporality' was previously published in *Borderlands e-journal* 4, 2 (2005).

Chapter 4, 'To Think the New in the Absence of its Conditions: Althusser and Negri on the Philosophy of Primitive Accumulation' was previously published in *Encountering Althusser*: *Politics and Materialism in Contemporary Radical Thought*, edited by Katja Diegenbach et al. (New York: Continuum, 2013): 261–72.

Chapter 5, 'A Universal History of Contingency: Deleuze and Guattari on the History of Capitalism' was previously published in *Borderlands e-journal*, 2, 3 (2003).

Chapter 6, 'The Age of Cynicism: Deleuze and Guattari on the Political Logic of Contemporary Capitalism' was previously published in *Deleuze and Politics*, edited by Ian Buchanan and Nick Thoburn (Edinburgh: Edinburgh University, 2008): 139–59.

Chapter 7, 'The Fetish is Always Actual, Revolution is Always Virtual: Marx and Deleuze' was previously published in *Deleuze Studies: Deleuze and Marx*, edited by Dhruv Jain, Volume 3, 2 (2009): 78–101.

Chapter 8, "The Affective Economy: Producing and Consuming Affects in Deleuze and Guattari" was previously published in *Deleuze and the Passions*, Edited by Ceciel Meiborg and Sjoerd van Tunien (New York: Punctum, 2016): 103–24

Chapter 9, 'Beyond Enslavement and Subjection: Deviations from Deleuze and Guattari' is an expanded version of a paper presented at the Deleuze and Foucault Conference, Purdue University, 2015.

Chapter 10, 'The *Potentia* of Living Labor: Negri's Practice of Philosophy' was previously published in *The Philosophy of Antonio Negri, Volume Two: Revolution in Theory*, edited by Timothy Murphy and Abdul-Karim Mustapha (London: Pluto, 2007), 28–51.

Chapter 11, 'The Order and Connection of Ideas: Theoretical Practice in Macherey's Turn to Spinoza' was previously published in *Rethinking Marxism* 19, 4 (2007): 517–37.

Chapter 12, 'Desire is Man's Very Essence: Spinoza and Hegel as Philosophers of Transindividuality' was previously published in *Hegel after Spinoza: Critical Essays*, edited by Hasana Sharp and Jason Smith (New York: Continuum, 2012): 42–60.

Chapter 13, 'The Order and Connection of Ideology is the same as the Order and Connection of Exploitation: Or, Towards a Bestiary of the Capitalist Imagination', *Philosophy Today* (Spring 2015): 175–89.

Chapter 14, 'Conscienta sive Ideologica: On the Spontaneity of ideology' is an expanded version of a paper presented at the Althusser Conference, Duke University, December 2016.

Chapter 15, 'A Genealogy of Homo-Economicus: Foucault, Neoliberalism, and the Production of Subjectivity', *A Foucault for the 21st Century: Governmentality, Biopolitics and Discipline in the New Millennium*, edited by Sam Binkley and Jorge Capetillo (Newcastle: Cambridge Scholars Press, 2009): 2–15.

Chapter 16, 'Abstract Materialism: Alfred Sohn-Rethel and the Task of Materialist Philosophy' is an expanded version of a paper originally presented at the Rethinking Marxism conference in 2009.

Chapter 17, 'The Production of Subjectivity: From Transindividuality to the Common' was previously published in *New Formations: A Journal of Culture/Theory/Politics*, 70 (2010): 113–31.

Chapter 18, 'Man is a Werewolf to Man: *Capital* and the Limits of Political Anthropology' was previously published in a special issue of *Continental Thought and Theory* dedicated to 150 Years of Capital, Volume One, Issue 4, 2017.

Chapter 19, 'The "Other Scene" of Political Anthropology: Between Transindividuality and Equaliberty' was originally published in *Balibar and the Citizen Subject*, edited by Warren Montag and Hanan Elsayed (Edinburgh: Edinburg University Press 2017), 111–31.

Chapter 20, 'Anthropocene and Anthropogenesis: Philosophical Anthropology and the Ends of Man' was originally published in a special issue of the *South Atlantic Quarterly* on Autonomism in the Anthropocene, edited by Bruce Braun and Sarah Nelson, 116, 2 (April 2017): 257–73.

Introduction

Marxist philosophy is by definition a strange and perhaps even oxymoronic project. This is not just because any such endeavour necessarily ignores the Eleventh Thesis on Feuerbach, which drew a sharp divide between interpreting and changing the world, a claim often understood as Marx's parting words on philosophy, but also because unlike other philosophical specialisations, say in Plato, Kant or Hegel, the task of Marxist philosophy necessarily exceeds exegesis. This is in part because, as Étienne Balibar writes, Marx's philosophy is both constantly falling short of and going beyond philosophy: 'falling short' in that the philosophical statements that characterise Marx's later writings often appear as fragments in a larger political and historical analysis, but also going beyond in that Marx often subjects philosophy itself to a critical examination of its pretensions, situating philosophy within a history that exceeds it.[1] Marx goes beyond philosophy by revealing philosophy's own limitations; its failure to not only transform the world but to even comprehend it, and comprehend itself. If Marxist philosophy is to be anything other than an oxymoron it must constantly address both the limitations of Marx's philosophical project while being aware of the limitations of philosophy itself as a discipline that seeks to interpret the world. The confrontation of these two limitations often produces the need for invention, to create new ways of doing and engaging philosophy. This brings us to the second reason as to why Marxist philosophy is something other than an exegesis of the central texts. At the centre of Marx's philosophy is the critique of not just political economy as a way of knowing the world but the capitalist mode of production itself, an object that is by Marx's own definition not only historical, as everything is, but dramatically so, caught in a process of constant transformation. For this reason a Marxist philosophy most necessarily invent new ways to make sense of transformations and mutations of capitalism. Despite the image of Marxist philosophy as a dogmatic enterprise that can only cite the same official sources in order to arrive at the same official doctrine, Marxist philosophy must necessarily reinvent and re-examine its own presuppositions in order to stay abreast of the 'constant revolutionising' nature of the history of capitalism. Or, to cite Louis Althusser, 'Marxist theory can fall behind history, and even behind itself, if it ever believes that it has arrived'.[2]

---

1 Balibar 2017, p. 4.
2 Althusser 1990a, p. 230.

The essays collected here trace a particular path of invention that can be broadly encapsulated by the phrase 'the production of subjectivity'. The production of subjectivity has to be understood in both senses of the genitive, as how subjectivity is produced, by the relations of production, ideology, and so on, but also as how subjectivity is productive, including producing effects that exceed the production and reproduction of capital.[3] In its initial conception 'the production of subjectivity' can be understood to be indebted not only to Althusser, whose reconceptualisation of ideology had at its basis the recognition that capital, like any mode of production, must reproduce itself as a social relation, as subjectivity, in order to reproduce itself, but to a broader engagement with poststructuralist thinkers such as Michel Foucault, Gilles Deleuze, and Félix Guattari. Lest this appear as a (fairly) recent trend, limited to the intersection between French philosophy and Marxism, the essays in this collection also demonstrate that the 'production of subjectivity', the way in which capital, as every mode of production, produces individuals encompasses the Frankfurt School in the form of Theodor Adorno and Alfred Sohn-Rethel as well as Italian Marxist thinkers often grouped together under the heading of autonomist such as Antonio Negri, Paolo Virno, and Maurizio Lazzarato. Moreover, just as every philosopher creates his or her predecessors, making possible new understandings of what came before, the production of subjectivity makes possible a reexamination of not only of Marx's texts, but his philosophical predecessors, most notably Hegel and Spinoza. The latter's rejection of mankind as a 'kingdom within a kingdom' makes it possible to examine the way in which desire, knowledge, and imagination, the constitutive elements of subjectivity, are assembled.

That Hegel is an important precursor to Marx's thought is acknowledged by nearly everyone, starting with Marx himself who referred to his debt and critical distance in nearly every text from the 1844 manuscripts to *Capital*. Spinoza is perhaps more surprising, or would be if there had not been for at least the last half century a growing literature from Althusser to such contemporary thinkers as Frédéric Lordon and Yves Citton, who have argued not so much for the influence of Spinoza on Marx, but for their points of overlap and connection. Of course a full genealogy of the Marx-Spinoza relation could be extended back to Plekhanov and Labriola, but such a genealogy is beyond the scope of this project. More to the point, I argue that the contemporary turn to Spinoza, despite all of the differences and deviations, converges around the production of subjectivity, as Spinoza's account of the historical formation of

---

3   On this point see Read 2003, and, more recently, Mezzadra 2018.

desire and imagination converges with Marx's emphasis on the historical transformation of production. Or, put more simply, Spinoza and Marx can both be
understood as theorists of the production of subjectivity. It is thus no accident
that this turn starts in the 1960s, with texts by Alexandre Matheron and Louis
Althusser, with arguments about the immanence of subjectivity to history. A
theoretical shift that begins just as the relation between subjectivity and capitalism is going through a massive restructuring that is often summed up by such
phrases as neoliberalism, real subsumption, or, more optimistically, late capitalism. Which is to add, last but not least, that the production of subjectivity
must be oriented not just towards philosophy, but also towards an understanding of and an intervention in contemporary capitalism. The essays collected
here examine colonialism, neoliberalism, the anthropocene, and contemporary forms of surveillance and exploitation. The production of subjectivity is
not just a new interpretation of the world, but also an understanding of how it
is changing in order to change it differently.

The essays collected here are organised in four sections. The first, 'Becoming
Contingent: Philosophy, Violence, History' is framed around the final chapters
of *Capital* dedicated to 'So-Called Primitive Accumulation'. The point is not to
read this chapter as a history of capitalism as much as it is to conceptualise
capital and history from the perspective of primitive accumulation. Doing so
not only underscores the violence at the heart of capitalism, but also its fundamental contingency. Recognising the contingency of capitalism as a social relation underscores the extent to which its reproduction must be perpetually reinforced. The first essay in this section, 'Primitive Accumulation: The Aleatory
Foundation of Capitalism' takes a broad view of the different attempts by Louis
Althusser, Antonio Negri, and Gilles Deleuze and Félix Guattari to read primitive accumulation as not just an account of the history of capitalism, one that
stresses the violence and overdetermination of the history of capitalism, but as
a philosophical concept that articulates the relationship between violence and
order, between contingency and necessity. Reading *Capital* backwards, starting with primitive accumulation rather than commodity fetishism, produces a
different understanding not only of capitalism, but of the production of subjectivity and historical change. The final essay in this section, 'To Think the
New in the Absence of its Conditions: Althusser and Negri on the Philosophy of
Primitive Accumulation' returns to this contested ground of readings of primitive accumulation, examining the works of Negri and Althusser through their
different way of understanding the foundation of capitalism. The other two
essays in this section, 'The Present as Pre-History: Adorno and Balibar on the
Transformation of Labor' and 'The Althusser Effect: Philosophy, History, and
Temporality', are less concerned with the passages on primitive accumulation

than on the general set of problems regarding transformation, contingency, and the temporality of transformation that primitive accumulation opens up. Viewing capitalism from its prehistory is the best way to grasp its current transformations.

The second section is dedicated to a reading of certain Marxist concepts through problems in Gilles Deleuze and Félix Guattari's two volume *Capitalism and Schizophrenia*. The point is neither to argue for some kind of Marxist pedigree of Deleuze and Guattari's text nor to position them an updating of Marx's corpus. Rather, it is to read Marx through the lens of Deleuze and Guattari and vice versa. Integral to this refraction is the role of subjectivity in terms of desire, beliefs, and affects. Deleuze and Guattari proclaim that desire is part of the infrastructure; in other words, that far from being a simple ideological effect the most private and intimate aspects of our lives are the conditions for the reproduction of the relations of production. The first essay in this section, 'A Universal History of Contingency: Deleuze and Guattari on the History of Capitalism' overlaps with previous section, which is understandable given that Deleuze and Guattari were very influenced by *Lire Le Capital* and their understanding of the contingent basis of capitalism prefigures Althusser's later concept of aleatory materialism. Or at the very least it suggests that aleatory materialism is a concept framed by Deleuze and Guattari reading Althusser reading Marx. The concept is produced in the overlap of readings and problems. Deleuze and Guattari are also drawn towards primitive accumulation less as a historical account of capitalism's emergence from violence than as an examination of how the mode of production cannot be separated from the production of subjectivity. Or, as Marx put it, 'The advance of capitalist production develops a working class which by education [*Erziehung*], tradition, and habit [*Gewohneit*] looks upon the requirements of that mode of production as self-evident natural laws'.[4] The remaining four essays in this section are aimed less at the relation between Deleuze and Guattari and Marxist traditions and instead focus on what reading *Capitalism and Schizophrenia* as a contribution to the critique of political economy reveals about contemporary capitalism. The production of subjectivity does not end with the formation of a working class but continues and changes with each change of capitalism. Marx in the unpublished Sixth Chapter of *Capital* argued that the worker under capitalism is compelled more by internal compulsions than external conditions, or, in Deleuze and Guattari's terms, subjection rather than enslavement. In the years since Deleuze and Guattari wrote, this intensive aspect has only increased

---

4   Marx 1977, p. 899.

as the labour relation has become even more isolated and workers are expected to show a great deal of motivation for little money. As I argue in 'Beyond Enslavement and Subjection: Deviations from Deleuze and Guattari' this is why Deleuze and Guattari's concept of subjection continues to be an important point of reference for such contemporary philosophers as Yves Citton and Maurizio Lazzarato. Ultimately, Deleuze and Guattari's assertion that 'desire is part of the superstructure' cuts both ways, it makes it possible to understand the immanence of subjectivity in the economy, the role of affects and habits in production, but also the economy in subjectivity, the way that capital is manifest in daily cynicism and fear.

The third section has as its central theme the importance of Spinoza for Marx. The Spinoza/Marx relation is unusual in the history of philosophy since as much as Spinoza comes before Marx the relation between the two is neither one of influence (as in the case of Hegel and Marx) or opposition (also in the case of Hegel and Marx) at least predominantly. The Spinoza/Marx relation has more to do with a series of problems in which the two intersect. As three essays in this section demonstrate, one of the central problems of the Marx/Spinoza relation is that of ideology, or understood more broadly, the material basis and effect of ideas. Two essays examine this problem by looking at one of the most famous, and most misunderstood Propositions from the *Ethics*, 'The order and connection of things is the same as the order and connection of ideas (EIIP7)' Following such interpretations as Pierre Macherey, Frédérique Lordon, and Yves Citton I argue that this proposition can help us understand the conditions and effects of ideology. Ideology is understood less as a representation of reality than another way in which reality is manifest. In terms of the former it is a matter of grasping what could be called, following Althusser, the 'spontaneity' of ideology, its emergence from historical practice and relations. The Spinoza/Marx relation is not limited to the critique of ideology, but also encompasses their shared commitment to an idea of social relations that is neither reducible to individual wills and intentions nor inter-subjective relations. In 'Desire is Man's Very Essence: Spinoza and Hegel as Philosophers of Transindividuality' I argue that Spinoza and Marx can be considered thinkers of transindividuality, of social relations that are neither the sum total of individual actions or a totality existing above them. While Althusser argues that Spinoza's epistemology, the division between the spontaneous imagination and the work of reason, was a philosophy for Marxism and Antonio Negri argued that it was Spinoza's ontology of power that could expand and revitalise Marx's critique of the power of capital, I argue, following Yves Citton and Frédéric Lordon, that it is Spinoza's anthropology, his account of desire, imagination, and affects, that is most useful for contemporary Marxism.

The final section, 'Returns of Philosophical Anthropology: New Subjections/ New Transformations', brings together the philosophical examinations of the production of subjectivity with new transformations of capital and its production of subjectivity. As the title of this section suggests, capitalism has increasingly taken on an anthropological dimension. It is part of neoliberalism's intellectual revolution to complete Adam Smith's justification of capitalism as part of humanity's natural tendency to 'barter, truck, and exchange' to the point where market relations become the key to understanding not only the economy but all human actions. This anthropological turn is met from a different direction with the concept of the anthropocene, the argument that humanity has become a world-altering geological force. Between these two anthropological tendencies (which are dealt with in 'A Genealogy of Homo-Economicus: Foucault, Neoliberalism, and the Production of Subjectivity' and 'Anthropology and Anthropogenesis: Philosophical Anthropology and the Ends of Man') there is a need to re-examine the intersection of philosophical anthropology and the critique of political economy, to understand humanity as a 'real abstraction' produced as an afterimage of the transformations of capital. In this final section the 'anthropological turn' of Etienne Balibar and Paolo Virno is examined alongside a critical examination of the invocation of humanity and inhumanity in Marx's *Capital*.

The itinerary of this book follows a kind of zig zag dictated by Marx's tendency to 'fall short of' and 'go beyond' philosophy, as the production of subjectivity is constantly brought back to philosophy, to a reconsideration of Marx, Hegel, and Spinoza, only to then go beyond it, to engage with debates about neoliberalism and the Anthropocene.

PART 1

Becoming Contingent:
Philosophy, Violence, History

∵

CHAPTER 1

Primitive Accumulation: The Aleatory Foundation of Capitalism

It is a matter of common knowledge that Karl Marx presents the difference between his analysis and all previous (bourgeois) understandings of political economy as a historical versus an ahistorical conception of capitalism. What is considerably less certain is how Marx, or those who came after him, understood this disparity: that is, what are its theoretical grounds and what were or could be its effects in the realm of philosophy, historical understanding, and political practice? There have been many interpretations of this difference; in this day and age this difference is often represented as either an incorrect prophecy (capitalism will collapse) or a contribution to a vague and inconsequential awareness of history (something, some economy existed before capitalism). If it is possible today to propose another thought of the distinction between Marx and political economy, or to attempt to reanimate the question, problem, and lines of investigation from behind this accepted bit of academic common sense, I would suggest that for Marx this difference, the difference history makes, has entirely different grounds, and different effects, than mere prophecy, transforming what is understood by society, the economy, materiality, power and subjectivity.[1]

Marx's critique of the conception of human nature and subjectivity supporting bourgeois political economy, as well as his development, albeit partial and often incomplete, of a radically different thought of the historicity and materiality of subjectivity, are perhaps nowhere more forcefully developed than in the points where Marx presents his account of the formation of the capitalist mode of production and its radical difference from all prior modes of production. I am referring here to the final chapters of volume 1 of *Capital*, the chapters on 'so-called primitive accumulation'. These chapters have to be read as something other than either a debate with classical political economy or the history of capitalism in England. As Marxist philosophers as divergent as Louis Althusser[2] and Antonio Negri[3] have argued, Marx's theory of primitive accumulation can be read as a contribution to an understanding of the 'materiality'

---

1 Althusser and Balibar, p. 158.
2 Althusser 1994a.
3 Negri 1999.

of social relations and subjectivity, and ultimately, despite appearances, to an understanding of the capitalist mode of production itself.[4]

Of course the term 'mode of production' has a long history within Marxist philosophy and theory. The various different positions and debates within this history perhaps have as their foundation and precondition the complex and ambiguous sense that Marx gives the term 'mode of production'. As Althusser argues, Marx uses the term 'mode of production' to refer to two different relations: the relation between the forces and relations of production, in the narrow or restrictive sense (found most famously in the Preface to *The Contribution to the Critique of Political Economy*), and the relation between the base and superstructure, which encompasses all of the social relations within a determinant society (in the expansive sense of a mode of production developed in Marx's writings on pre-capitalist economic formations and underlying Marx's rewriting of universal history).[5] The second sense approaches a conception of the social totality, encompassing the economic, political, and social relations within a given historical period.[6] In the writing on the mode of production following Althusser, the first limited sense – 'the articulated combination of forces and relations of production structured by the dominance of the relations of production' – has been accepted as the legitimate meaning of the mode of production, while the larger sense has been thoroughly criticised for ascribing too much explanatory power to economic relations.[7] Following Althusser, the term 'social formation' has been adopted to designate a concrete society; the advantage of this later term is that it allows for the coexistence of multiple modes of production (capital, feudal, etc.), within a given social totality and their complex interaction.[8] Moreover, it is argued that it is only possible to grasp the overdetermined structure of any society through the concept of 'social formation', a structure that exceeds the economic determination of the mode of production.[9] Althusser and Negri's (somewhat) recent return to the problematic of

----

4 It is not my concern here to stage a philosophical reconciliation between Althusser and Negri. Which is not to suggest that such a project would not be interesting. However, such a project would have to include not only the lines of convergence of the later writings, commented on by Negri himself in 'Notes on the Evolution of the Thought of the Later Althusser', but would ultimately have to interrogate the commonplace acceptance of their divergence: a divergence which posits Althusser as the philosopher of a history as a process without subjects or goals and Negri as a philosopher concerned primarily with living labour as subjectivity.

5 Althusser 1995, p. 45.

6 Negri 1991, p. 151.

7 Hindess and Hirst 1975, p. 9.

8 Hindess and Hirst 1975, p. 13.

9 Resnick and Wolff 1987, p. 22.

primitive accumulation as constitutive of the very definition of the mode of production would seem to constitute an interesting addition to this debate in that it places dimensions of social existence generally seen as necessary supplements to the mode of production – the state, law, power relations and the constitution of subjectivity – as constitutive elements of it.[10] Thus, it is possible to glimpse in Marx's theory of primitive accumulation a 'non-economistic' account of the mode of production in which the mode of production does not simply designate a particular economic relation which has its linear effects on other social relations, but rather is the dense point of articulation of power relations. Moreover, to offer something of a provocation, while postmarxism and postmodernism stress contingency as a category fundamental to rethinking the constitution and transformation of social and political identities, arguing that the contingency of social relations and transformations is unthinkable from Marx's perspective of history viewed as the succession and transformation of modes of production, a re-reading of primitive accumulation makes it possible to think at one and the same time the contingency of social relations, their constitution by the encounter, and the materiality of social relations – their inscription within the mode of production.[11]

---

10   Fredric Jameson's insistence on maintaining the term 'mode of production' is worth noting at this point. Jameson argues that the term mode of production is essentially a differential term in that even in the attempt to specify one particular mode of production, such as the capitalist mode of production, it is necessary to think in terms of the manner in which it differentiates itself from other modes of production. Marx could not define the capitalist mode of production without differentiating it from feudalism, just as the capitalist mode of production exists in tension with other possible modes. However, Jameson rejects the term 'social formation' to account for this conflictual co-existence, arguing that it reintroduces the empiricism which the former term was intended to include, and instead suggests the term 'cultural revolution' to account for the dominance of one mode of production over others (Jameson 1988, p. 174). Jameson's understanding of 'cultural revolution', as a necessary supplement to the mode of production, comes very close to the interlinking between the mode of production and the 'mode of subjection' explored in this paper.

11   Here I am referring to Laclau and Mouffe 1985. In the companion volume to this work, Laclau, Butler and Zizek 2000, Slavoj Zizek entertains the idea that the understanding of politics as the contingent contestation of political hegemonies must necessarily repress the critique of political economy. I am indebted to Geoff Boucher for making the point that Althusser's work on aleatory materialism can be understood as an attempt to think and maintain contingency without necessarily dispensing with the materiality of the mode of production.

1   The Moral of Subjectivity

So-called primitive accumulation [*sogenannte ursprünglichen Akkumulation*]
is the answer posed by political economy to a seemingly irresolvable problem:
the fact that capitalist production would seem to continually presuppose itself.
It presupposes wealth in the hands of capitalists as well as a population of those
who have nothing but their labour power to sell. These elements, capital and
workers, are the preconditions of any capitalist production, yet they cannot be
explained from it. Capitalist accumulation would seem to be something of an
infinite regress, always presupposing its own conditions. In order to accumulate capital it is necessary to possess capital. There must then be an original or
previous accumulation: an accumulation which is not the result of the capitalist mode of production but rather its point of departure, and which constitutes
the originary differentiation between capital and workers. This foundational
distinction has generally been understood by political economy as a moral difference. As Marx writes:

> This primitive accumulation plays approximately the same role in polit-
> ical economy as original sin does in theology. Adam bit the apple, and
> thereupon sin fell on the human race. Its origin is supposed to be ex-
> plained when it is told as an anecdote about the past. Long, long ago there
> were two sorts of people; one the diligent, intelligent, and above all frugal
> elite; the other lazy rascals, spending their substance, and more, in riotous
> living. The legend of theological original sin tells us certainly how man
> came to be condemned to eat his bread by the sweat of his brow; but
> the history of economic original sin reveals to us that there are people
> to whom this is by no means essential. Never mind! Thus it came to pass
> that the former sort accumulated wealth, and the latter sort finally had
> nothing to sell except their own skins.[12]

Thus, as much as so-called primitive accumulation posits a theory of the formation of the capitalist mode of production, albeit one predicated on a presupposed division between the diligent and the lazy, it turns this explanation
toward the present in the form of a moral tale. The origin provides the present
with a moral alibi, dividing the capitalist and the worker along the lines of the
good and the bad.

---

12   Marx 1977, p. 873.

Not only does the theory of so-called primitive accumulation function in the present, aiming for the present or a particular moral characterisation of the present, it never leaves the present even as it offers itself as history. The theory of 'primitive accumulation' takes the idealised memory of an individual capitalist's accumulation – saving money, which itself is a morally coded, (or best case, ideological) presentation of accumulation within capitalism, and turns it into the conditions of capitalist accumulation in general.[13] It mistakes this memory for history, the conditions *within* capitalist accumulation for the conditions *of* capitalist accumulation. Étienne Balibar asserts: 'The analysis of primitive accumulation thus brings us into the presence of the radical *absence of memory* which characterises history (memory being only the reflection of history in certain predetermined sites – ideology or even law – and as such, anything but a faithful reflection)'.[14] As a theory of the capitalist mode of production, so-called primitive accumulation constitutes a failure to think different conditions, limitations, and effects in history, or to think history as difference – a failure that is perhaps not entirely explained by self-interest. So-called primitive accumulation can only extend the conditions of the capitalist mode of production infinitely backward in time: capitalism was (and always will be) possible; in order to become real, it only required the industriousness and intelligence of the first capitalist.

The fantasy of the thrifty proto-capitalist, whatever its function as nursery tale may be within the schoolbooks and ideologies of capital, is wholly inadequate to the task of accounting for the formation of the capitalist mode of production. The accumulation of money without the conditions to transform it into capital (such as workers or those who have only their labor power to sell) is not capitalist accumulation but 'hoarding' [*Shatzbildung*].[15] For Marx, 'hoarding' is a subjective disposition towards money, and in part produced by money,

---

13   It is important to distinguish between the classical texts of political economy, which present so-called primitive accumulation as primarily a moral difference between thrift and greed, and the *practical interventions* of some of the same early economists. As Michael Perelman has argued, often the same political economists who theoretically presented the accumulation of capital as a moral difference practically understood the necessity of actively destroying the pre-capitalist practices of subsistence through state power (Perelman 2000, p. 98). Marx recognised a similar duplicity in the early writings on the colonies (America) in which the scarcity of Europe did not yet exist. As Marx writes: 'In the old civilized countries the worker, although free, is by a law of nature dependent on the capitalist; in the colonies this dependence must be created by artificial means' (Marx 1977, p. 937).

14   Balibar 1975, p. 283.

15   Marx 1988, p. 144.

prior to capital – that is, prior to the possibility of investment or surplus value. 'Hoarding' as a disposition is constituted by money and its particular character of being qualitatively without limits – it has the power to stand in for any other commodity, for anything desired – and quantitatively limited; one always has a particular finite amount of money.[16] Thus as much as there is a long history of capitalist accumulation prior to the formation of the capitalist mode of production (in the forms of mercantile capital and money-lending), it occurs within certain relatively stable limits – limits imposed in part by the money form. What is interesting for our purpose here is that Marx's deduction of the affective comportment of hoarding from the money form as an unstable combination of work, thrift, and greed, reproduces at least a certain presupposition or assumption of the theory of so-called primitive accumulation – that desire and will are themselves sufficient to generate history – but parodically as farce. Without the proper historical conditions, the 'miser's' desire for accumulation is destined only to collide with certain structural limits. As Marx states, 'This contradiction between the quantitative limitation and the qualitative lack of limitation of money keeps driving the hoarder back to his Sisyphean task: accumulation. He is in the same situation as a world conqueror, who discovers a new boundary with each country he annexes'.[17] Assuming that hoarding or the desire for wealth is in some sense contemporary with the money form, and thus preexists capital, it is possible to invert Marx's formula and to argue that farce comes before tragedy.[18] (The comic image of the miser with his bags of money comes before the tragedy of capitalist accumulation and massive expropriation). The question then becomes, under what conditions, and through what other causes, is this desire actualised? How does accumulation cease to be the dream of the 'hoarder' and become an effective practice, one that constitutes an entire mode of production?[19]

---

16   Marx 1977, p. 230.

17   Marx 1977, p. 203.

18   The sentence I am referring to here is the famous sentence from *The Eighteenth Brumaire*: 'Hegel remarks somewhere that all facts and personages of great importance in world history occur, as it were, twice. He forgot to add: the first time as tragedy, the second as farce' (Karl Marx, *The Eighteenth Brumaire of Louis Bonaparte*, p. 15).

19   As Marx writes, drawing the parallel between the miser and the capitalist, 'This boundless drive for enrichment, this passionate chase after value, is common to the capitalist and the miser; but while the miser is merely a capitalist gone mad, the capitalist is a rational miser. The ceaseless augmentation of value, which the miser seeks to attain by saving his money from circulation, is achieved by the more acute capitalist by means of throwing his money again into circulation' (Marx 1977, p. 255). Gilles Deleuze and Félix Guattari explicitly pose the question of the formation of the capitalist mode of production in terms of the actualisation of desire in *Anti-Oedipus: Capitalism and Schizophrenia*.

In order for money to constitute capital, and in order for the desire to hoard to constitute capitalist accumulation, there must be the conditions for its investment: that is, the capitalist must be able to purchase both the means of production and labour. These elements must be dissociated from any form of property or social relation that would leave the 'means of production', tools, or the land in the hands of the producers. When capital controls the means of production it ceases to operate at the margins of society, as merchant capital or moneylending, and occupies centre stage, becoming directly productive as industrial capital. There thus are at least two conditions of the formation of the capitalist mode of production, two conditions that make possible the genera-tion of capital in production rather than in circulation or money-lending. As Marx writes, in a deceptively simple and frequently repeated formula:

> In themselves, money and commodities are no more capital than the means of production and subsistence are. They need to be transformed into capital. But this transformation can itself only take place under par-ticular circumstances [*bestimmten Umständen*], which meet together at this point: the confrontation of, and the contact between, two very differ-ent kinds of commodity owners; on the one hand, the owners of money, means of production, means of subsistence, who are eager to valorize the sum of values they have appropriated by buying the labor power of oth-ers; on the other hand, free workers, the sellers of their own labour power, and therefore the sellers of labour.[20]

The capitalist mode of production is formed by the conjunction of money, or possessors of money, and those who have only their labour power to sell. Marx calls this second group free or 'bird-free' [*vogelfrei*], meaning at one and the same time that while they are not property (as slaves) they are themselves without property and cast out of the human community, as a community of property owners. As Althusser argues, thinking the mode of production from its presuppositions entails thinking the mode of production from the moment where these presuppositions come together in time and space; it entails think-ing the mode of production from the 'encounter'. The constitutive elements of the formation of any mode of production, the elements that enter into relations, such as free labourers and money freed from any productive use, have different and divergent histories.[21] From the moment of the encounter,

---

20   Marx 1977, p. 874.
21   Marx 1994a, p. 571.

however, once the worker and the flows of money encounter each other within a determinate space – the space of wage labour – there is the emergence of a particular mode of production, with its attendant forms of necessity and stability. (To continue our example, one could think here of the multiple necessities of the capitalist mode of production: the necessity of getting a job, to produce commodities, to extract surplus value, and to realise a profit, to name a few, all of which impose themselves to different degrees and for different groups within the mode of production). The encounter itself is contingent. As Deleuze and Guattari argue, 'The encounter might not have taken place, with the free workers and the money-capital existing "virtually" side by side'.[22] Necessity, or the regular reproduction of a mode of production, is itself generated by contingency, and as such it is perhaps never free of it. This imposes a particular demand on how one thinks of the mode of production. As Althusser writes, 'Instead of thinking of contingency as a modality of or an exception to the necessary, one must think necessity as the becoming-necessary of contingent encounters'.[23] A 'becoming-necessary', a process, and not a simple transition from contingency to necessity, because the different elements of a mode of production – the social, technological, and political conditions – have independent histories and relations, and this independence threatens any mode of production with its dissolution or transformation. As Marx has repeatedly indicated, capital is constantly threatened by the unhinging of its two constitutive elements: the flow of workers could dry up or leave, and capital could be wasted rather than invested. The encounter is not only the contingency of the origin but also the uncertainty of the future.

The 'encounter' replaces the teleological logic of intentions and their realisation underlying classical political economy with a logic of encounters, detours, and effects which are not the realisation of intentions but are constitutive of them. However, it is not only within classical political economy that historical teleology and the continuity between the past and future is posited through

---

22   Deleuze and Guattari 1983, p. 225. At several points in *Anti-Oedipus* Deleuze and Guattari seem to prefigure statements found in Althusser's essay on the materialism of the encounter: for example, in both texts the encounter between 'money and those who have only their labor power to sell' becomes grounds for speculation on the materiality of the event. While it is possible that Althusser had read or considered Deleuze and Guattari's text it is also worth noting, in this note towards a philology, that Deleuze and Guattari were reading and drawing from Balibar's contribution to *Lire le Capital*. Althusser also implicitly draws from this text in stressing the divergent and contradictory histories that pre-exist the formation of capitalism. Thus it is possible that Deleuze and Guattari's text only serves to magnify tendencies already at work in the previous project.

23   Althusser 1994a, p. 566, my translation.

the figure of a subject. In Marx's other writings (most famously *The Communist Manifesto*) it is the bourgeoisie as collective subject whose will and desire constitute the capitalist mode of production. Thus Althusser[24] criticises Marx's sloppy use of the term bourgeoisie as the name of both the social force destructive of feudalism and the dominant class within the new order. Such a narrative effaces the constitutive power of the encounter, the event, the fact that the capitalist class, like the proletariat, cannot exist prior to the series of encounters constitutive of capitalism. The term 'bourgeoisie' subsumes the facticity of the event under a logic of predestination. Paradoxically, 'so-called primitive accumulation' and the polemics of the manifesto both efface the constitutive difference of history with a single figure, that of the bourgeois or proto-capitalist, which is situated both before and after the capitalist mode of production. Thus, Althusser draws a line of demarcation within Marx's corpus not between the early and late Marx, as he so famously did earlier, but between two divergent materialisms at work in Marx's writing: a materialism of the event or the encounter versus a materialism of teleology and necessity. This line of demarcation also cuts through different conceptions of subjectivity. This division is not between subjectivity understood as the self-expression or alienation of the humanist subject and subjectivity understood as the bearer (*Träger*) of social processes, as Althusser's early work infamously tried to argue, but between subjectivity as a necessary cause or effect of the capitalist mode of production and subjectivity as constituted by and constitutive of the encounter. Althusser places two seemingly opposed conceptions of subjectivity within the same schema of necessity: the bourgeoisie as cause of capitalism and the proletariat as automatically produced by capital. To these conceptions, each of which is governed by a certain teleology or necessity (whether it is a telos of the will, in the first case, or the necessary effect of the economy, in the second), Althusser juxtaposes another conception of subjectivity, found in the chapters on primitive accumulation.[25]

---

24   Althusser 1994a.
25   Althusser does not explicitly name subjectivity as the deciding factor in distinguishing between these two different conceptions of the mode of production. However, his central example in defining what he calls the essentialist and philosophical conception of the mode of production is Marx's thought of the proletariat as automatically produced and reproduced by capital (Marx 1994a, p. 573). As I have noted, in a latter portion of the manuscript Althusser also criticises the idea of a bourgeoisie that pre-exists capital (Althusser 1994a, p. 575). In each of these cases, and in different ways, subjectivity is linked to necessity, as either effect or cause. Thus, reading Althusser's fragmented manuscript somewhat symptomatically, Althusser's aleatory conception of the mode of production must have a different relationship to subjectivity than is suggested by these concepts.

The conjunction of the flow of money, on one hand, and a flow of those who only have their labor power to sell, on the other, as the necessary or minimal constitution of capitalist accumulation, would seem to indicate that the capitalist mode of production cannot, in either its constitution or definition, be considered as a simple effect of one term or element: it is a relation, or an ensemble of relations.[26] To argue that the capitalist mode of production ought to be grasped as an 'ensemble of relations' is, in a primary and almost entirely negative (or critical) sense, to separate a thought of the capitalist mode of production from a thought of 'human nature'. The capitalist mode of production cannot be understood as a simple expression or deviation of human nature: it is neither the realisation of a fundamental and originary desire to hoard nor the suppression of an ancient communal essence.

In the *Theses on Feuerbach* Marx uses the term 'ensemble of human relations' to displace the question of the human essence. Marx argues against Feuerbach's concept of the abstract human essence and its alienation in religion: 'But the human essence is no abstraction inherent in each single individual. In its reality (*in seiner Wirklichkeit*) it is the ensemble of the social relations (*das Ensemble der gesellschaftlichen Verhältnisse*)'. Marx's statement 'displaces' the question of the human essence in that it does not argue against essence in general, but rather proposes that such an essence does not exist in an idea, but rather exists, or effectively exists, in the multiple and active relations that individuals establish with each other.[27] What human individuals have 'in common' is not some abstract idea of humanity but their specific relations: relations that are constituted each moment, through various encounters, in multiple forms. There is an affirmative aspect of this concept of an 'ensemble' which follows this displacement: just because capital cannot be related back to some abstract essence of humanity does not mean that it is separable from human desires, human intentions, or human subjectivity altogether, but rather, these desires must be considered from the particular relations and the history of these relations. Or, put otherwise, the formation of the capitalist mode of production is not reducible to the simple desire to accumulate on the part of the capitalist, or to the simple moral difference between capital and worker, although it involves and implicates desire as well as an entire moral discourse on the values of saving and spending as its component elements.[28] However,

---

26   Althusser and Balibar 1975, p. 215.

27   Balibar 2017b, p. 30.

28   As early as the *1844 Manuscripts* Marx recognised in political economy a self-contradictory moral discourse on the values of thrift and spending, which Marx believed to be something of a reflection of the contradictory tendencies of reducing 'necessary labour' while selling more commodities (Marx 1964, p. 150).

these elements or relations do not have as their cause some abstract nature of humanity, but rather, their causes are other relations: relations which coexist with and precede this particular ensemble of relations. As Althusser writes in his remarks towards a general theory of aleatory materialism, every 'thing' (body, subject, social relation) must itself be viewed as an effect of a series of different encounters, an effect that, once constituted, has its own particular causality or effectivity.[29]

For Marx, the relations that form the capitalist mode of production are 'the product of many economic revolutions, of the extinction of a whole series of older formations of social production', the most direct and immediate extinction being the breakdown of the feudal mode of production.[30] The 'extinction' of the feudal mode of production encompasses multiple elements and trajectories. It includes the dissolution of the regime of the guilds, the breakdown of the system of peasant land-ownership, and the massive disintegration of existing structures of wealth and prestige through merchant capital and usury.[31] These elements of dissolution are not the effects of a single strategy or aspects of a single process; they are, rather, entirely disparate. Étienne Balibar explains that '... the elements combined by the capitalist mode of production have different and independent origins'.[32] These elements of dissolution, such as usury, often stem from the margins and pores of the old society, and only begin to occupy centre stage in terms of their effects – the effects of constituting a new economy and a new mode of production. Whatever intelligibility or unity they have is produced after the fact, when they retroactively become the conditions of the capitalist mode of production.

Where the theory of so-called primitive accumulation imagines a vague identity of past and present, unified by a particular memory, morality, and subject, Marx finds the intersection of disparate historical trajectories and itineraries that only come together in the common space that they mutually create. For example, the laws and acts which turned common lands into pasture and forced the peasantry off the land did not have as their goal the creation of the 'proletariat' as a propertyless working class; this was rather an unintended effect that was later seized by other agents and actors.[33] 'The knights

29   Althusser 1994a, p. 565.
30   Marx 1977, p. 273.
31   It should be clear given these particulars that Marx, following the political economists he is critiquing, is primarily concerned with western Europe, particularly England, and to a lesser extent North America.
32   Balibar 1975, p. 281.
33   Louis Althusser calls this process by which the effects of a particular process are seized

of industry, however, only succeeded in supplanting the knights of the sword by making use of events in which they had played no part in whatsoever'.[34] To continue the comparison between 'so-called primitive accumulation' and primitive accumulation, we could add that where the theorists, or apologists, of political economy find an idyllic and moralising transformation, Marx finds violence and bloodshed. This violent transformation has two acts. First, as I have noted, there are multiple conditions of expropriation, including usury, which quite literally tear the producers from their means of production, most importantly the land.[35] Expropriation in itself does not produce 'free workers', however, only disenfranchised peasants and artisans looking for work, who are just as likely to resort to beggary or crime as they are to show up at the doors of the factories and mills of the newly emergent capitalist class. As Marx writes in the *Grundrisse*: 'The propertyless are more inclined to become vagabonds and robbers and beggars than workers'.[36] The period of expropriation is followed by the period of 'bloody legislation': laws are drawn up and regimes of penalisation and torture are enacted to curtail criminality and control the new class of criminals.

> Hence at the end of the fifteenth and during the whole of the sixteenth centuries, a bloody legislation against vagabondage was enforced throughout Western Europe. The fathers of the present working class were chastised for their enforced transformation into vagabonds and paupers. Legislation treated them as 'voluntary' criminals, and assumed that it was entirely within their powers to go on working under the old conditions which in fact no longer existed.[37]

---

and turned to other purposes and other ends *détournement*: 'This "detouring" is the mark of the non-teleology of the process and the inscription of its result in a process which has rendered it possible and which was totally alien to it' (Althusser 1994a, p. 572, my translation).

34   Marx 1977, p. 875.

35   In *Capital* Volume I, in the chapters on 'so-called primitive accumulation', Marx primarily deals with the expropriation of peasants from the land, and he is primarily concerned with the legal, or state centred, elements of this process. In *Capital* Volume III Marx provides something of a complement to this analysis in his analysis of the effects of usury and merchant capital on pre-capitalist property and social relations. What is important, I will argue, about the relation between these two chapters, and volumes, is not that they complete the picture, as it were, comprising two sides of a finished picture, but that they open the formation of the capitalist mode of production, and the mode of production itself, up to its constitutive complexity (Marx 1981, pp. 728–48).

36   Marx 1973, p. 736.

37   Marx 1977, p. 896.

While such laws are founded on the fantasy that it is possible to go on being a peasant after feudalism, their secondary, and perhaps unintended, effect is the control and containment of a 'working class' – of those who have only their labour power to sell. Those 'freed' from previous forms of labour and existence must be violently coerced and contained into the new structures of labour and existence. 'Centuries are required before the "free" worker, owing to the greater development of the capitalist mode of production, makes a voluntary agreement, i.e. is compelled by social conditions to sell the whole of his act-ive life, his very capacity for labour, in return for the price of his customary means of subsistence, to sell his birthright for a mess of pottage'.[38] The trans-ition from feudalism to capitalism is neither smooth nor easy, and it requires the necessary intervention of law, the state, and new forms of police to trans-form disenfranchised peasants and artisans into subjects of labour. As Marx argues, the state, and particularly its powers of police and violence, are then a contingent but necessary condition of the capitalist mode of production.[39]

The perspective that Marx assumes in the section on primitive accumula-tion is similar to that of Machiavelli.[40] It is situated at the historical perspective of the emergence of capital, an emergence it views from the people: in other words, it views the origins of capital from its initial victims, the violently disap-propriated peasantry.[41] Although Marx does not share Machiavelli's solitude, his historical vantage point of being a witness to the formation of the nation state (or, in this case, capital), through his research on primitive accumulation in England and in the colonies, he excavates the violent encounter of founda-tion that classical political economy effaces.[42] Whereas the perspective of clas-

---

38   Marx 1977, p. 382.

39   Marx 1977, p. 899.

40   Althusser makes a direct analogy between Machiavelli and Marx referring to 'primitive political accumulation' in the former, that is, the accumulation of the people and arms necessary to the constitution of the state. As Althusser writes: 'We are all familiar with Part VIII of the first volume of *Capital* in which Marx tackles so-called 'original [or prim-itive] accumulation'. In this original accumulation, the ideologists of capitalism told the edifying story of the rise of capital just as the philosophers of natural law told the story of the rise of the state. In the beginning there was an independent worker who worked so enthusiastically, intelligently and economically that he was able to save and then exchange ... Hence the accumulation of capital: by labor thrift and generosity. We know how Marx replied: with a story of pillage, theft, exaction, of the violent dispossession of the English peasantry ... with quite a different story and one far more gripping than the moralizing platitudes of the ideologists of capitalism' (Althusser 1999, p. 125).

41   Montag 1996, p. 97.

42   In a published lecture course titled '*Il Faut Défendre la Société*' Foucault offers a genea-logy of the counter-discourse of war and struggle, conceived as either a war of races or

sical political economy assumes the formation of capital as an accomplished fact, which it retroactively justifies through a moral difference, Marx writes from the perspective of the aleatory formation of capital. Thus Marx can be juxtaposed with classical political economy in the same way that Machiavelli can be opposed to the philosophers of natural law, such as Hobbes: in each case the moral discourse of right is replaced with a materialist understanding of force. Machiavelli's writing cannot simply be identified with the figure of the founding violence of the 'prince', it also includes his enumeration of the multiple aleatory conditions [*fortuna*] which both limit and make possible the prince's assumption of power.[43] The perspective of the aleatory beginning, which Marx and Machiavelli share, does not simply oppose the contingency of the event to the moral narrative of origins, but thinks the event in the overdetermination of its conditions.

The difference between Marx and the narrative of 'so-called primitive accumulation' is not simply framed at the level of their respective ideologies: it is not simply a matter of replacing a tale of the moral foundation with a tale of the a-moral origins of capital. The difference at the origin is carried over into the present. Just as Machiavelli's account of the violent interruption of the state into feudal conditions cannot simply be adjudicated with the moral discourse of natural law, as two different perspectives on the same 'thing', Marx's account of primitive accumulation constitutes a fundamental transformation of the object under consideration. The violence of primitive accumulation cannot appear within the discourse of classical political economy, given the manner in which it constructs its object – it conforms neither to the moral discourse underpinning classical political economy nor to its conception of the market as an invisible hand functioning without state intervention.[44] Primitive accumulation is the constitutive blind spot of classical political economy.

---

classes. While Foucault recognises a similar strategic significance to the discourse on war, an overturning of a moral discourse of right through an insistence on the violent conditions of the foundation of the state or social order, he explicitly rejects Machiavelli and Marx as 'pretenders' to this counter-discourse. As Foucault writes: 'the dialectic assures the constitution, across history, of a universal subject, a reconciled truth, a right in which all particulars would have their ordained place. The Hegelian dialectic, and all that have followed ... must be understood ... as the authoritarian colonization and pacification, by philosophy and right, of a historico-political discourse that is at the same time a statement, a proclamation, and a practice of social warfare' (Foucault 1997, p. 50, my translation). It would seem, however, that Foucault's categorical denunciation overlooks the constitutive tension that Althusser underscores between the aleatory materialism of primitive accumulation and the teleology of other logics in Marx.

43   Althusser 1999, p. 74.
44   Perelman 2000, p. 196.

As I have suggested, it is through the critique of so-called primitive accumulation that the elements of the historical definition of the capitalist mode of production are given. So far these elements are perhaps only given in a dim outline through the points of contrast with the moralists of so-called primitive accumulation. First, a mode of production is irreducible to, and in excess of, the intentions of an individual subject. While the 'fairy tale' of primitive accumulation founds the possibility of historical transformation and capitalist accumulation on individual intent and the morality of those that save rather than squander, Marx argues through the character of the miser not only that intentions in general cannot be actualised without their material conditions, but that these conditions are constitutive of intentions. Subjectivity is inseparable from the ensemble of relations which makes it possible. There is perhaps a second, albeit more oblique, element to this materialist critique of intentionality. Marx's account of the disparate conditions of primitive accumulation would seem to separate this thought of the mode of production from a subject of history. It is not the same subject, subjects, wills or desires that dissolve the old mode of production and produce the new one. Althusser has shown how this dimension of Marx's thought of primitive accumulation can be turned back against some of the cruder formulations of Marxism. At the most rudimentary level this means that Marx's thought of the historicity of the capitalist mode of production is completely separated from any attempt to write a 'great man' philosophy of history, in which history is nothing more than the realisation of ideas and intentions within a neutral and passive space of history. If Marx's history is not simply the *tabula rasa* upon which the actions and events of great men are unfolded, it is also not the eternal battle (now hidden, now open) of two classes. Classes are constituted by and constitutive of the aleatory encounter of material conditions. There are no laws of history, or epic agents, engaged in struggle, on the multiple overlapping effects of encounters. Finally, Marx's critique of so-called primitive accumulation begins to point to a specific problem within the mode of production – the manner in which a mode of production is constitutive and constituted by desires, forms of living, and intentions: subjectivity.

2   Economy of Force

While Marx's critique of so-called primitive accumulation provides a beginning point from which to think the conditions and constitutive elements of the capitalist mode of production, it is a paradoxical starting point from which to elucidate a consideration of the capitalist mode of production. Paradoxical, because it is unclear where or within what mode of production the conditions of primitive accumulation are to be located according to a historical periodisation: they could be placed within the feudal mode of production, from whose dissolution they stem, or within the capitalist mode of production, whose birth it represents. Primitive accumulation is situated between two types of violence and two types of power, between the feudal forms of servitude that it destroys and the capitalist forms of exploitation that it renders possible. Thus primitive accumulation would seem to exceed any strict periodisation, or division of history into a succession of modes of production (Asiatic, ancient, feudal, capitalist, and communist). It is, rather, a point of passage and transition.

It is unclear, however, whether primitive accumulation can simply be relegated to a moment of transition in the pre-history of the capitalist mode of production. As a process of accumulation it would seem to encompass both the conditions for the historical formation of capital, and its extension into other spaces and other modes of production. As Marx writes in a passage illustrating the overdetermined historical appearance of capital:

> The discovery of gold and silver in America, the extirpation, enslavement and entombment in mines of the indigenous population of that continent, the beginnings of the conquest and plunder of India, and the conversion of Africa into a preserve for the commercial hunting of blackskins, are all things which characterize the dawn of early capitalist production ... These different moments are systematically combined together [*systematisch zusammengeßt*] at the end of the seventeenth century in England; the combination embraces the colonies, the national debt, the modern tax system, and the system of protection. These methods depend on brute force [*brutalser Gewalt*], for instance the colonial system. But they all employ the power of the state, the concentrated and organized force of society [*Gewalt der Gesellschaft*], to hasten, as in a hothouse, the process of transformation of the feudal mode of production into the capitalist mode, and to shorten the transition. Force is the midwife of every old society which is pregnant with a new one. It is itself an economic power [*ökonomische Potenz*].[45]

As the passage above indicates, primitive accumulation is situated both at the historical formation of the capitalist mode of production as well as at the point of its extension into other modes of production through the violence of colon-

---

45   Marx 1977, p. 915.

isation. Primitive accumulation serves as the name not only for an event, but a process, the expropriation and legislation necessary to destroy other economic and social relations in order to make them productive for capital. Thus primitive accumulation becomes not only a cause of the capitalist mode of production but its effect. The two essential results of primitive accumulation – workers with only their labour power to sell and capital free to invest anywhere – are also effects of the capitalist mode of production's encounter with other modes and economies. While the above quote crosses a multitude of questions and problems regarding the relationship between capitalism and colonialism (introducing a series of questions which cannot be dealt with here), it opens up the possibility of understanding primitive accumulation as the long process by which capital expands to other spaces across the globe.

The assertion that 'force' [Gewalt] is the transforming agent, the common ground where the disparate strategies of colonisation and accumulation meet, would seem to suggest another sense in which primitive accumulation continues beyond the transition from feudalism to capitalism. Even if we bracket for a moment the forms of colonisation and neo-colonisation that would make primitive accumulation a continual process, these questions are difficult to answer due to the intimate relationship that the violence of primitive accumulation has with the new order it engenders. Poised as it were at the point of transformation, the moment of violence almost disappears in its execution.[46] Thus the violence of primitive accumulation is immediately justified within and by the new order that it constitutes. For example, the destruction of the common lands by the enclosure acts only appears violent from the perspective of the old order and practices that it destroys, from the new order, from the expansion of wage relations which have as their presupposition a mass of disenfranchised individuals and an entirely new relation between property, law,

---

46   Gilles Deleuze and Félix Guattari have related Marx's critique of political economy to a particular type of violence that is difficult to critique because it is always presented as pre-accomplished and carrying its justification. As Deleuze and Guattari write: 'Hence the very particular character of state violence: it is very difficult to pinpoint this violence because it always presents itself as pre-accomplished. It is not even adequate to say that the violence rests with the mode of production. Marx made the observation in the case of capitalism: there is a violence that necessarily operates through the state, precedes the capitalist mode of production, constitutes the primitive accumulation and makes possible the capitalist mode of production itself. From a standpoint within the capitalist mode of production, it is very difficult to say who is the thief and who is the victim, or even where the violence resides. That is because the worker is born entirely naked and the capitalist objectively 'clothed' as an independent owner. That which gave the worker and the capitalist this form eludes us because it operated in other modes of production' (Deleuze and Guattari 1987, p. 447).

and labour, it cannot appear as violent, or even appear at all. As Michel Foucault argues, the period of primitive accumulation entails a fundamental transformation of the definition of illegality and property: the longstanding relations of traditional use surrounding land (free pasture, wood collecting etc.) were replaced by a new regime of property. '… [L]anded property became absolute property; all the tolerated 'rights' that the peasantry had acquired or preserved were now rejected by the new owners who regarded it simply as theft'.[47] It is not by accident, or even through the cunning of the emergent bourgeoisie that primitive accumulation is characterised by an intermingling of violence and law. In fact, it is this intermingling of violence and law, the simultaneity of accumulation and the right to accumulate that Marx understands as primitive accumulation. As Antonio Negri writes with respect to primitive accumulation: 'Violence thus constitutes the vehicle between accumulation and right'.[48]

If the violence of primitive accumulation is difficult to locate as an event because it loses itself in the law and the new society that it produces, it is also difficult to locate because it is always situated with respect to a transformation of violence – the emergence of a new type of violence. In the long passage from feudalism to capitalism this transformation is in the first instance the passage from the dispersed violence of feudal lords to violence monopolised and standardised by law and the bourgeois state. As Marx states, in the beginning, '[t]he rising bourgeoisie needs the power of the state, and uses it to "regulate" wages, i.e., to force them into the limits suitable for making a profit, to lengthen the working day, and to keep the worker himself at his normal level of dependence. This is an essential part of so-called primitive accumulation'.[49] In the first instance the sporadic and excessive feudal forms of violence pass into the universality of law, but this is not the entirety of the transformation. Marx also seems to indicate a second moment of this transformation of violence in which violence disappears not into the neutrality of law, but into the quotidian relations that are the effects and cause of the law. In Marx's words: 'The silent compulsion of economic relations sets the seal on the domination of the capitalist over the worker. Direct extra-economic force is still of course used, but only in exceptional cases'.[50] Marx is somewhat ambiguous with respect to the closure of primitive accumulation, and the relation to the mode of production it engenders. At times, Marx seems to argue that primitive accumulation and the overt violence it involves ends in the day-to-day relations of exploitation.

---

47   Foucault 1977, p. 85.
48   Negri 1999, p. 254.
49   Marx 1977, p. 899.
50   Marx 1977, p. 899.

While at other times it appears that the violent law-making power of primitive accumulation is merely privatised and brought indoors into the factory. Marx emphatically illustrates the order of discipline imposed by the factory codes:

> The overseer's book of penalties replaces the slave-driver's lash. All punishments naturally resolve themselves into fines and deductions from wages, and the law-giving talent of the factory Lycurgus so arranges matters that a violation of these laws is, if possible, more profitable to him than the keeping of them.[51]

Marx suggests that there is a qualitative difference between primitive accumulation and the capitalist economy it engenders, in terms of the former's bloody discontinuity and the latter's continuity and silent functioning. At the same time, however, Marx would suggest that this qualitative change is perhaps best understood as a change in the form of violence itself. Capitalist accumulation is nothing other than primitive accumulation continued onto the shop floor, and thus nothing other than a continuation of the modification of violence begun with 'bloody legislation' and the enclosure acts.

Primitive accumulation cannot be reduced to a dialectic of 'law-producing' and 'law-conserving' violence since it entails a transformation of violence itself.[52] 'The immediate violence of the exploitation and the juridical superstructure becomes a mediated violence and a structure internal to the productive process. The law – or really, the form of violence – becomes a machine, or really, a permanent procedure, its constant innovation and its rigid discipline'.[53] Reading *Capital* for its nascent theory of power reveals that force does not simply end with the moment of primitive accumulation but migrates into the process of production itself. As Foucault summarises, '… [O]ne can find between the lines of *Capital* an analysis, or at least the sketch of an analysis, which would be the history of the technology of power, such as it was exercised in the workshops and factories'.[54] Furthermore, Foucault's own theory of disciplinary power can be understood as the conceptualisation of a thought of violence that is articulated 'without concept' through Marx's multiple allusions

---

51   Marx 1977, p. 550.

52   The concept of law-making violence, the violence that instantiates a new legal order, as well as the distinction between law-making and law-preserving violence, the violence that maintains an existing order, is drawn from Walter Benjamin's influential essay 'The Critique of Violence' (p. 280).

53   Negri 1999, p. 257.

54   Foucault 1994, p. 189.

to the power of ancient despots internalised in the capitalist mode of production.[55] Thus Foucault, at least in his writing of the 1970s, can be understood to be producing a sort of 'symptomatic reading' of Marx's theory of power, one that destablises any opposition between primitive accumulation as contingent event and the capitalist mode of production as silent necessity.

The problem of the relation between primitive accumulation and the capitalist mode of production opens onto yet another problem: the definition of the capitalist mode of production, or stated otherwise, the difference between capitalism thought as a mode of production and capitalism thought as an 'economy'. What is at stake in such a distinction is the understanding of the continuity of capital, the reproduction of the forces and relations of production over time. To understand capital as a mode of production is, in some readings, to insist upon the necessarily complex conditions of this continuity – an entire series of complex factors including the state, law, and ideology are necessary to the functioning of capital. To understand capitalism, or any other mode of production, as an economy is to lapse into an 'economism' of sorts. 'Economism', briefly, is the guarantee of the adequacy of the economy to its own reproduction without the necessary implication of other factors, or elements, such as the state, ideology, law, or subjectivity. Economism takes the law-like nature of the economy as a given, and understands its effects on other elements to be that of a simple linear cause. To return to an ambiguity indicated above with respect to the closure of primitive accumulation, we can see the possibility of interpreting the 'silent compulsion of economic relations' as either the dominance of the economy over other instances of the social, or, following Marx's statements regarding the disciplinary power of the capitalist, as the internalisation of the violence within the system itself.

---

55   In 'Les mailles du pouvoir' Foucault goes so far as to argue for the reciprocal determination of disciplinary power and capitalism: capital requires disciplinary power and disciplinary power makes capitalism possible (Foucault 1994, p. 200). This lecture, which was originally presented in Brazil in 1981, constitutes Foucault's most appreciative estimation of the influence of Foucault's relation to Marx. In this lecture not only does Foucault explicitly link the rise of capitalism with disciplinary power, a statement which can be found throughout Foucault's work, but more importantly, and uncharacteristically, he locates in Marx's work a complex thought of power. This final statement stands in sharp contrast to statements made in *The History of Sexuality* and *Power/Knowledge* in which Foucault argues that Marx, and more importantly, Marxism, remains trapped in a 'sovereign' concept of power in which power is viewed as something that can be possessed, rather than as a relation.

3   The Difference of Primitive Accumulation

At the level of individual quotes and citations, the problem of the contours and complexity of the mode of production is strictly speaking irresolvable; it will always be possible to oppose an 'economist' Marx to a 'non-economist' Marx – the entire history of Marxism bears witness to this possibility. In order to get beyond the seemingly endless back and forth of this or that statement, or concept, of Marx's writing, it is necessary to pose another seemingly unrelated question, the question of the place of primitive accumulation in the exposition, or logic, of Marx's *Capital*. Louis Althusser has argued that Marx's later writings, especially the first volume of *Capital* (since it was completed by Marx) engage philosophical problems articulated through their very exposition, in the order of chapters, and the logic of categories. Marx himself writes in the afterward to the second edition of *Capital*:

> Of course the method of presentation [*Darstellung*] must differ in form from that of inquiry [*Forschung*]. The latter has to appropriate the material in detail, to analyze its different forms of development and to track down their inner connection. Only after this work has been done can the real movement be appropriately presented.[56]

Capital, according to Althusser, is not an incomplete manuscript, a manifesto, or a series of notes 'written for self clarification'; it is a completed text, or at least part of one, and as such it engages and enacts a particular question: the question of its exposition or logic. That is, the relation between abstract concepts, examples and historical events, a relation which poses the problem of the presentation, or even the representation of something called the capitalist mode of production itself. We have already perhaps glimpsed something of this problem in the critique of so-called primitive accumulation. In part, and if it is possible to put aside the clear differences of ideology and politics, *the difference between the bourgeois theory of primitive accumulation and Marx's theory can be expressed as a difference of representation.* For the bourgeois theorist before Marx, the moral difference between thrift and expenditure is adequate to the representation of capital as a social relation; whereas for Marx the presentation of primitive accumulation and the formation of capital involved not only fundamentally different elements, such as the entire history of the dissolution of the feudal mode of production, the violent formation of the capitalist mode

---

56   Marx 1988, p. 27.

of production, and the history of colonialism, but also the question of the relations between these elements. If there is a specifically materialist dialectic, as
a thought of contradiction, antagonism, and relation, or if Marx is something
other than Hegel turned upside-down, Hegel applied to the material world,
then this 'dialectic' (if that word is still appropriate) would have to be found
in the logic of the presentation of *Capital*.

Marx cannot give a definition of the capitalist mode of production; any such
definition would belie its fundamental complexity and overdetermination.[57]
What is being represented is not a simple object for thought, but a relation
or series of relations and their particular dynamism and tensions.[58] That is,
Marx's text deals with the problem of the relations between structures, the
division of labour, the relations of production, etc., which are different elements of a larger structure, the capitalist mode of production.[59] The relation
between these structures cannot be contained or presented within existing
models of causality (they are not simply the causes or effects of each other
in a mechanical or expressive sense) or presentation (most notably the often
presupposed division between essence and appearance); rather, this relation is
one of immanent causality: the cause, or structure, is immanent in its effects,
there is nothing outside of its effects. Thus there is no simple division or pri-

---

57   In the first edition of *Lire le Capital* Althusser expanded upon the extent to which this idea
     of *Darstellung* necessarily intersected with the problems of representation, and aesthetic
     representation through a comparison/etymology of the terms *Darstellung* and *Vorstel-*
     lung. As Althusser writes: 'In *Vorstellung*, one certainly has to do with a position, but one
     which is presented *out front*, which thus supposes something which is kept *behind* this
     pre-position, something which is *represented* by that which is kept out in front [represen-
     ted] by its emissary: the *Vorstellung*. In *Darstellung* on the contrary, *there is nothing behind*:
     the very thing is there, 'da' presented in the position of presence' (Althusser and Balibar
     1965, p. 646). For this point regarding the significance of the concept of structure/*Darstel-*
     lung and its history in Althusser's thought I am indebted to Michael Sprinker's *Imaginary*
     Relations: Aesthetics and Ideology in the Theory of Historical Materialism, whose transla-
     tion of the passage from Althusser I have relied upon here (p. 291), and Warren Montag's
     'Althusser's Nominalism: Structure and Singularity'.

58   Marx 1973, p. 102.

59   Althusser in his contribution seems to refer to this relation as that between the regional
     mode of production and the global mode of production (Althusser and Balibar 1975,
     p. 397), in a sense giving the term mode of production, at the global level, a larger, more
     inclusive sense that goes beyond the economic proper, which would seem to be a regional
     mode of production. It is this distinction that would justify Fredric Jameson's claim that:
     'If therefore one wishes to characterize Althusser's Marxism as a structuralism, one must
     complete the characterization with the essential provision that it is a structuralism for
     which only *one* structure exists: namely the mode of production itself, or the synchronic
     system of social relations as a whole' (Jameson 1988, p. 36).

ority between cause and effect: every effect is equally and at the same time a cause.[60] This cause is both immanent and absent, because to be immanent and present in its effects is also to be un-localisable. This cause cannot be present or empirically given at any one point, hence the other name that Althusser gives it: 'metonymical causality'. Classical political economy is trapped in a 'fetishisa- tion' of the concrete in that it understands the capitalist mode of production to be constituted by the simple moral difference between thrift and greed: it fails to recognise the overdetermination of any cause. To risk something of an example of this overdetermined relation: elements of the capitalist mode of production that would seem to be its effects, such as the desire for accumu- lation on the part of the capitalist, or 'rationalised' hoarding, must equally be thought as causes and elements of its functioning. Without necessarily follow- ing all of the ramifications of Althusser's reading of *Capital*, it is important to indicate that Althusser's insistence on the intimate relation between present- ation, or philosophical exposition, and structure and the relations of the mode of production, displaces the earlier question regarding the place of transition or transformation in the mode of production from the infinite and inexhaust- ible series of quotes and counter-quotes of 'what Marx thought' to another and different problem – that of the exposition or logics (holding open for a second that there at least may be more than one) at work in Marx's text.

Marx's re-writing of the fantasy of primitive accumulation poses particular problems when placed within this question of textual presentation. Although primitive accumulation deals with the intersecting questions of the real rela- tions which have formed the capitalist mode of production, the dissolution of feudalism, and the imaginary apprehension of those relations (the moral- ity tale) it is placed at the end of *Capital* in the final chapters. There is thus a considerable difference between the presentation of primitive accumulation within the articulation of *Capital*, and its place in the historical formation. The text, *Capital*, begins from the famous analysis of the commodity form which constitutes the phenomenological appearance and common sense of the cap- italist mode of production, where '... [t]he wealth of societies in which the capitalist mode of production prevails appears as an "immense collection of commodities [*ungeheure Warensammlung*] ..."'[61] Marx does not begin *Capital* with the question of origins but with an element of capital that is at once quo- tidian and all encompassing in its scope. Marx's decision to begin with the com- modity is also somewhat curious since as much as capital confronts us as 'an

---

60   Althusser and Balibar 1975, p. 191.
61   Marx 1977, p. 126.

immense accumulation of commodities' it is not at all possible to equate capitalism with commodity production: the commodity, an object produced for the market, necessarily pre-exists the capitalist mode of production.[62] From the starting point of the commodity form, Marx develops the contradictory relationship between exchange and use values and abstract and concrete labour. Without attempting to offer anything like an overview or synopsis of the exposition of *Capital*, I will attempt to indicate something of the difference between primitive accumulation as the historical emergence of capital and the commodity form as the starting point for the presentation of capital. The difference between these two points is not only the difference between the synchronic articulation of the relations of capital and its historical emergence; it is also the difference between two different tendencies within the presentation [*Darstellung*] of the capitalist mode of production.

In a posthumously published text titled *Marx dans ses limites*, Althusser argues that Marx's writings, in even mature texts such as *Capital*, cannot be reduced to the articulation of a single presentation, but rather must be understood as themselves determined and constructed by multiple presentations and multiple logics. Thus in this later text (and others written at the same time) Althusser argues that it is no longer possible to separate Marx from the deviations of Marxism: that is, once it is recognised that the tendencies one is fighting against (most importantly economism and humanism) are not simply additions, or perversions, but have their condition of possibility in the tensions and divergent tendencies of Marx's own writing.[63] Despite the transformation of strategy in these later texts, Althusser's tactics remain the same: the tension between these different dimensions of Marx's thought are not located at the level of this or that quote, but must be extracted from the conflictual presentations or logics of Marx's writing. As with the later work on 'aleatory materialism', which it in some sense lays the ground for, this earlier division is not datable,

---

62   Marx considers the difference between a somewhat sporadic commodity production, excess goods sold to the market, and the commodity as general form of all production in an unpublished chapter of *Capital* (Marx 1977, p. 953).

63   Negri 1996a, p. 51. Of course it is possible to argue that this second 'moment' or strategy was always at work in the first, and thus that the entire self-presentation of the 'reconstruction' was an attempt to contend with certain political and ideological adversaries. 'For whatever may have been claimed, when [Althusser] enjoined us to "read *Capital*", it was not in order to restore some hypothetical purity of Marxism, but precisely in order to try to uncover the traces of the ideological class struggle of which Marx's text was itself a site, at the very moment and in the very forms in which Marx established the concepts that made it possible to theorize this struggle for the first time' (Lecourt 2001, p. 170).

with a definite before and after. Rather it manifests itself as an inner theoretical tension, which is the source of Marx's limits and productivity. As Balibar makes clear, the 'break' separating Marx's thought from its constitutive adversaries (classical political economy and Hegel) is not completed once and for all, but is continually reposed. 'Every break is at the same time irreversible and precarious, threatened with an impossible return to its ideological prehistory, without which it would not *last*, it would not *progress*'.[64]

There is a tension between the different beginnings of capital: a tension between the beginning of *Capital*, the commodity form, and the historical emergence of capitalism, primitive accumulation. The commodity form and the first chapter of capital proceed by a series of internal contradictions: from use value and exchange value, to abstract and concrete labor, and finally to surplus value itself. This movement is also the movement from the indeterminate abstraction of the commodity or value to what is finally the specific articulation of the capitalist mode of production including the day-to-day relations and struggles on the factory floor. It is in part due to the forceful linearity of this argument, in which the day to day struggles over the working day seem to unfold from the contradiction between use and exchange value, that many writers have argued that the 'commodity form' is itself the essence of the capitalist mode of production.[65]

The 'logic' that opens *Capital* Volume I does not account for the entirety of the text. Althusser contends that it is continually interrupted by chapters and analyses which incorporate relations and levels irreducible to the enfolding of the internal contradictions of the commodity form, and are outside the order of presentation [*hors ordre d'exposition*], constituting a break with its economistic logic.[66] While this rupture includes the chapters on primitive accumulation, and thus the problem of the foundation of the capitalist mode of production, it is not limited to it. This 'other' logic that breaks with economism includes the chapters on co-operation, the working day, and the chapters on machinery and large scale industry. What is at stake in this other logic that remains outside of the dominant order of exposition? How might an alternative be thought of in other than negative terms, as other than an interruption or

---

64   Balibar 1994, p. 172.
65   The opening paragraph of Lukács' 'Reification and the Consciousness of the Proletariat' reads as a definition of Althusser's concept of expressive causality. 'For at this stage in the history of mankind there is no problem that does not ultimately lead back to that question and there is no solution that could not be found in the solution to the riddle of commodity-structure' (p. 83).
66   Althusser 1994b, p. 397.

an outside to the dominant logic – a logic in which the relations and conflicts of capitalism all appear as simply effects of the contradictory essence of the commodity form?

The beginning of a response to these questions can be found in the disparity between the two starting points: the commodity form and primitive accumulation. The first assumes what the second puts into question by historicising – that is, the commodification of labour itself. Whereas primitive accumulation reveals the violent operations necessary to constitute a labouring subject, to constitute those who have only their labour power to sell, the analysis of the commodity form takes this condition as an already accomplished fact. Once the commodification of labor is assumed, surplus value or surplus labour is only the labour in excess of what is necessary to reproduce labour power: the value of what is produced over the value of what labor power costs.

> When you read Section 1 Book 1 of *Capital*, you find a theoretical present-ation of surplus value: it is an arithmetical presentation, in which surplus value is calculable, defined by a difference (in value) between the value produced by labor power on the one hand and the value of the commod-ities necessary for the reproduction of this labor power (wages) on the other. And in this arithmetical presentation of surplus value, labor figures purely and simply as a commodity.[67]

The 'arithmetical presentation' assumes abstract labour: that is, it assumes labour power as an anthropological constant. Human beings are already ex-changeable as different deposits of labour power and thus capitalism is always possible.[68]

---

67   Althusser 1979, p. 233.
68   It is precisely this aspect of Marxism, its anthropology of labour, that Foucault rejects. 'So I don't think that we can accept the traditional Marxist analysis, which assumes that, labor being man's concrete essence, the capitalist system is what transforms that labor into profit, into hyperprofit [*sur-profit*] or surplus value. The fact is, capitalism penetrates much more deeply into our existence. That system, as it was established in the nineteenth century, was obliged to elaborate a set of political techniques, techniques of power, by which people's bodies and their time would become labor power and labor time so as to be effectively used and thereby transformed into hyperprofit. But in order for there to be hyperprofit, there had to be an infra-power [*sous-pouvoir*]. A web of microscopic, capillary political power had to be established at the level of man's very existence, attaching men to the production apparatus, while making them into agents of production, into workers' (Foucault 2000, p. 86). Here once again the juxtaposition of Foucault and Althusser is use-ful: whereas the former's relationship to Marx vacillates from appreciation to dismissal, the latter recognises the vacillation internal to Marx's text.

In taking labour as always already constituted as a commodity, as already a quantifiable unit of abstract labour, what is overlooked are the interlacing apparatuses that transform bodies and relations into units of labour power – what Althusser famously explored through his examination of the ideological 'reproduction of the relations of production'.[69] What is overlooked are not only the aleatory conditions of capitalism, its constitution as a political, legal, and cultural order, but the overdetermined conditions of its survival. In Marx an indication of these necessary conditions (apparatuses or ensembles) are given through the analysis of primitive accumulation, albeit in the form of an almost negative outline. Antonio Negri indicates that the destruction and violence that defines primitive accumulation can only be understood if one posits forms of cooperation and social relations which pre-exist capital, and must be destroyed or seriously modified in order to produce the 'free worker' necessary to capitalist accumulation. In Negri's terms, 'in the period of primitive accumulation, when capital enveloped and constricted pre-existent labor forms to its own valorization, it was capital which posed the form of cooperation – and this consisted in the emptying of the pre-constituted connections of the traditional laboring subjects'.[70] The intimate relation between the formation of the capitalist mode of production and violence found in primitive accumulation has as its correlate the materiality of social relations that pre-exist capital. Thus it is possible to find in Marx a third moment of primitive accumulation, after the expropriation or destruction of the previous mode and its violent legislation, a moment of normalisation that bears on subjectivity and sociality itself. As Marx writes: 'The advance of capitalist production develops a working class which by education [*Erziehung*], tradition, and habit [*Gewohnheit*] looks upon the requirements of that mode of production as self evident natural laws'.[71] The violence and dissolution of the old mode of production is followed by the normalisation of the new mode of production, a normalisation which obliterates the memory of the past mode of production as well as any traces of the violent foundation of the new mode of production. This normalisation constitutive of the regularity and functioning of the capitalist mode of production is actualised not only at the levels of laws or institutions but also at the level of subjectivity.[72] In order for a new mode of production such as capital to be instituted it is not sufficient for it to simply form a new economy, or write new laws, it must institute itself in the quotidian dimensions of existence – it must

---

69   Negri 1996a, p. 52.
70   Negri 1996b, p. 165.
71   Marx 1977, p. 899.
72   Albiac 1996, p. 13.

become habit (what Althusser termed the 'society effect'). This is one aspect of the 'becoming necessary' of the mode of production in its constitution – it makes it impossible to live or imagine another world. Whereas the chapters on the commodity and on abstract labour would seem to present labour as an anthropological constant, the section on primitive accumulation reminds us that '[t]he positing of the individual as worker, in this nakedness, is itself a product of history'.[73] What 'primitive accumulation' reveals is that there is no *mode of production* without a corresponding *mode of subjection*, or a production of subjectivity.[74] The 'economy', as something isolated and quantifiable, only exists insofar as it is sustained by its inscription in the state, the law, habits, and desires.

4   Primitive Accumulation Today

The continuation of primitive accumulation would then encompass all of the dimensions of the concept sketched out above. What primitive accumulation reveals through its sheer violence is that the capitalist mode of production cannot simply be equated with a market or an economy; its origin cannot be accounted for through a narrative of thrift and greed or buying and selling. In order for the capitalist mode of production to assert itself historically it must destroy the pre-existing economies of subsistence and their corresponding ways of life. Thus, primitive accumulation continues wherever the capitalist mode of production produces its own legality, norms, and its own forms of sub-

---

73   Marx 1973, p. 472.
74   The following quote from Balibar would seem to be instructive here, provided that one keeps in mind that for Balibar (and Althusser) 'ideology' is nothing other than the material production of subjectivity. 'I even think that we can describe what such a schema would ideally consist of. It would not be the sum of a 'base' and a 'superstructure,' working like a complement or supplement of historicity, but rather the combination of two 'bases' of explanation or two determinations both incompatible and indissociable: the *mode of subjection* and the *mode of production* (or, more generally, the ideological mode and the generalised economic mode). Both are material, although in the opposite sense. To name these different senses of the materiality of subjection and production, the traditional terms *imaginary* and *reality* suggest themselves. One can adopt them, provided that one keep in mind that in any historical conjuncture, the effects of the imaginary can only appear through and by means of the real, and the effects of the real through and by means of the imaginary; in other words, the structural law of causality in history is the *detour through and by means of the other scene*. Let us say, parodying Marx, that economy has no more a "history of its own" than does ideology, since each has its history only through the other that is the efficient cause of its own effects' (Balibar 1995, p. 160).

jectivity. That is to say, if in this first sense primitive accumulation refers to the necessary non-economic conditions of the capitalist mode of production, its inscription in laws, codes of behavior, and habits, then primitive accumulation, or the production of subjectivity associated with it, is coextensive with the capitalist mode of production. Thus Althusser's turn to primitive accumulation in the essay on 'aleatory materialism' follows one of his most important theoretical innovations: that there is no simple functioning of a mode of production without ideological and cultural conditions, conditions which constitute individuals as subjects of the mode of production.

Moreover, if one wanted to look for the relevance of primitive accumulation for capitalism today, then it is also necessary to pose the question as to what are the contemporary equivalents of 'the commons'. If primitive accumulation in its classical sense used a combination of force and law to dismantle relations of labouring cooperation, then the question is what are the currently existing relations of cooperation and sociality that are being dismantled. As Michael Hardt and Antonio Negri contend, there is today a sort of neo-primitive accumulation, an accumulation not simply of wealth and workers but of subjective potentials, desires, and knowledges, many of which were formed outside of capitalism, in the public sector and in the interstices of commodified existence.[75] Moreover, it is increasingly the power of life itself, the capacity to reproduce and live, from the genetic code to the basic necessities of existence, that like the feudal commons, is increasingly coming under the rule of 'absolute private property'.

As much as these two instances, primitive accumulation as the accumulation of subjectivity necessary to any mode of production and the accumulation of the remaining non-commodified spaces, point to the continued relevance of the concept today, its relevance is not limited to detailing the entrenched status and absolute reach of the capitalist mode of production. There is also finally a 'revolutionary' status of primitive accumulation, or at least one oriented towards a thought of social transformation. Primitive accumulation is the persistence of the encounter at the heart of the capitalist mode of production. It is the insistence of the encounter in the simple fact that the constitutive elements of the mode of production, money, desires, bodies, beliefs, etc. can always become unhinged from their particular articulation. Primitive accumulation insofar as it deals with the overdetermined and complex conditions of the capitalist mode of production, attests to the persistence of non-capitalist

---

75   Hardt and Negri 2000, p. 258.

social relations, of the cooperative multitude that threatens capitalism.[76] The fact that multiple conditions, multiple relations of force, law, and ideology, are necessary for the constitution of the capitalist mode of production also means that its reproduction is not guaranteed, and thus constitutes the possibility of its transformation: overdetermination is inseparable from underdetermination.[77]

The placement of 'primitive accumulation' at the end of Volume I of *Capital* can thus also be understood as a reminder of the sheer contingency of the mode of production, the possibility that things could be and thus can still be otherwise. As Althusser writes: '[Primitive accumulation] continues to today, not just in the visible example of the third world, but as a constant process that inscribes the aleatory at the heart of the capitalist mode of production'.[78] Thus primitive accumulation opens a space between the orthodox Marxist belief in the inevitable collapse of capitalism and current ideologies that argue that capitalism is eternal. There are no such guarantees, only the overlapping histories of the encounter – in the space between these encounters there is the possibility for invention.

---

76   Negri 1999, p. 259.
77   Balibar 1996, p. 115.
78   Althusser 1994a, p. 573, my translation.

CHAPTER 2

The Present as Pre-History: Adorno and Balibar on the Transformation of Labor

> Horror consists in its always remaining the same – the persistence of 'pre-history' – but is realized as constantly different, unforeseen, exceeding all expectation, the faithful shadow of developing productive forces.
>
> THEODOR ADORNO

∴

As a problem or topic for discussion, the 'division of mental and manual labour' is perhaps as awkward as the phrase itself. This is in part due to the fact that the phrase would seem to belong to that long night of Marxist thought in which various quotes and concepts were mined from Marx's various writings in order to become explanatory concepts and slogans. If we move beyond the connotations of the term and its specific history and try to focus on it as an object or problem it only becomes more unwieldy. Initially, it would appear to be entirely an anthropological problem, a division fundamental to the very structure of *homo sapiens*, or, at the very least, a division that would have to be situated at the origin of human society, at the foundation of culture. At the same time, it is a contemporary problem, referring not only to the division of planning and execution in the labour process, but also to the various bureaucracies of expertise that structure political life. However, it is perhaps inaccurate to refer to the reorganisation of life through the various hierarchies of command and obedience as a problem, since this aspect of existence has become so pervasive, becoming a part of all walks of life, so as to be accepted as natural. Thus the phrase 'division of mental and manual labour' would gravitate towards a definition that is at once transcendental and quotidian, anthropological and historical. The instability of the term, its inability to remain within a specific area of knowledge and thus to intersect with the very definition of humanity and the foundation of the state, would suggest an interest and productivity beyond its apparent dogmatic inflexibility. Between the closure of the slogan and the plurality of the problems that it points to, the division of mental and manual labour remains a missed encounter as a concept and a problem.

In order to return to this missed encounter, to this overlooked possibility, it is necessary first to return to the primary text of its development. In *The German Ideology* Marx ascribes a central place to the division between mental and manual labour in the genealogy of the specific ideology of Germany, an ideology which turns out to be nothing other than philosophy itself, or more specifically, German Idealism. The division of mental and manual labour is not only the necessary precondition of ideology, of a set of beliefs separated from their organic connection with a particular form of life, but it intensifies and exasperates the alienating effects of the division of labour. As Marx writes, 'Division of labor only becomes truly such from the moment when a division of material and mental labor appears'.[1] To which he adds in a marginal note, perhaps anticipating Nietzsche, 'The first form of ideologists, priests, is concurrent'. It is the division of mental and manual labour that constitutes the division of society into two different classes with distinct modes of life: 'the division of labor implies the possibility, nay the fact, that intellectual and material activity – enjoyment and labor, production and consumption – devolve onto different individuals'.[2] Despite the central role that the division of mental and manual labour plays in the articulation of the concept of ideology, this division and the very idea of mental activity as labour is given little critical attention in the rest of Marx's writings. In *The German Ideology* the division of mental and manual labour is integral to the very definition of ideology, in later works it is subordinated to the general critique of capitalist exploitation, becoming merely another of its multiple effects. Thus, while ideology became central to Marxist philosophy and political practice, the concept integral to its initial formation fell by the wayside.

One could infer multiple reasons for this omission. The first is the immense historical and anthropological problems that this division opens at the heart of Marx's critique of political economy. The division of mental and manual labour is located not at the onset of capitalist production, with the integration of science into the apparatuses of machinery, but in the obscure mists of its prehistory. In Marx's text, it is situated sometime after the most ancient and anthropological division, the sexual division of labour, and before the formation of the state and the beginning of recorded history. Despite its ancient origin it is not one of those elements of prehistory that dissipates with the

---

1   Marx and Engels 1970, p. 51.
2   Marx and Engels 1970, p. 52.

formation of capital, as 'all that is solid melts into air'. While the specific holy proclamations of the different priests may have been rendered profane with the march of history, the very division between thought and existence that makes the priestly caste possible has not made it to the dustbin of history. On the contrary, this division has only continued; new figures take the place of the priest – philosopher, bureaucrat, scientist. At the same time the very idea of a division between mental and manual labour presupposes that all activities, physical and mental, can be considered 'labour', an idea which presupposes the generalisation of wage labour, and thus capitalism.[3] The very idea of such a division of labour is at once ancient and contemporary. Thus what Marx's idea calls into question is the very idea of a history that is at the very least linear if not progressive, an idea which rightly or wrongly has been identified with Marx. The very idea of the division of labour, as an ancient form of domination, dwelling within the modern state and the contemporary production process, would appear to throw a stick in the spokes of the idea of capitalism as a 'modernization without mercy'.

As a philosophical concept or theme the division of mental and manual labour would seem to be as embarrassing for philosophy as it is unwieldy. Not only does it exceed its position within any historical, sociological, or political logic, but it exposes philosophy to the scandal of its conditions. Philosophy remains a product of the very division which it attempts to master and transform.

1   Odysseus, or a Genealogy of the Intellectual

The historical instability of the division of mental and manual labour, its status as pre-historical, which Marx avoided, is explicitly taken up by Theodor Adorno. It is possible to read Horkheimer and Adorno's discussion of the transition from myth to enlightenment in the *Dialectic of Enlightenment* as an expansion of Marx's marginal remark on the first form of ideologist, the priest. For Adorno and Horkheimer the very separation of subject from object, which makes possible both substitutions of religious sacrifice, and the abstraction of enlightenment, are founded upon the material conditions that separate mastery and labour. The fundamental illustration of this division, and the domination it entails, is Odysseus who, lashed to the mast, is able to hear and contemplate the song of the sirens because the oarsmen continue to row on, deaf

---

3   Balibar 1985, p. 29.

to the song or what it means. Intellectual labour, the work of abstraction or even the idle reflection of aesthetic enjoyment, presupposes the domination over manual labour for its very existence. As Adorno and Horkheimer write: 'The universality of ideas as developed by discursive logic, domination in the conceptual sphere is raised up on the basis of actual domination'.[4]

Horkheimer and Adorno's assertion regarding the history of this division, as well as their general claim that Odysseus is the prototypical bourgeois, whose narrative of self-sacrifice and renunciation is nothing other than the epic form of modern subject formation, stretches any claim of historical credibility. However, that would seem to be precisely the point: history, the recording of events and narratives, is already on this side of the division. The division between mental and manual labour is necessarily prehistorical, constituting an unthinkable other-side of what is recordable and thinkable. Adorno's rewriting of Marx's account of the division of mental and manual labour does not only assign it a different origin with an earlier date, but in doing so radicalizes the problem from the realm of a sociology of knowledge to a philosophical problem; that is, it is no longer limited to the specific realm of say, the sociology of work, but becomes a fundamental question to the very idea or practice of philosophy.

If Odysseus's contemplation of the song of the siren had as its material condition the oarsmen who were willing to do his dirty work, our contemporary equivalent is the commodity form. The world confronts us as an immense accumulation of commodities and this accumulation, and its corresponding production, division, and specialisation is the material condition of thought in general. By this I do not merely intend to raise the banal point that we write papers because we are not foraging for food, and so on, but as Adorno argues in *Negative Dialectics*, the fundamental aspect of thought, the unifying of disparate phenomena under concepts, has the commodity form as its precondition. Before the world can be unified under the concept, it must be unified under the generality of exchange. While it is impossible to follow all of what Adorno means by identity in that work, and the role identity has in thought here, it is at least possible to follow him in the argument that this unification and purging of differences, or what he calls 'identification', arrives on the scene first as practical matter before becoming fundamental to thought. As Adorno writes:

> The exchange principle [*Tauschprinzip*] the reduction of human labor to the abstract universal concept of average working hours, is fundamentally

---

4   Adorno and Horkheimer 1987, p. 14.

akin to the principle of identification. Barter [*Tausch*] is the social model of the principle and without the principle there would be no barter; it is through barter that the non-identical individuals and performances become commensurable and identical.[5]

It is the action of exchange in which fundamentally disparate objects and activities, from objects to labour time, are rendered equivalent and interchangeable. The ability that thought or logic has to do the same, to posit pure concepts abstract and indifferent to their concrete contents, is only an after-image of a fundamental transformation of material existence.[6] The abstractions of thought arrive after, or at least along with, the material abstractions of money and the commodity, which are their material preconditions.

At this point it might seem that we have drifted from the problem of the division of mental and manual labour from *The German Ideology* to an investigation of the commodity form. Moreover, since the commodity form is all pervasive, it is no longer clear that we are dealing with a division of mental and manual labour, at least in the sense that would separate a class of manual from the class of intellectual labourers. The commodity form, and its division of exchange and use value, can be understood as a migration of this division from society in general to each and every individual. Commodities are purchased on the basis of their particular qualities, their use value, while it is this particularity that becomes the object of mental and affective evaluation, it is the universality of exchange value that actually constitutes the ground of their exchange.[7] Exchange value is not a mental approximation of the different commodities, but a concrete effect of the labour process. There is a division between mental labour, the desire or consciousness of the individual who wants this or that particular commodity, and manual labour, the actual practical relations, from the labour process to the market, that constitute the value of the commodity. With the commodity form the relation between the division of mental and manual labour is reversed, the concrete particularity is a fetish of consciousness and the abstract equivalence is produced in and through practical relations. This

---

5 Adorno 1992, p. 146.
6 On this point see Theodor Adorno's *Introduction to Sociology*, where Adorno writes: 'The abstract element here is not an idea which is content with the trifling observation that everything is connected with everything else ... The abstraction in question is really the specific form of the exchange process itself, the underlying social fact through which socialization first comes about' (Adorno 2000, p. 31).
7 Alfred Sohn-Rethel writes: 'In commodity exchange the action and the consciousness of people go separate ways. Only the action is abstract; the consciousness of the actors is not' (Sohn-Rethel 1978, p. 30).

division, between the material abstractions of exchange and value which run the world and particular drives and tastes which are only the window dressing of the commodity, condemns the work of the intellectual to a particular kind of impotence. As Adorno writes:

> The intellectual, particularly when philosophically inclined, is cut off from practical life: revulsion from it has driven him to concern himself with so-called things of the mind. But material practice is not only the pre-condition of his existence, it is basic to the world which he criticizes in his work. If he knows nothing of this basis he shoots into thin air ... [H]e hypostatizes as an absolute his intellect which was only formed through contact with economic reality and abstract exchange relations, and which can become intellect solely by reflecting on its own conditions.[8]

Adorno's diagnosis here is a negative one: the less the intellectual thinks of economic reality, the more she thinks in line with it, perpetuating the ideal of consciousness separate from material reality. However, if she turns towards economic reality, she risks losing the autonomy necessary to criticise it. 'Intellectual business is helped, by the isolation of intellect from business, to become a comfortable ideology'. The division between mental and manual labour, between pure thought and the practical matters of existence, only reinforces their relation, a relation of identity in non-identity. The more that intellectual work sees itself as separate from its material conditions the more it functions in the service of these same conditions. We are not too far from Odysseus on the mast, free to wail and scream, but cut off from anything that can be heard by the oarsmen.

While passages on the exchange principle and identification from *Negative Dialectics* update Adorno's remarks from the primordial division between head and hand to the contemporary condition of an existence thoroughly structured by exchange value, it is not without a great deal of ambiguity. There is a productive uncertainty in Adorno's writing on the commodity form, between a socio-economic critique of the dominance of exchange value over use value and a philosophical critique of the formalism, and identity, of the concept. It is possible to understand this uncertainty as a particular kind of chicken and egg problem: what came first, the economic relations of exchange which quantified the disparate products and activities of human existence, or the basic will to master reality by dominating it and classifying it? Of course, much of the nov-

---

8   Adorno 1974, p. 132.

elty and importance of Adorno's writing will be overlooked if this is presented as a matter of either/or, of choosing one of these two theoretical alternatives. Adorno is refusing to place economic exploitation or a more primordial will to domination in the place of the last instance.

The coexistence of these two modes of explanation in Adorno has a dialectical structure, a dialectic of tension that is not sublated into some higher term. Exploitation and domination coexist as two different narratives, each offering a different explanation. Thus it is possible, even necessary, to find both a primordial will to dominate the world and the traces of the commodity form in the activity and concepts of thought. Adorno's dialectic of exploitation and domination, of history and nature, refuses both a vulgar Marxism, which reduces all domination to exploitation, and a vulgar anthropology, which finds an ahistorical antisocial tendency underlying all of human history.[9] While the first of these was more of a problem in Adorno's time than in ours, the second has become the spontaneous philosophy underlying all of the various racisms, cynicisms, and philosophies of the clash of civilisations.[10] At the same time that Adorno refuses these ideologies, it suggests a new type of investigation that has interesting similarities with Étienne Balibar's exploration of 'philosophical anthropology'.

2   Intellectual Difference

Balibar's conception of philosophical anthropology is not a return to pure speculation about the nature of man, as if the various critiques (feminist, postcolonial, post-structural, etc.) of this object had never taken place, but rather an investigation into the unstable, but unavoidable question or image of the human. Balibar is primarily concerned with what he calls 'anthropological difference', a difference that fulfills two conditions: first, it is a necessary component of any definition of the human (such as language); and second, the dividing line can never finally be objectively drawn.[11] Examples of this would include

---

9   Marx, of course, suspects all anthropology and carefully refrains from locating antagonism in human nature or in primitive times, which he paints according to the cliché of the Golden Age; but this makes him only more stubborn in his insistence on the historical necessity of antagonism. Economics is said to come before dominion, which must not be deduced otherwise than economically (Adorno 1992, p. 321).

10   Although it is possible to suggest that vulgar Marxism has been replaced by vulgar-liberalism with its belief in the free market as the necessary and sufficient condition of all future freedoms.

11   Balibar 2004, p. 240, n. 21.

sexual difference and the difference between sickness and health. In each case there is no division of humanity into men and women (or the healthy and the sick) without remainders, intersections, and identities that would ultimately need to be policed and patrolled. Balibar includes the division of labour, or what he calls 'intellectual difference', within this category. Humankind cannot be defined without the idea of thought (as Spinoza writes: 'Man thinks'), but this general definition is divided by the practices and institutions which determine and dictate the division between the 'ignorant' and the 'educated' or between 'manual' and 'mental' labour.

The division of mental and manual labour, or what Balibar calls 'intellectual difference', is constitutive of subjectivity, the subjectivity of the manual worker and the intellectual, who are constituted by the separation and antagonism of such a division.[12] As such, this division is complicated by technological history, which continually redraws the line between head and hand, through automation and labour-saving devices, thus fundamentally rewriting the very schema or idea of the human body. Through the use of computers and technology, intellectual operations are broken down and subject to the same mechanisation as physical operations, while at the same time other intellectual operations are 'somatised', inscribed in the body, as in 'the aesthetisation of the executive as decision maker, intellectual, and athlete'.[13] The division between head and hand determines and modifies the very figure, and ideal, of humanity into 'body-men' and 'men without bodies'. These images of perversions of the human are ambiguous objects of both fear and idealisation.[14] For example, 'body-men', or human beings reduced to brute physicality by the labour process, are objects of both an aesthetisation and idealisation as athletes, and of fear, as contemporary savages. As such, the division between mental and manual labour is integral to, without determining, the imagery of various racisms and other forms of conflict, which are in part conflicts over the proper identity of the human, over the ideal of the 'correct' integration of mind and body. The division of mental and manual labour is the point of intersection of the figure

---

12   Balibar 2017b, p. 50.

13   Balibar 1991, p. 212.

14   'This process modifies the status of the human body (the human status of the body): it creates *body men*, men whose body is a machine body, that is fragmented and dominated, and used to perform one isolable function or gesture, being both destroyed in its integrity and fetishized, atrophied and hyterophied in its useful organs ... This is an unbearable process for the worker, but one which is not more 'acceptable', without ideological and phantasmic elaboration, for the worker's masters: the fact that there are body men means that there are *men without bodies*' (Balibar 1991, p. 211).

of the idea of humanity as it is envisioned and lived, and the historical transformations of technology and the economy.

As much as 'intellectual difference' underlies all of the various social imaginaries of race and class, in which the human being is presented as an unstable and asymmetrical mixture of 'mind' and 'body', 'animal' and 'human', it would be wrong to look at it as a purely ideological concept. The division of mental and manual labour transforms actual lives, bodies, and subjectivities. Marx initially indicated this in the *Economic and Philosophical Manuscripts of 1844*, in which he writes, reflecting on the division of labour, 'It replaces labour by machines – but some of the workers it throws back into a barbarous type of labour, and the other workers it turns into machines. It produces intelligence – but for the worker idiocy, cretinism'.[15] In that early text, as much as Marx criticised capitalism for alienating mankind's 'species being', the generic essence of humanity, he also recognised capitalism's capacity to transform humanity, to divide it into human beings reduced to bodies or minds, to the point in which it no longer has a common essence.[16] Marx continued to develop this idea of the dissolution of the unity of the human body in *Capital*, in which the development of large scale industry and automation transforms and destroys the unity of the worker's body as organising principle. At the end point of the process, at least as far as Marx could envision it, the workers become 'conscious organs' subordinated to the logic and force of the machinery.[17] It is worth noting that the division here is no longer symmetrical; Marx is no longer proposing a division between human beings who only think and those who only work with their bodies, but human beings who lend their eyes, ears, and to a lesser extent, minds to a productive apparatus which exceeds them.[18]

---

15   Marx 1964, p. 110.

16   The imagery of mankind divided into classes of 'mind men' and 'body men' is repeated throughout science fiction. See for example H.G. Well's *Time Machine* and, for a contemporary retelling in the age of temp work and downsizing, James Hynes' *Kings of Infinite Space*.

17   Marx 1977, p. 544.

18   There are perhaps historical as well as philosophical reasons for the fact that Marx focuses on the reduction of mankind to 'conscious organs' of machines, and not human beings reduced to the mere physical capacity to labour. Historically, at the time of Marx's writing, machinery was more physical than mental. Thus, it was perhaps not possible for Marx to even imagine the various machines which take up the work of mental labour, leaving human beings to do the physical work. Secondly, Marx argues that a mental component differentiates human labour from animal work. As Marx famously writes, 'But what distinguishes the worst architect from the best of bees is that the architect builds the cell in his mind before he constructs it in wax' (Marx 1977, p. 284).

What Marx initially understands as an antagonistic division of society (into producers and consumers, bodies and minds) through the division of mental and manual labour finally becomes identified as the destruction or at least transformation of the subject of labour. The individual with his or her tool is replaced by a series of organs disseminated across the productive process.[19] Balibar pushes Marx's argument to a higher level, arguing that the history of the transformations of the division of mental and manual labour entail not just a destruction of *homo faber*, the labouring individual, but 'political individuality'. As Balibar argues, the ideal of a unity of mind and body is not just at the basis of an anthropology of labour, but is situated at the foundation of the ontology of western democracy.[20] Balibar's point of reference here is C.B. Macpherson's influential study of Hobbes and Locke in *The Political Theory of Possessive Individualism*. Property in oneself, or a certain kind of self-possession, is not just the basis of the acquisition of property, but is also at the basis of political citizenship. 'To possess things one must, in effect, first "possess oneself", and this self-possession is nothing other than the generic concept of intelligence'.[21] Intelligence, a certain link between mind and hand (to use Locke's term), is what links the capacity to labour with the capacity to deliberate and participate politically. As intelligence is automatised, removed from the day to day intersection with ways of life and materialised in abstract systems, disciplines and codes, this unity is fractured. Following some of Marx's suggestive remarks in the *Grundrisse*, and recent history, Balibar is not just referring to the automatisation of knowledge in the factory, as skill and knowhow are materialised in the gears and motions of machinery, but to the larger process in which human knowledge is 'automatised' from the concrete human relations which produce it and 'materialised' in machines, databases, and institutions. As Balibar states:

---

19 This image or idea of the machine breaking up the body, and attaching parts of the body to it, is not unique to Marx: it can also be found in Henry Ford's autobiography. As Mark Seltzer writes: 'The production of the Model T required 7,882 distinct work operations, but, Ford observed, only twelve percent of these tasks – only 949 operations – required "strong, able-bodied, and practically physically perfect men". Of the remainder – and this is certainly what Ford saw as the central achievement of his method of production – "we found that 670 could be filled by legless men, 2,637 by one legged men, two by armless men, 715 by one-armed men and ten by blind men". If from one point of view such a fantasy projects a violent dismemberment of the natural body and an emptying out of human agency, from another it projects a transcendence of the natural body and the extension of human agency through the forms of technology that supplement it' (Seltzer 1993, p. 99).

20 Balibar 2002a, p. 300.

21 Balibar 1994b, p. 58.

This process of autonomisation-intellectualisation-materialisation of 'knowledge' determines more and more the exercise of the 'property rights' and thereby individuality. But at the same time it renders more and more uncertain the identity of proprietors, the identity of the 'subject' of property. Then we are no longer dealing merely with a mechanism of division of human nature that practically contradicts the requirement of freedom and equality. Instead we are dealing with a *dissolution* of political individuality.[22]

Just as the independent craftsperson has been engulfed by the vast network of machines and apparatuses that make him or her a functioning part, adjacent to rather than mastering these networks, the individual is no longer an origin for political right or obligation. Of course Marx, and Marxists, have never ceased to denounce such 'Robisonades' of liberal thought, which make the individual outside of history the basis and principle of society, but such an ideology falls increasingly out of step with transformations of social relations. Networks, machines and process (not individuals) create an immense wealth of knowledge that is the precondition not just for the accumulation of wealth, but for social participation altogether.

There is a fundamental ambiguity to this historical situation according to Balibar. The dissolution of a particular form of political individuality, or a particular ontology, of individuality, carries with it possibilities for liberation. Since the knowledge and information which is at the basis of appropriation (programs, copyrights, genomes, codes) cannot be strictly mastered or possessed, it reopens the question of the political function of property, questions which were declared closed and dead with the collapse of 'actually existing socialism'.[23] Moreover, since these ultimately 'inappropriable conditions of appropriation' directly intersect with social relations from the most fundamental and basic (agriculture, medicine, etc.) to the most public dimensions of existence (information, culture, knowledge), the question of property, or 'the administration of things', can no longer be separated from politics proper, whether it be conceived of as action, public opinion, or the conflict of ideologies. 'Property (*dominium*) reenters domination (*imperium*)'.[24]

Within this transformation there is grounds for a reconsideration of the political, the formation of new forms of political belonging, new collectivities, and new forms of action. At this point Balibar's assertion intersects with

---

22   Balibar 1994b, ibid.
23   Balibar 1994b, p. 222.
24   Ibid.

the work of Paolo Virno, Antonio Negri, and Michael Hardt, who see in the rise of networks and flows of social knowledge (what they call, following Marx, 'the general intellect') not just the dissolution of old forms of political belonging (worker or citizen) but the formation of a new political subjectivity, 'the multitude', and a new practice of politics, one which takes the intersection of property and politics, labour and action as its starting point.[25] However, Balibar stresses that this transformation is itself thoroughly ambiguous, or perhaps more precisely, this transformation like all transformations of capital must be viewed dialectically with its risks and destructions as well as its promises. The ambiguity lies with a division that is not only the division between types of labour but also a division of political belonging.

The contemporary mode of production, which is often summed up by the unavoidable term 'globalisation', is characterised by both a fundamental transformation of the role of knowledge in the production process, and by a new division. A division that is not internal to production (as between conception and execution) but external to production while at the same time internal to the market. As Balibar writes:

> [T]he situation is that millions of disposable human beings are at the same time excluded from labor – that is, *economic activity* – and kept within the boundaries of the *market*, since the market is an absolute; it has no *external limits*. The Market is the World. When it excludes you, you cannot leave it, search for another America, settle there and start again ...[26]

Not just individuals, but entire regions of the world are situated at this paradoxical limit of the globe, outside production but inside of the market, destitute and seen as expendable. They are left to starve, subject to the ravages of AIDS, exposed to whatever calamity may befall them. The world is divided into 'life zones' and 'death zones'. 'At the moment at which humankind becomes economically and, to some extent, culturally 'united', it is violently divided "biopolitically"'.[27] The outside of production is also and at the same time the outside of the networks of publicity, knowledge, and representation. Which means that these individuals cannot control or even influence the conditions of their own appearance in the media, and thus, in the consciousness, ideologies, and politics of the world. To the rest of the world, and under the existing conditions of

---

25   Virno 2004, p. 49.
26   Balibar 2002b. p. 142. An amended and extended version of this essay is in *La Crainte des masses: Politique et philosophie avant et après Marx*. Paris: Galilée 1997.
27   Balibar 2004, p. 130.

global media hegemony, 'they cannot represent themselves, they must be represented'.[28] The conditions of these representations at times follow the dictates and demands of the politics of the global north, which makes some 'victims' visible and some invisible in order to legitimate various wars and interventions, but mostly it follows the logic of the divisions between mental and manual labour, producing a violence and a destitution which appears to be natural. As Balibar argues:

> The 'disposable human being' is indeed a social phenomenon, but it tends to look, at least in some cases, like a 'natural' phenomenon, or a phenomenon of violence in which the boundaries between what is human and what is natural, or what is post-human and what is post-natural, tend to become blurred; what I would be tempted to call an *ultra-objective* form of violence, or *cruelty without a face*; whereas the practices and theories of ethnic cleansing confront us with what I would call *ultra-subjective* forms of violence, or *cruelty with a Medusa face*.[29]

The 'ultra-objective' forms of violence, the structures of the market, the histories of exploitation and domination, which are unrepresentable because they are impersonal, complex, and overdetermined, give rise to the 'ultra-subjective' forms of violence, which serve as the former's alibi. The desire to know and comprehend the world latches onto the most visible and dramatic indicators of difference, failing to see to what extent these indicators are themselves effects of global divisions and relations.[30] Since the conditions of the various divisions of the world are continually occluded by the strictures of representation and politics of publicity, they primarily appear as the resurfacing of ancient, and thus unintelligible conflicts, or as a fundamental 'clash' of opposed civilisations.

As with Adorno's critique of the position of the intellectual, the less one thinks of material conditions, the global division of labour and market, the more one thinks in line with its demands, producing a narrative of crisis

---

28   Marx 1963a, p. 124.

29   Balibar 2002b, p. 143.

30   As Balibar argues, academic and popular racist theories are persuasive precisely because they render the causes of social conflict immediately intelligible based on visible evidence (somatic markers of distinction). 'I shall therefore venture the idea that the racist complex inextricably combines a crucial function of *misrecognition* (without which the violence would not be tolerable to the very people engaging in it) and a "will to know", a violent *desire for* immediate *knowledge* of social relations' ("Is there a 'Neo-Racism'," Balibar 1991, p. 19).

and clash which can justify infinite repressions.[31] The division of mental and manual labour makes it possible to situate and comprehend these narratives, to see in the pessimistic image of a mankind hopelessly locked in the most primitive conflicts of self and other, the effects of global conditions of production and reproduction.

3   By Way of a Conclusion

Thus the division of mental and manual labour returns us to the problem of the intersection of anthropology, history, and politics, but in a much more complex manner than was first imagined. What Marx, or Marxists after him, saw as perhaps most questionable about the division of mental and manual labour – the difficulty in locating it within the historical progression of capital – becomes in Adorno's and Balibar's writing the benefit of thinking from the problem. For Adorno, the inability to derive this division from exploitation forces us to recognise other histories at work in the present, other than that of the development of capitalism. We are living and thinking in a present that is inhabited not only by the innovations and transformations of commodity production but by the traces of our ancient fear and mastery of the natural world.[32] Our thinking carries with it, as Gramsci argued, 'elements of the cave man, and principles of the most modern and advanced learning, shabby local prejudices of all past historical phases and intuitions of a future philosophy'.[33]

Thus to understand Adorno's dialectic through Balibar, is to think of it as overdetermined, not just by the intersection of the economic and the political, but by the different epochs of history, the presence of different pasts.[34] It is not just that there are two different ways of viewing history, through the lens of exploitation or domination, but that these registers continually intersect through the figure of humanity, as it is imagined and lived, which continues

31   The exemplary text here is Samuel Huntington's *The Clash of Civilizations*. For Balibar's critique of Huntington's tendency to create 'Schmittian' divisions of 'friend' and 'enemy' out of the geopolitical divisions of the existing world order see *L'Europe, L'Amérique, La guerre: Réflexions sur la médiation européen*. Paris: La Découverte, pp. 141–57.

32   'Intelligence and thought are imbued with the history of the whole species, and one may also say with the whole of society' (Adorno 2000, p. 16).

33   Gramsci 1971, p. 59.

34   Despite the rather obvious differences between the two schools of thought, Fredric Jameson has suggested a fundamental similarity between Althusser and Balibar's idea of 'overdetermination' and Adorno's concept of constellations, insofar as they deal with the question of the representation of capital (Jameson 1990, p. 244).

to be an unavoidable referent of the various political imaginaries and ideologies throughout history.[35] Odysseus' simultaneous mastery *over* and alienation *from* the oarsmen, and hence the body and non-human nature, is continually repeated as mankind continues to divide itself.

As Balibar argues the various epochs of politics can be roughly characterised as the ancient, in which the very idea of the political and the citizen is conditioned by the anthropological difference of free man and slave; modern, which can be characterised as the long struggle to purge the citizen of any anthropological reference; and finally the 'postmodern', which is confronted with a recognition of the limitations of a politics of the abstract conception of man. If this is true, then the investigation of the division of mental and manual labour shows us that these stages do not surpass each other: 'anthropological difference' has not been purged from politics, it is continually reinvented by transformations of the mode of production, which paradoxically produces new and more extreme divisions of humanity, at the same time that it unifies all of humanity within one world/market.[36]

Thus, to return to a remark made earlier, it is perhaps the very awkwardness of the idea of the division between mental and manual labour, the way in which it forces us to think about both the foundation of human existence as well as the latest transformation of knowledge and body, that is the strength of its particular provocation: it forces us to recognise that we are products of a history which exceeds historicisation. The past that returns as ancient crusades are waged once again, and cultures clash for eternity, is not the 'pure past' frozen and brought into the present, but a production made possible by the conflicts and divisions of the present. The recognition of the disjunctive temporality of the present makes possible a future which can be something other than a repetition of the continued horror of the existing world order.

35   Heller 1984, p. 50.
36   Balibar 1994b, p. 59.

CHAPTER 3

The Althusser Effect: Philosophy, History, and Temporality

> The person who is addressing you is, like all the rest of us, merely a particular structural effect of this conjuncture, an effect that, like each and every one of us, has a proper name. The theoretical conjuncture that dominates us has produced an Althusser-effect ...
>
> LOUIS ALTHUSSER, 1966[1]

∵

Philosophy has an ambiguous relation with its history. On the one hand, in terms of both pedagogy and research, philosophy is defined by its rumination on its history, its canon: the major philosophers running the gambit from Anaximander to Žižek. Students are required to take courses in ancient, modern, and contemporary philosophy, at both the undergraduate and graduate level, and proficiency is often measured by one's ability to master a period, or, better yet, to produce a reinterpretation of some canonical figure or to argue for the continued relevance of some long-forgotten thinker. Every year works are published on the 'new' Nietzsche, Bergson, Spinoza, or Sartre. Thus, philosophy as a discipline in part distinguishes itself from other disciplines for which historical concerns constitute at best an offshoot of the discipline itself: histories of anthropology, sociology, chemistry, etc. are not to be confused with actual work in those disciplines.[2] Despite this constant return to the past, to what is called 'the history of philosophy', philosophy's relation to its past remains for the most part unhistorical, or at least unhistorical in most senses that would be recognised by historians. What is called the history of philosophy is usually nothing more than a collection of philosophical works or authors according to a chronological timeline; for example, ancient philosophy from Plato to Aristotle or modern philosophy from Descartes to Kant. In these courses history appears –

---

1 Althusser 2003, p. 17.
2 Ree 1978, p. 1.

if at all – as a few remarks of context, a mention of Galileo, the Thirty-Years War, or the French Revolution. In the various arguments for the continued or renewed relevance of this or that philosopher there is little – if any – discussion on why thoughts from several centuries ago might bear reexamination now. To borrow a phrase from Louis Althusser, philosophy has a history, but it has no concept of its history, no understanding of its relation to the passage of time, the 'progress' of perspectives, or of the regressions and returns that make old perspectives relevant.

In invoking the name of Althusser it would appear that I have already slipped into one of the methods I have disparaged above. Is it time for a 'new Althusser', for a reconsideration of a philosopher who was invoked and debated so much in the 1960s and 70s only to be eclipsed by his own personal crises and the general crisis of Marxism? Perhaps, but that is not my concern here; rather my intent is to trace some of Althusser's speculations about the situation of philosophy, its conditions, effects, and history, with all of their concomitant provocations and limitations. These speculations extend beyond Althusser's work, establishing the idea of a philosophy in the conjuncture as a general problem for those who come after (to lapse into chronology again). In doing so I will argue that Althusser's work makes possible a rethinking of the paradox of the history of philosophy as a 'history without history'.

1   Part 1: The (Specific) Temporality of Philosophy

The writings of 1965, *For Marx* and *Reading Capital*, which made Althusser's reputation, are concerned primarily with the status of Marx's theory and do not have much to say about the history of philosophy. In *Reading Capital*, where Althusser does address the history of philosophy, it functions primarily as an example within the general critique of historicism. To demonstrate that history must be thought according to the specific and differential temporalities of the various elements of the social structure (legal, ideological, etc., down to the history of technology and the economic base), Althusser takes as his example the history of philosophy, or more specifically, the eclipse and return of the philosophical legacy of Spinoza, to show that history cannot be measured against one standard timeline. As I will argue, however, the appearance of the history of philosophy as merely an example, as if Althusser could have made his point with any other specific history (such as the history of technology or of chemistry), is more than a bit deceiving. In Althusser's critique of historicism the history of philosophy is more than just an example, because philosophy cannot be separated from the history of philosophy, which is to say that thought cannot be separated from the history of thought. More to the point, Althusser must contend with the history of philosophy in order to address and define the specificity of Marx's thought, as a philosophy that is something other than another ideology of its age.

Marx often presents his critique of political economy as a simple historicisation of political economy, a simple matter of arguing that the categories of political economy are themselves products of a specific history, that, far from being the timeless condition of the production and accumulation of wealth, capital was a specific moment in the history of the relations of production. As Marx wrote as early as *The Poverty of Philosophy*: 'Economists express the relations of bourgeois production, the division of labour, credit, money, etc. as fixed, immutable, eternal categories'.[3] If this is the fault of political economy, then the critique must only historicise: that is, it must chart and date the emergence of these concepts, tying them to their particular social conditions of emergence and their eventual disappearance. Criticism, the critique of political economy, becomes synonymous with historicisation; it ultimately becomes an act of revealing the transitory, relative, and provisional validity of everything that is thought to be eternal and necessary. This understanding of Marx's critique of political economy leads to a general identification of Marx, and Marxism, with historicism, in which not only the concepts and categories of political economy, but also politics and philosophy, are revealed to be the specific products of specific periods in history.[4] The eternal truths of philosophy, the timeless works of literature and art, are revealed to be nothing more than products of a particular time, effects (and conditions) of a particular mode of production. The problem with this understanding of Marx, Althusser states, is that history is undefined, or, and this amounts to the same thing, it is understood to be completely obvious and self-evident. History is not conceptualised, it is assumed as a fact, a fact that connects events – political, philosophical, or economic – by the simple coincidence of their date.

For Althusser, historicism ultimately rests on a 'Hegelian' conception of time, which has two mutually reinforcing defining characteristics: 'the homogeneous continuity of time' and 'the contemporaneity of time'. These two ideas find their philosophical expression in Hegel's understanding of history as the self-development of the Idea or Spirit. Spirit develops along a timeline which is both continuous, moving forward without loss and delay, and self-identical, in which each period, each epoch can be grasped as the articulation of one

---

3 Marx 1963b, p. 104.
4 Althusser 1970, p. 93.

central contradiction. What matters to Althusser is less the epithet of 'Hegelianism' than the manner in which this 'Hegelian' understanding of time is present even in the most obvious or empirical understandings of history. As Althusser argues, it is this conception of time that underlies any understanding of history as divided into 'periods'. Periods of history are assumed to be homogeneous (making up a single slice of time) and self-identical (in which everything in the period is *of* the period). Periods do not get ahead of themselves or lag behind themselves, and this unarticulated understanding of historical time, Althusser contends, is the unstated backdrop of all of the questions of history which seek to draw the lines between this or that period (medieval, modern or postmodern) or situate each event in its proper epoch.[5] This conception of historical time, as Althusser labels it, transcends the more overt differences of perspective or method that would distinguish materialist (feudalism, capitalism, and communism) or idealist (the ancient world, the Germanic world, the Enlightenment) periodisations of history. Since the history of philosophy is almost always presented as a series of periods (e.g., ancient, medieval, or modern), it could be argued that this concept of time underlies the history of philosophy as well.

Althusser's goal is less to unmask the Hegelian dimensions of other understandings of history or of empirical work in history (revealing once again the looming figure of Hegel lurking behind every attempt to escape his influence), than to underscore the limitations of this concept of time that Hegel and others have in common, as well as to chart the gulf that separates Marx from it. For Althusser it is less a matter of Hegel's lingering influence on all that comes after him than it is a matter of his implication within an understanding of time that appears to be self-evident. Althusser somewhat cryptically states that the origins of this conception of time are to be found in 'the false obviousness of everyday practice'.[6] Hegel is instructive not as the originator of a particular understanding of time and history, but as the one who perhaps first rendered it explicit. As Althusser reminds us, one of the consequences of Hegel's understanding of history is his particular understanding of not only his own philosophical position, but of the history of philosophy in general. As Hegel writes in *Elements of the Philosophy of Right*, '... philosophy ... is its own time comprehended in thought. It is just as foolish to imagine that any philosophy can transcend its contemporary world as that an individual can overleap his own time ...'[7] Philosophy is entirely a product of its time because

---

5 Althusser 1970, p. 94.
6 Althusser 1970, p. 96.
7 Hegel 1991a, p. 21.

nothing in its time is alien to it. It expresses the central contradictions of its time because all conflicts, all *contradictions*, are ultimately contradictions of consciousness. The Hegelian understanding of historical time, a linear progression of periods that are unified and self-contained, is an effect of the Hegelian dialectic, which, Althusser contends, is centred on one central contradiction of recognition and misrecognition, as a dialectic of consciousness.[8] Hegel's historicisation of philosophy, his assertion that no philosophy can outrun its historical moment, only appears to denigrate philosophy (destroying its pretension to universality and trans-historical validity); philosophy cannot outrun its period because it entirely comprehends it in thought. For Hegel, to understand ancient Athens, one only needs to read Plato, who expresses not its basic identity, but its conflict and contradiction (between the unity of the *polis* and the freedom of the individual).[9]

The difference between the Hegelian concept of the social totality (presented figuratively as interconnected spheres) and the Marxist totality (the 'topography' of base and superstructure) is a matter not only of different conceptions of historical time, but also of different understandings of thought, and of the history of philosophy. If the Hegelian understanding of historical time must be extracted from Hegel's understanding of the social totality, as a totality of spheres centred around a central philosophical contradiction, then the Marxist understanding must in a similar fashion be found in Marx's understanding of society. Marx's understanding of society is founded on a topographical figure: this is, of course, Marx's famous schema of the base and superstructure. Marx's social totality is not a series of circles centred on one central contradiction, but rather a complex whole of different relations: there are the effects of economic conflicts on the superstructure of law and ideology, but also the effects of ideological struggles on the base. The 'relative autonomy' of these different levels, their independence and effects on each other, is reflected in their history, in a *differential* history. Such a history is differential because it is not enough to simply state, as many historians have, that law, art, or philosophy each has its own history with its own rate, events, and temporality, but rather that since the independence of these different instances of the social totality is only relative, each instance is only relatively autonomous and its history must be situated against its interrelations with each of the other instances of the social totality. As Althusser writes: '... [T]he mode and degree of independence of each time and history is therefore necessarily determined by

8   Balibar 1994a, p. 164.
9   Hegel 1991a, p. 20.

the mode and degree of dependence of each level within the set of articula-tions of the whole'.[10] Relative autonomy means that the history of each aspect of society, each practice – legal, political, scientific or ideological – must be thought as both distinct from and in relation to each of the others. Finally, this history is differential because it is removed from any standard timeline from which the different histories could be identified as more or less advanced. As Althusser argues, terms used within Marxist analysis such as 'uneven devel-opment', 'underdevelopment', 'backwardness', and 'residual elements', address the complexity of historical time, but do so in such a way that differences are still related to one standard timeline. There is not one timeline, a continuous and homogenous timeline upon which events and practices could be marked as 'backwards' or 'emergent'. The specific temporality of each instance, of each social structure, must be constructed. As Althusser argues, it is necessary to fol-low Marx in understanding capitalism not just as a specific moment of history, as a specific mode of production, but also as a specific mode of temporality and a particular way of articulating the different rhythms of production, consump-tion, and circulation.

In order to illustrate this differential history, Althusser takes as his example not the specific temporality of capitalism, a task whose importance and diffi-culty is only remarked in passing, but the history of philosophy. Constructing a history of philosophy means first of all dispensing with its immediate and obvious history, a history that is often nothing more than a chronology of major works and figures. As Althusser writes:

> The time of the history of philosophy is not immediately legible either: of course, in historical chronology we do see philosophers following one another, and it would be possible to take this sequence for history itself. Here, too, we must renounce the ideological pre-judgment of visible suc-cession, and undertake *to construct the concept of the time of the history of philosophy*, and, in order to understand this concept, it is absolutely essential to define the specific difference of the philosophical as one of the existing cultural formations (the ideological and scientific form-ations) ...[11]

What the chronology of works – the lining up of different texts in histories and syllabi according to the date of their publication – leaves out of the picture

---

10   Althusser 1970, p. 100.
11   Althusser 1970, p. 101.

is precisely what is most important to address: the conditions and effects of philosophy. The questions that such a chronology cannot address are the conditions of philosophy (how and why a given philosophical position emerges at a particular juncture in time) and its effects (how and why it acts on different practices, on political ideologies, on morality, etc). As Althusser briefly illustrates with respect to Spinoza, such a history of conditions and effects deviates greatly from a linear chronology. 'The history of philosophy's repressed Spinozism thus unfolded as a subterranean history acting at *other* sites (*autres lieux*), in political and religious ideology (deism) and in the sciences, but not on the illuminated stage of visible of philosophy'.[12] As Althusser will argue in the closing passages of *Reading Capital*, Spinoza's effect on philosophy is not to be found in those works and authors that are chronologically closest, who for the most part misread Spinoza or repressed him as scandalous, but only after the works of Hegel and Marx (not to mention Freud and Lacan) make possible a recognition of his revolutionary idea of 'structural causality'. Structural causality, the idea of a cause that only exists through its effects, which Spinoza used to understand the relation of god to the universe, of creator to created, comes to fruition as a way of understanding capitalism as that which only exists in and through its effects – cultural, legal, and ideological.[13] Spinoza's effects travel through politics and the sciences, existing primarily as point of heresy, in order to emerge by way of the nineteenth-century as part of a revolutionary rethinking of the idea of society.

Constructing the concept of the history of philosophy is a matter of first dispensing with the linear chronology of philosophical works. The real transformations and effects of philosophy are not measured by the ordering of copyright dates, but by subterranean histories and unexpected divisions. Spinoza's belated effect on philosophy and Marx's break with humanism are two examples of the absolute inadequacy of chronology for understanding the history of philosophy. In the first case, effects follow long after the date of publication, passing through science and politics, while in the second, the division is not the immediately apparent distinction between different authors, but is internal to the works of one author, even to one text. Grasping these delayed effects and divisions entails constructing the concept of the specific history of philosophy, a history that can only be grasped 'differentially' according to its relations (in terms of both conditions and effects) with other practices, most importantly with other theoretical practices – science and politics.

---

12   Althusser 1970, p. 102.

13   Althusser 1970, p. 189.

2   Part 2: Between Conditions and Effects

Marx, Althusser never tires of reminding us, never wrote his 'dialectic', his understanding of his particular way of doing philosophy, his particular 'theoretical practice'.[14] From this absence Althusser assumed a particular task and a general problem. The particular task is a matter of understanding how Marx produced a particular revolution in philosophy; that is, how a philosophy emerges from particular historical and ideological conditions, breaking with and ultimately transforming those conditions. Althusser attempted to understand this 'revolution' on rigorously materialist grounds, without recourse to an ideology of genius or divine insight. Which leads Althusser to a more general problem, a materialist understanding of philosophy, or how theory as a kind of practice emerges from particular conditions only to transform them. The very idea of such a general theory would seem to be at odds with the specific understanding of conditions and effects, the specific differential history of the philosophy of conditions and effects sketched out in *Reading Capital*. It is perhaps because of this internal tension (as well as the external criticism of such positions as the 'epistemological break' brought on by his increased visibility as a Marxist philosopher) that Althusser spent much of the late sixties and early seventies in attempts to revise and rearticulate his understanding of philosophy as a specific kind of practice. This work took many forms: a proposed but never completed book on the unity of theory and practice, as well as a series of lectures, manuscripts, and collective programmes for research. As some of this material has been published in recent years it is now possible to follow the development of the provocative remarks made in *Reading Capital* regarding the specific history and situation of philosophy, in terms of its conditions and effects, towards the development of a materialist understanding of philosophy.

Althusser's project during these years is riddled with false starts, self-critiques and dead-ends, culminating in piles of texts 'left to the gnawing criticism of the mice' and an increasingly self-destructive process of self-criticism. It is possible to view the entire project as something of a failure: such an evaluation would not only overlook the insights developed over the course of the project, but its almost insurmountable constitutive difficulties. These difficulties begin with Marx. From *The German Ideology* onwards, with its infamous identification of philosophy as ideology, Marx's corpus has pursued a (sometimes hidden, sometimes open) assault on philosophy's self-understanding as

---

14   Althusser 1969, p. 174.

an autonomous search for truth independent of its (material) historical conditions. As Althusser writes: 'Marx's scientific revolution contains an unprecedented philosophical revolution which, by forcing philosophy to think its relationship to history, profoundly alters the economy of philosophy'.[15] This assault is at once polemical and highly uneven, even ambiguous. Ambiguous because it takes the form of condemnations of philosophy, departures from philosophy (the famous eleventh thesis on Feuerbach), and returns to philosophical problems, for example the section on 'commodity fetishism', which is nothing less than a rumination on the problem of universals and value. As Balibar identifies, the unevenness of this legacy is a 'permanent oscillation between "falling short of" and "going beyond" philosophy', a combination of philosophical statements without premises and a socio-historical situating of philosophy itself.[16] This unevenness has made it possible to purge not only Marx from philosophy, but to dispense with the series of questions that he opens with respect to the relation between philosophy and its historical, social, and political conditions.

As we have seen, it is Althusser's attempt to complete what Marx began, to read between the lines of his various political interventions, critiques of political economy, and theoretical works, both the philosophy and the *critique* of philosophy that Marx was not able (nor inclined to) write. This reconstruction cannot simply be a matter of finding the appropriate quotes from Marx's writings, but takes the form of a demanding theoretical intervention. Althusser takes his general bearings from Marx's topography, the articulation of society according to base and superstructure. For Althusser the 'topography' is less a definite answer, declaring once and for all the role of economics, ideology, and philosophy in history, than a problem: the problem of the relations of force and effectivity which situate the different aspects of social existence. Philosophy is of course situated in the superstructure, as one of the elements of what Althusser calls 'the theoretical', along with science and politics. Marx's writing does not simply sketch this topography, it also intervenes in a particular way: Marxism, Althusser maintains, is itself an uneven combination of a science (historical materialism) and a philosophy (dialectical materialism).[17] To risk stating the obvious, it should be added that Marxism is a politics as well, a point that Althusser stressed in later works. The three dimensions, science, politics, and philosophy (perhaps a more generic version of Lenin's three sources) are conditions of Marx's particular philosophy and, in a different manner, philosophy in general. Althusser's thought continually moves from this particular

---

15   Althusser 2003, p. 230.
16   Balibar 2017b, p. 4.
17   Althusser 1972, p. 165.

instance, Marx's transformation of philosophy, to the general problem, the conditions of philosophical change in general, and back again.

Philosophy is situated between science and politics, between the breaks of science and the political revolutions and counter-revolutions that provide the content of ideology.[18] Althusser illustrates this assertion with respect to two examples, which are also two turning points in the history of philosophy, Plato and Descartes. Plato and Descartes can both be situated after a revolution of science, the opening of a new continent, the mathematics of Thales (Plato) and the physics of Galileo (Descartes).[19] The two philosophers can also be situated with respect to a political or social revolution; Althusser cites, in remarks that are really more sketches in a notebook than historical arguments, the democracy of Pericles in the case of Plato and, in the case of Descartes, the emergence of bourgeois right, or a system of standardised law under Absolute Monarchy.[20] All philosophy is determined, doubly determined by its place within 'the theoretical' (which could less awkwardly, but perhaps also less accurately, be called the ways of knowing and perceiving within a given historical moment), and the transformations of science and the conflicts of politics, conflicts that are ultimately conditioned by the class struggle. In a word, philosophy is 'overdetermined'. Althusser argues that this overdetermination follows a particular law of causality:

> This 'overdetermination' of philosophy by these two events obeys the following law: the determination in the last instance of philosophical events by ideological events (the *ideological revolutions* of the class struggle), determination by scientific events (the breaks) only in the second instance.[21]

All philosophy (Plato, Descartes, Marx, Althusser) is situated with respect to this double determination, a determination by science and by politics. Science, with its transformation of rationalities and abstract objects, determines in part the form philosophy takes, its particular logic, while its content is determined in ideological struggle. These two terms 'politics' and 'science' gesture towards areas of reality that could be taken as self-evident. However, Althusser spends much of the period of the sixties refining what he means by both of these terms, and defining the relative importance of 'politics' and 'science' to philosophy.

---

18   Althusser 1995c, p. 307.
19   Althusser 1995c, p. 307.
20   Althusser 1995c, p. 38.
21   Althusser 1995, p. 308, my translation.

As Pierre Macherey argues, the political determination of philosophy takes on increasing importance in the decisive of year of 1968.[22]

Science and politics are not just distinguished by the role they have in philosophy, as form and content, but more importantly by their specific temporality and modality of change. Science transforms itself and develops through a series of breaks, by transformations that are definitive and decisive. This linear progression of decisive breaks and transformations, of discoveries that are unambiguous and universally acknowledged, is often the envy of philosophers, forming a model of 'progress'. Althusser argues that even those philosophers who would appear to have nothing to do with science, or are even opposed to it (for example Heidegger), must confront it.[23] Politics is transformed by revolutions, revolutions that are 'historical facts', not 'theoretical facts'.[24] It is perhaps because of this that political revolutions have an ambiguous relation to philosophy. Unlike the history of science, a history that confronts philosophy with a model of linear and irreversible progression, political revolutions can be philosophically denied or repressed. In general, philosophers believe themselves to be above the fray of such political struggles, expounding universal and timeless truths. However, as Althusser demonstrates in his interpretations of Montesquieu and Rousseau, philosophy always carries the scars and symptoms of its political conjuncture.[25]

These two different timelines, of necessary breaks and ambiguous revolutions, must intersect and affect each other; if not, then Althusser's differential history would give way to a purely pluralist and autonomous history of different times, one for science and one for politics. The question is how to posit both the distinction and connection of science and politics, a question that is crucial for defining philosophy. What defines science is less its specific content than its practice, the production of new objects of knowledge. While politics is defined primarily by ideology, what Althusser calls the various practical ideologies (such as law, morality, and ethics, which shape 'notions-representations-images' into 'behaviour-conduct-attitude-gestures'), are determined in the last instance by class struggle.[26] Science produces knowledge, what Althusser calls 'knowledge effects', while ideology makes behaviors, actions, and ultimately history. This division between knowledge and action, between the 'is' and the 'ought', is always unstable, with the one blurring into the other. The 'knowledge-

---

22   Macherey 1999, p. 265.
23   Althusser 1995a, p. 259.
24   Althusser 1995a, p. 309.
25   Althusser 1972, p. 159.
26   Althusser 1990b, p. 83.

effect' produced by science becomes part of the general social knowledge of a given society, informing its ideologies, while, at the same time, the practical ideologies of day-to-day contact have their effects on scientific practice as well.[27] This blurring of the 'ought' into the 'is' (and vice versa) is in some respects the condition of philosophy.

Within this over, or double, determination, the case of Marx is unique. First, because the scientific event, what Althusser calls the 'discovery of the continent of history', is not an event situated in the general milieu of Marx's writing, as Galileo was for Descartes, but is a product of Marx's own thought. Which does not mean that Marxists, or even Marx himself, grasps what this 'event' in the science of history means for philosophy. This is ultimately the significance of the division into historical materialism (science) and dialectical materialism (philosophy), terms that Althusser borrows from Engels (and Stalin) to express the lag that separates philosophy from science.[28] For Althusser these terms indicate the unevenness of Marx's theoretical development: philosophically Marx did not write anything that would compare with his development of the science of history, *Capital*. That Marxist philosophy lags behind science is for Althusser ultimately a specific case of a general rule. 'Philosophy only exists by virtue of the distance it lags behind its scientific inducement'.[29] Second, the object of Marx's science is concerned with nothing other than the general transformation of society, a transformation which includes the effects of social transformations on the instances of science and philosophy. Marx's 'topography' is nothing other than an attempt to think the 'place' of philosophy, the conditions of its enunciation, and the limitation of its effects.[30]

The 'double determination' of philosophy between the 'breaks' and discoveries of science and the 'revolutions' of ideology provides a way of rethinking the conditions of philosophy, of understanding the causal conditions which situate a particular philosophy, but it says little about the effects of philosophy, of what it does with these conditions. It only allows us to grasp the history that is made in philosophy, a history that is the effect of exterior events, such as the transformations of science and ideology, not to grasp the history that philosophy makes. This is in part because for Althusser it is not clear that philosophy has a history. Much of Althusser's reflection on the history of philosophy in the late 1960s takes the form of a reflection of Marx's basic idea that 'morality,

27   Althusser 1995b, p. 314.
28   Althusser 1972, p. 167.
29   Althusser 1971, p. 42.
30   Althusser 1990c, p. 220.

religion, metaphysics ... have no history'.[31] As Althusser interprets Marx's formula, 'philosophy has no real history'.[32] For Althusser this idea is not simply
the grounds for a dismissal of philosophy, but a paradoxical reconsideration of
its history.[33] In a negative sense this idea designates that in philosophy, unlike
science (and perhaps even politics), there are no irreversible events, no discoveries or transformations that do not need to be repeated: there are no 'breaks'
in philosophy. The institutionalised practices of philosophy testify to this fact:
despite the pages and pages of criticism, there is no philosopher who is ever
finally dead and buried, there is always room for a 'return' to Hegel, Sartre,
Spinoza, even Althusser. Althusser also wants to maintain a positive sense of
this absence, in which the absence of history designates something like an
omni-historical reality. Althusser's assertion that philosophy does not have a
history would seem to be a repetition of his infamous assertion that ideology
does not have a history.[34] While in the former, the phrase indicated the permanence of a structure, ideology as a necessary dimension to the functioning of any
society, in the latter it designates the permanence of a site. Philosophy has no
history, because its site, the theoretical, the point where science, ideology, religion, and the various practical ideologies (of politics and morality) effect and
transform each other, is permanent, is a permanent site of contestation and
demarcation. The absence of history does not mean that philosophy has always
existed, as an eternal dimension of thought; it can only exist in the presence of
its conditions, in societies that meet the two conditions of science, an abstract
and necessary form of knowledge, and the class struggle.[35]

It is from this absence of history that it is possible, paradoxically, to understand the particular effect that philosophy has on history. Philosophy, even
those philosophers that claim to be interested in a universal, impersonal, and
indifferent truth, acts by making an intervention. In the first instance this intervention is only an action that philosophy performs on itself, on its concepts
and modes of articulation. 'Philosophy intervenes in reality only by producing
results within itself. It acts outside of itself through the result that it produces
within itself'.[36] Every philosophy 'takes a position' within a field that is already
saturated, which is to say that every act of taking a position must involve a
seemingly infinite process of differentiation whereby every new position must

---

31   Marx 1970a, p. 47.
32   Althusser 1971, p. 55.
33   Macherey 1999, p. 283.
34   Althusser 1971, p. 161.
35   Althusser 1995b, p. 35.
36   Althusser 1990b, p. 107.

defend itself against the positions of other philosophers. It is this simultaneous condition of emptiness (the absence of 'real' history) and fullness (the saturation of the field of positions) that defines every philosophy as an intervention within a struggle. Philosophy acts on other philosophies, and in doing so it acts on the practical philosophies that make up religion and ideology. As much as philosophy, philosophical practice only acts on itself: producing effects in the world only insofar as it acts on itself, it does so in such a way that it acts on its own conditions, its own overdetermination. As Althusser argued in the lecture 'Lenin and Philosophy', referring to the two conditions of philosophy outlined above, 'Philosophy represents politics in the domain of theory, or to be more precise: with the sciences – and, vice versa, philosophy represents scientificity in politics, with the classes engaged in the class struggle'.[37] Philosophy intervenes in the very site where it is born, at the point of articulation and disarticulation of knowledge and action.

The first half of this formulation, politics in the sciences, is developed at length in Althusser's lecture course 'Philosophy and the Spontaneous Philosophy of the Scientists'. In this course Althusser argues that philosophy's role with respect to science is not to define its object or conditions of possibility, in the sense of a *philosophy of science*, but to draw a line of demarcation between the discoveries of scientists and the spontaneous philosophy of scientists (that is, the way in which scientists, as subjects to a given society and its ruling ideology, reinterpret their practice according to the dominant ideology – although Althusser gives only a few examples of this, it is possible to find examples in much science criticism, which repeatedly points out how scientists find the social order, the 'selfish gene', the investment of genetic material, in the natural world). Here philosophy intervenes not in philosophy proper, not in the arguments and counter-positions that make up the history of philosophy, but in a 'philosophy' which is embodied in the practical ideologies of behaviour.

What Althusser identifies as a spontaneous philosophy is very close to Gramsci's famous statement that 'everyone is a philosopher', his assertion that there is a philosophy, an interpretation of the world, at work in language, common sense, and culture.[38] The idea of a 'spontaneous philosophy' thus expands greatly the definition of philosophy, removing it from the ivory tower of intellectuals and bringing it into contact with reality.[39] As Gramsci writes:

---

37   Althusser 1971, p. 65.
38   Gramsci 1957, p. 58.
39   Balibar 1994a, p. 173.

The philosophy of an age is not the philosophy of this or that philosopher, of this or that group of intellectuals, of this or that broad section of the popular masses. It is a process of combination of all of these elements, which culminates in an overall trend, in which the culmination becomes a norm of collective action and becomes concrete and complete (integral) 'history'.[40]

Gramsci's attentiveness to philosophy as it exists in religion, common sense, and quotidian practices, underlies Althusser's examination of the 'spontaneous' philosophy of the scientists as well as the spontaneous ideologies of law and morality. However, as Gramsci's reference to 'the philosophy of an age' makes clear, it carries with it an avowed historicism, which Althusser was quick to criticise in *Reading Capital*.

But even in Marxist theory we read that ideologies may survive the structure that gave them birth (this is true for the majority of them: e.g., religion, ethics or ideological philosophy), as may certain elements of the politico-legal superstructure in the same way (Roman law!). As for science, it may well arise from an ideology, detach itself from its field in order to constitute itself as science, but precisely this detachment, this 'break', inaugurates a new form of historical existence and temporality which together save science (at least in certain historical conditions that ensure the real continuity of its own history – conditions that have not always existed) from the common fate of a single history; that of the historical bloc unifying structure and superstructure.[41]

What Gramsci's 'philosophy of the age' effaces is the differential temporality of philosophy, its manner of conserving the ideologies of the past, as well as its contact with scientific discoveries that make the future. It overlooks the fundamental difference between 'breaks' and 'revolutions', a difference which is integral to philosophy.

Althusser's second half of the formulation, 'philosophy represents science in politics', can be in part be understood as an assertion of this temporal heterogeneity. 'Science' in this formulation refers first of all to Marx, to historical materialism, which brings knowledge of history, of the mode of production and its topography, to the ideological conflicts of politics. This is at least the initial

---

40   Gramsci 1971, p. 345.
41   Althusser 1970, p. 133.

meaning, and as such it would tie the formulation to Althusser's early argument regarding the scientific status of Marx's thought. In later years, however, Althusser develops a different interpretation of science, one that is tied less to Marx, to include specific discoveries of physics and mathematics. As Althusser responds to Fernanda Navarro's question regarding the importance he gives to the triad philosophy-politics-ideology:

> We are able to say that historically philosophy is born from religion, from which it inherits specific questions, which it then converts to the grand themes of philosophy, with all of their different responses: for example the origin or the end of man, of history, and of the world. Nevertheless, I maintain that philosophy constitutes itself as such, in a rigorous sense, when it encounters the first science: mathematics ... From this moment ... one has to begin to reason in a different manner and on different objects: abstract objects.[42]

Althusser's response bears a striking resemblance to Spinoza's formulation in the appendix of Part One of the *Ethics* where he reflects on the powerful influence that superstition has on the thought of mankind.

> This alone, of course, would have caused the truth to be hidden from the human race to eternity, if mathematics, which is concerned not with ends, but only with the essences and properties of figures, had not shown men another standard of truth. And besides mathematics, we can assign other causes also (which it is unnecessary to enumerate here), which were able to bring it about that men would notice these common prejudices and be led to the true knowledge of things.
> EIApp

What remains constant throughout Althusser's reflection on science is the fundamental difference between ideology, which is ultimately concerned with the origin and end of things, and science, which posits not only abstract objects, but a causal order which is indifferent to meaning and ends. It is this difference in logic, between causes and ends, rather than an assumed epistemological hierarchy, that distinguishes science from ideology.[43] The difference between science and ideology is thus more of a matter of practice, of a manner of produ-

---

42   Althusser 1994c, p. 49.
43   Badiou 1993, p. 33.

cing objects for investigation and concepts, than specific content or authority. Science is thus radically distinct from the various practical ideologies, and day-to-day common sense, which we use to make sense of the world. Thus, science is always out of sync with ideology (and philosophy), disturbing the unity of any 'age'.

Althusser's writing on the history of philosophy, on the conditions and effects of theoretical practice, is as uneven as it is promising. Much of this unevenness reflects a tension between thinking through the specific effects of the theoretical practice of Marx and a general theory of theoretical practice. This tension can be seen in the manner in which Althusser's general rule, the rule that philosophy lags behind science, a rule drawn from the specific experience of Marxism, itself 'lags behind' the provocations outlined in *Reading Capital*. Althusser's differential history outlined in that text does not have a general rule for the chronological relation between philosophy and science; philosophy may lag behind science or jump ahead. In a similar manner Althusser later argues that philosophy may 'fall behind' or 'leap ahead' of ideological transformations.[44] To which we could add that a philosophy too can fall behind itself, a fact that Althusser's thought demonstrates. Althusser's own self-criticism, his reconsideration of his thesis regarding a radical break in Marx's thought, forces him to rethink philosophical progress in general. It is no longer a matter of finding some break that transforms a philosopher's thought once and for all, but understanding how every rupture with existing ideologies, every break with existing knowledges, is unstable, leading to regressions and lags.[45] Philosophy does not just lag behind science, but also behind itself. As Balibar argues, in this latter period Althusser is less interested in identifying definitive 'breaks' (or ruptures) in philosophy than in recognising the relation between transformations (of knowledge and ideologies) and practice. 'Every break is at the same time irreversible and precarious, threatened with an impossible return to its ideological prehistory, without which it would not *last*, it would not *progress*'.[46]

In the work of the 1960s Althusser's thought specifically lags behind itself as it tries to make Marx's thought a general model of the relation between philosophy, politics, and science. When Althusser imposes a kind of symmetry on Marx's thought, making it another example of the effects of scientific breaks and ideological revolution alongside Plato and Descartes, he loses not only the specificity of the conjectural dimension of philosophy, but returns to concepts

---

44   Althusser 1995a, p. 307.
45   Althusser 1994b, p. 363.
46   Balibar 1994a, p. 172.

specifically criticised in early texts. In 'Marx's Relation to Hegel' Althusser even goes so far as to argue that the three great revolutions in scientific knowledge, mathematics, physics, and history, constitute the major dates in the periodisation of philosophy, the ancient period (Plato), the modern period (Descartes) and the period of Marxist philosophy.[47] This dividing up of philosophy into periods, which Althusser had criticised as an effect of the Hegelian conception of historical time, ironically returns to crown Marx's achievement in philosophy. Marx's differential history, a history that argued against the very idea of a single and irreversible timeline upon which all events could be measured, is effaced in favor of a new period, 'the age of Marxism'. Moreover, such periods of philosophy, tied to particular scientific events, blur the distinction between scientific breaks, political and ideological revolutions, and philosophical struggle, thus eclipsing the fundamental difference of temporality that not only defines these events but is also the condition for an articulation of a differential history of the relations between science, politics, and ideology. This is not to suggest that Althusser's thought on the history of philosophy is burdened by his allegiance to Marx, as if it was possible to imagine something like a 'de-Marxified' Althusser who can take his place within the history of philosophy, but that it falls behind itself as it loses track of the singularity of Marx's thought. This singularity is perhaps restored in Althusser's last published works in which Marx is no longer the proper name of the general rules of philosophical production, of the relation of philosophy to science, but the material condition of an understanding of the situation of philosophy, its place in the superstructure, alongside science, religion, and morality. As Althusser states in 'Marxism Today', in substantial revision of Marx's materialism:

> The measure of Marx's materialism is less the materialist content of his theory than the acute, practical consciousness of the conditions, forms and limits within which these ideas can become active. Hence their double inscription in the topography.[48]

What Althusser earlier perceived as a lack becomes instead a kind of surplus; it is because Marx did not produce a philosophy, a system, a discourse of the ultimate origin and ends of knowledge, but instead sought to situate philosophy, to see its effects and limitations, that his thought makes possible an understanding of the specific practice of philosophy. The philosophical problem that Marx

---

47   Althusser 1972, p. 167.
48   Althusser 1990a, p. 275.

left in his wake is not a reconstruction of the dialectic method he never had time to write, but how to think the specific site of philosophy.

3   Conclusion: Thought of/in the Conjuncture

It is impossible, or at least irrelevant, to have any kind of last word on Althusser's particular intervention in the history of philosophy. As Althusser's history of Spinoza's thought claims, and as the later history of Spinoza scholarship testifies (a history that includes Étienne Balibar, Pierre Macherey, and others influenced by Althusser himself), last words on any philosophy are always premature: the eternal history without history that is the history of philosophy provokes new readings, new interpretations, which are provoked as much by ongoing political and ideological struggles as they are by the supposed inexhaustible 'richness' of any philosophical text. However, it is possible to at least trace some of the effects that Althusser has had on thought about the history of philosophy.

These effects are most noticeable in the works of Pierre Macherey and Étienne Balibar. Macherey states that it is necessary to remove Althusser's problem, the historical condition and effect of philosophy, from the specific situation of its articulation, the contested terrain of Marxism as a science, the split between Marxist and Maoist parties, and his own ambiguous fame and infamy.[49] This is not an attempt to water Althusser down, or to steer clear of controversy, but to draw out a thread of research that is often overlooked in the attention to the major controversies. At the same time that Althusser was developing, defending, and rethinking his argument regarding Marx's 'epistemological break', he was researching the specific philosophical conjuncture in France, a conjuncture shaped by the history of spiritualism (de Tracy, Cousin, Bergson) and rationalism (the legacy of Descartes) in French philosophy.[50] Macherey continues this work, developing a historical perspective on French philosophy that addresses the institutional and cultural conditions of its transmission. Philosophy does not exist independently of its pedagogical conditions, its situation within a university, conditions which are often determined by questions of the status of a discipline and national politics, politics concerned with the identity of the nation.[51] Macherey's reflection on this history does not take the form of a sociology of knowledge; that is, it

---

49   Macherey 1999, p. 279.
50   Althusser 2003, p. 4.
51   Macherey 1998, p. 20.

does not simply chart this history from the outside without also reflecting on the nature of philosophy itself. Rather, it is precisely this opposition between 'outside' (institutional context and constraint) and 'inside' (concepts, ideas, and arguments) that Macherey's work on the history of philosophy contests. As Macherey argues, philosophy must be thought as an operation that works within the determinate conditions and constraints of its historical and political conjuncture, rather than as an action that starts out from its own free possibility and dictates to the world what principles it should follow. Macherey takes the term 'operation' from a distinction that Spinoza makes in the *Ethics*, a distinction that is lost in most English translations:

> That thing is called free which exists from the necessity of its nature alone and is determined to act by itself alone. But a thing is called necessary, or rather compelled, which is determined by another to exist and to *operate* in a certain and determinate manner.
>
> EID7 and MACHEREY 1992, p. 72

To define philosophy as an operation is to accept that all philosophy is impure, burdened by concepts and content whose conditions and causality it cannot choose. This constraint is the condition for a production of effects.

In a similar manner, Etienne Balibar argues that all philosophy can be viewed as a particular intervention in a conjuncture, an intervention in a conjuncture by *writing*, by connecting the immediacy of the overdetermined now with the historicity of traditions.

> We must therefore think through together both determinations of philosophical practice: its necessary relation to conjunctures (which leads philosophical texts to organize themselves into sets that are themselves dependent on a conjuncture) and its relation to writing as permanent short-circuit or short-cut between the immediacy of thinking and its longer history.[52]

For Balibar, philosophy's relation to the conjuncture not only makes possible new interpretations of its past (readings of Spinoza, Locke, Fichte, etc), but also a new practice in the present. Balibar's writing on the political questions of violence, citizenship, and the border works from the premise that these concepts are not just ideas for political philosophers, but concepts which are

---

52   Balibar 1995, p. 148.

transformed by the vicissitudes of history, by singular events and material transformations.[53] The conjuncture becomes the condition for the renewal of philosophical practice.

Traces of this 'Althusser effect' can also be found in the works of philosophers who do not consciously affirm their connection with Althusser. Alain Badiou's writing on the non-philosophical 'conditions' of philosophy, mathematics, poetics, political invention, and love also seeks to grasp philosophy as an activity which is situated by the 'truth procedures' which are its conditions.[54] Badiou, like Althusser, situates Plato with respect to the conditions of mathematics and politics. As Badiou writes in a formulation that echoes his early work with Althusser on the history of philosophy 'How are mathematics and political ontology compossible? Such was the Platonic question to which the operator of the form came to provide the main fulcrum of a resolution'.[55] Plato's position in philosophy has less to do with his particular genius, or with the metaphysical destiny of the West, than with the way in which his philosophy operates on its existing political and scientific conditions, what Badiou refers to as the 'truth' of science and politics. Badiou's thought is in part founded on an attempt to go beyond Althusser, in thinking both the plurality of the conditions of philosophy, adding aesthetics and love to science and mathematics, and the specific autonomy of philosophy to its conditions, its ability to produce the new, to name the event.[56]

What matters here is less a full account of all of the traces of Althusser's rethinking the history of philosophy – as I have noted above, such a procedure is impossible, the last word is always yet to be written – than the affirmation of a singular idea. This idea is quite simply that philosophy as a discipline, but more importantly as an activity, can be renewed and reinvigorated, not by prostrating itself before its 'metaphysical excesses' (as in the 'end of philosophy') nor by purging itself from its connection to existing reality (ethics and the 'pure ought' of normativity as the last refuge of philosophy), but by thinking itself as profoundly conditioned by other transformations of the 'theoretical' (science, politics, and ideology). It is only by thinking itself as conditioned, and by attempting to understand how, that philosophy can have any effect, any relevance. Althusser's researches into the history of philosophy and the place of theoretical practice are far from being the last words on this subject: they are in some sense only an initial condition, the effects of which it still remains to trace

---

53   Balibar 2004, p. viii.
54   Badiou 1999, p. 38.
55   Badiou 1999, ibid.
56   Badiou 1993, p. 42.

and develop. After a long history of its effects (and their erasure) in politics, literature, and cultural studies, it is perhaps time to bring Althusser's thought back to the site of its enunciation, the history of philosophy, in order to grasp the extent, and the unrealised possibility, of the 'Althusser effect'.

CHAPTER 4

To Think the New in the Absence of Its Conditions: Althusser and Negri and the Philosophy of Primitive Accumulation

Louis Althusser and Antonio Negri are two of the most influential Marxist philosophers of the (late) twentieth century. Despite their influence, influence that extends into the same spheres of theoretical and philosophical discussion, there has been little discussion and debate of their relation, at least in the Anglo-American world. This is perhaps because the lines of demarcation would seem to be drawn up in advance: Althusser is the philosopher of history as a process without subjects or goals, while Negri is the philosopher of living labour as subjectivity. They even draw from different texts: for Althusser, at least initially, Marx's philosophy is found in the structure of *Capital*, albeit often between the lines, while Negri turns to the *Grundrisse*, a series of notes written in a time of crisis, to find the force of antagonism. The combined effect of their seemingly opposed positions with respect to subjectivity and the emphasis on different texts has set up a relation of either absolute opposition or indifference. This despite the fact that in later years, the final years of Althusser's life and some of Negri's more recent texts, the two writers began to construct and draw on the same lineage of Machiavelli and Spinoza, as well as Marx, in order to construct their philosophy. Beneath the crude oppositions between structuralism and autonomism, there emerges the overlapping, but not necessarily shared, project of reconstructing a materialist philosophy.

In order to relate Althusser and Negri I would like to begin not with their respective readings of Machiavelli or Spinoza, but with their engagement with Marx's writings on primitive accumulation. Althusser turns to primitive accumulation in the final pages of his essay on aleatory materialism, remarking that everything that comes before, the fragmentary notes on Machiavelli, Spinoza, and Rousseau, is a prelude to his engagement with the problem of materialism in Marx. Negri's reflections on primitive accumulation appear in the penultimate chapter of the book on constitutive power (*Insurgencies* in the English translation), in which Marx's concept of living labour is considered to be the fullest development of a constitutive ontology. In each case, primitive accumulation, Marx's account of the violent and contingent formation of capitalism, is understood to be a philosophical problem, a problem of ontology, and not simply a political or economic problem. This differentiates Althusser and Negri from much of the current revival of interest in primitive accumulation, most of which is orientated towards understanding the violence intrinsic to new strategies of accumulation associated with the privatisation of public sectors and the breakdown of commons. What Althusser and Negri seek, in different ways, can be considered an attempt to reconstruct if not Marx's philosophy, than a materialist philosophy from these writings on the violent foundation of the capitalist mode of production. Which is to say that the reading of primitive accumulation will have effects on philosophy, not only in terms of creating a lineage that incorporates Machiavelli and Spinoza, but, more importantly, in terms of what constitutes the relevant problems and concepts of philosophy. Such a philosophy will necessarily be different from more familiar attempts to ground a Marxist philosophy on reification, alienation, or the historical process in general, but such comparisons remain outside of the purview of this essay.

First, a provisional definition of primitive accumulation. In the final pages of *Capital* Marx does two things: he counters the dominant conception of capitalist accumulation and provides an alternate account. The dominant conception of the accumulation of capital, the story of so-called primitive accumulation, is a morality tale in which one group, future capitalists, saves, while another, future workers, squanders. In this 'ant and grasshopper' tale moral differences are adequate to make history. Against this Marx stresses the fundamental complexity of the formation of capital. In order for capitalism to constitute itself as a mode of production it is not enough for some to save and others to squander: there must be the accumulation of wealth, made possible by the breakdown of laws regarding usury and the reign of mercantile capitalism, and, more importantly, there must be the disappropriation of peasants from the land. They must be separated from the means of production in order to become workers. This is made possible by violence, by the laws of bloody legislation that separate individuals from the land. In place of the simplicity of moral intent, Marx places the complexity of conditions and the transformative force of violence. In his narrative, primitive accumulation cannot be the simple effect of a moral intention, but must be the encounter of radically heterogeneous strategies. In order to understand how there could be an encounter between wealth on one hand and a group of people with nothing but their labour power to sell on the other, it is necessary to take into consideration a whole series of disparate and disconnected events, from the rise of usury, the destruction of the commons, and the wealth generated from colonialism and the slave trade. As Marx writes, 'The knights of industry, however, only succeeded in supplanting the knights of the sword by making use of events in which they had played no part in whatsoever'.[1]

---

1 Marx 1977, p. 875.

Whereas 'so-called primitive accumulation', the tale told by capitalists, presents a straight line in which the morality of intentions are rewarded, Marx's account presents a history of multiple encounters and violent transformations in which effects are never reducible to intentions.

1   Becoming Necessary

Althusser's essay, even though it is presented as developing a new conception of materialism, and thus a new ontology, does not begin with a consideration of Marx at all, but with a long survey of the history of philosophy. This materialism, as much as it makes reference to the philosophies of Epicurus and even Heidegger, is primarily developed through political texts; its primary metaphors or concepts are the figures of Machiavelli's prince and Rousseau's forest primeval. This follows, or radicalises, Althusser's earlier claim that it is 'necessary to get rid of the suspect division between philosophy and politics which at one and the same time treats the political figures as inferior – that is, as non-philosophers or Sunday afternoon philosophers – and also implies that the political positions of philosophers must be sought exclusively in the texts in which they talk about philosophy'.[2] This is perhaps one of the most persistent tenets of Althusser's philosophy, from the early investigations which more or less reconstructed the philosophy Marx neglected to write from the pages of *Capital*, to the remarks on class struggle in theory, Althusser disrupts the separations and hierarchies that distinguish political philosophy from philosophy, knowledge from action. Althusser's overcoming of such reified and established categorisations is undertaken in the name of another demarcation, one that is produced rather than assumed. This is what Althusser refers to as a transformation of the practice of philosophy.[3] This division goes by different names in Althusser's writing – sometimes it is the division between idealism and materialism, while in other periods it is the conflict between ideology and science, before developing into the thesis of philosophy as class struggle. All of this is prior to the material on aleatory materialism, which produces yet another division. What remains constant, however, is that in each case the division refers to a fundamental conflict at the heart of philosophy itself, the stakes of which are practical as much as they are conceptual. These divisions are simultaneously inside and outside of philosophy: they are

---

2   Althusser 1990d, p. 206.
3   Althusser 1990c, p. 249.

internal to its concepts and categories, cutting through the facile categorisations that separate politics from epistemology, but these internal divisions are ultimately the effects of external divisions, the situation of philosophy in a field of forces.

It is through this break with the dominant categories of philosophy that we can understand Althusser's turn to political philosophy in order to articulate a philosophy of the encounter. If the dominant tradition of philosophy has been to posit reason and necessity underneath apparently disparate and heterogeneous phenomena, then it is only through politics that the aleatory dimension, that contingency, can come into full light. Althusser's position here is profoundly Machiavellian, not just in the sense that the latter's idea of the encounter between virtú and fortune provides the basis for the meditation of the encounter at the heart of aleatory materialism, but also in the sense that, like Machiavelli, such a philosophy can only be developed through an active refusal of all hitherto existing philosophy. As Althusser writes, Machiavelli must repudiate all classical conceptions of politics, conceptions that in various ways posit a principle, a morality, existing behind the world in order to explain it.[4] Machiavelli's refusal of such political utopias is also a refusal of the dominant schema of metaphysics, which explains the apparent contingency of the world by some underlying necessity, positing the cycles of political regimes beyond the apparent contingencies of political fortunes. What defines politics is not the essence of the various regimes or their passage into each other, but the encounter between the skill of the prince (virtú) and its conditions. As Machiavelli defines this encounter, 'Without that first opportunity their strength [virtù] of purpose would never have been revealed. Without their strength [virtù] of purpose, the opportunity they were offered would not have amounted to anything'.[5] The focus on the singular conditions of the encounter does not mean that Machiavelli is an empiricist for whom the facts of history make it possible to dispense with the concept altogether: Althusser insists that Machiavelli produces the concepts of the event. It is not a matter of opposing philosophy to history, but of a new practice of history, new protocols for the production of concepts.[6] Just as Machiavelli turns towards history in order to recognise the reality of contingency, Althusser turns to political philosophy to construct a philosophy of the event. Althusser overshoots Machiavelli's target: the task is not just to turn to political history to clear the dead weight of utopian

---

4   Althusser 2006b, p. 174.
5   Machiavelli, p. 18.
6   Althusser 2006a, p. 198.

metaphysics underlying political philosophy, but to turn to political philosophy in order to produce an ontology of the event, a new materialism.[7]

Althusser's aleatory materialism has as its defining characteristic the primacy of the event, the contingent encounter, over the constituted forms that it produces. The central ontological claim of the text, however, or at least the line of demarcation that has the greatest effect, is Althusser's reversal of the relationship between necessity and contingency. 'Instead of thinking contingency as a modality of necessity, or an exception to it, we must think necessity as the becoming necessary of the encounter of contingencies'.[8] Contingency is not just some exception to the general rule, but as Althusser wrote earlier with respect to the conjuncture, the exception is the general rule.[9] Events do not rupture the continuity and necessity that is the norm of history and of being, but are themselves the exceptional norm. 'Every encounter is aleatory, not only in its origins, but also in its effects'.[10] Everything would seem to rest, then, on how we understand this becoming necessary, how necessity or at least the appearance of necessity emerges in a world of contingency. It is also with respect to this point that tension opens up between the political texts, Machiavelli, Rousseau, and Marx, and the metaphysical problem. This can be seen by asking the question: how are we to understand this becoming necessary? Machiavelli, Rousseau, and Marx all offer different answers, and these different answers constitute the bulk of their political philosophy. For Machiavelli this necessity is identified with the figure of the prince: the contingent event, the prince seizing power, can sustain itself or maintain itself if the prince possesses sufficient virtú – if he is skilful enough to manage his appearance amongst the people, the affects of hatred and fear, then his power will last. For Rousseau, whose *Discourse on the Origin of Inequality* puts forward the audacious thesis of the 'radical absence of society as the essence of society', the becoming necessary of society is constituted by the increased specialisation and hierarchy constituted by society itself. Once instituted, society becomes its own rationale: 'as soon as one man needed the help of another, as soon as one man realized that it was useful for a single man to have provisions for two, equality disappeared, property came into existence, labor became necessary'.[11] For Marx the becoming necessary of the contingent encounter of workers and capitalist is the transition from the force of the state to the compulsion of the economy.

---

7   Althusser 1999, p. 73.
8   Althusser 2006b, p. 193.
9   Althusser 1969, p. 104.
10   Althusser 2006b, p. 193.
11   Rousseau, p. 51.

As Marx writes, 'The silent compulsion of economic relations sets the seal on the domination of the capitalist over the worker. Direct extra-economic force is still of course used, but only in exceptional cases'.[12] Becoming necessary, the transformation of the encounter into something necessary, is considered in terms of political strategy, social dependency, and economic compulsion.

Politics, society, and economics, three figures of becoming necessary that in most accounts would be differentiated, distinguished by their relative degrees of necessity, are considered to be simply different versions of the same general problem, of the becoming necessary of the contingent encounter. Althusser's refusal of the existing categories of politics, sociology, and economics, categories that have often contained an implicit hierarchy between the contingent and shifting terrains of politics and the necessity of economic laws, is quite strong. This becomes focused in the final polemic on Marx, which draws a line between two concepts of the mode of production in Marx's writing: the first, which stresses the aleatory nature of capitalism's origin, is found in the writings on primitive accumulation and the Asiatic mode of production; while the second is found in the 'great pages in *Capital* on the essence of capitalism'. The second concept, which Althusser acknowledges dominates much of the Marxist tradition, understands capital, or any mode of production, to have a necessary logic and development.

Althusser is particularly critical of the role that the concept of the bourgeoisie plays in Marx's theory, specifically the way in which the term is used to name both the destructive force in the old order and the dominant class in the new order. The bourgeoisie is a unity, an imagined unity made up primarily of adjectives, that would seem to preexist its conditions: they would be capitalists before capitalism, effacing the aleatory foundation beneath the unified intention of a subject.[13] Althusser makes similar remarks with respect to the proletariat, which Marx often presents as a simple effect of the capitalist mode of production. The final remarks, at least in terms of the edition of the manuscript, clarify and justify Althusser's flattening of the economic, social and political dimension of becoming necessary onto one plane. There is only one meaningful distinction to be made, between a philosophy that treats the established order as an accomplished fact, and one that treats it as 'a fact to be accomplished'. In the first case, order and unity are assumed as given; the problem is in understanding destruction and change. While in the second, aleatory

---

12   Marx 1977, p. 899.
13   Althusser 2006a, p. 202.

dispersion is seen as primary, and unity becomes a problem. It is only from the perspective of the contingency of the social order that it is possible to pose the question of its reproduction, its specific becoming necessary.

The line of demarcation that Althusser draws between the necessary and contingent concepts of the mode of production, which is a reflection of the idealist and aleatory materialist forces within the history of philosophy itself, cuts right through the centre of Althusser's work, returning to the fundamental problems of reproduction, ideology, subjectivity, and the causality of the structure. Years earlier, in *Reading Capital*, Althusser had named the particular way in which a society coheres 'the society effect'. As Althusser argues:

> The mechanism of the production of this 'society effect' is only complete when all the effects of the mechanism have been expounded, down to the point where they are produced in the form of the very effects that constitute the concrete, conscious or unconscious relation of the individuals to the society as a society, i.e., down to the effects of the fetishism of ideology (or 'forms of social consciousness' – *Preface* to *A Contribution ...*), in which men consciously or unconsciously live their lives, their projects, their actions, their attitudes and their functions as *social*.[14]

This is the classic problem of ideology, which Althusser has often identified with reproduction, a kind of becoming necessary of a specific mode of production. As Althusser's argument regarding the two modes of production suggests, this reproduction has often been understood as a kind of supplement to an already given economic necessity, what Marx referred to as the 'silent compulsion of economic relations'. The turn to primitive accumulation, and the economy itself as one instance of a general becoming necessary, subverts this tendency. The economic order itself is not somehow more necessary than politics, but must itself be seen as contingent. The economy is not a cause existing outside or beyond the various dimensions of becoming necessary; it is another modality, or, to recall Althusser's reference to Aristotle in the essay on ideology, another sense of becoming necessary.

To draw these two lines together, that of the economy as contingent and yet part of the general becoming necessary, we could say that the becoming necessary in its different aspects, political, social, and economic, converges around a representation of the world, a kind of necessity effect. Ultimately we can then see the role that Spinoza plays in the construction of aleatory material-

---

14   Althusser and Balibar 1970, p. 66.

ism. While Spinoza's thought of a universe of absolute necessary immanent causality would seem to be out of place in a philosophy of contingency, he provides a necessary component in thinking the given world, the world perceived in its necessity as an effect of the imagination. As Althusser writes, 'the imagination is not by any means a faculty, but fundamentally only the only world itself in its "givenness"'.[15] While Althusser initially frames his idea of the 'becoming necessary' of contingent encounters as an ontological proposition that inverts the relation between contingency and necessity, the examples of Machiavelli, Spinoza, Rousseau, and Marx would seem to indicate that it is as much about the constitution of the world through the practices of politics and ideology as it is about the world as such. Spinoza is inscribed twice in this ontology: once as a critic of the imaginary fullness that constitutes the world as it is perceived and lived, and a second time, as a general thought of the primacy of relations that subtends such a world. As Althusser writes, one of the central premises of aleatory materialism is the primacy of the encounter, of the relations to being. These encounters always start with two, fortune and virtú or labour power and money, but proliferate beyond that to encompass other relations, other series. Althusser's reference to Spinoza within the essay on aleatory materialism is to the parallelism of attributes as a kind of non-relation of encounter. It would seem, however, that the true point of reference would seem to be structural causality, the idea of a cause that exists only in its effects. In this case, the cause is not some stable or timeless structure, an idea which burdened Althusser's early writings on the concept, but is nothing other than the encounter, the relation itself. The encounter exists only in its effects, and the effects are nothing other than a becoming necessary of the contingent encounter.

Ultimately, Althusser does not just turn to politics to construct a new ontology, one that places the event and change over stability and order, but returns this ontology to the field of politics itself. It is only through aleatory materialism that the central political question of reproduction, the political, social, and economic becoming necessary of a given social order, comes to light. As Althusser writes, the task of aleatory materialism is to think the 'reality of politics' and the 'essence of practice' and most importantly the encounter of these two realities in struggle.[16]

---

15   Althusser 2006b, p. 179.
16   Althusser 2006a, p. 188.

2   Becoming Constituent

It is at this point that we can see the proximity and distance that relates
Althusser's thought to some of the latter work of Antonio Negri. This proximity is not simply a matter of the shared lineage of Machiavelli, Spinoza, and
Marx, but of a shared problem, a rigorous thought of a materialist constitution of this world, which is to say a world constituted through practical activity
without preconditions or end. As Negri says, it is a matter of thinking the new
in the absence of its conditions. This distance and proximity can be charted
by the way that they interpret primitive accumulation. Like Althusser, Negri
sees primitive accumulation as foundational for not only a new understanding of capitalism, one that eschews the necessity and teleology underlying
its history as the history of different modes production, but a new ontology
as well. Like Althusser, Negri's turn to primitive accumulation, to a reading
of Marx, is situated at the end of a text that undertakes a long survey of the
history of philosophy that encompasses Machiavelli, Rousseau, and Spinoza.
Negri's interpretation reads these philosophers in the light of the revolutionary sequence that runs through the American, French, and Russian Revolution.
Negri's study of constituent power, published in English as *Insurgencies*, begins
from a simple assertion: democracy is founded on constituent power, the will
or consent of the people.[17] This fundamental axiom conceals a problem. As
much as constituent power appears in the history of political thought, it is
immediately concealed or effaced. Constituent power is transformed into an
exceptional event, as in the case of the founding moments (or 'founding fathers') or it is assumed to express itself fully and adequately in a constitution,
a series of formal structures that realise and tame it. Negri's central political
question is how can there be a constituent power that will not alienate itself
in a constituted order, in a structure. This is nothing less than the question of
revolution, of revolution not simply as the foundation of a new order but of a
transformation of the very idea of political order, of the state, what used to be
called 'permanent revolution'.

   This question frames Negri's reading of the history of revolutionary thought,
which runs from Machiavelli through the American, French, and Russian Revolutions. At first glance Negri's examination would appear to belong more properly in the realm of political philosophy, but as with Althusser's aleatory materialism, this political thought cannot be separated from an ontological dimension. Ontology asserts itself first in terms of a limit, a barrier, of what it makes
it possible to think. If, as we have seen, the barrier that aleatory materialism

---

17   Negri 1999, p. 1.

comes up against is necessity, the assumed necessity of the social order, the barrier that constituent power comes up against is also that of order, but it is not just order as necessity, but order as a pregiven structure that production and practice would only actualise. Order is teleology, the prefiguration of what is possible and can be done. As Negri writes of constitutive power, 'The political is here production, production "par excellence", collective and non-teleological'.[18] Althusser and Negri are both trying to think the reality of politics, of practice, and this can only be done if one dispenses with the idea of anything that politics would be a realisation of, any order or necessity existing beyond or beneath the play of forces.

Negri's genealogy of constituent power begins with Machiavelli's *Prince*, with the encounter of virtú and fortune. For Negri, however, virtú and fortune are not simply the terms of an aleatory encounter, but are fundamentally asymmetrical. Fortune is the dead weight of history, the given situation, within which virtú intervenes. As much as Machiavelli poses the radical figure of this eruption, of a practice that constitutes a new order in an interruption in what already exists, he does so in a fundamentally limited manner. Constituent thought is radically atheistic not just in that it dispenses with god, but in that it dispenses with any pregiven structure, any unity or reality that practice is said to realise. Thus, for Negri Machiavelli is a fundamentally stalled figure of constitutive practice in that the multiplicity of practice is subordinated to the unified figure of the Prince. The task then is a matter of reading the revolutionary process through a sequence that begins with Machiavelli and extends through Spinoza and Marx, each of which will be seen as an increasingly adequate figure. Negri's genealogy is almost the reverse of Althusser's: while Althusser turned to political philosophy to produce an ontology that would assert the priority of contingency over necessity, Negri turns to the history of metaphysics to find a figure of constitutive practice. For Negri 'the real political science of modernity lies in metaphysics'.[19] The strong opposition is only apparent, however: Negri's conception of metaphysics is eccentric to say the least, determined by figures outside of the dominant tradition and turning to texts not understood to be properly philosophical. Of the three philosophers that make up this genealogy, Machiavelli, Spinoza, and Marx, only the second, Spinoza, is generally understood to be a metaphysical thinker, but for Negri even Spinoza's metaphysics necessarily passes through politics, through the constitutive role of the imagination.[20]

---

18   Negri 1999, p. 28.
19   Negri 1999 p. 305.
20   Negri 1991b p. 122.

Negri's particular understanding of the relationship between metaphysics and politics comes to light in his interpretation of Marx on primitive accumulation. As with Althusser, Negri first locates in the violence of primitive accumulation the absence of any preexisting foundation; there is only the encounter in the here and now, drawing together the constitutive elements. Negri adds that this violent foundation is immediately constitutive of not only a new order, a new regime of accumulation, but also a new form of right. Primitive accumulation is also always an immediately political accumulation, the constitution of a new form of authority. It is possible to see this accumulation of right as part of the 'becoming necessary' of the contingency, the legitimation that transforms a contingent fact into a legitimate result. What interests Negri is the manner in which capital constitutes a social order that constitutes its own ever-shifting foundation, actively destroying, through the violence of primitive accumulation, the traditions that constituted the social. However, according to Negri, taken by itself primitive accumulation is indequate to account for the constitution of the capitalist order. The account of primitive accumulation needs to be coupled with the chapter from *Capital* on cooperation. As Negri writes: 'Cooperation is, in fact, in itself an essentially productive force'.[21] As with Althusser's reading of primitive accumulation, the reading extracts an ontology from what is otherwise a historical examination. Cooperative labour, like the violence of accumulation, constitutes a world but it does so according to a fundamentally different account of right. Capitalist accumulation and cooperation both constitute a form of right, and 'between equal rights, force decides'.[22] History is the relation between these two different 'rights', two different modes of association: capitalist violence, which imposes its form of labour and socialisation, and the socialisation produced in the networks of labour.[23] Negri considers this relation to be more antagonistic than dialectical, there is no mediation or synthesis of one by the other. Nonetheless, there is a gradual transformation, and development, a telos even, as the constitutive process encompasses more and more aspects of reality. This telos culminates in a reversal of the relation between force and constitution: primitive accumulation begins with capitalism imposing a form of cooperation on disparate bodies, but in the end cooperation is external and prior to capital. Capital is no longer necessary to constitute the cooperative powers of labour, but becomes an extrinsic parasitic force, expropriating a cooperative force that exceeds it.

---

21   Negri 1999, p. 259.
22   Marx 1977, p. 344.
23   Negri 1996b, p. 165.

Negri's thought, like Althusser's, crosses the terrain from the political, to the social, and the economic, which are not just different figures of the becoming necessary, of the inscription of the event in a structure and a rule, but are increasingly adequate figures of this constituent process. Against the tendency of bourgeois political philosophy to subordinate the constituent process to a distant event, or to contain it in a formal structure, ironically, it is Marx's critique of political economy that provides the adequate concept of the constituent power. Living labour, the productive force of cooperation beset by the constituted authority of accumulation, constantly recreates the world again. As Negri writes, 'Living labour constitutes the world, by creatively modeling *ex novo*, the materials that it touches ... its constructions are constructions of new being'.[24] Marx resolves the problem of constituent power by removing the division between the political, social, and economic dimensions of existence, by flattening them onto the terrain of cooperation and accumulation where existence is created and recreated through the quotidian experience of labour. Thus, the political problem can only be solved through metaphysics, a metaphysics that is in some sense the absence of metaphysics, or a metaphysics that finds its only possible expression in the multiple relations of constituent power. It is a metaphysics of production, not the instrumental action of an individual on an object, but production as the multiple relations of affecting and being affected – production is nothing other than finite modal existence.

As with Althusser's reading, what is at stake in this interpretation is nothing less than the fundamental problem of a materialist philosophy, and as with Althusser this involves a reinterpretation of the fundamental problem of a mode of production. One could say that Negri's analysis also draws a line of demarcation, not between necessity and contingency in the mode of production, but between a restricted and expansive definition of the mode of production. For Negri the mode of production must be understood not simply as an economic base underlying the superstructure of society, but as the general relation of cooperation and command in society. This expansive sense of the term is made possible by focusing on labour, on living labour, which is always something more than an element in a combinatory that combines 'forces' and 'relations'. For Negri the purely economic understanding of the mode of production mirrors the purely formal and political understanding of the constitution. In each case the actual dynamic of the economics, politics, and ontology are overlooked. This dynamic dimension is labour itself, labour understood in its antagonistic materiality. 'Marx brought to light a commonality of the social,

24   Negri 1999, p. 326.

the political, and being that is traversed and always newly defined by living labour its subsidiary associations, and the subjectivities that emerge within it – in short, by constituent power'.[25] It is through living labour, through its encounter and struggle with the constituted force of capital that the political and economic structure is transformed, a struggle which can only be understood if it is examined ontologically, as a struggle of being itself.

The encounter between the virtú of the prince and the accumulated force of fortune is the first figure of this conflict. Machiavelli's prince refers this encounter back to an almost transcendental figure. The task for Negri is to retain this eruption of the new, the transformative force without mythologising it, to make it absolutely immanent and quotidian. The transformative force of Machiavelli's prince must be democratised by Spinoza's multitude, by the multiple productive relations of affecting and being affected. Marx's 'living labour' is the culmination of this series, a culmination that is only possible if the three philosophers are read together, through the intersection of politics and metaphysics.

3   Philosophy's Outside

From this provisional sketch of the differences between Negri and Althusser it is possible to see the way in which their different attempts to extract an ontology from the dense critical historical narrative of primitive accumulation oppose each other. In Althusser the emphasis is on the contingency of the event, an event that underlies the constitution of any world, undermining its rationality and necessity, but the process of becoming necessary is less clear. The multiple figures of this becoming necessary from Machiavelli to Marx develop its expansive sense, but these senses converge on the imaginary constitution of the world, which is considered more as a given fact than a constitutive process. In sharp contrast to this Negri underscores the way in which the opening of primitive accumulation lends itself to a understanding of the way in which the world is created, or constituted, anew from the practical contestation of accumulation and cooperation. From primitive accumulation Althusser constructs an ontology of the event, making the event less a historical exception than a general category of being; Negri, on the other hand, turns less towards the event itself than to the constitutive dimension of practice that it makes possible. These differences become all the more extreme

---

25   Negri 1999, p. 327.

when viewed in light of the other thinker's limitations: Althusser's 'becoming necessary' is broadened to encompass politics, society, and economics, but the practical dimension of this process is never revealed, leaving it somewhat mystified; Negri, on the other hand, provides an ontology of the constitution of a social order, focusing on living labour as the nexus by which political and social structures are constituted and contested, but does so by returning linearity and teleology to the process. Telos is a word that runs through Negri's thought; sometimes it is limited to the desire and intentionality underlying human action. However, Negri's history of constitutive power, a history in which the various figurations, from Machiavelli's prince to Marx's labour power, become more and more adequate to the constitutive process, indicates a much deeper sense of linearity. Thus, despite my initial words of caution, it is possible to view each as the other's antithesis. However, it is also possible to see in each of their respective processes an attempt to renew and deepen the relation between conditions and activity, conjuncture and practice.

Althusser and Negri offer a renewal of Marxist philosophy. They do so not just by inventing a trajectory that passes through Machiavelli and Spinoza, thus uprooting Marx from a limited (and endlessly debated) relation with Hegel, but by determining its specific practice. Materialist philosophy is hostile to the divisions that would not only separate politics and economics, but both from ontology. Which is not to say that everything collapses into a mechanistic assertion of the identity of matter. Overcoming the separation between politics, economics, and ontology makes it possible to frame new lines of demarcation, lines that are drawn from the reality of political and ideological struggle rather than from the textbooks of philosophy.

In Althusser and Negri's view the limitations of confronting this problem are as much conceptual as they are conjunctural; thinking revolution, change, and the event means breaking with a tradition that places necessity over contingency, constituted things over the constitutive process. As much as primitive accumulation makes possible a philosophical rather than just an economic or political investigation, it is an investigation provoked by the event itself, by the vicissitude of history. History means something different in each case. For Althusser, at least during the period of 'aleatory materialism', history is defined by the collapse of the determinations that were to function as the fundamental guarantee and justification of the Marxist project – the inevitable collapse of capitalism. It was Althusser's profound insight to see these determinations as fetters rather than guarantees: the promise of an ultimate direction of history fundamentally obscures the reality of history itself, the reproduction and transformation of the mode of production. For Negri history is defined by a profound mutation of the relationship between subjectivity, labour, and capital.

In each case 'something has snapped', but in Althusser's case it is the project
of finding an ultimate guarantee of the Marxist project, while for Negri it is
the relation between command and labour that has characterised the capital
worker relationship.[26] It is possible to see Negri's project as more 'historicist' in
orientation, as more dependent on a particular understanding of the current
moment as defined by the hegemony of immaterial labour, and thus having
missed Althusser's fundamental insight regarding the absence of telos of history.[27] It is possible, even easy, to interpret the relationship this way, however, it
is also possible to see a historical dimension to Althusser's text as well, not just
in the aleatory turn to a contingent history, but in the increased attention to
'becoming necessary' as a fundamental transformation of the imagination and
subjectivity. Between the lines of Althusser's articulation of an aleatory materialism, and definitely in the closing lines on the two concepts of the mode of
production, there is a focus on the materialist dimension of the imagination
as part of becoming necessary. This becomes abundantly clear if read in light
of Althusser's earlier texts on reproduction. Althusser and Negri's renewal of
materialism is also a response to the increasing incorporation of subjectivity
into the productive process. On this point Althusser and Negri are opposed as
well, but it is not the static opposition between structure and subject, conjuncture and historicism, but a dynamic opposition that foregrounds the political
problem, the forces of labour and subjection that determine the terrain for
communist struggle. Thus, the ultimate merit of Althusser and Negri's projects
is to turn our attention towards the core of a materialist philosophy, the point
where the power of thought, its ability to construct new concepts and break
through ossified structures, is determined by the event, by a history that constitutes its necessary outside.

26   Althusser 1979, p. 226.
27   Hardt and Negri 2004, p. 109.

PART 2

Putting the Capitalism Back into Capitalism and Schizophrenia: On Deleuze and Guattari

∵

A Universal History of Contingency: Deleuze and Guattari on the History of Capitalism

One of the difficult characteristics of the writing of Gilles Deleuze, alone and in collaboration with Félix Guattari, is, in Deleuze's terms, its extremely 'untimely' nature. Philosophical and theoretical positions that have generally been abandoned or rendered untenable by the passage of time are advocated by Deleuze and Guattari and subsequently twisted so as to be rendered unrecognisable. There are multiple specific examples of this: the turn to vitalism, to naturalism, or to pre-critical philosophical positions, but more generally it is possible to say that Deleuze and Guattari write as if the general breakdown of the lofty aspirations of philosophy, the critique of metaphysics and of the systematising pretensions of philosophy, had not happened. Or do they? Even as Deleuze and Guattari seem to produce a metaphysics and even a cosmology that encompasses everything from the geological history of the earth to the contemporary technological and political transformations of capital they do so with such a perverse humour that it is impossible to assume what is at stake in such writing. Is this simply the worst sort of totalising metaphysical philosophising, or is it all just some sort of joke? Or is something altogether different happening – another practice of philosophy, that is neither a return of the grand systematic aspirations of philosophy nor the dismantling of it?

Perhaps the most perplexing philosophical position that Deleuze and Guattari assume is the invocation of universal history throughout the two volumes of *Capitalism and Schizophrenia*. Universal history would seem to be a mode of practising philosophy incapable of being redeemed today. Has not universal history been exposed as, at best, the fantasy of armchair historians and, at worst, the apology for western imperialism? Yet Deleuze and Guattari insist on rewriting universal history. This rewriting of universal history is animated by questions which have been adopted from Marx, or Marxist history; namely, they are the question of the origin and formation of capitalism, its specific difference with respect to previous economic forms, or modes of production, and the relation of the formation of capital to the formation of the state. While Deleuze and Guattari pose and examine these questions which have been the bread and butter of Marxist theorising, they inflict them with an emphasis on a question which is somewhat novel – the examination of the relationship between the transformations of the mode of production and the production of subjectivity. In other words, Deleuze and Guattari ask the question: what sort of subject (what sort of desires and beliefs) does capital, or each of the other modes of production, require? How is this subject produced? What sort of limits or resistances does this production come up against? And, ultimately, what are the conditions for a different production, for new ways of living and desiring? It is this series of questions, questions which lead in the direction of what Foucault called a 'historical ontology of ourselves' that end up having transformative effects on the more established 'Marxist' questions. Rather than see the universal history, a history of epochs of civilisation or modes of production, and genealogy, a history of desires and subjectivity, as fundamentally opposed projects and perspectives, Deleuze and Guattari suggest that they are necessarily intertwined. The central (and not so central) questions of Marxist history and philosophy are engaged throughout Deleuze and Guattari's writing, but their sense and meaning has been fundamentally rewritten in light of the question of desire, of the generation and corruption of different forms of subjectivity.

The specific form that the borrowing of these questions takes, as well as the texts and modes of inquiry chosen to respond to them, vary in each of Deleuze and Guattari's collaborative efforts, from the re-reading of the relationship between Marxism and anthropology in *Anti-Oedipus* to the use of the work of Fernand Braudel to construct a 'geophilosophy' in *What is Philosophy?*, constituting something of a minor intellectual history in itself. Within this trajectory there are, however, several constant themes; most notably in *Anti-Oedipus* Deleuze and Guattari announce against Hegel that 'universal history is the history of contingencies, and not the history of necessity'. This meditation on the contingent and the event runs throughout their writing on history.[1] It would seem that such an announcement would run against Marx as well, against the comprehension of history as the universal, necessary, and teleological passage from one mode of production to another, culminating in communism (whether governed by class struggle or the conflict between the forces and relations of production as the determining instance). The gulf that separates Deleuze and Guattari's sense of history and Marx would appear to deepen as they add that universal history is 'retrospective, ... contingent, singular, ironic, and critical'.[2] In *Anti-Oedipus* Deleuze and Guattari argue, however, that in thinking history as a series of singular encounters and accidents they are following exactly 'the rules formulated by Marx'. Moreover, in *Anti-Oedipus*, a

---

1   Deleuze and Guattari 1983, p. 140.
2   Deleuze and Guattari 1983, ibid.

text that I will argue sets down the basic problems and terms of Deleuze and Guattari's reflections on 'universal history', they proceed through a reading of Marx's notebooks posthumously titled 'Pre-Capitalist Economic Formations' [*Formen, die der kapitalistischen Produktion vorhergehen*] in the *Grundrisse*. In this regard *Anti-Oedipus* is more important for understanding the relationship of Deleuze and Guattari to Marx than *A Thousand Plateaus* (which is not to suggest that Marx, or an engagement with a Marxist conception of history, entirely disappears from the later text – in fact, the discussion of capital in terms of the difference of code and axioms is one of the few things which persists in the later volume). Thus, the initial question provoked by Deleuze and Guattari's 'untimely' return to universal history, a question of how to read such an invocation, ultimately becomes a question of how to read Marx as well. Reading Marx not for the necessity, universality, and dry seriousness that we are told awaits us there, but for contingency, singularity, and a critical sense of irony. For Deleuze and Guattari the name Marx and the texts of Marx do not constitute the invocation of proper pedigree, but rather are subject to selection, transformation, and ultimately the production of something new.

In *Anti-Oedipus* the selection of 'Pre-Capitalist Economic Formations' as a central text of their engagement with Marx would already seem to locate Deleuze and Guattari at the margins of Marx's thought. They do not begin with the problem of alienation, ideology, the labour theory of value, or commodity fetishism, problems or concepts that have a long history in Marxist social theory, but with the odd prehistory of capitalism. The text opens with a consideration of the basic historical preconditions and presuppositions of the capitalist mode of production, which are presented not as inevitable effects of the collapse of the previous (feudal) mode of production, but as something that is simply given. As Marx writes: '[Capital's] *original formation [Urbildung]* is that, through the historic process of the dissolution of the old mode of production, value existing as money-wealth is enabled, on one side *to buy* the objective conditions of labor; on the other side, to exchange money for the *living labor* of the workers who have been set free'.[3] Of course this formulation could be understood as a historical shorthand, stressing the two fundamental elements of the capitalist mode of production, money and workers. In order for the capitalist mode of production to exist there must be, on the one hand, money that is no longer invested in land, and on the other, workers stripped of the means of production. What is emphasised in this text, however, is not the universality of the two constituent elements, but rather the singularity of the encounter. The

---

3   Marx 1973, p. 507.

conditions are necessary, but not sufficient to the formation of capital, as Marx demonstrates with respect to the plebeians of ancient Rome:

> Thus one fine morning there were to be found on the one hand free men stripped of everything except their labor power, and on the other, the owners of all the acquired wealth ready to exploit this labor. What happened? The Roman proletarians became not wage laborers but a *mob* of do-nothings more abject than those known as 'poor whites' in the South of the United States, and alongside them there developed a mode of production which was not capitalist but based on slavery. Thus events strikingly analogous but taking place in different historical surroundings led to totally different results. By studying each of these forms of evolution separately and then comparing them one can easily find the clue to this phenomenon, but one will never arrive there by using as one's master key a general historico-philosophical theory, the supreme virtue of which consists in being supra-historical.[4]

The encounter takes place under certain determinate conditions, conditions that necessarily presuppose a series of other conditions, and it is only under these conditions that capitalism is formed. As Deleuze and Guattari argue: 'The encounter might not have taken place, with the free workers and the money-capital existing "virtually" side by side'.[5]

Marx gives the contingency of this encounter of wealth and workers its clearest historical and philosophical illustration and elaboration in the chapters on 'Primitive Accumulation' that end Volume I of *Capital*. (These chapters simultaneously illustrate and complicate the remarks on the 'original formation' of capital in 'Pre-capitalist Economic Formations', providing historical specificity and depth to a general formula). In these chapters Marx criticises the moral narrative of thrift and greed of 'so-called primitive accumulation' offered by classical political economy. This narrative is offered to answer a seemingly irresolvable problem: if all capitalist accumulation presupposes capital to invest and workers to hire in a seemingly infinite regress there must be an original or previous accumulation that makes capital possible. Classical political economy argues that it was the thrift of the first proto-capitalists that made capitalism possible. As Marx writes:

---

4   Marx and Engels 1955, p. 294.
5   Deleuze and Guattari 1983, p. 225.

This primitive accumulation plays approximately the same role in political economy as original sin does in theology. Adam bit the apple, and thereupon sin fell on the human race. Its origin is supposed to be explained when it is told as an anecdote about the past. Long, long ago there were two sorts of people; one the diligent, intelligent, and above all frugal elite; the other lazy rascals, spending their subsistence, and more, in riotous living.[6]

For Marx this moral or ideological presentation of the formation of capitalism fails to encompass the double-sided nature of the formation of capital; there must be both wealth (capital) and dispossessed individuals (workers), a double-sided nature that on closer inspection turns out to be multiple. The saving or hoarding of wealth only accounts for one of the two elements of the encounter; there must also be a dispossession of the means of production, land, tools, etc., from those who own it. This process of dispossession is itself brutal and violent, as the old structures of property, such as the commons, are destroyed and a new form of right and property is created. These two different elements constitute two very different histories and strategies: on the one side there is the accumulation of wealth that includes the early emergence of mercantile capital, colonialism, and the beginning of the credit system, and on the other there is the destruction of the commons and the guild system.[7] These two different histories cannot be reduced to a single logic, intention, or historical subject, but must be thought as themselves constituted by a multiplicity of encounters.[8] The capitalist mode of production is not the simple result of the intention of a subject, or subjects, nor is it generated as if from the womb of the previous (feudal) mode of production: it is made possible by a series of events whose results must be seized and turned towards different ends. These events take place at the margins of the previous mode of production; they only take

---

6 Marx 1977, p. 873.
7 Deleuze and Guattari 1983, p. 225; here Deleuze and Guattari are drawing from Étienne Balibar's contribution to *Reading Capital*: 'in the examples analysed by Marx, the formation of free laborers appears mainly in the form of transformations of agrarian structures, while the constitution of wealth is the result of merchant's capital and finance capital, whose movements take place outside those structures, "marginally", or "in the pores of society"' (Althusser and Balibar 1970, p. 281).
8 In a provocative essay written in the 1980s, Louis Althusser argues that 'primitive accumulation' constitutes a different thought of materialism than the one generally attributed to Marx; a materialism of the 'encounter' and the event, rather than a materialism of necessity and teleology, working from some of the same passages and texts that Deleuze and Guattari draw from – see Althusser 1994a.

centre stage retroactively as the 'prehistory' of the mode of production that follows. Althusser calls the process by which the effects of a particular process are seized and turned to other purposes and other ends *détournement*: 'This "detouring" is the mark of the non-teleology of the process and the inscription of its result in a process which has rendered it possible and which was totally alien to it'.[9]

In 'Pre-Capitalist Economic Formations' the contingency of the encounter, the fact that every mode of production must begin from presuppositions which are not produced by it but are presupposed by it, is immediately intertwined with a second problem – the manner in which every mode of production conceals its own contingency, its historicity, and, ultimately, its vulnerability. Thus, what is being proposed here, placing the contingent encounter of money and workers at the centre of Marx's account of the constitution of the capitalist mode of production, is not to be confused with the simple assertion that 'everything is contingent'. Such a statement would have as its necessary political correlate the statement 'everything is possible', and would thus be tantamount to an idealism of political practice. At the core of Marx's thought is the investigation into the material conditions and limits of any practice and activity (one possible definition of the mode of production), and this is not changed by the stress placed here on the contingency of the encounter. It is not that one is catapulted from a world of necessity to a world of contingency, but that the relation between the necessary and contingent must be rethought from the ground up. As Althusser writes: 'Instead of thinking of contingency as a modality of or an exception to the necessary, one must think necessity as the becoming-necessary of contingent encounters'.[10] A 'becoming necessary', a process, and not a simple transition from contingency to necessity, because the different elements of a mode of production – the social, technological, and political conditions – have independent histories and relations, and this independence threatens any mode of production with its dissolution or transformation. Therefore, while it is possible to think of each mode of production as entailing certain dimensions of necessity (for example in capital it is necessary to valorise existing capital, to reproduce a docile and competent labour force, and so on), the contingent encounter that formed the mode of production haunts it as the threat of its dissolution. As Althusser writes: '[Primitive accumulation] continues today, not just in the visible example of the third world, but as a constant process that inscribes the aleatory at the heart of the capitalist mode of production'.[11]

---

9   Althusser 1994a, p. 572.
10   Althusser 1994a, p. 566.
11   Althusser 1994a, p. 573.

Deleuze and Guattari name this threat of dissolution 'desiring-production', which can be at least provisionally defined as desire that is at odds with the goals and presuppositions of social production. 'To code – desire and the fear, the anguish of decoded flows – is the business of the socius'.[12] In translating the general problem of the possible dissolution of the capitalist mode of production into the problem of the coding of desire, Deleuze and Guattari underscore the fact that what threatens a specific mode of production most of all is not some objective fact – war, disaster, or famine – but the failure of a mode of production to reproduce the subjective desires necessary for its reproduction. Thus 'coding' entails a wedding of desire to the particular mode of production. This in part involves a particular presentation or engagement with the historical preconditions of the mode of production. One way to code desire, to identify its goals with the goals of social reproduction, is to foreclose the contingency and historicity of the specific mode of production. As Marx demonstrates with respect to the critique of 'so-called primitive accumulation', the presentation of the complex and violent history of the formation of capital as a moral narrative of thrift and waste serves not only to justify the existing class divisions of capital, but to present capitalism as an ever present possibility. That is not to suggest, however, that this illusion is a sort of 'noble lie' invented to keep the exploited in their place; rather, and here we come closer to Deleuze and Guattari's concept of coding, this misrecognition of the historical conditions of capital is produced by the very structures and relations of capital. It should be noted that the term 'coding' is not entirely accurate with respect to capitalism. Deleuze and Guattari follow Marx's project in the notebooks in developing a general theory of the mode of production, within which the specificity – economic, political, and cultural – of capitalism can be articulated. While every mode of production must conceal its contingency, historicity, and instability, only precapitalist societies do so through a code, which could also be understood as a dominant ideology or mythology. In capitalism there is no one such structure of beliefs, rather, the various codes are broken down by the abstract rules of exchange (which accept not higher authority), becoming privatised (the terms that Deleuze and Guattari use for this privatisation of code – the breakdown of the unifying belief system of a society into private beliefs that are all the more effective, in terms of social regulation, in that they are private – are 'recoding' and 'reterritorialisation'). Capitalism cannot offer, or tolerate, a new mythos other than that of the market itself – it can only offer private moralities.

'So called primitive accumulation', the narratives and myths of the formation of capital offered by classical political economy, replaces history with memory,

---

12   Deleuze and Guattari 1983, p. 139.

the conditions of accumulation within capital for the conditions of the formation of the capitalist mode of production. A narrative of private success, saving
rather than spending, becomes not only a moral rule – save rather than spend –
but also a general representation for the historical transformation of capitalism – as if the entire lengthy history of the transformation from pre-capitalism
to capitalism could be understood as the expression of rational self-interest.
In other words, in capitalism the only representation of all of society or the
common good is that of individual self-interest.[13] As Étienne Balibar writes:
'The analysis of primitive accumulation thus brings us into the presence of the
radical *absence of memory* which characterizes history (memory being only the
reflection of history in certain predetermined sites – ideology or even law – and
as such, anything but a faithful reflection)'.[14] So called primitive accumulation
is not just a moral justification of the class divisions of capitalism, but an inability to grasp the historicity of the capitalist mode of production, the fact that
capital was formed through a particular conjunction of events, desires, and processes, a conjunction which exceeds the moral difference between saving and
squandering. This inability to grasp the historicity of the mode of production
is not simply disseminated through the ideological structures and relations of
the mode of production, but is inscribed as what Deleuze and Guattari call an
'apparent objective movement' in the very structures and institutions of the
mode of production itself.

The theme of an 'apparent objective movement', or an illusion that is neither
hardwired in the structures of human consciousness, as in the Kantian aporias,
nor perpetrated by a knowing subject operating behind the scenes, but is
produced by a particular social formation, runs throughout Marx's writing.
It underlies the idea of ideology as an 'objective' illusion both produced and
necessitated by the division of labour, specifically the division of mental and
manual labour, and commodity fetishism as an 'objective' illusion produced by
the pervasiveness of market relations. Étienne Balibar has argued that these
two problems, the problem of ideology and the problem of fetishism, are perhaps two different problems. In the former, there is the combination of objective conditions such as the division between mental and manual labour and a
subjective class point of view, the ideas of the ruling class, while in the latter,
the fetish is objectively produced by the mechanisms of commodity production.[15] It is perhaps for this reason that while Deleuze and Guattari dispense

---

13   Massumi 1992, p. 140.
14   Althusser and Balibar 1970, p. 283.
15   Balibar 2017b, p. 60.

with the notion of ideology, and its corresponding ideas of false and true consciousness, they retain the term 'fetishism' to refer to this 'apparent objective
movement'.

In 'Pre-capitalist Economic Formations' Marx offers not so much a general
theory of the production of this 'objective' illusion, but rather shows how in
the various pre-capitalist modes of production this illusion bears on the historical presuppositions of the mode of production. In all modes of production the
conditions of existence are produced and reproduced as the practical effects
of labour and desire, but this production and reproduction starts from certain
presuppositions. At the very basis these presuppositions include the earth as
the natural conditions of labour. 'The earth is the great workshop, the arsenal
which furnishes both means and material of labor, as well as the seat, the base
of the community'.[16] That the earth is not itself produced but is the precondition of all productive activity would seem to be a simple and banal fact hardly
worth mentioning. Marx argues, however, that this basic condition of all production never appears in its pure form – it is always-already mediated by the
particular social relation, the particular community that one enters. What is
presupposed, placed at the origin, is not simply the earth, and the fact of biological existence, but the social conditions which assume the responsibility for
this 'divine gift'.

> The *real appropriation* through the labor process happens under these
> *presuppositions*, which are not themselves the *product* of labor, but appear
> as its natural or *divine* presuppositions [*natürlichen oder göttlichen
> Voraussetzungen erschein*]. This form, with the same land-relation as its
> foundation, can realize itself in very different ways [*kann sich selbst sehr
> vershieden realisieren*].[17]

The different ways that this 'divine presupposition' can realise itself includes at
the most basic level the tribe or community of a primitive communism, but it
also includes Asiatic despotism. Marx argues that in the Asiatic mode of production it is the despot himself and not simply the earth that appears to be
the necessary precondition for labor and the existence of social relations. In
placing Asiatic despotism within 'this same form' Marx passes from a banal
problem, that there are always preconditions that one starts somewhere in history, to a different problem – that of the social and political reproduction of the
mode of production.

---

16   Marx 1973, p. 472.
17   Marx 1973, Ibid.

The Asiatic mode of production is perhaps one of the most controversial aspects of Marx's thought, and the history of its development is a history of debate and controversy. Although in some sense this history is inseparable from its own particular pre-history of presuppositions, in that the image of a despotic 'Orient' dating back to at least Aristotle has been continually reasserted by Western philosophy from Montesquieu to Hegel, all the while shifting from Persia to India and China, following the trajectory of western imperialism (it is due to this rather tainted intellectual history that Perry Anderson argues that this 'notion should be given the decent burial that it deserves').[18] Within Marxism the concept of a specifically Asiatic mode of production initially seemed to violate the linear progression that ran from ancient to feudal to the capitalist mode of production. This violation took on added importance in Russia and China, countries that were at one point or another identified with the 'bureaucratic commune' of the Asiatic mode of production, and for which the question of their place within Marx's historical periodisation took on immediate political importance. Moreover, the Asiatic mode of production not only stands outside of the history of pre-capitalism (keeping in mind that for Marx all considerations of feudalism and other modes of production are only genealogies of the present), but also stands outside of the general conceptual scheme of this history – it is posited as static, as a political formation which remains stubbornly the same as all else changes.[19] The Asiatic mode of production, in that it has as one of its defining characteristics despotic state power prior to the formation of capital, also suggests another thought of the genesis and function of the state form, one which is not grounded on class struggle or reducible to an instrument of the ruling class. This made it possible to utilise the Asiatic mode of production to criticise the bureaucracy of the Soviet Union and China, to turn one of Marx's concepts against the revolutions carried out in his name.[20] Finally, a third moment in the history of the concept of the Asiatic mode of production entails the project to expand Marxism into a general theory of social relations, beyond the criticism of the capitalist mode of production, a project which involves an encounter with anthropology.[21] Deleuze and Guattari's point of entry into these debates is oblique (and almost guaranteed to be overlooked by many readers). What matters for them is less a decision about these various questions, and more a use of the Asiatic mode of production to interrogate the logic and limits of the Marxist conception of history.

---

18   Anderson 1974, p. 548.

19   Spivak 1999, p. 91.

20   e.g. Wittfogel 1957.

21   e.g., Hindess and Hirst 1975.

What Marx is outlining with this idea of an Asiatic despot, and what Deleuze and Guattari underscore, is the fact that because a mode of production is constituted as a contingent encounter of different political and social processes, an encounter which is continually threatened by its own unraveling, it must produce, artificially as it were, its own stability. This production of stability entails in part a coding (or recoding) of desire; or rather, a production of a particular subjectivity that recognises itself and its desires in the mode of production. Marx refers to this production of subjectivity through what he calls the 'inorganic body' from which subjectivity is produced; that is, the mode of production reproduces itself by providing the raw material of subjectivity in the form of the 'inorganic' material of beliefs, language, and desires.[22] Althusser names this dimension, or problem, the 'society effect' (*l'effet de société*).

> The mechanism of the production of this 'society effect' is only complete when all the effects of the mechanism have been expounded, down to the point where they are produced in the form of the very effects that constitute the concrete, conscious or unconscious relation of the individuals to the society as a society, i.e., down to the effects of the fetishism of ideology (or 'forms of social consciousness' – *Preface* to *A Contribution ...*), in which men consciously or unconsciously live their lives, their projects, their actions, their attitudes and their functions as *social*.[23]

In one of the un-credited citations of *Reading Capital* Deleuze and Guattari rename this problem the socius. Deleuze and Guattari stress what the definition offered above eclipses – that this society effect, or socius, must also and at the same time be a cause; that is, it must have its own particular effects and productivity.

> ... the forms of social production, like those of desiring production, involve an unengendered nonproductive attitude, an element of anti-production coupled with the process, a full body that functions as a *socius*. This socius may be the body of the earth, that of the tyrant, or capital. This is the body that Marx is referring to when he says that it is not the product of labor, but rather appears as its natural or divine presuppositions. In fact, it does not restrict itself merely to opposing productive forces in and of themselves. It falls back on [*il se rabat sur*] all production, constituting

---

22   Marx 1973, p. 490.
23   Althusser and Balibar 1970, p. 66.

a surface over which the forces and agents of production are distributed, thereby appropriating for itself all surplus production and arrogating to itself both the whole and the parts of the process, which now seem to emanate from it as a quasi-cause.[24]

Every society, or social machine, has an aspect that appears as the condition, or cause, rather than the effect, of the productive relations, the desires and labours of society. Paradoxically, this 'quasi-cause' appears to be a cause of production, because it is itself not productive, or, more precisely, it is 'anti-productive'. It appropriates the excessive forces of production, distributing some for the reproduction of society and wasting most (in the form of tribal honours, palaces, and ultimately war). Eugene Holland underscores the centrality of 'anti-production' of an expenditure which is at once useless (constituting a vast appropriation of productive forces for excess and expenditure) and useful (reproducing the relations) and thus does not fit within a neat Marxist conceptualisation of 'forces' and 'relations' of production.[25]

The socius is not an effect, but a cause, a production of authority, prestige, and belief, what is referred to as both the recording of production and the production of recording. However, Deleuze and Guattari's reinscription of the society effect as cause is not an actual deviation from Althusser, but rather a return of Althusser's concept of the 'society effect' to his most important theoretical innovation, 'immanent causality'. While several Althusserians dismiss the idea of the 'society effect' as a wrong turn for Althusser,[26] Balibar continues to utilise and expand on this concept, arguing that the 'society effect' and the particular mode of subjection it entails must be thought in terms of its own particular materiality and effectivity.[27]

The reading that Althusser performs in *Reading Capital* has more than superficial similarities with Deleuze's reading of Spinoza in *Expressionism in Philosophy: Spinoza*. In each case there is a reading that produces a concept that is not named as such but functions or is illustrated through the entire organisation of the work; 'immanent causality' in the former and 'expression' in the latter. Moreover, in which the concept in question both functions immanently in relation to the text, as the unnamed articulation of its movement, and is a question of immanence in the world. As Pierre Macherey notes with respect to Deleuze's book on Spinoza, the inability for the respective authors (Marx and

---

24 Deleuze and Guattari 1983, p. 10.
25 Holland 1999, pp. 62–3.
26 e.g., Callari and Ruccio 1996, p. 2.
27 Balibar 2002c.

Spinoza) to name the concept is not simply an error or subjective failure, but has more to do with a concept which is more of function, or a producer of certain effects, than an object of representation.[28] In *Reading Capital* Althusser argues that Marx's *Capital*, at least the first volume completed by Marx in his lifetime, produces a concept which is never named as such, but accounts for the very organisation and structure of the volume. The cause or structure is immanent in its effects because it is nothing outside of its effects. This cause is both immanent and absent, because to be immanent and present in its effects is also to be un-localisable. This cause cannot be present or empirically given at any one point, hence the other name that Althusser gives it: 'metonymical causality'.[29] Althusser argues that Marx breaks decisively with the two dominant models of causality within the western philosophical tradition: 'expressive causality' (Hegel), in which a single cause, or contradiction, expresses itself in various effects which are merely epiphenomena of this cause, and mechanical causality, in which causes and effects interact, all the while remaining completely independent of each other. This break with all pre-existing thoughts of causality is not so much announced by Marx but is illustrated by the entire presentation of *Capital*. What is illustrated and put to work by the particular combination of philosophical arguments, critiques of existing works of political economy, historical accounts of struggles, and descriptions of the factory is a particular thought of causality in which every effect of the capitalist mode of production must also and at the same time be a cause. There is thus a relation between this 'new' thought of causality and the entire presentation [*Darstellung*] of *Capital*.

> Now we can recall that highly symptomatic term '*Darstellung*', compare it with this 'machinery' and take it literally, as the very existence of this machinery in its effects: the mode of existence of the stage direction [*mise en scène*] of the theatre which is simultaneously its own stage, its own script, its own actors, the theatre whose spectators can, on occasion, be spectators only because they are first of all forced to be its actors, caught by the constraints of a script and parts whose authors they cannot be, since it is in essence an authorless theatre.[30]

In *Anti-Oedipus* Deleuze and Guattari criticise not only psychoanalysis but also Althusser for reintroducing a 'theatrics of representation' after their respective

---

28   Macherey 1996.
29   Althusser and Balibar 1970, p. 191.
30   Althusser and Balibar 1970, p. 193.

critiques of the idealist protocols of representation. As Deleuze and Guattari write: 'Even in Louis Althusser we are witness to the following operation: the discovery of social production as a "machine" or "machinery", irreducible to the world of objective representation (*Vorstellung*); but immediately the reduction of the machine to structure, the identification of production with a structural and theatrical representation (*Darstellung*)'.[31] However, Deleuze and Guattari's criticism traces the line of Althusser's own self-criticism: Althusser cut many of the passages referring to a theater in the second edition of *Lire le Capital*.[32] Specifically, Althusser cut all of the passages in which the metaphor of the theatre reintroduces a concealed or latent structure, the script or the direction, existing behind or beyond the immanent taking place of the specific actions and interactions on stage. Thus in each case – the rewriting of the socius as both effect and cause and the critique of 'theatrical representation' – Deleuze and Guattari offer not so much a criticism of Althusser, but sketch out internal lines of demarcation between different tendencies within the same 'problematic'.

> What do we mean here by immanent cause? It is a cause which is realized, integrated and distinguished in its effect. Or rather the immanent cause is realized, integrated and distinguished by its effect. In this way there is a correlation or mutual presupposition between cause and effect, between abstract machine and concrete assemblages (it is for the later that Foucault most often reserves the term 'mechanisms' [*dispositif*]). If the effects realize something, this is because the relations between forces, or power relations, are merely virtual, potential, unstable, vanishing and molecular, and define only possibilities of interaction, so long as they do not enter into a macroscopic whole capable of giving form to their fluid matter and their diffuse function. But realization is equally an integration, a collection of progressive integrations that are initially local and then become or tend to become global, aligning, homogenizing and summarizing relations between forces ...[33]

In each case this demarcation is drawn in relation to production. For Deleuze and Guattari a general ontology or an expansive sense of production must conceptually underwrite immanence and immanent causality.

---

31   Deleuze and Guattari 1983, p. 306.
32   Montag 1998, p. 71; for more on the importance of 'theater' in Althusser's thought; see also Montag 2003.
33   Deleuze 1988, p. 37.

> ... [T]he real truth of the matter ... is that there is no such thing as rel-
> atively independent spheres or circuits: production is immediately con-
> sumption and a recording process [*enregistrement*], without any sort of
> mediation, and the recording process and consumption directly determ-
> ine production, though they do so within the production process itself.
> Hence everything is production: *production of productions*, of actions and
> of passions; *production of recording processes*, of distributions and of co-
> ordinates that serve as points of reference; *productions of consumptions*,
> of sensual pleasures, of anxieties, and of pain.[34]

The conceptual precursor of this expansive sense of production is found in
Marx's '1857 Introduction'. In that text Marx critically reexamines the three concepts of classical political economy: production, distribution, and consumption. These three concepts contain the logic of political economy, a logic that
is not without its specific anthropology and ontology.

> Thus [in political economy] production, distribution, exchange and con-
> sumption form a regular syllogism; production is the generality, distri-
> bution and exchange the particularity [*Besonderheit*], and consumption
> the singularity [*Einzelnheit*] in which the whole is joined together. This
> is admittedly a coherence, but a shallow one. Production is determined
> by general natural laws, distribution by social accident, and the latter
> may therefore promote production to a greater or lesser extent; exchange
> stands between the two as a formal social movement; and the conclud-
> ing act, consumption, which is conceived not only as a terminal point
> [*Endziel*] but also as an end-in-itself [*Endzweck*], actually belongs out-
> side of economics except in so far as it reacts in turn upon the point of
> departure and initiates the whole process anew.[35]

In this logic it is only distribution, the property relations of a given society,
which has a history that is not determined by nature. It is thus only distribution that has any real history or effectivity. Production is an ontological and
anthropological given. The effect of consumption is only to start the process
anew, to set the wheels of the economy in motion. Against this articulation
of the relation between the three concepts, Marx proposes an understanding
of production, consumption, and distribution in which all three are histor-

---

34   Deleuze and Guattari 1983, p. 4.
35   Marx 1973, p. 89.

ical, and all three act on and determine each other. As Marx indicates, production and consumption seem to have an immediate identity, as well as an opposition, in the simple fact that all production involves consumption of raw materials and at the same time all consumption would seem to immediately produce something, if only the energy for production. Beyond this immediate identity Marx asserts that there is a more intimate relation of co-implication that encompasses and enfolds the supposed exterior and a-historical ground of need and nature. As Marx writes:

> Production not only supplies a material for the need, but it also supplies a need for the material. As soon as consumption emerges from its initial state of natural crudity and immediacy – and, if it remained at that stage, this would be because production itself had been arrested there – it becomes itself mediated as a drive by the object. The need which consumption feels for the object is created by the perception of it. The object of art – like every other product – creates a public which is sensitive to art and enjoys beauty. Production thus not only creates an object for the subject, but also a subject for the object ... Consumption likewise produces the producer's *inclination* by beckoning to him as an aim determining need.[36]

Production produces consumption, producing not only its object but its particular mode and subject, and in turn consumption acts on production, in effect producing it. As Marx explains: 'consumption ideally posits the object of production as an internal image, as a need, as a drive and a purpose. It creates the objects of production in a still subjective form'.[37]

Marx's concept of a mode of production, of the manner in which production, distribution, and consumption all act on each other, delineating a particular form of life, breaks with both the economism and the humanism of classical political economy. It breaks with economism because it is no longer possible to take the relations of distribution – property relations and exchange – as the determinate conditions of production. These relations are effected and determined by the technological, cultural, and political transformations of production and consumption. At the same time it is no longer possible to ground the economy on either the natural needs or the given productive capacities of an assumed human subject, needs and desires are transformed (and transforming) along with the development of the mode of production.[38]

---

36   Marx 1973, p. 92.
37   Marx 1973, Ibid.
38   On the 'anthropology' of classical political economy, see Althusser and Balibar 1970, p. 162.

Deleuze and Guattari appropriate Marx's general problem, lifting it from its Hegelian terminology toward a general problematic of production, or rather a problematic of generalised production. Every aspect of social existence, from technological conditions to desires, dreams, and fantasies, insofar as they have effects on each other must be considered productive. At the same time, Deleuze and Guattari recognize the risk underlying this formulation; the risk that an insistence that 'everything is production' can be the equivalent of a 'night when all cows are black'. As much as the insistence of productive, or effective dimensions, breaks with any pre-given schema of causality, such as the relation between base and superstructure, it risks flattening the distinctions between the various dimensions out to the point where there is only a vague assertion that everything has effects. Deleuze and Guattari thus reinsert differences internal to production, not a difference which would posit a history against and outside of nature or a difference that would inscribe a hierarchy of effectivity between base and superstructure, but in Deleuze and Guattari's terms the difference between 'desiring production' and 'social production'. These two concepts do not correspond to the distinction between any of the three types of productive relations above, consumption, distribution, and production; however, it is through these concepts that we can understand the particular articulation or relation of these three activities within a given social formation. If one wanted to search Marx for conceptual precursors to 'desiring' and 'social' production one would have to turn to the relation between 'abstract labour' and 'living labour'. In Marx's writing, 'abstract labour' refers to the abstraction necessary to quantify the activity of diverse bodies. In order for commodities to be exchanged, labour must be organised so that it is indifferent to who performs it. Abstract labour is not simply a mental generalisation necessary for the record books and calculations of political economy, but it is a real abstraction necessary to the functioning of capital. Abstract labour implies a deterritorialisation, a separation of the body from any code or tradition that would tie it to a particular body or type of knowledge and a practice of discipline that renders every body indifferent and interchangeable. The concept of 'abstract labour' is inseparable from a political and economic strategy – the reduction of all labour to simple abstract labour, and the destruction of skills. Abstract labour is a reduction of the worker, of subjectivity, to the minimum required for the reproduction of the capitalist system. This strategy, sometimes called 'proletarianisation', which Marx at times identified as the dominant tendency if not the destiny of capitalism, runs up against certain limits, not the least of which is 'living labour' as the internal limit of abstract labour. Living labour is the inverse of abstract labour, it can be described by the same attributes – indifference to the content of activity, flexibility, even poverty – but these qualities now appear as sources of its strength.

> This living labor, existing as an *abstraction* from these moments of its actual reality [raw-material, instrument of labor, etc.] (also, not value); this complete denudation, purely subjective existence of labor, stripped of all objectivity. Labor as *absolute poverty*; poverty not as shortage, but as total exclusion of objective wealth ... Labor not as an object, but as activity; not as itself value, but as the *living source of value*. ... Thus, it is not at all contradictory, or, rather, the in-every-way mutually contradictory statements that labor is *absolute poverty as object*, on one side, and is, on the other side, the *general possibility* [*allgemeine Möglichkeit*] of wealth as subject and as activity, are reciprocally determined and follow from the essence of labor, such as it is *presupposed* by capital as its contradiction and as its contradictory being [*gegensätzliches Dasein*], and such as it, in turn, presupposes capital.[39]

Living labour, however, is not just the terminological opposite of abstract labour. Unlike 'concrete labour', which is defined as the specific form labour takes in this or that trade performed by this or that individual and thus stands in nearly static opposition to abstract labour, 'living labour' is only occasionally named by Marx as another way of understanding the flexibility and force of labor, as antagonistic force.[40] It appears throughout Marx's writings at every point that capital necessarily develops and relies upon the subjective capacities of labour, its ability to not only produce wealth but to communicate and constitute new social relations. From the assemblage of bodies under the same roof in the factory to the flexible and cooperative networks of labour required for contemporary capitalist valorisation, capitalism necessarily develops the power of living labour.[41] What is important here in making the transition from the concepts of 'abstract' and 'living' labour to 'desiring production' and 'social production' is that this distinction is fully immanent and fully internal: there is no spatial or temporal division or distinction between abstract or living labour. Just as 'living labour' is both the internal condition and potential disruption of abstract labour, desiring production is the internal condition and limit of social production.

---

39   Marx 1973, p. 296.
40   For a more detailed discussion of 'living labor', and its role in Marx's thought, see chapter 2 of Read 2003.
41   For a reading of Marx that draws out the political and philosophical implications of 'living labour' see Negri 1999.

At the same time that Deleuze and Guattari adopt the general thought of an immanent and internal antagonism from Marx they expand it beyond its limited application to capital (for Marx abstract and living labour are strictly terms which can be applied within capital) to generalise it as the problem of every social machine. For Deleuze and Guattari 'human anatomy contains a key to the anatomy of the ape': the conflict between the flexibility and relationality of living labour and the discipline, goals and norms of abstract labour can, with some modification, be extended backwards in time as a general social conflict.[42] More precisely, it is not that the conflict between 'living' and 'abstract' labour can be turned into the supra-historical condition of universal history, but that all social machines prior to capital dread what 'abstract' and 'living' labour have in common – a thoroughly abstract potentiality of desire and productivity, free of any tradition, code, or value. The previous social machines, tribal and despotic, dread the levelling potential of money and the disruptive desires it brings; it is for this reason that they limit its use and application through 'code', through a set of prescriptives and limitations bearing on power, knowledge, and desire. For Deleuze and Guattari capital is the relative limit of all previous social formations. While other social formations code, or, in Marx's terms, tether production to the reproduction of a particular social relation, capitalism decodes, playing fast and loose with the sacred meanings of past societies – ancient religions, temples, and beliefs become commodities. The capitalist social machine is not, however, the absolute limit or the completion of the conflict between desire and uncoded flows – the 'end of history'. It has its own conflict: one that illustrates and exemplifies the distinction between desiring and social production.

It is from the difference between desiring production and social production that Deleuze and Guattari reinterpret the difference and indices of effectivity of the different productions, productions of production, consumption, and distribution. There is a fundamental difference between the 'recording' and 'production' of production. 'Production is not recorded in the same way it is produced, however. Or rather, it is not reproduced within the same way in which it is produced within the process of constitution'.[43] This difference would, at first glance, appear to be grounded on an almost phenomenological impossibility, the impossibility of presenting or imagining the immanent relations and potentials of desiring production. Just as the mode of production effaces the

42   For Deleuze and Guattari Marx's discovery of abstract labour, or abstract subjective potential, is similar in many ways to Freud's discovery of the drives; see Deleuze and Guattari 1983, p. 270.

43   Deleuze and Guattari 1983, p. 12.

contingency, force, and difference at origin, it also effaces the material conditions of its existence by continually coding, or relating, its existence to particular images and ideals. Production, the force and activity of bodies and actions, is unrepresentable, in excess of any image society may have of itself. At the same time, however, it is possible to understand this difference to stem from the fact that all labour, even that undertaken under the most rudimentary conditions, is always 'superadequate' to its own reproduction, so that a surplus is intrinsic to the goals and aims of social production rather than being added on after the fact.[44] This surplus is not just a surplus of objects, wealth, or commodities, but of meaning and desire. The 'recording of production' is a fundamental displacement or misrecognition of the productive capacities of living labour made possible by the relations and structures of the mode of production, it is the mystified image that the mode of production produces of itself.

> Let us remember once again one of Marx's caveats: we cannot tell from the mere taste of the wheat who grew it; the product gives us no hint as to the system and relations of production. The product appears to be all the more specific, incredibly specific and readily describable, the more closely the theoretician relates it to *ideal forms of causation, comprehension, or expression*, rather than to *the real process of production on which it depends*.[45]

Deleuze and Guattari provide two examples of this: in the first case, 'the Asiatic mode of production', the mode of production is characterised by large collective works, dams, irrigation, temples etc., large works that appear to emanate from the despot himself, to be products of his divine authority and not the thousands of hands which have produced them. 'He is the sole quasi cause, the source and fountainhead and estuary of the apparent objective movement'.[46] There is a misrecognition of the source of production, production is recorded differently than it is produced, but this mystification is in turn productive, producing obedience and docility. The temples, pyramids, and irrigation projects produced for the despot become palpable symbols of his power. This is what Deleuze and Guattari mean by 'quasi-cause'. It is an effect of particular social and political conditions that in turn acts on those conditions as cause – appear-

---

44 Spivak employs the term 'super-adequate' to draw our attention to a simple but overlooked element of Marx's thought of 'labour-power': at the basis of this concept is the power to exceed the givenness of its condition; see Spivak 1988, p. 154.

45 Deleuze and Guattari 1983, p. 24.

46 Deleuze and Guattari 1983, p. 194.

ing to preexist its conditions. Étienne Balibar offers a schema that captures some of what is implied here with respect to the quasi-cause, or the effectivity of 'imaginary' or representational elements.

> I even think that we can describe what such a schema would ideally consist of. It would not be the sum of a 'base' and a 'superstructure', working like a complement or supplement of historicity, but rather the combination of two 'bases' of explanation or two determinations both incompatible and indissociable: the *mode of subjection* and the *mode of production* (or, more generally, the ideological mode and the generalized economic mode). Both are material, although in the opposite sense. To name these different senses of the materiality of subjection and production, the traditional terms *imaginary* and *reality* suggest themselves. One can adopt them, provided that one keep in mind that in any historical conjuncture, the effects of the imaginary can only appear through and by means of the real, and the effects of the real through and by means of the imaginary; in other words, the structural law of causality in history is the *detour through and by means of the other scene*. Let us say, parodying Marx, that economy has no more a 'history of its own' than does ideology, since each has its history only through the other that is the efficient cause of its own effects.[47]

In the capitalist mode of production 'capital' – in the form of both fixed capital (machinery) and money – appears to be productive apart from and without the productive capacity of labour, without the networks of desire and production which make capital possible.

> Capital is indeed the body without organs of the capitalist, or rather of the capitalist being. But as such it is not only the fluid and petrified substance of money, for it will give to the sterility of money the form whereby money produces money. It produces surplus value, just as the body without organs reproduces itself, puts forth shoots, and branches out to the farthest corners of the universe. It makes the machine responsible for producing a relative surplus value, while embodying itself in the machine as fixed capital.[48]

---

47   Balibar 1995, p. 160.
48   Deleuze and Guattari 1983, p. 10.

In each, the Asiatic mode of production and the capitalist mode of production, the socius, or quasi-cause, is at one and the same time a displacement of the productive capacities of desire and a materialisation of these capacities in some other instance or institution. This legitimates Deleuze and Guattari's use of the term 'fetish' as another name for the socius or quasi-cause.[49] In the famous chapter on commodity fetishism Marx demonstrates how (exchange) value appears to be an attribute of things, rather than the product of a specific social and political order; in short, a relation between people appears as a relation between things. This process is one both of idealisation (the displacement of a quality of social relations onto some object or representation of social relations) and of materialisation (this object is material, it is a thing in the world), a process that in capitalism culminates in money as the 'real abstraction'.[50] This misrecognition of the productive powers of labour and desire, as it is displaced onto a quasi-cause (capital or the despot) also entails a prescriptive dimension: it determines not just what individuals should perceive but how they should act.

Deleuze and Guattari's idea of the socius as a necessary condition of the coding of desire and subjectivity would seem to eclipse the difference between the Asiatic and capitalist mode of production. Would this not constitute the worst sort of denial of history, in which historical difference is only the difference of different institutions or structures filling the same roles or place holders, in this case the despot or capital as socius? In the first place it should be noted that the 'structural' similarities that Deleuze and Guattari point to here have their condition of possibility in Marx's own writing. Despite the fact that the Asiatic mode of production was often presented as the complete other of capitalism, Marx also suggested that there is a fundamental similarity between the two at the level of mystification. As Marx writes: 'The power of Asiatic and Egyptian kings, of Etruscan theocrats, etc. has in modern society been transferred to the capitalist, whether he appears as an isolated individual or, as in the case of joint stock companies, in combination with others'.[51] As much as its seems Marx inherited the Eurocentric distinction between the West as the land of freedom and history and Asia as static and despotic this inheritance is complicated by the (mostly polemical) parallels that Marx draws between capitalism and the Asiatic mode of production. While Marx's statement has in the first place an immediate polemical significance (exposing the mystification and tyranny at the heart of enlightened and democratic capitalist modernity) it also points

---

49   Massumi 1992, p. 187.

50   Balibar 2017b, p. 63.

51   Marx 1977, p. 452.

to a more basic similarity of the two modes of production. Capitalism and the Asiatic mode of production are both totalities structured according to a singular determinant instance, the economy in the case of the former and political power in the case of the latter. According to Balibar the similarity between the Asiatic mode of production and capitalism is to be explained by their relative simplicity at the level of determination. Other modes of production, such as the feudal mode of production, are founded on a distinction and difference between the dominant instance, or the instance determined as dominant, for example the church or politics, and the determinate instance, which is the economy (Balibar's distinction between determinant and dominant is founded almost exclusively on one passage from Marx's *Capital*, where Marx states that 'it is the manner in which [societies] gained their livelihood [*Die Art und Wiese, wie sie ihr Leben gewannen*] which explains why in [the ancient world] politics, in [the middle ages] Catholicism, played the chief part [*die Hauptrolle spielte*]').[52] As Balibar writes: 'In different structures, *the economy is determinant in that it determines which of the instances of the social structure occupies the determinant place*. Not a simple relation, but rather a relation between relations; not a transitive causality, but rather a structural causality'.[53] Another way of understanding this is that in other modes of production, such as feudalism, there is a palpable distinction between necessary and surplus labour that is lived in the form of a spatial and temporal division between work performed for survival and work performed for the state. Capital and the Asiatic despot efface this difference. Capital does so through the wage, which effaces any difference between necessary and surplus labour, and the Asiatic despot does so through generalised slavery in which all labour is labour for the despot. Determination is not displaced to another scene, such as religion or politics, but what is 'fetishised' is the determinant instance itself in that it appears to be entirely self sufficient and autonomous, not to mention transcendent and perhaps even metaphysical. The socius in the form of the Asiatic despot and capital thus bare a stronger resemblance to fetishism than to ideology; there is no attempt to conceal or evade the relations of determination, rather the determining instance is elevated to the point where it appears to be the sole cause and not the effect of actions – it appears to transcend its conditions.

For Marx any similarity between the Asiatic and capitalist mode of production must be complicated and qualified by the fact that the most significant historical break in a history of breaks and encounters is the one that separates

---

52   Marx 1977, p. 176.
53   Althusser and Balibar 1970, p. 224; see also his discussion in Balibar 1996.

capitalism from pre-capitalism. The pre-capitalist modes of production should be more accurately called modes of reproduction in that productive activity is subordinated to the reproduction of particular social and political relations, a particular community – that is also a particular form of subjectivity. It is only in capital that production becomes unfettered from the reproduction of a particular social relation, or form of life, and is subordinated to nothing other than the production of more wealth: production generates production. Marx is thoroughly 'dialectical' on this point, revealing the extent to which this production for the sake of production is both 'alienation' and the precondition for liberation.

> Thus the old view, in which the human being appears as the aim of production, regardless of his limited national, religious, political character, seems to me to be lofty when contrasted to the modern world, where production appears as the aim of mankind and wealth as the aim of production. In fact, however, when the limited bourgeois form is stripped away, what is wealth other than the universality of human needs, capacities, pleasures, productive forces etc., created through universal exchange? The full development of human mastery over the forces of nature, those of so-called nature as well as humanity's own nature? The absolute working out of his creative potentialities, with no presupposition other than the previous historical development ... In bourgeois economics – and in the epoch of production to which it corresponds – this complete working-out of the human content appears as a complete emptying out, this universal objectification as total alienation, and the tearing down of all limited, one-sided aims as sacrifice of the human end-in-itself to an entirely external end.[54]

Thus, in 'Pre-Capitalist Economic Formations' Marx elaborates and expands upon a historical argument that is given its most famous theoretical elaboration in *The Communist Manifesto*: that capitalism washes away the old relations of hierarchy and subordination with a tide of abstract money. Whereas the other modes of production were intrinsically conservative, capitalism is intrinsically revolutionary. 'Constant revolutionizing of production, uninterrupted disturbance of all social conditions, everlasting uncertainty and agitation distinguished the bourgeois epoch from all earlier ones'. However, the slight difference is that while in the latter text this historical transformation is

---

54   Marx 1973, p. 488.

characterised as a shift in power relations, as the final chapter in the long history of class struggle in which the masks and illusions of hierarchy are finally
stripped away, in the former the transformation is presented as completely
modifying the production of subjectivity. While the subject (slave to the despot or peasant) of a pre-capitalist mode of production is immersed in a social
space or world (the inorganic body) that sustains and subjugates him or her, the
subject in capital is stripped bare and exposed to the necessary contingency of
having to sell his or her labour power. 'The positing of the individual as worker,
in this nakedness, is itself a product of history'.[55]

    In many ways, some of Deleuze and Guattari's conceptual innovations
(deterritorialisation, reterritorialisation, codes, and axioms) can be at least initially or provisionally understood as an interpretation of this epochal divide
and an examination of its political, social, and libidinal effects and conditions.[56] While there is not enough space here to follow all of these intersections
it is at least possible to demonstrate how Deleuze and Guattari reconceptual-
ise the distinction between pre-capitalist and capitalist modes of production as
the difference between societies which stave off the threat of contingency and
desire through 'code' or through 'axioms'. In doing so it is possible to show how
Deleuze and Guattari follow the line of thought of 'Pre-capitalist Economic
Formations' by focusing on the difference of the production of subjectivity in
each, rather than the line of thought of *The Communist Manifesto*, in which the
history of capitalism is understood through the simplification of class antagonisms. Deleuze and Guattari develop their understanding of code from Althusser
and Balibar's distinction between dominant and determination. As Deleuze
and Guattari define code:

> All of these code characteristics – indirect, qualitative, and limited – are
> sufficient to show that a code is not, and can never be economic: on
> the contrary, it expresses the apparent objective movement according to
> which the economic forces or productive connections are attributed to
> an extraeconomic instance as if they emanated from it, an instance that
> serves as a support and an agent of inscription. That is what Althusser and
> Balibar show so well: how juridical and political relations are *determined*
> *as dominant* – in the case of feudalism, for example – because surplus
> labor as a form of surplus value constitutes a flux that is qualitatively and

55   Marx 1973, p. 472.
56   Fredric Jameson has recently insisted on the centrality of Marx's account of the transition
      from pre-capitalism to capitalism to the concept of deterritorialisation, an intuition that
      can be found in many readers of Deleuze and Guattari; see Jameson 1997.

temporally distinct from that of labor, and consequently must enter into
a composite that is itself qualitative and implies noneconomic factors ...
That is why the sign of desire, as an economic sign that consists in producing and breaking flows, is accompanied by a sign of necessarily extrae-
conomic power, although its causes and effects lie within the economy.
Or – what amounts to the same thing – surplus value here is determined
as a surplus value of code.[57]

The subordination of productive activity to the reproduction of a particular
social relation, and its corresponding forms of hierarchy, has as its effect what
Deleuze and Guattari call a 'surplus value of code'. The surplus that is produced
is turned over to some other social practice or instance, the chief, church, or
despot, and this surplus bestows this practice with particular value or meaning.
Thus it is possible to say that code produces a certain kind of belief or meaning as an after-effect of this appropriation of surplus; however, it is necessary
to add that this belief in turn becomes a cause in that it is belief in the symbolic powers of the surplus that sustains the pre-capitalist mode of production.
Axioms are distinct from codes in that they do not require belief in order to
function. It might be more accurate to say that axioms are concerned more with
what should be done rather than what must be believed. Axioms relate to no
other scene or sphere, such as religion, politics, or law, which would provide
their ground or justification. They are merely differential relations between
abstract and quantitative flows. In capitalism two such flows are the flow of
labour power available on the market and the flow of capital. These two flows
conjoin at a particular time and place, and this conjunction establishes a differential relation between the two flows.[58] Once such a relation is established,
setting up a particular relation between a specific quantity of labour and a
specific quantity of capital, or wage, the axiomatic is effective. It cannot be
avoided; one can only add new axioms to the system. Deleuze and Guattari
utilise the formula dx/dy to express a relation between two values that is indifferent to their specific content. 'Dx and dy are nothing independent of their
relation, which determines the one as a pure quality of the flow of labor and the
other as pure quality of the flow of capital'.[59] There is no possible contestation
at the level of code or belief; in fact the differential relations and their concrete
effects remain in place; they are functional whether or not they are believed.
This is why Deleuze and Guattari refer to capitalism as 'the age of cynicism'. The

57   Deleuze and Guattari 1983, p. 248.
58   Deleuze and Guattari 1983, p. 249.
59   Deleuze and Guattari 1983, Ibid.

'setting up' of axioms between abstract quantities is an aspect of what Deleuze and Guattari call 'reterritorialisation', the regulation of the abstract quantities as abstract quantities. 'It may be all but impossible to distinguish deterritorialization from reterritorialization, since they are mutually enmeshed, or like opposite faces of one and the same process'.[60] To return to the example of commodity fetishism, the equivalence between a quantity of abstract labour and money displaces the abstract potentiality of labour onto money itself, setting up an artificial territory – it now appears as if it is money itself that is productive. The epochal distinction between pre-capitalist and the capitalist mode of production is not only a distinction between subjective and objective domination, but a shift in how this domination is lived. Whereas prior to capitalism it is lived through the coded structures of belief and personal subjugation, in capitalism it is lived through abstract operative rules, which are not necessarily believed or even grasped.

Returning to the question of the odd similarities of the Asiatic despot to capital it seems that both the 'structural' interpretation of this overlap provided by Balibar, as two modes of production constituted by a single site of determination and difference, and the merely rhetorical relation proposed by Marx, the ancient mysticism at the heart of capital, would seem to miss the point. The responses of both Balibar and Marx overlook what has to be explained: the resurgence of mystification of an almost divine power at the heart of capital. Deleuze and Guattari identify this 'return of the repressed' with the problem of the state:

> The special situation of the State as a category – oblivion and return – has to be explained. To begin with, it should be said that the primordial despotic state is not a historical break like any other. Of all the institutions, it is perhaps the only one to appear fully armed in the brain of those who institute it, 'the artists with the look of bronze'. That is why Marxism didn't quite know what to make of it ... It is not one formation among others, nor is it the transition from one formation to another. It appears to be set back at a remove from what it transects and what it resects, as though it were giving evidence of another dimension, a cerebral ideality that is added to, superimposed on the material evolution of societies, a regulating idea or principle of reflection (terror) that organizes the parts and the flows into a whole.[61]

---

60   Deleuze and Guattari 1983, p. 258.
61   Deleuze and Guattari 1983, p. 219.

Deleuze and Guattari thus break not only with the linear account of Marxist history, the progression of the different modes of production one after the other, but with the totality and closure that such a progression implies.[62] History is not the history of bounded and clearly defined unities that pass into each other without remainder, anticipation, or residue, but is a much more fundamentally 'anachronic' process in which the present contains elements of the past and future (however, 'past' and 'present' are not entirely useful here since they imply what Althusser calls 'an ideological base time' as the standard against which something can be identified as 'residual' or 'emergent', and given, therefore, the absence of a present against which differences can be measured, Althusser suggests we think in terms of differential temporality).[63]

> To speak of differential historical temporality therefore absolutely obliges us to situate *this site* and to think, in its particular articulation, the *function* of such an element or such a level in the current configuration of the whole; it is to determine the relation of articulation of this element as a function of other elements, or this structure as a function of other structures, it obliges us to define what has been called its overdetermination or underdetermination as a function of the structure of the determination of the whole.[64]

This temporal torsion is already at work in the various ways in which each mode of production effaces its own conditions of emergence; producing its own images of eternity – capital has always been possible, the despot has always ruled. Moreover, it is exemplified in the manner in which elements of bygone modes of production continue to outlive their usefulness. This is precisely the problem that any historicism or functionalism cannot explain; seemingly archaic elements – the state, roman law, the family, and various tribal identities – show no signs of being washed away with the axioms of capital, but remain and even resurface in more virulent forms. Deleuze and Guattari locate in 'Pre-capitalist Economic Formations' a universal history that not only gives centre-stage to contingency and the event, but also breaks with the linear model of progress espoused in *The Communist Manifesto*.[65] The fetish, the des-

---

62   Deleuze and Guattari's understanding of history is indebted to Althusser's critique of historicism – see Patton 2000, p. 88.

63   See Althusser and Balibar 1970, pp. 105–6.

64   Althusser and Balibar 1970, p. 106.

65   Claude Lefort argues that there is tension between the linear version of history in the *Manifesto* and what he argues is a cyclical version in 'Pre-capitalist Economic Formations';

pot, money, all of these supposedly bypassed images and their corresponding relations of power resurface and are reanimated by capital making it a 'motley painting of everything that has ever been believed'.[66]

At this point it is possible to interpret the difference and identity of the Asiatic despot to capital, or the return of the old tyranny of the despot in the impersonal flows of money. As Deleuze and Guattari write, there are two fundamental elements of the constitution of capital, of its massive deterritorialisation of the old beliefs and systems. These two elements are: commodity and private property. These two elements are in tension: the tension between the releasing of unfettered forces of production no longer subordinated to any code or authority on the one hand, and on the other, the need to continually tie this productivity to the realisation of surplus value and the maintenance of existing wealth, the bourgeois limitations indicated above. This tension can be understood as an interpretation of Marx's famous statement regarding the contradiction between 'forces' and 'relations' of production, in which the productive forces are continually exceeding the existing legal and political limitations, eventually arriving at communism. Or, and this is the direction Deleuze and Guattari generally work in, this tension can be presented as 'the tendency of the rate of profit to fall', that is less as an inevitable telos and more as tension without end, or tendency which cannot be separated from its various countertendencies. Thus, Deleuze and Guattari prefer to frame it as a tension between two poles, rather than a contradiction:

> The social axiomatic of modern societies is caught between two poles, and is constantly oscillating from one pole to the other. Born of decoding and deterritorialization, on the ruins of the despotic machine, these societies are caught between the Urstaat that they would like to resuscitate as an overcoding and reterritorializing unity, and the unfettered flows that carry them toward an absolute threshold. They recode with all of their might, with world-wide dictatorship, local dictators, and an all powerful police, while decoding – or allowing the decoding of – the fluent quantities of their capital and their populations. They are torn in two directions: archaism and futurism, neoarchaism and ex-futurism, paranoia and schizophrenia.[67]

---

see Lefort 1992, pp. 139–80.

66   Deleuze and Guattari 1983, p. 34; Deleuze and Guattari citing, with some modification, Nietzsche here; compare Nietzsche 1969, p. 143.

67   Deleuze and Guattari 1983, p. 260.

Thus Marx may have been correct in identifying capitalism with its own specific temporality, but was perhaps incorrect in identifying, as he did in the *Manifesto*, this temporality with unfettered transformation – 'everything solid melts into air'. This famous statement only covers one pole of capital, the pole corresponding to the continual transformations brought about by the abstract potentiality of labour, and the commodification of new spaces and desires; there is also at the same time the need to subordinate this potentiality to existing wealth and values. It is in order to preserve these old values that the power of the despot continually returns. The despot returns, but it is impossible for it to do so exactly the same way as it did when it left. The breakdown of codes, of belief as a collective and social phenomenon investing all dimensions of the body politic, is an irreversible event. Belief and desire have not only become abstract, subordinated to money, that unique object which can stand in for any object whatsoever, but have been 'privatized' as well – disinvested from the public works and spectacle of the despot. The codes that used to dictate and control social life and invest it with belief have become privatised and interiorised, retreating into the private space and desires of the home.

> Civilized modern societies are defined by processes of decoding and deterritorialization. But *what they deterritorialize with one hand, they reterritorialize with the other*. These neoterritorialities are often artificial, residual, archaic; but they are archaisms having a perfectly current function, our modern way of 'imbricating', of sectioning off, of reintroducing code fragments, resuscitating old codes, inventing pseudo codes or jargons ... These modern archaisms are extremely complex and varied ... Some of these archaisms take form as if spontaneously in the current of the movement of deterritorialization ... Others are organized and promoted by the state, even though they might turn against the state and cause it serious problems (regionalism, nationalism).[68]

Thus, as much as the temporal torsion between capital and the state takes place publicly, it also exists as a private interiorised struggle, a struggle at the heart of subjectivity, between the possibility for a new future and the ghosts of the Old World. The despot returns but he is split in half, in a division that corresponds to the dual origins of capital, the two facets of deterritorialisation – 'commodification' and 'privatisation' – the flow of money and the flow of labour power. As quasi-cause or displaced representative of the productive power of desiring production, he appears in the form of capital, as a pure quantity to which one

---

68   Deleuze and Guattari 1983, p. 258.

responds without necessarily believing. As the over-coding unity of desires and social activity, he appears in the form of the private codes that restore meaning to existence. Thus, it is possible to understand Deleuze and Guattari's argument on an existential level in which the return of codes is an attempt to compensate for the 'cynicism' or absence of meaning imposed by the abstract quantities of money and labour power. 'These are the two aspects of a becoming of the State: its internalization in a field of increasingly decoded social forces forming a physical system; its spiritualization in a supraterrestrial field that increasingly overcodes, forming a metaphysical system'.[69] The first of these poles makes possible the second; it is only once the specific codes of belief and desire as conditions for social production and reproduction have been replaced by the abstract conditions of money and labour that anything like a private life is possible.[70] It is between these two poles that 'we moderns' live.

> It is no longer the age of cruelty or the age of terror, but the age of cynicism, accompanied by a strange piety. (The two taken together constitute humanism: cynicism is the physical immanence of the social field, and piety is the maintenance of a spiritualized Urstaat; cynicism is capital as the means of extorting surplus labor, but piety is this same capital as God-capital, whence all the forces of labor seem to emanate).[71]

This interplay of cynicism and piety, of the cold, hard facts of life and moral belief, can be found in the ideological narrative of 'so-called primitive accumulation', which combines a recognition of the necessity of exploitation with a moral justification of that necessity. If someone is going to be exploited it might as well be those who are lazy. Thus, if one wanted to depart from the specific language and concepts of Deleuze and Guattari's thought, it is possible to argue that Deleuze and Guattari's specific provocation here is to posit the privatised and closed-off realm of individual desire as a from of subjection no less pervasive and powerful than that wielded by the legendary despot.

'In a word, universal history is not only retrospective, it is also contingent, singular, ironic, and critical'.[72] It is ironic in the sense that it ends not in the completion of spirit, or the realisation of communism, but it ends in the privatised spaces of the family where we all reinvent our own codes and recreate our own little despots. However, this is not the only possible end: as Deleuze

---

69   Deleuze and Guattari 1983, p. 222.

70   See Deleuze and Guattari 1983, p. 251; Massumi 1992, p. 136.

71   Deleuze and Guattari 1983, p. 255.

72   Deleuze and Guattari 1983, p. 140.

and Guattari argue, universal history must also be self-critical, able to grasp its own contingency and limits. Deleuze and Guattari present something like a genealogy of the contemporary subject, a genealogy that, although it takes the desires of the oedipalised psychoanalytic subject as its object, would be quite at home in the age of the 'return to family values' or the reign of self help – anything that elevates the interiorised and privatised space of the family into transcendental conditions for subjectivity. Thus it might be possible to understand Deleuze and Guattari's relationship to these narratives of the constitution of subjectivity to be similar to Marx's relationship to the idyllic narratives of primitive accumulation: in each case an ahistorical narrative, a narrative of what has always existed or what has always been possible, is historicised by a narrative of contingency and force. Such an analogy is strengthened by the fact that primitive accumulation in Marx was not simply an accumulation of wealth and labouring bodies, but an accumulation of obedience to the new system – a primitive accumulation of subjectivity.[73] As Marx writes: 'The advance of capitalist production develops a working class which by education [*Erziehung*], tradition, and habit [*Gewohneit*] looks upon the requirements of that mode of production as self-evident natural laws'.[74] Deleuze and Guattari show how this subjectivity is produced between the flows of money, which incorporate the 'desire of the most disadvantaged creature' into the capitalist system as a whole, and the private space of the home, where one is left to tinker with one's own little codes. Moreover, Deleuze and Guattari produce a reading of Marx which extracts the strongest elements of his understanding of the difference between pre-capitalist and capitalist modes of production, the fundamental transformation of the form and function of power and obedience, without reproducing Marx's particular prejudices and limitations with respect to this difference; capital as the progressive 'becoming-transparent' of social conflicts, as modernisation without remainder. At the centre of Deleuze and Guattari's neologisms and conceptual inventiveness is an attempt to produce a reading of Marx that is not only adequate to the production of desire necessary to so-called consumer society, but to the various 'neo-conservatisms' that seize hold of desire. Beyond these possible uses, Deleuze and Guattari present us with a new possibility of thinking history after Marx: not a history of necessity, or even a historicism of completed epochs, but a contingent and differential history of the lines of force, and desire making and unmaking us in the present. It is these lines of force and their relations that are the precondition for a future different from the present.

---

73   Albiac 1996, pp. 11–17.

74   Marx 1977, p. 899.

CHAPTER 6

The Age of Cynicism: Deleuze and Guattari on the Production of Subjectivity in Capitalism

Gilles Deleuze argues that Spinoza's assertion 'we do not know what a body can do' functions as a 'war cry' cutting through the conceptual divisions of soul, mind, and consciousness, defining a new concept of power, philosophy and subjectivity.[1] Deleuze's assertion suggests, albeit obliquely, that works of philosophy can be interpreted through not just their central insight, or main points, but their 'war cry', the formulation that expresses the battle they wage against other philosophies, and conceptions of the world. The 'war cry' or slogan (as in *mot d'ordre*) that could be used to sum up Deleuze and Guattari's two volumes of *Capitalism and Schizophrenia* is 'desire belongs to the infrastructure'.[2] With this phrase Deleuze and Guattari reject any dualisms or hierarchies between the mental and the material, subjective and objective, or social and libidinal, that would make either the subjective an effect of the material (as in most Marxisms) or the social an effect of the libidinal (as in psychoanalysis). In the first volume, *Anti-Oedipus*, this assertion is the basis of the polemics against psychoanalysis: for psychoanalysis, desire and its anxieties are necessarily mediated through the family, which provides both their cause and condition of intelligibility. This assertion of the immanence of desiring production to social production, or, in the terms of *A Thousand Plateaus*, machinic assemblages of bodies to collective assemblages of enunciation, persists through the two volumes of *Capitalism and Schizophrenia*, becoming a central philosophical assertion, as many of the polemics against psychoanalysis of the first volume are left by the wayside.[3] Deleuze and Guattari's particular position is a refusal of the mediations or levels that relate and separate the economy from subjectivity. It is an assertion of what Paolo Virno calls 'immediate coincidence'. As Virno writes in a passage that could be applied to Deleuze and Guattari:

> What is involved here is the conceptualization of the field of *immediate coincidence* between production and ethics, structure and superstruc-

---

1 Deleuze 1990, p. 255.
2 Deleuze and Guattari 1983, p. 348.
3 Deleuze and Guattari 1987, p. 89.

ture, between the revolution of labour process and the revolution of sentiments, between technology and emotional tonality, between material development and culture. By confining ourselves narrowly to this dichotomy, however, we fatally renew the metaphysical split between 'lower' and higher, animal and rational, body and soul – and it makes little difference if we boast of our pretensions to historical materialism. If we fail to perceive the points of identity between labour practices and modes of life, we will comprehend nothing of the changes taking place in present-day production and misunderstand a great deal about the forms of contemporary culture.[4]

Hints of this 'immediate coincidence' can be found in Marx's own writing, most notably in the polemics of *The Communist Manifesto*. The broad impassioned tones of Marx's manifesto assert a connection between the capitalist mode of production and a particular ethos, a particular social logic, and subjectivity. In the *Manifesto* this connection is direct, immediate, it does not pass through the superstructures of politics, law, and ideology. For Marx, at least the Marx of the *Manifesto*, the specificity of the capitalist mode of production, its specific temporality, sociality, and way of life, is to be found in its revolutionary nature, its destruction of all previous traditions, hierarchies, and values. 'Constant revolutionizing of production, uninterrupted disturbance of all social conditions, everlasting uncertainty and agitation distinguish the bourgeois epoch from all earlier ones'.[5] The strength of Deleuze and Guattari's writing is that it extends and deepens this assertion of a particular capitalist ethos, or production of subjectivity, extending it from a polemic to a philosophical assertion and method. In doing so they are able to address, and even answer, problems that undermine contemporary Marxism: namely, the persistence of capitalism, the collapse of the working class as an antagonist form of subjectivity, and the return of seemingly outmoded beliefs and subjectivities.

1   **From Codes to Axioms**

While the immediate coincidence of production and desire bears a superficial relationship to the polemics of the *Manifesto*, it would seem to contradict the rest of Marx's writing. Most notably it contradicts the model of base and super-

---

4   Virno 1996a, p. 14.
5   Marx and Engels 1978, p. 476.

structure, which places ideology, beliefs, desires, and subjectivity, on top of, and thus dependent on, material transformations in the realm of production. However, Marx's writings offer other models for thinking about the connection of production and subjectivity, most notably the notebooks collected in the *Grundrisse* known as 'Pre-capitalist Economic Formations'. Marx's dominant philosophical concern in these notebooks is the nature and the ground of the difference between capitalism and pre-capitalist modes of production: to grasp the unique and singular nature of capitalism. Although this is by no means Marx's only concern, the notebooks also trace the genealogy of the capitalist mode of production through the breakdown and collapse of the previous modes of production. Moreover, in this text Marx advances an expansive theory of the mode of production, one that does not limit the mode of production to a particular technical or economic manner of producing things, but understands a mode of production to constitute a particular form of life. Every *mode of production* is inseparable from a *mode of subjection*, which is not added on as a supplement, or a simple effect, but immanent and necessary to its existence.[6] This general philosophical point does not only apply to the pre-capitalist modes of production, which are so clearly oriented towards reproducing a particular form of existence, (as Marx reminds us, the question in ancient Greece was 'which mode of property creates the best citizens?'), but to capitalism as well, in which it would appear that the *reproduction* of a way of life is entirely secondary to the *production* of surplus value. Capitalism too must reproduce particular forms of subjectivity, particular forms of technological competence and political subjection, but it must do so while simultaneously breaking with the past. As Marx writes: 'The advance of capitalist production develops a working class which by education, tradition, and habit looks upon the requirements of that mode of production as self evident natural laws'.[7] It is because of the peculiar way in which the notebooks on pre-capitalism articulate the intersection between production and subjectivity, that they provide the theoretical backdrop for Deleuze and Guattari's examination of the affective politics of capitalism.

For Marx the specifically pre-capitalist modes of production (Asiatic, Ancient, and Feudal) are necessarily conservative in that they have as their specific goal the reproduction of a particular form of property and a particular social relation. Reproduction of a social relation is also reproduction of a particular form of subjectivity. What characterises the different pre-capitalist

---

6   On this point see my *The Micro-Politics of Capital: Marx and the Prehistory of the Present*: Read 2003.

7   Marx 1977, p. 899.

modes of production is not just their intrinsically conservative nature, but also that subjectivity is inseparable from its collective social conditions. The subject is not exposed to whatever existence he or she can get in exchange for his or her labour power, as in capitalism, but is embedded in cultural, technical and political conditions that he or she in turn works to reproduce. These conditions are what Deleuze and Guattari call 'codes'. Codes can be thought of as tradition, or prescriptions and rules bearing on the production and distribution of goods, prestige, and desire. As such they are inseparable form a particular relation to the past – a relation of repetition. With codes actions and desires in the present are immediately related to the past, to an inscription of memory, 'this is how things are done, how they have always been done'.

The codes become part of the 'inorganic body' of the individual in pre-capitalist modes of production; that is, conditions of production and reproduction of subjectivity that constitute a kind of second nature. Marx defines the inorganic body as follows:

> These natural conditions of existence, to which he relates as to his own inorganic body, are themselves double: (1) of a subjective and (2) of an objective nature. He finds himself a member of a family, clan, tribe, etc. – which then, in a historic process of intermixture and antithesis with others, takes on a different shape; and as such a member, he relates to a specific nature (say, here, still earth, land, soil) as his own inorganic being, as a condition of his production and reproduction.[8]

The first model of the 'inorganic body' is the earth itself as the original condition of all production; it is 'primitive, savage unity of desire and production'.[9] However, Marx's general formula of 'Pre-capitalist Economic Formations' stresses that this 'divine presupposition of production' can realise itself in different ways, appearing first as the earth, then the primitive community, or even the Asiatic despot.[10] It is this displacement, or, more accurately, deterritorialisation, that forms the basis of Deleuze and Guattari's concept of the full body, or the body without organs. What Deleuze and Guattari stress is the connection between production and an unproductive, or anti-productive, element that falls back onto production appropriating the forces of production. As Deleuze and Guattari write:

---

8   Marx 1973, p. 490.

9   Deleuze and Guattari 1983, p. 140.

10   Marx 1973, p. 472.

... the forms of social production, like those of desiring production, involve an unengendered non-productive attitude, an element of anti-production coupled with the process, a full body that functions as a *socius*. This socius may be the body of the earth, that of the tyrant, or capital. This is the body that Marx is referring to when he says that it is not the product of labour, but rather appears as its natural or divine presuppositions. In fact, it does not restrict itself merely to opposing productive forces in and of themselves. It falls back on [*il se rabat sur*] all production, constituting a surface over which the forces and agents of production are distributed, thereby appropriating for itself all surplus production and arrogating to itself both the whole and the parts of the process, which now seem to emanate from it as a quasi-cause.[11]

Every society, or form of social production, has an aspect that appears as the condition, or cause, rather than the effect of the productive relations, the desires and labours of society. Paradoxically, this 'quasi-cause' appears to be a cause of production, because it is itself not productive, or, more precisely, 'anti-productive'. It appropriates the excessive forces of production, distributing some for the reproduction of society and wasting most in excessive expenditure (such as tribal honours, palaces, and ultimately war). As Marx argues, the Asiatic despot appears to be the cause, and not the effect, of the productive powers of society, the massive public works, such as irrigation, that define the 'Asiatic mode of production' for Marx: it appropriates for itself the productive powers of society.

Each of the pre-capitalist modes of production is constituted by a fundamental misrecognition, what is produced by the labour of the community and appears as its precondition, as an element of divine authority. This misrecognition stems from a fundamental difference, a basic gap, between production, and the recording, or representation, of production. 'Production is not recorded in the same way that it is produced'.[12] Deleuze and Guattari thus utilize Marx's theory of pre-capitalist economic formations to intervene within the general question of ideology, the way in which societies reproduce themselves through a fundamental misrecognition of their constitutive conditions. What Deleuze and Guattari draw from Marx is less a theory of ideology in which a particular class or group disseminates particular ideas than a theory of 'fetishism' in which a society, a particular mode of production, produces its own particular

---

11   Deleuze and Guattari 1983, p. 10.
12   Deleuze and Guattari 1983, p. 12.

form of appearance, its apparent objective movement.[13] Marx argued that the commodity as fetish obscures the conditions of its production in a dazzling display of its value. Deleuze and Guattari's concept of a *'socius'* is thus close to what Louis Althusser refers to as 'the society effect'. As Althusser writes:

> The mechanism of the production of this 'society effect' is only complete when all the effects of the mechanism have been expounded, down to the point where they are produced in the form of the very effects that constitute the concrete, conscious or unconscious relation of the individuals to the society as a society, i.e., down to the effects of the fetishism of ideology (or 'forms of social consciousness' – *Preface* to *A Contribution* ...), in which men consciously or unconsciously live their lives, their projects, their actions, their attitudes and their functions as *social*.[14]

What Deleuze and Guattari stress is that this 'effect', or what they term 'the recording of production', must also be thought as productive: it is not only an effect, it produces effects as well. Most importantly what is produced by such effect is the obedience, the belief and desire, necessary to the functioning of the particular mode of production.

Deleuze and Guattari's interpretation of Marx's theory of pre-capitalist economic formations, and subsequent rewriting of a theory of the production of subjectivity, attaches an almost disproportionate emphasis to the Asiatic mode of production. This is in part due to what Jean-Jacques Lecercle calls Deleuze and Guattari's 'displacement' of Marxism, viewing his theory of the mode of production from its 'most eccentric element': the only one situated outside of

---

13   The theme of an 'apparent objective movement', or an illusion that is neither hardwired in the structures of human consciousness, as in the Kantian aporias, nor perpetrated by a knowing subject operating behind the scenes, but rather is produced by a particular social formation, runs throughout Marx's writing. It underlies the idea of ideology as an 'objective' illusion both produced and necessitated by the division of labour, specifically the division of mental and manual labour, and commodity fetishism as an 'objective' illusion produced by the pervasiveness of market relations. Étienne Balibar has argued that these two problems, the problem of ideology and the problem of fetishism, are perhaps two different problems. In the former, there is the combination of objective conditions such as the division between mental and manual labour and a subjective class point of view, the ideas of the ruling class, while in the latter, the fetish is objectively produced by the mechanisms of commodity production (Balibar 2017b, p. 60). It is perhaps for this reason that while Deleuze and Guattari dispense with the notion of ideology, and its corresponding ideas of false and true consciousness, they retain the term 'fetishism' to refer to this 'apparent objective movement'.

14   Althusser and Balibar 1970, p. 66.

Europe, identified by a geographic place rather than a historical period, and consequently the cause of much controversy within Marxism.[15] Deleuze and Guattari use this infamously allusive and problematic element of Marx's theory to address a famous omission of Marx's philosophy: the state. Deleuze and Guattari do not offer so much a theory of the state, an enterprise they dismiss as tautological, but a series of relations through which to consider the state.[16] First, and this is something that Deleuze and Guattari borrow directly from Marx, the state, or the despot, comes into existence as something that subordinates pre-existing communities, clans, and groups. It makes these diverse points 'resonate' by relating them to a central institution or structure.[17]

Étienne Balibar has offered what could be considered an illustration of this relation of resonance: 'States cannot become *nation-states* if they do not appropriate the sacred, not only at the level of representations of a more or less secularised 'sovereignty', but also the day to day level of legitimation, implying the control of births and deaths, marriages or their substitutes, inheritance and the like. States thus tend to withdraw control of these functions from clans, families, and, above all, churches or religious sects'.[18] In other words, the state overcodes the existing codes and values, becoming the central term around which their meaning gravitates. 'The essential action of the State, therefore, is the creation of a second inscription by which the new full body – immobile, monumental, immutable – appropriates all the forces and agents of production; but this inscription of the State allows the old territorial inscriptions to subsist, as "bricks" on the new surface'.[19] Secondly, Deleuze and Guattari argue that the concept of the state is formed all at once, not gradually, hence their interest in ancient despotisms and the archaeological evidence for complex bureaucracies and systems of taxation in the ancient world.[20] The state is not one institution among others, developing gradually over time, but an idea, if

---

15   Lecercle 2005, p. 42.
16   Deleuze and Guattari 1987, p. 427.
17   Deleuze and Guattari 1987, p. 433.
18   Balibar 2004, p. 20.
19   Deleuze and Guattari 1987, p. 198.
20   Deleuze and Guattari 1983, p. 217; In his earlier writings Gilles Deleuze referred to this condition in which the state is formed all at once as Levi-Strauss's or, referring to the Crusoe's situation stranded on a desert isle, Robinson's paradox. As Deleuze writes: 'Any society whatsoever has all of its rules at once – juridical, religious, political, economic; laws governing love and labor, kinship and marriage, servitude and freedom, life and death. But the conquest of nature, without which it would no longer be a society, is achieved progressively, from one source of energy to another, from one object to another' (Deleuze 1990, p. 49).

not ideality itself. Thus, '... giving evidence of another dimension, a cerebral ideality that is added to, superimposed on the material evolution of societies, a regulating idea or principle of reflection (terror) that organizes the parts and the flows into a whole'.[21] This leads to one of the most difficult, but also persistent, elements of Deleuze (and Guattari's) thought, the mutually reinforcing connection between thought and the state, in which thought, or philosophy, borrows its model from the state ('a republic of free spirits whose prince would be the idea of the Supreme being'), and in turn, the state is legitimated by thought ('the more you obey, the more you will be master, for you will only be obeying pure reason, in other words yourself ...').[22] Deleuze and Guattari's political thought is situated between capital and the state, which are both abstractions, processes of deterritorialisation, that nonetheless have very different concrete effects in the realm of politics and subjectivity.

In the pre-capitalist modes of production, productive activity is subordinated to reproduction: all productive activity aims to reproduce the community, the codes, and the relations of subordination. Capitalism can be partially defined by the liberation of production from such demands of the reproduction of a particular form of life. In capitalism production does not aim at anything other than itself, than the production of more capital, or, insofar as it does produce something other than itself, what it produces is abstract, purely quantitative. Capitalism does not have a particular organisation of desire, a particular code or social organization as its historical presupposition. Its only presupposition, as Marx demonstrated, is the encounter between, on the one hand, a multitude of individuals who have only their labour power to sell, and on the other, a flow of money free to purchase labour power. In each case the constitution of these two flows of bodies and money presupposes the breakdown of codes. A breakdown of the codes that anchored labour to any community, tradition, or hierarchies of knowledge (as in the guilds or feudalism), as well as a breakdown of anything that links money to specific places and uses, to a restricted economy of prestige. 'Hence capitalism differentiates itself from any other *socius* or full body, inasmuch as capital itself figures as a directly

---

21   Deleuze and Guattari 1983, p. 219.
22   Deleuze and Guattari 1987, p. 376; the problem of the image of thought first appears in Deleuze's *Difference and Repetition*. Although the state is not specifically mentioned, the defining characteristics of state thought, most notably a presupposed universality ('everybody knows, no one can deny') appear under the name of good sense (Deleuze 1994, p. 130). The idea that all thought, all philosophy, presupposes a particular image, a particular idea of what it means to think, also appears in Deleuze and Guattari's final coauthored book *What is Philosophy?*

economic instance, and falls back on production without interposing extra-economic factors that would be inscribed in the form of a code'.[23] Labour and wealth have become deterritorialised; have become stripped of any code that would tie them to any determinate relation to the past. Rather than coding the various practices and desires constitutive of the society, capitalism functions by setting up quantitative relations between the two flows, labour and capital, establishing as axiomatic an equivalence between a particular amount of labour time and a particular amount of money. Axioms are distinct from codes in that they do not require belief in order to function. Axioms relate to no other scene or sphere, such as religion, politics, or law, which would provide their ground or justification.[24] Axioms simply are: they lay down a particular formula, a particular system of equivalences, and this cannot be argued with – it is only possible to add new axioms to the system. In order for capitalism to function, one does not need to believe in anything, *even in it*; one only needs to act in accordance with the quantitative flows, selling one's labour, etc. Capitalism is a revolution at the mode of subjection as well as the mode of production, a revolution that appears as liberation, a rupturing of the old codes, and the death of the despot. Part of Deleuze and Guattari's project is to reveal the new forms of constraint in this revolution; that is, the way in which capitalism continually reterritorialises what escapes it.

2   The Age of Cynicism

Capitalism does not tarry with belief, with codes and traditions, it operates through the abstractions of money and labour, which are all the more effective

---

23   Deleuze and Guattari 1983, p. 249.

24   Jameson 1997, p. 398; Deleuze and Guattari's distinction can be read through not only Marx's text but also Althusser and Balibar's *Lire le Capital*. As Balibar argues, in all pre-capitalist economic formations there is a temporal and spatial distinction between labour and the extraction of surplus. Thus, in pre-capitalist modes of production the extraction of a surplus is always accompanied by a 'non-economic' instance determined as dominant (politics or religion) which renders visible and palpable the division between necessary and surplus labour, but in the capitalist mode of production this division is in some sense invisible. As Balibar argues, in capitalism the labourer works in the production process, and its temporality (the working day) and relations (such as the relation between the individual worker and capitalist) constitute lived experience, while the 'valorization' process and its division between necessary and surplus labour never takes place in the lived present. In the capitalist mode of production there is no spatial or temporal division between necessary and surplus labor: thus in some sense, exploitation is invisible, or at least potentially invisible, taking place behind one's back (Althusser and Balibar 1970, p. 223).

in that they are not believed or even grasped. This does not mean that capitalism is absolutely indifferent to the forms of existence, the desires, and affects of those who live and work in it. Like every mode of production capitalism must produce its subjects, the workers and consumers, or rather individuals who identify themselves as workers and consumers, in order to perpetuate itself. Its apparent indifference to the beliefs and desires of its subjects, its ability to tolerate everything, to turn every scandal and taboo into a commodity, must itself be seen as a kind of social subjection to capital. Deleuze and Guattari begin to illustrate this, by suggesting that the gap that exists in capital between what one believes and what one does already carries with it a subjective and affective component. As they write:

> It is no longer the age of cruelty or the age of terror, but the age of cynicism, accompanied by a strange piety. (The two taken together constitute humanism: cynicism is the physical immanence of the social field, and piety is the maintenance of a spiritualized Urstaat; cynicism is capital as the means of extorting surplus labour, but piety is this same capital as God-capital, whence all the forces of labour seem to emanate).[25]

Deleuze and Guattari are not simply offering a moral definition of cynicism, or a moralising critique: cynicism is a structural effect of a social system, a social machine, in which axioms replace codes. Deleuze and Guattari's distinction between code and axioms underscores one of Marx's central points about capitalism, that it is a form of power in which individuals are 'ruled by abstractions', rather than other individuals, as in the case of Feudalism.[26] As Marx writes in *Capital*, assuming the voice of the worker in a complaint against the capitalist: 'You may be a model citizen, perhaps a member of the R.S.P.C.A. [Royal Society for the Prevention of Cruelty to Animals], and you may be in the odour of sanctity as well; but the thing you represent when you come face to face with me has no heart in its breast'.[27] In capitalism power is indifferent to intentions of its rulers. As an economic, political, and cultural system it opens up a gap between intentions and effects, between piety and cynicism. Thus Deleuze and Guattari extend the point that Marx makes polemically, ultimately arguing that the defining characteristic of capital is not simply the difference between being ruled by individuals or abstractions, but that 'being ruled by abstractions' produces and presupposes its own particular form of subjectivity.

---

25   Deleuze and Guattari 1983, p. 225.
26   Marx 1973, p. 164.
27   Marx 1977, p. 343.

Deleuze and Guattari's invocation of a 'spiritualized Urstaat' against the 'immanence of the social forces' invokes Marx's early criticism of capitalism in 'On the Jewish Question'. As Marx argues, the problem of the 'Jewish question' reveals the limitations of what he calls political emancipation. In political emancipation the state declares itself to be indifferent to matters of wealth, status, and title, declaring everyone to be equal before the law. The emancipation of the individual from these distinctions is really the emancipation of the state from social distinctions; it washes its hands of the inequality of the social sphere, privatising inequality. As Marx is quick to point out, the distinctions of property, education, rank, and ethnicity continue to matter in the social realm, in the realm of civil society, even after the state has declared them irrelevant. This leads to a splitting of the subject, and of existence, in which mankind lives as both a citizen, an equal participant in the ideology of collective life, and a member of civil society, unequal and concerned only with one's private self-interest. The matter for Marx is not how the state should recognise religion, but how the state is already 'religious', with all of the criticism that the word entails for Marx. As Marx writes: 'The political state is as spiritual in relation to civil society as heaven is in relation to earth'.[28] As Peter Sloterdijk argues in the *Critique of Cynical Reason*, the backdrop of Marx's analysis is the emergence of what he calls modern cynical consciousness, characterised by the combination of a rigorous *cynicism of means*, a thoroughly instrumental consciousness in which everything is permissible in the name of self-interest, and an equally rigid *moralism of ends*, values which are clung to even tighter as they come into conflict with reality.[29] The state, and with it the church, becomes the guarantor of ends, with the ideals of the citizen and the general good, and means are left to the private realm, to the market of competing interests.

Marx's early critique of the state posits a division or a split between ideal and existence, mind and matter, mental and manual labour, with the exception that this is not a division between two classes, two groups, but a division that cuts internally; we all live as private members of civil society, pursuing our individual interests, and as citizens of the state, concerned with the general good. We are all cynics and pious. This theme of a fundamental division or splitting of the subject is continued through Marx's critique of commodity fetishism. In the act of exchanging and buying commodities what one focuses on is the concrete particularity of this or that commodity, its use or its image, but in the act of buying and selling what matters is not its particularity, but the

28   Marx 1978, p. 34.
29   Sloterdijk 1987, p. 192.

abstract labour time necessary to its production. As Alfred Sohn-Rethel writes: 'The consciousness and the action of people part company in exchange and go different ways'.[30] Or, to offer another example, we might know that money is just a social convention, but we cannot help but act as if it is the physical embodiment of value.[31] The fetish is not something we recognise, or something we are aware of, we do not purchase commodities because of exchange value, because of their abstract equivalences, but because of their particularity, their particular use, colour, taste, etc. The fetish character is what Sohn-Rethel calls a 'real abstraction'.[32] What Sohn-Rethel details is a fundamental splitting of consciousness in capitalism between use, which is consciously recognised and private, and exchange, which is public and effective without being consciously recognised, a splitting that duplicates Marx's split between citizen and self-interested individual (as well as Deleuze and Guattari's split between cynicism and piety). Only the terms have been reversed: belief has become a private matter, attached to use, while publicly the only value that matters is price, exchange value. We may have our own particular values, our own piety about the importance of books, organic food, etc. but that does not keep us from acting, in our quotidian existence, as if everything including labour power is exchangeable for everything else. Capitalism is a massive privatisation of desire. 'The person has become "private" in reality, insofar as he derives from abstract quantities and becomes concrete in the becoming concrete of these same quantities. It is these quantities that are marked, no longer the persons themselves: *your capital or your labour capacity*, the rest is not important ...'[33] Thus the point where Sohn-Rethel and Deleuze and Guattari overlap (not to mention Zizek and Sloterdijk) is that they locate in Marx's analysis of the commodity-form a schema of what could be called the political unconscious: the unconscious is not a bundle of drives in need of socialisation, but desires which are already organised by the practices and relations (what Deleuze and Guattari call flows) of capitalism.[34]

For Deleuze and Guattari, cynicism, like desire, is directly a part of the infrastructure. It is this point that differentiates their analysis from the related pronouncements of Slavoj Zizek and Peter Sloterdijk. Cynicism is thus directly related to the 'real abstractions' of the commodity-form and wage labour, which makes heterogeneous objects and activities interchangeable and thus equival-

---

30   Sohn-Rethel 1978, p. 26.
31   Zizek 1989, p. 31.
32   Sohn-Rethel 1978, p. 20.
33   Deleuze and Guattari 1983, p. 251.
34   Deleuze 2004, p. 262.

ent. Capitalism begins with the encounter of two flows of abstractive subjective potential, the pure capacity of labour, and money, abstract wealth.[35] This is what Marx calls 'formal subsumption', the imposition of the commodity form and wage labour over a pre-existing technical and social order. From this point capitalism 'concretises', transforms the technological and social conditions that it initially takes as given. This is what Marx calls 'real subsumption'. As Deleuze and Guattari write, citing one of Marx's more cryptic formulations: 'History proceeds from the abstract to the concrete'.[36] Capitalism transforms general knowledge of society into a productive force, liberating the various 'codes' that kept knowledge subordinated to different hierarchies and subordinating them only to the axioms of profit. 'Knowledge, information, and specialized education are just as much parts of capital ("knowledge capital") as is the most elementary labour of the worker'.[37] The real abstraction ceases to be the abstract flows of money and wealth, and becomes what Marx calls 'the general intellect', the general knowledge of society.[38] Antonio Negri has emphasised the often overlooked connection between Deleuze and Guattari's writing and Marx's seemingly prescient description of a stage of capitalism in which knowledge and desire have become directly productive forces: a connection brought to light by the phrase 'desiring machine', which scrambles the divisions between man and nature, fixed capital and variable capital.[39] Negri argues that underneath Deleuze and Guattari's prolific series of neologisms, there is a description, even a 'phenomenology', of the present formation of capital in which the old division between man and machine can no longer account for the intersections between desire, machines, and subjectivity that produce and circulate commodities and information.

Paolo Virno relates the transition from formal to real subsumption to a transformation of cynicism, a transformation that could be referred to as a deepening of cynicism. The abstractions of formal subsumption at least had to acknowledge the principle of equality. As Marx demonstrates in *Capital*, the fundamental rule of exchange is that equivalent is exchanged for equivalent, hence the riddle of the first part of the book: How is difference, surplus value, produced in a system based upon the exchange of equivalents? The answer is to be found in the hidden abode of production. Labour power is the non-equivalent, the commodity that produces more than it costs, that makes

---

35   Deleuze and Guattari 1987, p. 452.
36   Deleuze and Guattari 1983, p. 221.
37   Deleuze and Guattari 1983, p. 234.
38   Marx 1973, p. 706.
39   Negri 1995, p. 93.

possible the exchange of equivalents. Even at the level of production, at the level of abstract labour power, however, capital posits equality in making the labour of diverse individuals, men, women, children, interchangeable. Behind the equality of exchange, the realm of 'freedom, equality, and Bentham', there is equally the capacity to be exploited.[40] This is abstract labour. As Marx argues, capitalism, which is based upon the exploitation of homogeneous human labour, finds its religious form in Christianity, 'with its religious cult of man in the abstract'.[41] The real abstractions of formal subsumption have the potential for subversion. This is lost as productive power turns to knowledge, to different programmes or paradigms, which are instrumentalised and subordinated to the search for profit. As Virno writes:

> The cynic recognizes, in the particular context in which he operates, the predominate role played by certain epistemological premises and the simultaneous absence of real equivalences. To prevent disillusion, he forgoes any aspiration to dialogic and transparent communication. He renounces from the beginning the search for an intersubjective found- ation for his practice and for a shared criterion of moral value ... The decline of the principle of equivalence, a principle intimately connec- ted to commerce and exchange, can be seen in the cynic's behaviour, in his impatient abandon of the demand for equality. He entrusts his own affirmation of self to the multiplication and fluidification of hierarchies and unequal distributions that the unexpected centrality of knowledge in production seems to imply.[42]

Formal subsumption was cynical and pious, producing a split between one's existence in the marketplace, subject to the axioms of capital, and one's 'pri- vate' existence, left to whatever piety or value one wanted to cling to. In con- trast to this, the cynicism of real subsumption, of the productive powers of the general intellect, is a cynicism without reserve, in which every aspect of one's existence, knowledge, communicative abilities, and desires becomes product- ive. In the terms of *A Thousand Plateaus* this could be described as a change from 'social subjection', in which an individual is subordinated as a subject to a higher unity, such as a machine, to 'machinic enslavement', in which a human being is reduced to a constituent part of a machine. Capitalism, at its initial stage, is identified with social subjection; workers are not slaves, or even feudal

---

40   Marx 1977, p. 280.
41   Marx 1977, p. 72.
42   Virno 1996, p. 24.

serfs, but are individuals, free to enter into any labour contract. This changes as knowledge, and with it subjectivity in general, becomes part of the productive process. As Deleuze and Guattari write:

> In the organic composition of capital, variable capital defines a regime of subjection of the worker (human surplus value), the principal framework of which is the business or factory. But with automation comes a progressive increase in the proportion of constant capital; we then see a new kind of enslavement: at the same time the work regime changes, surplus value becomes machinic, and the framework expands to all of society. It could be said that a small amount of subjectification took us away from machinic enslavement, but a large amount brings us back to it.[43]

Cynicism is the point at which it is not just the world, but subjectivity, human existence itself, which is reduced to its market value. The struggle to maximize one's human capital, one's competitive advantage, replaces demands for equality.

3   Capitalist Majority

At this point Deleuze and Guattari's rewriting of the pre-history of capitalism seems to for the most part follow the general narrative of modernisation Marx outlines in the *Manifesto*, with one noticeable exception. History proceeds from pre-capitalist modes of production in which exploitation is coded over, mystified by traditions and beliefs that establish the tribe and the despot as necessary preconditions of production, to capitalism in which belief is no longer necessary, everything is expressible in the form of quantitative relations. '[A]ll that is holy is profaned, and man is at last compelled to face with sober senses, his real conditions of life, and his relations with his kind'.[44] Deleuze and Guattari would appear to retain the basic narrative of this general history of demystification, only to have it end with a generalised cynicism, in which exploitation comes to be seen as a fact of life, part of the general human condition, rather than as the impetus for revolutionary awakening.

Cynicism is not capitalism's last word on the production of subjectivity, on social subjection. It is because exploitation in capital is stripped of any polit-

---

43   Deleuze and Guattari 1987, p. 458.
44   Marx and Engels 1978, p. 476.

ical or religious alibi, any meaning that would tie it to a determinant system of belief, that capitalism generates its own mystifications and illusions. What is 'mystified' is no longer some political or social relation that appears to be dominant, but the determining instance, the economy itself. Deleuze and Guattari follow Marx in recognising that money constitutes a massive reorganisation of desire, money is that object that has the potential to stand in for all possible objects – it becomes the universal object of desire. What capital loses in terms of belief it more than regains as an object of desire. Of course this restructuring of desire pre-exists capitalism emerging with the beginning of a monetary economy. Prior to capitalism, however, it manifests itself as a contradiction, a contradiction between money as the unqualified desire for any object whatsoever and money as quantitatively limited, as a finite amount of money. 'This contradiction between the quantitative limitation and the qualitative lack of limitation of money keeps driving the hoarder back to his Sisyphean task: accumulation. He is in the same situation as a world conqueror, who discovers a new boundary with each country he annexes'.[45] With the formation of capitalism the contradiction of hoarding is displaced, it is no longer necessary to decide between spending and saving, since capitalism can be defined by the formula 'spending in order to accumulate'. This only displaces the contradiction, however, to the point where it is no longer a contradiction between two different dimensions of money, a qualitative lack of limit and quantitative limit of money, but of two different functions of money within capitalism: money as capital, as means of investment, and money as wages, as means of consumption. According to Deleuze and Guattari: 'Measuring the two orders of magnitude in terms of the same analytical unit is a pure fiction, a cosmic swindle, as if one were to measure intergalactic or intra-atomic distance in meters and centimetres. There is no common measure between the value of enterprises and that of the labour capacity of wage earners'.[46]

Deleuze and Guattari follow Suzanne de Brunhoff in arguing that money is not simply a quantity, a unit of measure, but a complex relation that cuts across different relations of credit, finance, and speculation, and the axioms of their relations.[47] Money is not a measure, a simple quantity, but heterogeneous phenomena encompassing ancient (means of payment) and new (financial speculation) functions. While de Brunhoff focuses on the critique of the quantitative theory of money, Deleuze and Guattari focus on the effects that the idea of money, money or capital as quasi-cause, have on subjectivity. The fact

---

45   Marx 1977, p. 277.
46   Deleuze and Guattari 1983, p. 230.
47   de Brunhoff 1976, p. 90.

that this gulf, the gulf that separates wage earners and capitalists, is effaced by the same object and symbol, by money, has very definite and divergent effects. First, it is the condition for the incorporation of desire into capitalism. Money extends the illusion that we all participate in the system as equals; the dollars you and I earn are the same dollars that the wealthy invest to make billions. It makes it appear as if the dollars that we carry in our wallet are made of the same substance as the money that is capital. The difference between rich and poor, exploiters and exploited, is not coded in language of blood, honour, or race: it is expressed as a purely quantitative difference. Thus it is possible to believe that only a few dollars more will enable one to cross the line, to invest, to become rich. Capital does not spread the wealth, only the idea that we all could become wealthy.

The system of axioms is much more flexible than a code. These axioms effectively do away with the proletariat as a class which 'has nothing to lose but it chains', adding a few stock options here, readily available consumer credit there, or even 'individual social security' accounts, all of which produce investments of desire without changing the basic relations of production. 'You say you want an axiom for wage earners, for the working class and the unions? Well then, let us see what we can do – and thereafter profit will flow alongside wages, side by side, reflux and afflux'.[48] Deleuze and Guattari do not deny the fact of exploitation, but argue that exploitation in itself is insufficient to account for the production of subjectivity in capital. The axioms of capital reintegrate the subjectivity of the working class: as Maurizio Lazzarato argues, workers are exploited insofar as they sell their labour to capital, but they are also investors, investors through pension plans and stock options.[49] As Lazzarato states, following Deleuze and Guattari, the 'working class', or those that sell their wage labour, have been incorporated in the capitalist 'majority'. The majority is not defined numerically but by the way in which a particular form of existence becomes the norm. 'Majority implies a constant, of expression or content, serving as a standard measure by which to evaluate it'.[50] In the case of capitalism investing becomes the norm of economic participation; for example, the stock market, and not wages, becomes the standard through which the economy is evaluated, regardless of the fact that it does not benefit everyone. Thus, in capitalism 'Desire of the most disadvantaged creature will invest with all its strength, irrespective of any economic understanding or lack of it, in the

---

48   Deleuze and Guattari 1983, p. 238.
49   Lazzarato 2004, p. 241.
50   Deleuze and Guattari 1987, p. 105.

capitalist social field as a whole'.[51] What capitalism loses in terms of belief by 'decoding' all of the hierarchies of authority and prestige, reducing them to the purely quantitative calculation of payment, it more than regains in the form of 'investment' of desire. Desire directly invests in the flows, and fluxes, of capital, and it is at this level, at the level of the most quotidian and economic relations, and not exclusively at the level of ideology, or the superstructure, that we should look for the production of subjectivity in capital.

The deterritorialisation of desire in capitalism, as much as it makes possible a strong identification between the desire of the individual and the capitalist system, also continually threatens it. In giving up belief, in giving up the coding that constitutes pre-capitalist societies, capitalism gives up a great deal of control. It is a system that seems to make everything, every desire possible. It continually produces new desires while at the same time limiting the possibility for the actualisation of those desires. This is a problem that the other modes of production do not have to contend with since the distance that separates wealth and poverty is always coded, or over-coded, by symbolic economies of prestige, honour, and tradition.[52] In capitalism all of these codes have been decoded, or deterritorialised, ripped from their moorings in practices and beliefs by the flows of money and abstract labour. Desires for freedom and equality circulate along with money and abstract labour as their bothersome afterimages. Money and the wage make it possible to fight for not just the specific conditions of one's existence, but anything one desires; moreover, the abstract and indifferent labour that capital requires is inseparable from a new sociality of flexibility and cooperation. As capital turns to the productive power of science, knowledge, and communication, it must deterritorialise these powers as well, decode the structures which keep them locked in particular locales (such as the university, or intellectual copyright) making them part of the general knowledge of society, that is, 'common'.[53] Deleuze and Guattari's critique of capitalism focuses not on the contradictions of capital, but its lines of flight: in

---

51   Deleuze and Guattari 1983, p. 229.

52   As Immanuel Wallerstein argues: 'While privilege earned by inheritance has long been at least marginally acceptable to the oppressed on the basis of mystical or fatalistic beliefs in an eternal order ... privilege earned because one is possibly smarter and certainly better educated than someone else is extremely difficult to swallow, except by the few who are basically scrambling up the ladder. Nobody who is not a yuppie loves or admires a yuppie. Princes at least may seem to be kindly father figures. A yuppie is nothing but an overprivileged sibling. The meritocratic system is politically one of the least stable systems. And it is precisely because of this political fragility that racism and sexism enter the picture' (Wallerstein 1991, p. 32).

53   Virno 2004, p. 37.

this case, forms of aesthetic and scientific experimentation that open up new ways of perceiving and feeling.[54] Deterritorialisation threatens capitalism as much as it nourishes it.

It is against the backdrop of this threat that we can understand capitalism's most potent form of subjection, beyond the cynicism of privatised belief, and the stimulation of desire by money. Capitalism does not just 'decode' the old beliefs and traditions, wash them away in the 'cold water of egotistical calculation', it continually resuscitates them, gives them new life. As Deleuze and Guattari write:

> Civilized modern societies are defined by processes of decoding and deterritorialization. But *what they deterritorialize with one hand, they reterritorialize with the other.* These neoterritorialities are often artificial, residual, archaic; but they are archaisms having a perfectly current function, our modern way of 'imbricating', of sectioning off, of reintroducing code fragments, resuscitating old codes inventing pseudo codes or jargons ... These modern archaisms are extremely complex and varied. Some are mainly folkloric, but they nonetheless represent social and potentially political forces ... Others are enclaves whose archaism is just as capable of nourishing a modern fascism as of freeing a revolutionary charge ... Some of these archaisms take form as if spontaneously in the current of the movement of deterritorialization ... Others are organized and promoted by the state, even though they might turn against the state and cause it serious problems (regionalism, nationalism).[55]

Deleuze and Guattari insist that the process of deterritorialisation, the breakdown of codes and traditions by the abstract quantities of labour and desire, is inseparable from a process of reterritorialisation. For Deleuze and Guattari modernisation is always uneven, reviving antiquated beliefs and political forms, 'archaisms', as some melt away. This is not due to some grand conflict of

---

54   Deleuze and Guattari would appear to argue at least implicitly that capitalism's lines of flight are primarily aesthetic and scientific rather than political. As they write: 'Why this appeal to art and science, in a world where scientists and technicians and even artists, and science and art themselves, work so closely with the established sovereignties – if only because of the structures of financing? Because art, as soon as it attains its own grandeur, its own genius, creates chains of decoding and deterritorialization that serve as the foundation for desiring machines, and make them function' (Deleuze and Guattari 1983, p. 368). A similar argument underlies their later theory of 'nomadic thought': which takes science and art as its model.

55   Deleuze and Guattari 1983, p. 258.

cultures (Jihad vs. McWorld), as some political analysts claim, or some internal conflict between the global scale and lightning pace of contemporary culture and our necessarily tribal and patriarchal minds, as some socio-biologists claim, but between two sides of capitalism itself. It is a conflict between capitalism's tendency to create new desires, new needs, new experiences and possibilities, and the tendency to subordinate this potential to the over-arching need of maintaining and reproducing the existing distribution of wealth and property. This conflict animates the relation between capitalism and the state. Capital by definition is global; this is necessary to its very reproduction. No less necessary to the functioning of capital is the state. 'The internationalism of capital is thus accomplished by national and state structures that curb capital even as they make it work; these archaic structures have genuine functions'.[56] The state is the ultimate archaism, in fact Deleuze and Guattari argue that the modern state is nothing less than the ancient despot brought back to life. It is revived, but with an important difference, it no longer stands above society, overcoding the various social collectivities. Now it is the state that produces and reproduces the necessary dimensions of code, of social subjection, which counteract and make possible deterritorialised flows of subjectivity necessary to capitalism. The state is a model of realisation for capital. 'Social subjection proportions itself to the model of realization, just as machinic enslavement expands to meet the dimensions of the axiomatic that is effectuated in the model'.[57] What Deleuze and Guattari insist on, and this makes up the heart of the idea of reterritorialisation, is that capitalism produces subjectivity, not in spite of its disruptive cultural and political force, but through it. Modern subjectivity is split between axioms and codes, machinic enslavement and social subjection, between cynicism and piety, between the past and the future. Deleuze and Guattari's insistence on the 'immediate coincidence' of subjectivity and production makes it possible to see this split as a political division, a division between capital and the state, rather than an existential division, between the meaninglessness of capital and the search for some meaning in tradition.

4   Conclusion

Deleuze and Guattari's articulation of the historical and cultural logic of capitalism through such concepts as code, axiom, deterritorialisation, and reterritorialisation, concepts which often appear daunting, even incomprehensible, is

---

56   Deleuze 2004, p. 196.
57   Deleuze and Guattari 1987, p. 459.

oriented towards dismantling an entrenched set of oppositions, between economy and affect, subjectivity and objectivity, and base and superstructure. It is in undoing these oppositions, recognising the way in which 'desire is part of the infrastructure', that Deleuze and Guattari argue it is possible to grasp the realities of the present. These realities include the persistence of capitalism long past the date that its social, political, and ecological contradictions were to bring about its inevitable demise. As Deleuze and Guattari argue, we should look to understand the persistence of capital not simply on the side of the economy, examining the tendency of the rate of profit to fall and economic crises, but on the side of subjectivity, at the way in which capitalism captures not only labour power, but also desire and the imagination. Thus, Deleuze and Guattari offer the starting point of what Paolo Virno calls a 'noneconomic critique of political economy'.[58] A critique which promises to make possible a way to understand what is most perplexing about the present, its tendency to be both 'behind and ahead of itself'; that is, the coexistence of the archaic and the modern.[59] There are multiple examples of this from the current political scene in the United States, which presents itself as the search for a perfect synthesis between the 'new economy' of high speed digital transactions and the 'traditional values' of family, state and God to the resurgence of ethnic identities and hatreds (so called neo-tribalisms) in the face of a world order which purports to be 'global', and thus beyond nationalities and the nation state. This coexistence cannot be explained by looking simply at the economy, by studying the connection between underdevelopment and development, or by looking at subjective factors, alienation or the inevitable 'clash of civilizations'. It can only be grasped by examining the way in which the mode of production and the mode of subjection, desiring production and social production, intersect and affect each other. Finally, despite the fact that Deleuze and Guattari do not offer an explicit programme for a new political order, their method does suggest a new way of doing politics, one that focuses not simply on 'real' economic issues or cultural questions of recognition, exclusion, and desire, but the point where the two intersect.

58   Virno 1996b, p. 271.
59   Deleuze and Guattari 1983, p. 260.

CHAPTER 7

The Fetish is Always Actual, Revolution is Always Virtual: From Noology to Noopolitics

The obvious starting point for any discussion of the relation between Marx and Deleuze would seem to be the two volumes of *Capitalism and Schizophrenia*, in which Marx's texts provide the backdrop for the conceptualisation of deterritorialisation, desiring production, and abstract machines. However, in *Difference and Repetition*, there are a few references to Marx that, although disparate and oblique, suggest a fundamental overlap of central problems. As an initial point of provocation and orientation, we can begin with the following two statements: 'The natural object of social consciousness or common sense with regard to the recognition of value is the fetish', and, secondly, a few lines later, 'The transcendent object of the faculty of sociability is revolution'.[1] In these passages we see two of the central terms that represent the alpha and omega of Marx's thought, fetishism and revolution; the first is synonymous with false consciousness, a fundamental misapprehension of the world, while the second is the overturning of that perspective and that world. The citation of these terms is situated within Deleuze's project of transforming the very image of thought, from one based on recognition and identity to a paradoxical thought of difference. Of course it is possible to argue that what links these two thinkers and problems is nothing but the contingent and superficial connection of a context: Marx was a central, even obligatory point of reference during the 1960s in France, and thus the invocation of his name is nothing more than the by-product of writing during a particular place and time. If one scratches beneath the surface, however, it is possible to see that this superficial pairing of problems indicates a much more significant intersection, one based on the fundamental problem of what could be called the politics of thought: a politics that examines how certain images of thought emerge from different social relations, and how they in turn affect these relations.

This problem takes on different forms, concepts, and names in each thinker. For Deleuze, it emerges in *Difference and Repetition* as the problem of the dominant image of thought in philosophy, and continues through the collaborations with Guattari as noology, which they define as 'the study of the images

---

1   Deleuze 1994, p. 208.

of thought and their historicity'.[2] Deleuze (and Guattari's) fundamental point is that despite philosophy's attempt to function without presuppositions, to engender itself through a fundamentally grounded and rational discourse, it always rests on an implicit idea of what it means to think, an image of thought that ultimately serves power. The problem of the politics of thought takes on a somewhat different form in Marx's writing, so much so that it might not even appear to be a problem that Marx's work addresses at all. However, as Marx argued in *The German Ideology*, the fundamental mistake of German Idealism, and thus to some extent all of philosophy, has been to overlook its connections with 'its material conditions'.[3] The central political and philosophical concepts of Marx's work – mode of production, ideology and commodity fetishism – all address, in one form or another, the relation between thought and its conditions, conditions that are not conceptual, but material, the social conditions that are the constitutive outside for any philosophy, for any thought. It might appear that in each case what is meant by presuppositions is fundamentally opposed. In the first case they are conceptual, the orientation and image, that all thinking must assume; while in the second the presuppositions concern material conditions that by definition are lived rather than thought, reflected in Marx's fundamental assertion that *'Life is not determined by consciousness, but consciousness by life'.*[4] My point is not that Deleuze and Marx are the same, rather that it's the differences between the two, the former's focus on the preconceptual assumptions underlying conceptual thought and the latter's focus on the material conditions that make thought possible, that give shape and meaning to a fundamental philosophical problem. This fundamental problem is formed and transformed through Deleuze and Guattari's writing that continues this problem of the image of thought, from *Difference and Repetition* through the two volumes of *Capitalism and Schizophrenia*, a problem that remains strongly connected to the general problem of materiality and abstraction. As we will see, the vicissitudes of this problem are determined as much by extrinsic conditions, by the changing relationship between thought and labour in contemporary capitalism, as they are by intrinsic factors, the development and revision of a line of thought. It is through tracing this connection between

---

2 Deleuze and Guattari 1987, p. 376.

3 Pierre Macherey underscores this dimension of *The German Ideology*, writing the following: 'Hence this notion that Marxism was the first to explore: philosophy is not an independent speculative activity, as would be a pure speculation, but is tied to "real" conditions, which are its historical conditions; and this is why, let it be said in passing, there is a history of philosophy, which can be retraced and understood' (Macherey 1998, p. 9).

4 Marx and Engels 1970, p. 47.

material conditions and conceptual presuppositions that we can arrive at a new definition of revolutionary thought; revolutionary thought is no longer an eschatology, attempting to discern the signs of the future revolution in the present, but a thought oriented towards everything that exceeds the society as a fetish, exposing the virtual relations and micro-political transformations that constitute a sociality that exceeds any delimited society.

1   Society is a Fetish

In developing his idea of the image of thought, Deleuze takes as his initial focus not ideology, but the fetish, or commodity fetishism. In the initial gloss of Marx and Deleuze, we have treated these two problems, ideology and commodity fetishism, as relatively interchangeable, turning to *The German Ideology* for a general definition of Marx's interrogation of thought. Deleuze's rejection of the term ideology in the 1970s is well known; made famous in a discussion with Michel Foucault, ideology is rejected because of the manner in which it positions social relations, knowledge, and the intellectual. Ideology presupposes both masses who are deceived and an intellectual who possesses the truth. For Deleuze ideology obscures the real problem, the investments and productions of desire.[5] This explains the rejection of ideology, but not the adoption of fetishism. An examination of the general contours of the problem of commodity fetishism alongside Deleuze's general project of *Difference and Repetition* begins to establish a deeper connection, one that has less to do with the polemics of the role of the intellectual and more to do with the problem of the relationship between thought and the social order.

On first glance the choice of commodity fetishism as a model for a critique of an image of thought seems like a strange move; ideology would seem to be the obvious position from which to interrogate the relationship between thought and its presuppositions. After all, in *The German Ideology*, ideology was just another name for (German) idealism, for a mode of thinking which in ignoring its material conditions not only fails to grasp the real basis of society, but is unaware of the way in which it serves class interests. In contrast to this, commodity fetishism would seem to be restricted to a much more specific problem, that of the epistemological status of political economy, and its understanding of value. This is the difference if we focus on the objects of their respective criticism, namely philosophy and political economy. A different picture emerges,

---

5   Deleuze 2004b, p. 212.

however, if we examine the way in which each concept articulates the relationship between thought and its social presuppositions. While ideology, for
Marx, is rooted in social conditions, such as the division between mental and
manual labour and the consequent class divisions of capitalist society, there
is not a necessary relation between these conditions and either the form or
content of ideology. In other words, while there are material conditions that
make each ideology the ruling ideas of the ruling class, namely ownership of
the means of production, there is nothing to dictate the specific shape that
ideology takes, what these ideas are in each case. Thus, while it is possible that
Marx meant to indict the pretensions of philosophy tout court with his critique
of ideology, the term ideology is generally understood in the plural. There are
various ideologies, all of which have a merely historical extrinsic relationship
to thought. The fetishisation of the commodity-form, however, is a necessary
appearance of capitalist social relations. This is why the chapter on commodity fetishism ends with a discussion of different societies – Robinson Crusoe,
medieval society, and an 'association of free men' – fetishism can only be overcome practically through a change in social relations.[6] This is why the opposite
of fetishism is not enlightenment but revolution. In capitalist society, the isolation of the different producers, the separation of private industry, makes it
so that social relations appear in the form of the relation between things; the
value of the various commodities, a quality that appears to be as real as their
myriad qualities, is nothing other than the social relations of society in a distorted form. Two consequences follow from this; first, the emphasis is not on
the content but on the form. Any attempt to develop a critique of philosophy
from the commodity-form would take as its starting point not a criticism of
this or that content or concept, as in ideology critique, but would begin from
a much more troubling problem regarding the social causes of what is seemingly most necessary and inescapable for thought, its form.[7] Second, given that
the fetish is most fundamentally a misapprehension of social relations, seeing the social relations as the quality of things, the opposition is not simply
between truth and falsity, but between a thought of difference and identity, of
relations and things.[8] This is precisely what Deleuze stresses about commodity

---

6   Marx 1977, p. 171.
7   In this manner Deleuze's comparison of the form of thought with the commodity form, a
    form that privileges identity over difference, is similar to Theodor Adorno's critique in *Neg-
    ative Dialectics*.
8   John Holloway, following Lukács, Adorno, and Negri, has generalised this idea of fetishisation
    in terms of a rift between the doing and done, subject and object, difference and identity. His
    understanding, like Adorno's cited above, is not unrelated to the intersection of Deleuze and
    Marx. See *Change the World without Taking Power: The Meaning of Revolution Today*.

fetishism, as he writes: 'For example, according to Marx, fetishism is indeed an absurdity, an illusion of social consciousness, so long as we understand by this not a subjective illusion but an objective or transcendental illusion born out of the conditions of social consciousness in the course of its actualization'.[9] What is at stake for Deleuze in Marx's understanding of commodity fetishism is a new understanding of the limits of thought, not the empirical limits of error, or even the transcendental condition of illusions hard-wired into subjectivity, but the socially produced limits that transform relations into objects.

To grasp Deleuze's understanding of fetishism, and how it relates to Deleuze and Guattari's later engagement with Marxism, it is necessary to at least briefly clarify the concepts that form the critical backdrop of *Difference and Repetition*, specifically the critique of common sense as an image of thought. For Deleuze common sense is a particular presupposition of thought, a presupposition that is not objective, not a particular concept or definition, but an implied meaning of what it means to think. What is presupposed is an ideal of representation that posits an identical object, a thing which remains fundamentally the same, and a unity of the subject, as the various faculties converge on the same object; it is the same thing, which is felt, seen, and remembered by the same subject. Truth is recognition: error is misrecognition. Common sense is dominated by recognition; to know is to recognise, to extract the same from the multiplicity of its instances. Against this Deleuze suggests a counter-image of thought based not on recognition, but on an encounter. 'Something in the world forces us to think. This something is an object not of recognition but of a fundamental encounter'.[10] Whereas recognition is predicated on the convergence of the different faculties on the same object, the encounter, the break from common sense, is predicated on their fundamental discord. What is thought, sensed, or remembered, takes each of these faculties to its limit and does not communicate with the other faculties, except through a kind of crisis. This includes a sociability, which has its own disjoint relation to the faculties; it cannot be recognised, it is not an object for knowledge, it can only be lived. As Deleuze writes:

> Take the social multiplicity: it determines sociability as a faculty, but also the transcendent object of sociability which cannot be lived within actual societies in which the multiple is incarnated, but must be and can be lived only in the element of social upheaval (in other word, freedom, which is always hidden among the remains of an old order and the first fruits of a new).[11]

---

9   Deleuze 1994, p. 208.
10   Deleuze 1994, p. 139.
11   Deleuze 1994, p. 193.

Common sense objectifies sociality, makes society a thing that can be seen, remembered, and thought. To use a term that is not entirely out of place with Marx's understanding of commodity fetishism, common sense reifies sociability; it displaces the practice, the process of the constitution of social relations with the product. In contrast to this, in moments of upheaval and disruption, there appears a sociality that exceeds any actually existing society, a virtual society that is always in excess of any existing social order. In Deleuze's thought, virtual does not mean possible, a concept that is always derived from reality, caught in a relation of identity, nor is it unreal: it is, as Deleuze writes, abstract and real. It is the fact that every society, every social articulation, can be realised otherwise, can have different relations, and is thus surrounded by a virtual cloud.[12] At this point in *Difference and Repetition* this revolutionary idea, this idea of revolution, is only seen in the moment of disruption. It is thus no accident that in this text the transcendent object of sociability is named anarchy.[13] In Deleuze's later writings with Guattari, the connection between this virtual sociability and the economy, or, more specifically, labour, will be strengthened. The transition from anarchy to labour is not just a matter of reviving some nineteenth-century debate between anarchism and Marxism, but of shifting the focus from the virtual as a revolutionary moment to a persistent presence – an immanent condition.

2   Production/Representation

As Deleuze argues, the social idea, sociality as a virtual multiplicity, has to be seen as something of a structure, which different societies realise in myriad different ways. As Deleuze writes:

> The social Idea is the element of quantitability, qualitability, and potentiality of societies. It expresses a system of multiple ideal connections between differential elements: these include relations of production and property relations which are established not between concrete individuals but between atomic bearers of labour-power or representatives of property. The economic instance is constituted by such a social multiplicity – in other words, by the varieties of these differential relations.[14]

---

12   Deleuze 1997, p. 148.
13   Deleuze 1994, p. 143.
14   Deleuze 1994, p. 186.

Deleuze's nod here is to Louis Althusser and Étienne Balibar's reading of Marx, which makes it possible to grasp history not as the teleological unfolding of a fundamental contradiction, making possible the periodisation of history, but as the differential actualisation of a system of relations. In Althusser and Balibar's view the 'mode of production' is most fundamentally a 'relation between relations'.[15] This structure, or relation between relations, is made up of the different practices, economic, political, ideological etc, that act on and in relation to each other. In this structure or relations, the economic remains determining, but it does not simply act on the other aspects of society, imposing its brute necessity, but acts on them by determining their differential relations, determining which of these relations, or practices, is dominant. The classic example of this is drawn from Marx's discussion of feudalism, in which Marx argues that in the Middle Ages, religion was determined as dominant.[16] The constituting relations can be articulated in multiple different ways, with different practices, economic, political, or religious, occupying the dominant position, and different relations between these different instances. 'The economic instance is constituted by such a social multiplicity – in other words, by the varieties of these differential relations'.[17] Such a conception of the economy breaks with any teleology, any sense of the different modes of production following each other in a linear progression, in order to stress their differential articulation. While Deleuze stresses the determining nature of the economy, its determination is that of a problem, which is solved in different ways, not that of historical necessity or a base. The truth of social relations is not to be found in some concrete instance, but in the relations between the different social relations, thus in abstraction, in the virtual.

Deleuze deviates from Althusser and Balibar in placing 'abstract labour' at the foundation of this differential relation. As Deleuze writes, 'In what Marx calls 'abstract labour' abstraction is made from the particular qualities of the products of labour and the qualities of the labourers, but not from the conditions of productivity, the labour power and the means of labour in society'.[18] Deleuze's definition stresses two aspects of Marx's concept that will become increasingly important to his later work: abstraction as indifference to subject and object, yet socially determined. In *Anti-Oedipus*, Deleuze and Guattari foreground Marx's discovery of abstract labour, or rather his crediting of Adam Smith, and Ricardo for the discovery, in their development of desiring production. As Deleuze and Guattari write:

15   Althusser and Balibar 1970, p. 224.
16   Marx 1977, p. 176.
17   Deleuze 1994, p. 186.
18   Deleuze 1994, p. 186.

Marx said that Luther's merit was to have determined the essence of religion, no longer on the side of the object, but as an interior religiosity; that the merit of Adam Smith and Ricardo was to have determined the essence or nature of wealth no longer as an objective nature but as an abstract and deterritorialized subjective essence, the activity of production in general.[19]

This is a fundamental example, if not the paradigmatic instance of, deterritorialisation. Whereas prior political economists had initially sought the origin of wealth in a privileged object, such as the earth, or in a particular kind of activity, such as agricultural labour, the political economy of Smith and Ricardo recognises that at the basis of wealth, there is nothing other than labour as an abstract subjective activity. Deleuze and Guattari immediately assert that political economy no sooner discovers this abstract activity than it objectifies it, reterritorialising it by subordinating it to accumulated capital. Capitalism is thus the exemplary instance of Deleuze and Guattari's fundamental point: deterritorialisation is inseparable from reterritorialisation. This is how they introduce Marx's critique of political economy, as a critique that not only liberates abstract subjective activity from the territories of the earth, but also explores the way that this activity is appropriated by the territories of capital and the state.

Abstract labour, as Marx defines it in the opening section of *Capital*, is not only labour that it indifferent to, or abstracted from, its particular concrete mode of existence. It is also, and perhaps more importantly, labour that has been rendered interchangeable, equivalent, despite the different individuals performing it. It is that invisible but not impalpable unit that makes exchange value possible. Its invisibility outlines the fundamental problem of the question of value, and of commodity fetishism, in which the grounds for the equivalence of the various commodities is mysterious in theory because it is always already answered by practice. In practice, abstract labour is a socially necessary abstraction, an abstraction made possible by the machines and technologies that render different kinds of work interchangeable. It is felt as a practical reality whenever these social and technical realities change, whenever a new machine is invented or a new, more efficient labour process is invented.[20] As such, it arises only with the formation of capitalism. As Marx writes: 'the most general abstractions arise only in the midst of the richest possible

---

19   Deleuze and Guattari 1983, p. 270.
20   Marx 1977, p. 135.

concrete development'.[21] It is only in capitalist society, with the rise of monetary relations and the breakdown of traditional jobs and activities, that something like 'labour' as an abstract activity emerges, displacing the concrete activities. However, as Marx famously argues, 'human anatomy contains a key to
the anatomy of the ape': it is from the perspective of this historically produced
activity that we are able to make sense of other societies as determined by
modes of production, as based on the articulation, distribution, and use of
labour. This is precisely the position taken by Deleuze and Guattari with respect
to abstract subjective activity, or what they call desiring production, desiring
production continues Marx's positing of of an abstract indifferent activity, a
species activity, that is organized differently in different social forms only now
it is no longer limited to labour, to the production of things, to include the productive dimension of desire. This activity emerges at the end of history, in the
breakdown of codes and the general imperative to produce, but it makes possible an understanding of other societies, precisely in the manner in which
they code or repel desiring production. The most fundamental abstractions,
abstract labour or desiring production, are not found at the beginning of society, in some primitive state, but in the most complex societies.

Returning to the passages above from *Difference and Repetition* viewed now
through their development in *Anti-Oedipus*, we can see that in the former text
Deleuze draws together two very different strains of Marxist thought. The first,
which posits the economy as a series of differential relations, is drawn from
Althusser and Balibar, while the second, focusing on abstract labour, does not
seem to have a specific point of influence aside from Marx, but has resonances with the idea of 'real abstraction' developed in different senses by Alfred
Sohn-Rethel, Moishe Postone, and Paolo Virno. These two lines of thought
continue through Deleuze and Guattari's works: the first with its emphasis
on relations forms the basis of such concepts as abstract machines, while
the second underlies their conception of desiring production. Where these
two lines of thought converge is in their refiguring the notion of abstraction:
abstraction is no longer an activity of thought, but is the product of material relations, relations that remain in some sense unrepresentable. This claim
is in some sense already indebted to Marx's understanding of his own critical project, which paradoxically focuses on the status of the abstract concepts of 'abstract labour' and 'surplus value'.[22] It is only from the perspective
of the critique of capitalism that labour can appear as both absolutely neces-

---

21   Marx 1973, p. 104.
22   Althusser and Balibar 1970, p. 80.

sary, as part of man's metabolic interrelation with nature, and as fundamentally abstract, as an indifference to its specific object or subject. This indifference must be actualised, it must take the form of a particular kind of work,
of labour. This necessary abstraction can only appear in particular concrete
formulations. From this we can better grasp Deleuze's earlier assertion, in *Difference and Repetition*, that 'there are only economic social problems'.[23] The
economy is both absolutely necessary, something that meets the most fundamental needs of existence, and fundamentally abstract, made up of only
the differential relations between the various practices, and structures, which
become concrete only in their reciprocal relations. It is the problem that every
society faces, but a problem that can only be resolved in specific articulations,
in specific social formations. The economy, understood as the articulation of
abstractive subjective activity, of any-activity-whatsoever, is something that
exists only in its particular articulations, as specific concrete realisations of this
virtual set of relations. Deterritorialisation is inseparable from reterritorialisation.

In *Anti-Oedipus* the critique of recognition, of identity in thought, is res-
ituated from a critique of an image of thought to an opposition between production and representation. Much of this takes a polemical tone, in which the
theatre of Oedipus is opposed to the factory of the unconscious, the work of the
desiring machines. However, it also extends and deepens the idea of fetishism.
As Deleuze and Guattari write:

> Let us remember once again one of Marx's caveats: we cannot tell from
> the mere taste of the wheat who grew it; the product gives us no hint as
> to the system and relations of production. The product appears to be all
> the more specific, incredibly specific and readily describable, the more
> closely the theoretician relates it to *ideal forms of causation, comprehen-
> sion, or expression*, rather than to *the real process of production on which it
> depends*.[24]

Just as products, commodities, obscure the process of their production, institutions, structures, society itself, obscure the virtual relations that constitute
them; the solution conceals the problem from which it emerged. In *Anti-
Oedipus* Deleuze and Guattari expand upon and develop this idea of the fetish
from *Difference and Repetition*: the fetish becomes the socius. It is not just that

---

23   Deleuze 1994, p. 186.
24   Deleuze and Guattari 1983, p. 24.

the product, society, obscures the productive relations that generate it, it actively appropriates them. As Deleuze and Guattari write:

> ... the forms of social production, like those of desiring production, involve an unengendered nonproductive attitude, an element of antiproduction coupled with the process, a full body that functions as a *socius*. This socius may be the body of the earth, that of the tyrant, or capital. This is the body that Marx is referring to when he says that it is not the product of labour, but rather appears as its natural or divine presuppositions. In fact, it does not restrict itself merely to opposing productive forces in and of themselves. It falls back on [*il se rabat sur*] all production, constituting a surface over which the forces and agents of production are distributed, thereby appropriating for itself all surplus production and arrogating to itself both the whole and the parts of the process, which now seem to emanate from it as a quasi-cause.[25]

Just as the despot appears to be the cause and not the effect of subjection, capital appears to be the cause and not the effect of labour. Once disconnected from the conditions of production, from the virtual relations that make it possible, society, the socius, not only appears to be autonomous, in the form of money making money, but is an effect that appears as a cause. Society does not only appear to exist prior to the differential relations, the production and desire that constitute it, but it appears to stand above these relations as their necessary condition.[26] The fetish has become common sense in that we see society, with its structures, rules, and goals, as something that exists prior to and is constitutive of the social relations of desire, perception, and production.

---

25   Deleuze and Guattari 1983, p. 10.
26   Once again the point of reference would seem to be Althusser and Balibar's *Reading Capital*. In that text Althusser refers to the 'society effect' as the way in which the different and differential practices of society hold together through a form of subjection. As Althusser writes: 'The mechanism of the production of this "society effect" is only complete when all the effects of the mechanism have been expounded, down to the point where they are produced in the form of the very effects that constitute the concrete, conscious or unconscious relation of the individuals to the society as a society, i.e., down to the effects of the fetishism of ideology (or "forms of social consciousness" – *Preface to A Contribution* ...), in which men consciously or unconsciously live their lives, their projects, their actions, their attitudes and their functions as social' (Althusser and Balibar 1970, p. 66).

3   The Return to Noopolotics: The Problem of State Thought

Following the line of noology, of the politics of thought, from *Difference and Repetition* to *Anti-Oedipus*, leads to a rather strange deepening of the problem. In *Difference and Repetition* the criticism was focused on a particular 'image of thought', one that takes recognition as the fundamental function of thought. At the social level, this object of recognition, this identity between past, present, and future, is in some sense society as a fetish. Against this, Deleuze focused on the transcendent object of thought, on the abstract and differential relations that exceed any faculty of thought, any possible conceptualisation. The difference still passed within thought, opposing the provocations of thought to common sense. In *Anti-Oedipus*, however, the opposition shifts; it is no longer between different figures of thought, but between representation and the forces of production that exceed representation. The fundamental opposition is between how social relations are produced and how they are represented: or, as Deleuze and Guattari put it, how desire is produced and how it is recorded. It is for this reason that the image of thought, or what Deleuze and Guattari call noology, disappears from *Anti-Oedipus*. The entire problem of the image of thought disappears, to be replaced with the stark opposition between representation and production.[27]

Of the many shifts of terminology, content, and style that characterise the transition from *Anti-Oedipus* to *A Thousand Plateaus*, two are relevant for our project here: the first, as I have already acknowledged, is the return of noology, the image of thought as a problem, and the second is the disappearance of labour, or rather production, as that which exceeds representation. It might be more accurate to state that it is the polemical rift between production, or labour, and representation, or thought, that disappears in the later text; when labour does appear, it appears not as an absolute rupture with the logic of representation, but as a figure of capture and subjection. Taken together these two changes suggest a fundamental transformation of the opposition that characterised *Anti-Oedipus*, that of thought and production. Production is no longer the absolute outside of representation, nor is thought reduced to a representation that can never intersect with production: thought is no longer limited to

---

27   Étienne Balibar has offered an interpretation of the limitations of *The German Ideology* that is relevant here. As Balibar argues, the strong identification of idealism, ideology, and domination has as its corollary an identification of matter, production, and liberation in the body of the proletariat (Balibar 1994c, p. 93). Put simply, in Marx's text the proletariat has no ideology, no theory, as Marx argues, its theoretical illusions have been dissolved by the pure force of history.

the fetish of common sense – to tasting the wheat without ever grasping how it has been produced – but is itself a productive force. Thought and production become tied to the same relations of deterritorialisation and capture.

If we turn our attention briefly back to *Anti-Oedipus* we can see that the issue of labour was never quite as simple as it might first appear, that the transformation of the question of production was already indicated by tensions within that text. As much as Deleuze and Guattari based their concept of abstract subjective activity, or 'desiring production', on abstract labour, this understanding was perhaps always skewed with respect to Marx's text.[28] For Marx, abstract labour is the condition of possibility of exchange, of the exchange that makes capital possible; thus it is first and foremost an equivalence established between different types of concrete labour. Marx vacillates somewhat on the ground of this equivalence, sometimes attributing it to an anthropological constant, and at other times attributing it to the machines and techniques that render labour equivalent and exchangeable.[29] Deleuze and Guattari do not recognise the existence of anything like an anthropological constant underlying abstract labour, arguing that any idea of a standard amount of labour is itself the product of an arbitrary imposition. What Deleuze and Guattari focus on is not the equivalence underlying abstract labour, the fact that the labour of one person is equal to that of others, but its abstraction, or, more properly, deterritorialisation, its indifference to object or subject. It is perhaps for this reason that in *Anti-Oedipus* Deleuze and Guattari also consider the role of machines, actual machines, in the production of surplus value. If labour can be abstracted from particular forms of subjectivity, from the blacksmith or shoemaker as a particular kind of labourer, and from particular objects, from the land or industry, then why cannot it also be abstracted from humanity, from human hands and minds altogether? Abstract labour becomes part of the machine; not just in the sense that Marx might have argued, in which the pure motor force of the body is replaced by the machine, but in the sense that abstract subjectivity activity, including that of knowledge, can become part of the machine. As Deleuze and Guattari write, 'Knowledge, information, and specialized education are just as much parts of capital ("knowledge capital") as is the most elementary labour of the worker'.[30] Machinery has a fundamentally

---

28   One of the strangest elements of Deleuze and Guattari's text is that in referring to Marx's understanding of the break represented by Smith and Ricardo, they frequently cite Foucault's *The Order of Things*, locating in that text an epochal distinction between a classical age of representation and a modern age of production.

29   Read 2003, p. 74.

30   Deleuze and Guattari 1983, p. 234.

different role to play in each account: in Marx's account the machine internal-ises the skills and knowledge of the worker, leaving behind a residue of labour that is fundamentally abstract in that it can be performed by anyone, while in Deleuze and Guattari's understanding, the abstraction of subjectivity crosses the divide between machine and human, constituting and exceeding both. In the first instance the machine makes abstract labour possible, as a form of completely exchangeable human activity, while, in the second, the machine embodies abstract labour.

It is at this point where we can see the gulf that separates Marx's understand-ing of abstract labour from Deleuze and Guattari. For Marx, abstract labour is first and foremost an equivalent, it is what makes possible the exchange of the labour of one for others, while for Deleuze and Guattari abstract labour is primarily defined as a flow, as something separate from specific bodies and objects, the equivalent of which can only be the effect of a seizure by force. This last point is crucial: while Marx had always excavated the asymmetries of force underlying the equivalents of exchange, Deleuze and Guattari radicalise this point through their understanding of the primacy of difference over identity. In a seminar in the 1970s, Deleuze makes a distinction between an arithmetical and differential understanding of surplus value.[31] In the first, the quantifiable nature of labour is given, or assumed, and the only difference is a quantitative one between the wage (necessary labour) and profit. In the second, differen-tial understanding, there is no equivalence, just an encounter between a flow of labour and a flow of wages. There is no ground for the exchange between labour and capital, the very terms of the exchange are constituted by the rela-tion. The scandal of exploitation is not that labour is paid for at an insufficient rate, but that it is paid for at all: that a unit of money becomes equivalent to a unit of labour time.[32] This differential understanding also makes possible a theory of scientific or technical labour. Just as there is an encounter between a flow of labour and a flow of money, there is an encounter between a flow of money and a flow of knowledge. As Deleuze and Guattari argue, technological innovations are only introduced if they can increase surplus value. Technolo-gical innovations are dependent upon a flow of money for their realisation. This is dependent upon multiple factors, such as scale of production and cost of labour, factors that make possible an incredibly uneven development of tech-nology and social relations.[33] As with *Difference and Repetition*, society only

31   The lecture is dated 12/21/71 is available here: https://www.webdeleuze.com/textes/121
      Accessed 2/7/22.
32   Deleuze and Guattari 1983, p. 249.
33   Deleuze and Guattari 1983, p. 233.

exists as a set of differential relations between different flows: money, labour, and knowledge.

In *A Thousand Plateaus*, Deleuze and Guattari repeat their earlier formulation that presents capitalism as formed by the encounter between an unqualified activity, any activity whatsoever, and an unspecified object, any object whatsoever.[34] However, at this point, production, labour, is no longer presented as the paradigmatic instance of deterritorialised subjective activity; rather, it is integral to the manner through which this activity is seized by force: it is an apparatus of capture. The model of abstract subjective activity is no longer abstract labour, but free action: the figure of this abstract subjective activity is no longer the 'schizo', the factory of desiring production, but the nomad and its war-machine. This radical break at the level of names and figures risks concealing what is in many respects a continuation at the level of concepts and problems. As we have seen, when Deleuze and Guattari invoke abstract labour in *Anti-Oedipus*, it is never the quantifiable abstraction that is stressed, the capacity of rendering labour exchangeable and interchangeable, but its qualitative indifference to subjects and objects. In *A Thousand Plateaus*, it is precisely this capacity to render different activities comparable that is identified with the 'apparatus of capture'. Activity, free activity, is captured by being rendered comparable with other activities, by being subject to an abstract standard that defines it as work, a standard that is always inseparable from a surplus. The encounter between the two flows, money and labour, is always asymmetrical, with the first setting the terms of the relation. Surplus labour is not the simple quantitative difference of labour above and beyond what is necessary to survive, but the foundational excess that determines the terms of the equation. 'Surplus labour is not that which exceeds labour; on the contrary, labour is that which is subtracted from surplus labour and presupposes it'.[35] Labour does not exist as a generic human capacity, but is constituted by the very act that exploits it, that constitutes a surplus. As Deleuze and Guattari write:

> Impose the Work-model upon every activity, translate every act into possible or virtual work, discipline free action, or else (which amounts to the same thing) relegate it to 'leisure', which exists only by reference to work. We now understand why the Work-model, in both its physical and social aspects, is a fundamental part of the state apparatus.[36]

---

34   Deleuze and Guattari 1987, p. 453.
35   Deleuze and Guattari 1987, p. 441.
36   Deleuze and Guattari 1987, p. 490.

As the passage indicates, one of the fundamental roles of the state is creating work as the standard of the comparison of different activities. What is
excluded from this, what cannot be measured or exchanged, becomes unproductive labour, leisure. In something of a reversal of classic Marxist theory,
Deleuze and Guattari argue that the state as central force of command must
be prior to the economy as an organised set of relations between disparate
human endeavours. 'It is not the state that presupposes a mode of production;
quite the opposite, it is the state that makes production a mode'.[37] Moreover,
in attributing this process to the state, rather than the market, Deleuze and
Guattari begin to suggest that the two problems addressed above, the return of
noology and the changing status of labour, are in some sense related. The state
is not just the name of the relations of force that make possible the equivalence underlying the exchange of different labours (and the commodities and
surplus produced by this exchange), it is simultaneously a model of thought.
It is a model of thought that obscures the groundless nature of the differential relations between labour and capital, effacing the asymmetry of force with
the neutrality of law – state violence is inseparable from its justification. This
justification is not based on some specific narrative, some specific conceptual
content, that would make the state reasonable, but an identification of the state
with reason itself.

The critique of state thought develops from the critique of common sense,
in each case it is a matter of a presupposed unity, 'what everyone knows', but
in the case of the state, this unity is elevated to universality. As Deleuze and
Guattari write:

> The classical image of thought, and the striating of mental space it effects,
> aspires to universality. It in effect operates with two 'universals', the Whole
> as the final ground of being or all-encompassing horizon, and the Sub-
> ject as the principle that converts being into being-for-us. Imperium and
> republic.[38]

What is striking about this passage is that the identification of the state as functioning with two universals, the 'whole' and the 'subject', is very close to the general formula that Deleuze and Guattari use to identify capital: the encounter
between an unqualified subjective activity and an unspecified object. Both capital and the state, or at least state thought, function in relation to an object

---

37   Deleuze and Guattari 1987, p. 429.
38   Deleuze and Guattari 1987, p. 379.

and a subject that is in each case generic and universal. The crucial difference would seem to be that capital deals with differential relations between abstract activities and objects, while the state presents these abstract relations as equivalent, fundamentally overcoding the differential relations with an image of legitimacy. Capital is founded on the encounter between two flows, an asymmetrical, contingent, and groundless encounter that the state renders legitimate by presenting the terms, money and labour or worker and capitalist, as interchangeable. For the state the difference of class, of being a worker or capitalist, is irrelevant, they are equally subjects, motivated to exchange by interest and dwelling in 'the Eden of the innate rights of man'.[39] As Deleuze and Guattari argue, the interiority of state thought is primarily a relation of identity between capitalist and worker, or ruler and ruled, positing a common ground of reason amongst different subjects. 'The state must realize the distinction between legislator and the subject under formal conditions permitting thought, for its part, to conceptualize their identity'.[40] Deleuze and Guattari's criticism of capital and the state risks collapsing the distinction, not just to the point where the two are identified, capital and the state as both figures of universality and abstraction, but to the point where the opposition is reduced to a simple binary of the state versus nomadism (or, in *Anti-Oedipus*, fascism versus the schizo).

Despite the tendency to present the conflict between the state and the nomad as timeless, or at least metahistorical, Deleuze and Guattari fundamentally change the terms of the conflict by shifting it from philosophy, in which the conflict was between the long line of state thought, stretching from Descartes to Hegel, and nomadic thought, to science. As Deleuze and Guattari argue, state science is primarily hylemorphic, working with form and content, and privileging formed and fixed bodies. 'Nomadic science', however, works with movements, with singularities: the events through which qualitative transformations take place.[41] The opposition between these two forms of science is only apparent: state science constantly needs the discoveries of nomadic science. The fluctuations of nomadic science thus are reterritorialised onto the fixed coordinates and categories of state science. Two things can be said about this concept of science. First, it reiterates a theme that is central to *Anti-Oedipus*, in which knowledge is presented as a deterritorialising/deterritorialised force. Second, the situation is parallel to that of labour, which is deterritorialised only to be reterritorialised onto property and capital. The deterritorialisations of

---

39   Marx 1977, p. 280.
40   Deleuze and Guattari 1987, p. 376.
41   Deleuze and Guattari 1987, p. 372.

nomadic science are integral to state science, even as they are subordinated to measures and concepts that are alien to them. The idea of nomadic science allows Deleuze and Guattari to make a point they could not make with respect to the history of philosophy: state thought is dependent on nomadic thought, difference is prior to identity, deterritorialisation is primary to reterritorialisation. For Deleuze and Guattari knowledge and labour, thought and action, are subject to the same apparatus of capture, the same process of homogenisation and standardisation that constitutes quantitatively exchangeable units from differential relations of desire and action. In *A Thousand Plateaus* there is no longer a division between representation and production, or thought and action: each have their deterritorialised dimension, nomadic science and free activity, and are thus subject to similar apparatuses of capture. This similarity does not close the question of the relation of consciousness to life, but opens it to its historicity.

4   From Production to Invention: The Problem of Noopolitics

Of the many readers and commentators of Deleuze and Guattari's works, the Italian reception, specifically that of Antonio Negri and Maurizio Lazzarato, is unique in that it stresses the historical dimensions of their writing. To begin with, Negri's understanding of the historical dimension of Deleuze and Guattari's work is not the simple assertion that their thought represents an example of 'May '68' thought, of that bygone moment of exuberance and revolutionary excess. Rather, for Negri specifically, what is central is precisely what we are examining here: the changing structure of labour and its relation to the problem of thought. Negri argues that the machines that populate *Anti-Oedipus* are not metaphors, but attempts to grasp the complexity of the interactions of humanity and the machines that make up contemporary capitalism. The same could be said for the assemblages and machines that make up *A Thousand Plateaus*.[42] What Negri's reading underscores, and is often overlooked by many other readers, is that it is not simply because of theoretical sophistication that we do not accept a dualism between representation and production, but because such dualisms no longer fit the current reality, in which representations are themselves productive. The schema of labour, action, and intellect, first articulated by Aristotle and placed on a modern footing by Hannah Arendt, is itself out of touch with a reality in which knowledge is product-

---

42   Negri 1995, p. 104.

ive and the uncertainty and plurality of action has become part of the service industry.[43] Thus, the shift of philosophical positions regarding the relation of labour, subjectivity, and thought from *Anti-Oedipus* to *A Thousand Plateaus* is itself a product of the transformation of capital.

Negri's reading opens, or rather calls to attention to, a different way of approaching the relationship between Marx (or Marxist problematics) and Deleuze and Guattari. It is no longer simply a matter of the way in which particular problems from Marx and Marxists inform Deleuze's writing, providing the basis for understanding society as a fetish, but the way in which Deleuze and Guattari's writing provokes and continues a reexamination of Marx's concepts. Or more to the point, since such a division is artificial, what is important is the way in which the central problems and concerns of Marxist thought, that of the redefinition of labour in light of the contemporary transformations of capital, are integral to Deleuze and Guattari's understanding: just as Deleuze and Guattari's concepts of deterritorialisation, noology, and the virtual make possible a reexamination of Marx's thought.

Of all of the post-autonomist thinkers who have followed Negri in reading Deleuze and Guattari as thinkers of the present, the one who is perhaps most interesting or relevant to our concerns is Maurizio Lazzarato. Lazzarato's central project is in rethinking the current conjuncture from the perspective of both noology, the image of thought, and an examination of the intersection of abstract subjective activity and labour. Lazzarato takes as his starting point what Deleuze and Guattari define as the foundation of capital, the encounter between a generic subject, of any subjective activity whatever, and an unspecified object.[44] Picking up on Deleuze and Guattari's emphasis on deterritorialisation, on the abstraction from specific activities and objects, Lazzarato opens the question of the adequacy of thinking this abstract activity through the figure of work.[45] As much as Marx may ground his understanding of capital on an abstract subjective activity, labour, that works on any object whatsoever, the commodity, he still primarily thinks of this relation as the action of a subject on an object producing a product through the medium of a tool.[46] While we might add, in good dialectical fashion, that this action in turn transforms the subject, the fundamental question remains as to whether or not this schema of

---

43   This argument regarding the breakdown of the classic schema of labour (or poesis), action (or praxis) and thought (or theoria) is given its most concise formulation in the work of Paolo Virno 2004 (see *A Grammar of the Multitude*, p. 51).

44   Lazzarato 2004, p. 13.

45   Lazzarato 2004, Ibid.

46   Marx 1977, p. 284.

activity can account for contemporary relations of production in which work is not so much about transforming objects as it is about transforming perspectives, desires, and relations. Thus, for Lazzarato, Marx's perspective is limited on two counts: first, in that it takes as its general schema of labour the idea of a subject transforming an object, and, second, in that it understands this activity to be an abstract and interchangeable activity, positing subjects who interact only through the ground of this generic activity.[47] What is excluded in each case is difference, difference that is neither quantitative nor subject to the measure of labour time. The question is one of subjectivity, subjectivity not simply defined as the capacity to transform an object, but understood as temporality, invention, and relation.[48]

For Lazzarato, the true basis of an understanding of the abstract subjective activity underlying capital is not Marx but Gabriel Tarde, who tried to understand subjectivity as a relation of invention, imitation, and competition.[49] Lazzarato uses Tarde's reexamination of the sociality of subjectivity to redefine labour, or replace it with the idea of 'action at a distance', of minds affecting minds, and to return to the problem noology, or rather, noopolitics. Noopolitics is defined as the action of minds on minds, of subjectivities acting on each other at a distance, affecting memory, desires, and attention.[50] Despite the terminological similarity with Deleuze and Guattari's study of the images of thought, the 'nous' that underlies noology and noopolitics, Lazzarato's point of reference is less *A Thousand Plateaus*, with its battle between state thought and nomadic thought, than Deleuze's 'Postscript on Control Society', with its emphasis on forms of control that do not so much operate on the body as on the mind, through the new technologies of communication.[51] Lazzarato places Tarde's interest in the public, and the forms of media that were emerging in the nineteenth century, in a trajectory (borrowed from Foucault and Deleuze) in which power operates less and less on the flesh of the body, as in sovereign power, and more and more on perceptions, affections, and memories. Modern technologies such as the television, cinema, and the internet operate on minds; they are apparatuses of capture, capturing attention, memory, and imagination. Before products can be sold, or even made, attention and memory must be captured by the technologies that work on publics.[52] The emphasis is on a new

---

47   Lazzarato 2002, p. 25.
48   Lazzarato 2004, p. 144.
49   Lazzarato 2002, p. 39.
50   Lazzarato 2004, p. 85.
51   Deleuze 1995, p. 181.
52   Lazzarato 2004, p. 117.

form of capital that works more on memory (think of the various cinematic remakes that are nothing more than attempts to mine a reservoir of nostalgia), belief, and attention than the production of things. This action in which the mind acts on the mind, on thoughts, defines a new political or social relation: if the age of abstract labour corresponded to the political regime of discipline, which made disparate bodies and actions abstract and interchangeable, the age of highly deterritorialised labour corresponds to actions on disparate minds, memories, and perceptions. As Lazzarato writes: 'Noopolitics is exercised on the head, implicating attention in order to control the virtual power of memory. The modulation of memory would thus be the most important function of noopolitics'.[53] However, it should be noted, especially in the face of the many arguments levelled against epochal understandings of contemporary capital, in which the new is posited as a complete break with the past, immaterial labour replacing material labour, that Lazzarato's interest in Tarde is less about a transformation of the economy than a different understanding of the relationship between subjectivity and the economy. For Tarde, both Marxism and theories of marginal utility overlook the constitutive role of memory and desire in forming markets. Tarde's *La Psychologie Economique* argues that the 'economy', in the sense of the production and circulation of goods, is itself embedded in a larger economy, or circulation, of beliefs and desires which determine it.[54] Not only is there no separation between representation and production, belief and labour: the former is the ground of the latter. The immaterial, the virtual, becomes central to production, as goods and finance are increasingly dependent on the relations of belief.

As much as Lazzarato's argument can be understood as an argument against the Marxist idea of labour, especially against the gulf that separates production from representation, it is an argument that returns us to the identification of the economy and the virtual in *Difference and Repetition* (as well as the productive power of desire in *Anti-Oedipus*). Lazzarato argues that the dialectic of subject and object needs to be replaced by the relation of event and worlds. Capital is not simply the work of an abstract subject on an undetermined object, it is inseparable from the production of new worlds, new senses of possibility, belonging, and orientations of affects. Every product, every enterprise, entails not just the actualisation of particular material and technological possibilities, but the actualisation of particular subjective possibilities, ways of thinking and seeing. As Lazzarato writes, 'Capitalism is not a mode [mode] of

---

53   Lazzarato 2004, p. 85.
54   Lazzarato 2002, p. 28.

production, it is a production of worlds [mondes]'.[55] These worlds emerge from the virtual relations of belief and desire that define a particular sense of the possible. This is not only true of consumption in which every product is inseparable from its lifestyle, its habits and desire, but it also effects finance capital, in which corporations are valued primarily in terms of the level of expectations and belief.[56] The stock market is also immersed in a field of beliefs and desires that constitute the basis for value. This process of production and effectuation, or in Tarde's terms, invention and imitation, takes place through activity, activity understood broadly to include the actions that disseminate beliefs, ideas, and knowledge, activities that involve labour but exceed it. The two points of Deleuze's reading of Marx in *Difference and Repetition*, the economy as the articulation of differential relations and abstract labour, ultimately converge: the differential relations constitutive of society are actualized through abstract subjective activity.

5   Becoming Revolutionary without the Revolution

In *Difference and Repetition*, Deleuze argues that different societies can be understood as the actualisation, which is to say the solution, of a general problem that can be called, for lack of a better word, economic. The solution actualises one of a virtual multiplicity of relations, and in doing so obscures the problem from which it emerges. In *Anti-Oedipus*, this general problem takes on the specific form of the relation between desiring production and social production; every society, every form of social production is nothing but a specific organisation and articulation of desiring production, assigning it specific goals and aims. This task is in part completed by a representation of society itself, by the socius that presents society, in the form of the despot or capital, as something that exists prior to the various actions that constitute it. In *A Thousand Plateaus*, noology, the image of thought, returns; now it is situated within the conflict between the state and the nomad. This conflict between the images of thought is a conflict between a mode of thought that privileges fixed forms and stable movements versus 'thought without an image' that is founded upon difference and events. The differential relation of forces that constitutes capital is obscured by state thought that deals only with equal and interchangeable subjects. At this point, however, the relation is less an opposition than a process

---

55   Lazzarato 2004, p. 96.
56   Lazzarato 2004, p. 112.

by which the former is continually captured by the latter. State thought requires the deterritorialisation of nomad thought, just as capital requires labour. What this trajectory underscores is not just the virtual differential relations underlying any delimited society, that every society is the realisation and limitation of various social possibilities, but that these different relations are produced and actualised by abstract subjective activity.

Deleuze and Guattari thus offer a more radical, or at least more interesting, understanding of the phrase 'there is no such thing as society' than the one made famous by Margaret Thatcher: society is a fetish (albeit one with incredibly pervasive effects), but what it misrepresents is not some underlying reality of 'individuals and families', but an abstract subjective activity, which is another way of saying that what is real is the indetermination and transformative nature of activity itself. Deleuze and Guattari rearticulate a different link between labour and revolutionary consciousness than the one that has traditionally held sway in Marxism. It is not a matter of a dialectical negation, or a historical telos, labour power taking the subjective form of the proletariat as that class with nothing to lose but its chains. Production in Deleuze and Guattari is not the act of a subject at all, it is an abstract subjective activity, an activity that exceeds subjectivity and constitutes it. It even exceeds any attempt to delimit it to a specific type of activity, to designate it as labour. As Deleuze and Guattari argue, capitalism entails a fundamental, almost ontological transformation of what constitutes subjectivity and objectivity: an unqualified and global subjectivity encounters an unspecified object, or, in more conventional terms, labour power confronts the commodity. The connection between this activity and revolution does not pass through a subject of history, but rather passes through the relationship between the virtual and the actual, the creative activity constitutive of society and its actual articulation and concealment within a specific society.

This activity does not just produce the actual world, but as Lazzarato argues, the possible world as well, producing the halo of the virtual that accompanies the actual. To become revolutionary is to grasp this potential underlying the present, the virtual underlying the actual. The virtual is always already present in every labour, in every action. Politics is no longer a struggle over this world, even of its contradictions, but a production of new worlds. Another world is always possible.

CHAPTER 8

The Affective Economy: Producing and Consuming Affects in Deleuze and Guattari

The thought of Gilles Deleuze (and Félix Guattari) bears an ambiguous relation with respect to the 'affective turn' in social and political thought that it supposedly helped initiate. This ambiguity touches on the very role and meaning of affects. From Deleuze's writings on Nietzsche and Spinoza through the collaborations of *Capitalism and Schizophrenia* Deleuze and Guattari insist on the central role of the affects, joy, sadness, fear, and hope, as structuring individual and collective life. In that sense, Deleuze and Guattari are rightfully hailed as central figures in a turn towards affect. However, if, as some argue, the 'affective turn' is a turn towards the lived over the structural and the intimate over the public, then Deleuze and Guattari's thought has a much more complex relation to affects. The broader polemical target of Deleuze and Guattari's *Anti-Oedipus*, beyond the specific polemics with psychoanalysis, is any explanatory theory that would reduce social relations to expressions of individual passions and desires. Deleuze and Guattari's claim that there is only 'desire and the social, and nothing else' is oriented against such individualistic accounts of not only social relations but subjectivity as well. Moreover, Deleuze and Guattari's theory of capitalism argues that it reproduces itself in and through the encounter of abstract quantities of money and labour power, and as such is a social relation that is indifferent to the beliefs and meaning that we attach to it. Thus, if affect is central to Deleuze and Guattari's thought it is necessary to add the caveats that affect must be thought of as anti-individualistic rather than individualistic, as social rather than intimate, and as impersonal, reflecting the abstractions that dominate life.

The caveats with respect to affect are as much strengths as they are limitations. Which is to say that it is not a matter of simply reconciling the concept of affect with Deleuze and Guattari's critiques of oedipal explanations and theory of capital, but of producing a concept of affect which is both anti-individualistic and adequate to the real abstractions and structural complexities of contemporary capitalism. If affect is to be the basis of a critical theory of contemporary society it must be radically separated from individualist accounts of social relations, accounts that have become increasingly pervasive in a neoliberal self-help culture, on the one hand, and attuned to the 'real abstractions' of contemporary capitalism, on the other. Affect must be a way of grasping the abstractions that determine individual and collective life, rather than a retreat into an interior free of them.

1   Intensive Affects and Extensive Emotions

Deleuze's engagement with affects is framed by two different philosophers, Spinoza and Gilbert Simondon. It was Spinoza who recognised both the ontological dimensions of affects, defining everything by its capacity to affect and be affected, and the political and social dimension of affects, which is to say that affects orient not only individual striving but do so only in and through encounters and relations with others. Political collectives are defined more by common structures of feeling than common notions and ideas. The central task of politics, any politics, is then of organising and defining the affects. Affects are thus necessarily both anti-humanist, defining all of existence in various ways, and transindividual, passing in and through relations with others. Deleuze's definition, or use of affects, exceeds Spinoza's in that he adds another distinction, that of a distinction between the intensive order of affects and the extensive order of emotions. This definition is close to Simondon, as we will see below, for whom affects correspond to the intense and metastable dimension of existence, defined by tensions and transformations, while emotions are more defined and individuated. It is thus no surprise that this distinction has been read by affect theorists, such as Brian Massumi, to correspond to a distinction between affect, understood as an impersonal intensity, and emotion, understood as a subjectivised and individuated feeling. As Massumi writes,

> An emotion is a subjective content, the sociolinguistic fixing of the quality of an experience, which is from that point onward defined as personal. Emotion is qualified intensity, the conventional consensual point of insertion of intensity into semantically and semiotically formed progressions, into narrativizable action-reaction circuits, into function and meaning. It is owned and recognized. It is crucial to theorize the difference between affect and emotion.[1]

While such a distinction may help orient Deleuze's thought of affect, it is completely absent from Spinoza's work. Spinoza's use of the term affect, affectus in Latin, is absolutely and rigorously consistent; affects define not only the differ-

---

1   Massumi 2002, p. 28.

ent states of human subjective life, from the basic joy and sadness to the complex and ambivalent affects of jealousy and ambition, but define everything –
every finite thing has a capacity to affect or be affected. Affects are less some
uniquely human attribute, making us a kingdom within a kingdom, than the
general rule of existence of being modified or affected by encounters and relations, of which human life is only a particularly complex instance. For Spinoza
we are constituted and individuated through our affects, affective composition
differs from individual to individual, but this individuation does not take the
form of a distinction between affects and emotions.

Despite these terminological differences it is thus possible to understand
affect in Deleuze as reconciling two different problems, Spinoza's emphasis
on the political organisation of affect, and Simondon's emphasis on affects as
individuation. Simondon's thought is oriented around a central problematisa-
tion of the individual. Individuation has to be considered as a process and not
the default state of being. This process moves from a milieu that is considered
preindividual, made up of tensions and relations, to a process of individuation
that increasingly encompasses different levels and aspects, biological, psychic,
and social. The social is then not a negation of individuation, but its condition. Transindividuality is the fact that the social is not so much a suppression
of individuality, a loss of the individual in the collective, but its transformation and condition. Within this relation the distinction between affect and
emotion figures twice. First in that affects are less individuated than emotions:
while emotions are the emotions of specific subjects relating to specific objects,
affects are less differentiated and individuated, constitute more of an inchoate sense or sensibility. Second in that affects are intensive while emotions are
extensive. The passage from affects to emotions is part of general individuation,
and as such it necessarily passes through the constitution of collectivity. As
Simondon writes:

> If one is able to speak in a certain sense of the individuality of a group
> or such and such a people, it is not by virtue of a community of action,
> too discontinuous to be a solid base, nor of the identity of conscious rep-
> resentations, too large and too continuous to permit the segregation of
> groups; it is at the level of affective-emotional themes, mixtures of rep-
> resentation and action, that constitute collective groups.[2]

If it is to have any individuality at all, the individuality of the collective must be
sought at the level of particular affects and emotions, particular ways of feeling

---

2 Simondon 2005, p. 248.

and perceiving the world, which are often tied to particular objects. In place of the rigid distinction between affects and emotions, in which one is social and the other individual, Simondon argues that both individuals and collectives are constituted by affects and emotions; which is to say that individuals individuated as subjects and the individuation of collectivity, the constitution of definite collectives, are both constituted through the preindividual dimension of affects, and their increasing individuation into emotional evaluations. Collectives are defined by their 'structures of feeling'.

Despite the terminological difference of affect and emotion, both Spinoza and Simondon see affect as something that passes between the preindividual and the transindividual (even if these specific terms are missing from the former). For Simondon affects are part of the metastable milieu that remains even as individual emotions and perceptions are constituted. The affective dimension carries over from the preindividual, constituting a kind of indetermination at the heart of individuation, an indetermination that demands a social dimension in order to be at least partially resolved. In a similar fashion, Spinoza's affects are preindividual: they are less determinate states of individuals and properties of objects than passages and transformations, increases and decreases of power. Joy is nothing other than a passage from a lesser to a greater perfection and sadness is only the opposite. They are intensities, transformations of states, rather than determinate conditions. The states cannot be separated from their supposed opposites, from the ambivalence of the affects; sadness cannot be rigorously separated from joy, hate from love. As much as the affects are less determined states than an index of their transformation, constituting a process of the constitution and destruction of individuation, they are necessarily transindividual. Or, more to the point, it is because the affects are always situated in the increases and decreases of power that they are necessarily transindividual. For Simondon the progression of individuation that takes place between affects and emotions necessarily passes through the transindividual as affects coalesce around perceptual points of view and relations.[3] While in Spinoza it is not that one passes from the preindividual affects to individuated emotions, but the basic affects of love and hate enter into increasingly individuated combinations as they shape the affective composition of an individual. As Spinoza writes, 'each affect of each individual differs from the affect of another as much as the essence of one from the essence of the other' (EIIIP57). The different essences are nothing other than the different compositions and combinations of affects. Affects and emotions are the transindividual intersection between individual and collective individuation.

---

3   Simondon 2005, p. 261.

The difference of terminology between affect and emotion risks obscuring other, more salient, differences between Simondon and Spinoza. Spinoza's relational account of the various affects is oriented around a fundamental distinction, the fundamental axiological distinction of an increase or decrease in power.[4] It is this distinction that initially distinguishes joy and sadness, and is carried over into the various permutations of love and hate. This is not to suggest that this duality constitutes some kind of core that all of the affects could be reduced to, so all that matters is joy or sadness, increase or decrease in power. There is a constitutive tension between the basic orientation of joy and sadness and the constitutive complexity of the myriad ways sadness and joy are combined and articulated. Second, this duality of joy and sadness is divided again in the split between the joyful passive affects and the sad passive affects, between those affects which are joyful, reflecting an increase of power, but have an external cause, and those that have their own internal determination.[5] At the level of affects one divides into two. This complicates the initial axiology of joy and sadness, introducing the idea that there is a negative dimension to passive joys, a possibility that they can be excessive, and a positive dimension, or at the very least a utility, to such passive sad affects as fear and humility. Spinoza's definition of the affects is situated within the ethical horizon of becoming active.

Between Simondon and Spinoza we have the basic coordinates that orient Deleuze's thoughts on affect. Affects are situated within the process of collective and individual individuation, constituting the basis of both collective relations and individual subjectivity. The axis of the individual and collective is in turn bifurcated by the axis dividing the becoming active from becoming passive. Which is to argue that affects are the conditions of both subjection, and transformation, situated between power and individuation.

2   Consuming Affects

Anti-Oedipus, the first of the two volumes of *Capitalism and Schizophrenia*, opens with a citation of the fundamental political question of Spinoza's work, 'Why do men fight for their servitude as if it was salvation?'[6] Spinoza's answer to this question necessarily involved the affects of fear, ambition, and hope as they structure both political life and individual desires. Thus, it is somewhat odd to

---

4   Sharp 2011, p. 40.
5   Bove 1996, p. 130.
6   Deleuze and Guattari 1983, p. 29.

note that affect does not appear in *Anti-Oedipus*, at least by name. That it does not appear by name does not mean that it does not appear in *Anti-Oedipus*. Affect appears between the lines in terms of both the general problems outlined above, and, more importantly, *Anti-Oedipus* shifts the basic problem of servitude and salvation in Spinoza's thought from politics understood as the rule of tyranny to political economy.

Affect appears first in *Anti-Oedipus* under a different name, that of 'Stimmung', or mood. While the term 'Stimmung' suggests Heidegger, whom philosophers such as Étienne Balibar and Antonio Negri have recognised as the other, often opposed, philosopher of affect, the reference is to Nietzsche by way of Klossowski. Either way the fundamental effect suggests a broader basis for a philosophy of affect. What ties these different and disparate philosophies together is the assertion of the unavoidable affective or emotional dimension of all thought and practice, as a fundamentally orienting dimension of thought. Deleuze and Guattari situate Stimmung, the intensities of affect, with the third synthesis, that of the conjunctive synthesis of consumption. A few provisional conclusions can be drawn from this placement (without necessarily engaging Deleuze and Guattari's entire reading of syntheses). First and foremost: affects are consumed, this consumption comes after the synthesis of the production and the recording of desire. Deleuze and Guattari locate the subject on this synthesis. It comes after the production of desire and the recording of desire, caught between the tension between the forces that constitute the world and their inscription. As Deleuze and Guattari write,

> Thus this subject consumes and consummates each of the states through which it passes, and is born of each of them anew, continuously emerging from them as a part made up of parts, each one of which completely fills up the body without organs in the space of an instant.[7]

Deleuze and Guattari's conception of subject can be compared to Spinoza's assertion that we do not want something because it is good, but we call it good because we want it, desire it, and strive for it. Our affects come after the history, a history of production and recording, that determine them, and our awareness of affects comes even after that. Subjectivity is secondary to, and unaware of, the process that produces it. It is situated between desiring-production and the body without organs, between the process of production and its product, a product that in turn appropriates the various processes of production. Phrased

---

7 Deleuze and Guattari 1983, p. 41.

differently, we could say that affects, intensities, are always situated between the process of individuation, the production and practices that produce and exceed individuation, and its product, the individual, between the conditions of individuation and individuation itself. Affect is the instability and tension of the relation of individuation and production, and as such it can always misrecognise its conditions. As Deleuze and Guattari cite one of Marx's more prosaic statements, 'we cannot tell from the mere taste of wheat who grew it: the product gives us no hint as to the system and the relations of production'.[8] Deleuze and Guattari draw profound insights from this statement, connecting it to the idea of commodity fetishism, a process of production. This is the condition for oedipal subjectivity, a subject that continually misrecognises the conditions of its production, seeing itself as the product of the family rather than the historical process which has produced it.

What does it mean to consume affect, or think of affect as consumption, and how does it relate to both the theory of capital and the critique of Oedipus? Deleuze and Guattari's particular rewriting of the distinction between precapitalist and capitalist economic formations focuses on the role of the family in social production and reproduction. As Deleuze and Guattari argue, the various social formations that precede capitalism all have as their defining characteristic the fact that the very relations that produce and reproduce individuals are directly intertwined with the praxis and politics of social reproduction. Familial relations are directly both political and economic. It is only in capitalism, in the massive privatisation of desire, that there is a separation of reproduction from social production. Capital puts to work deterritorialised flows of labour; it is thus indifferent to the specific marking or memories of individuals. As Deleuze and Guattari write,

> The alliances and filiations no longer pass through people but through money; so the family becomes a microcosm, suited to expressing what it no longer dominates. In a certain sense the situation has not changed; for what is invested through the family is still the economic, political, and cultural social field, its breaks and flows. Private persons are an illusion, images of images or derivatives of derivatives.[9]

Of course the family still continues to reproduce social relations, but it does so paradoxically, through its separation and privatisation. The family becomes an

---

8   Deleuze and Guattari 1983, p. 24.
9   Deleuze and Guattari 1983, p. 264.

intimate space that represents social relations rather than reproducing them; all of society is seen through the idea of the father and the mother. Presidents and dictators become father figures and nations become motherlands: all of history and society is folded back into the family. This representation is itself a kind of reproduction, but one that has been privatised and depoliticized because it is outside of the conditions of social production.

Capitalism is defined by social production that passes through axioms of abstract quantities, flows of money and labour that are the real relations of alliance and filiation, rather than codes. Codes have become private matters, searches for meaning. This split between production and reproduction constitutes a very particular affective relation as well, which Deleuze and Guattari summarise as 'the age of cynicism, accompanied by a strange piety. (The two taken together constitute humanism: cynicism is the physical immanence of the social field, and piety is the maintenance of a spiritualized Urstaat)'.[10] These two affects, cynicism and piety, correspond to the division of social production and reproduction. In the first, in the axioms of capital, we have a social order that reproduces itself without meaning or code. Axioms merely set up a relation between two quantities, a flow of labour and a flow of money. One does not believe in, or justify, the rate at which labour is exchanged for money – it simply is. Cynicism is an affect attuned to the indifference of the axioms that produce and reproduce social life, the recognition that the flows of the market mean nothing, have no justification, than their brute effectivity. Piety, and belief, is reserved for the home, for the intimate sphere of reproduction that becomes the source of all pleasure and pain. Capitalism's affective economy of cynicism and piety is thus distinguished from the savage economy of cruelty and the barbarian economy of fear, both of which were public despite all of their cruelties. Deleuze and Guattari's division of affective life between cynicism and piety is given a contemporary update by Paolo Virno, who writes,

> It is no accident, therefore, that the most brazen cynicism is accompanied by unrestrained sentimentalism. The vital contents of emotion – excluded from the inventories of an experience that is above all else an experience of formalisms and abstractions – secretly returns simplified and unelaborated, as arrogant as they are puerile. Nothing is more common than the mass media technician who after a hard day at work, goes off to the movies and cries.[11]

---

10   Deleuze and Guattari 1983, p. 225.

11   Virno 2004, p. 18.

What connects these two theories of affect in contemporary society is that what is depleted from any affective investment in public life, in the activities of work and politics, returns in private life.

What ties together cynicism and piety, indifference and sentimentality, is that each affect is in some sense passive. These affects are passive in two senses. First, the conditions of their production are elsewhere, outside of the familial space in which they are produced. Secondly, the conditions of the production of affects cannot be acted on. The axioms remain outside the sphere of politics, of individual and collective action. They are each passive, but in different senses. Cynicism, the affect attached to the working of the economy, confronts an economy that is perceived as being indifferent to human actions, while piety attaches itself to the family, which is perceived as being absolutely ahistorical. Far from seeing the privatisation of desire and affects as liberation, as setting it free from the collective structures and relations, Deleuze and Guattari see it as its subjection. To be passive is to be acted on, without acting in turn. The Spinozist critique of passivity is coupled with Marx's critique of fetishism: it is not just that we are passive in the face of the structures and relations that determine us, we are unable to comprehend them, relating them back to ideal representations, the family, the father's love, rather than material conditions. Representation, especially the representation that passes through the interiorised conflicts and codes of the family, making the entire outside world an allegory for it, is the ultimate repression of production, of the productive powers of desire.

The genealogy of Oedipus is one in which intensity, what Deleuze and Guattari refer to as the 'immense germinal flow', desiring-production in all of its multiple connections and multivalent associations, is eventually interiorised, extended into representations. The process begins in the first coding of desire, the mnemotechnics that breed and constitute a 'man that can keep promises', and culminates in the private home. Affects have lost their intensity, their productivity and multiplicity, to become grounded in the family, to become representations of the world rather than its production. There is nonetheless a tension in *Anti-Oedipus* between a genealogy of the specific affects of cynicism and piety, affects that reflect the split between production and reproduction in capitalism, and a general critique of the reduction of the entire level of affect to consumption and representation, the reduction of intensity to extension, and production to representation. In the former the rise of Oedipus and capital is associated with particular 'sad affects', those of cynicism and piety, while in the latter it is a matter of not so much the particular constitution of affects, as a general reduction of affects to consumption, to representation, and privatisation.

3   Capturing Affects

Of the many conceptual and rhetorical changes that underlie the shift from *Anti-Oedipus* to *A Thousand Plateaus*, perhaps one of the most striking is the loss of Oedipus as a target of critique. The elimination of the entire polemic against Freud and psychoanalysis shifts fundamentally the status of affect. Affect is no longer associated with consumption, and thus with the privatisation of desire, but is part of a general dimension of the micropolitics of society. The ninth plateau on 'Micro-Politics and Segmentarity' resumes some of the central themes of *Anti-Oedipus'* social theory, only now they are presented less as a genealogy of oedipal subjectivity and more as a general theory of the micropolitics of all of society.

The first task of any such theory is to differentiate between the molecular and the molar. These terms do not address scale, with the molecular constituting the private spaces of home or family, and the molar addressing the state and its institutions. The molecular is not more individual than the molar, and the molar is not more collective than the molecular. Rather the molecular and the molar constantly intersect at all levels of society and subjectivity, framing two different ways of perceiving, two different politics. As Deleuze and Guattari write,

> In short, everything is political, but every politics is simultaneously a macropolitics and a micropolitics. Take aggregates of the perception or feeling type: their molar organization, their rigid segmentarity, does not preclude the existence of an entire world of unconscious micropercepts, unconscious affects, fine segmentations that grasp or experience different things, are distributed and operate differently. There is a micropolitics of perception, affection, conversation, and so forth.[12]

The terminology of the molecular and the molar was already at work in *Anti-Oedipus*, specifically in the final, programmatic section dedicated to schizoanalysis, but it operated in tension with the genealogy of Oedipus, and an ironic conception of history in which savagery, barbarism, and capitalism culminate in Oedipus, a kind of motley painting of everything ever believed.

A Thousand Plateaus could be understood as a culmination of the positive project of schizoanalysis over the polemical one, as the critique of Oedipus, of psychoanalysis, gives way to the construction of an ontology and politics of

---

12   Deleuze and Guattari 1987, p. 213.

assemblages, a nomadic politics. It is in many ways an an-oedipal book rather than an anti-oedipal book, which not only does not need to kill any fathers, Oedipus, Freud, Lacan, but also no longer pays tribute to any lineage, any fili-ation. In place of the multiple debts to Marx, Nietzsche, and even Artaud and Kafka, we get a series of nomadic borrowings and deterritorialisations from various fields and disciplines from ancient history to ethology and the study of birdsongs. While such a distinction captures much of the shift of tone and style between the books, it does not fully capture what is at stake. Eduardo Viveiros de Castro has offered two points of reorientation that shed light on the shift between the two volumes. As Viveiros de Castro argues, in the lat-ter volume 'becoming' plays the same cosmological and political role as pro-duction does in the former.[13] Desiring production is replaced by the various becomings, woman, animal, etc. This shift from production to becoming marks another shift, one in which filiation is no longer the privileged term of an ontology of social relations, but alliance is. In the first volume, filiation, the intense germinal influx of desire and production, was what every society must repress, and emerges in the productive capacity of capital. Alliance is always the inscription, the coding of this intensity into determinant subjects, goals and desires. It is only once filiation is coupled with alliance that we get social reproduction, the rule of the relations of production over the forces, while in the second volume it is alliance, the alliances between humans and anim-als, the nomads and the outside, that constitutes the basis for becoming and transformation. Filliation, the lines of descent, are always those of the state, of memory and authority. This shift could be understood as a shift of critical tar-gets, even politics, from the critique of capital, which appropriates the power of filiation, appearing as the quasi-cause of capitalist production, to the cri-tique of the state, which subordinates alliance to the state as a condition of belonging. The task of *Anti-Oedipus* was to think a production irreducible to teleological and instrumental logics of production, breaking production from the 'mirror of production', while the task of *A Thousand Plateaus* (at least some of the latter plateaus) is to think exchange irreducible to the possessive indi-vidualistic foundations of the social order. Thus, the first volume endeavored to break the production, an intensive filiation, free from its subordination to the inscription of dominant orders and relations, the domination of dead labour over the living, while the second endeavours to break alliance, an alliance of becoming free from the alliance of the state. As Viverios de Castro summarises this shift, 'The concept of becoming effectively plays the same axial cosmo-

---

13   Viveiros de Castro 2009, p. 133.

logical role in *A Thousand Plateaus* that the concept of production plays in *Anti-Oedipus*'.[14]

Returning to the question of affect, it is possible to ask what do these shifts of focus, alliance and filiation, production and becoming, relate to, and resituate the idea of affect. We have already seen how *Anti-Oedipus* juxtaposes the productive nature of desire, of affect, from its consumption in the family, effectively drawing a line of demarcation between two filiations, one intensive and productive, the other extensive and consumptive. What line of demarcation separates becoming from alliance organised under the categories of the state? For Deleuze and Guattari this distinction has to do with an apparatus of capture. An apparatus of capture functions through two terms, through direct comparison and monopolistic appropriation.[15] In the first case, direct comparison reduces the various activities to one homogenous activity, in the case of labour, or the various objects to instances of one homogenous object, in the case of the commodity. The second case, monopolistic appropriation, is not a secondary accumulation imposed upon this comparison but its necessary precondition. As Deleuze and Guattari write, 'Surplus labor is not that which exceeds labor; on the contrary, labor is that which is subtracted from surplus labor and presupposes it. It is only in this context that one may speak of labor value, and of an evaluation bearing on the quantity of social labor, whereas primitive groups were under a regime of free action or activity in continuous variation'.[16] It is the monopoly, the appropriation by force which constitutes the very ground that compares different activities, different objects, making them interchangeable.

The point of contrast to this apparatus of capture is becoming. Becoming establishes a relation, between man and woman, humanity and animals, but it is never a relation predicated on a shared identity, is never an exchange. 'A becoming is not a correspondence between relations. But neither is it a resemblance, an imitation, or, at the limit, an identification'.[17] A becoming is a transformation, but not one that passes in and through discernible identities, not a matter of some thing becoming some thing else, but is a transformation at the level of the preindividual, a reorganisation at the level of the very conditions of individuation. If capture passes through hierarchy and identity, revealing the secret unity that connects identity to hierarchy, then becoming passes through immanence and transformation, undoing both iden-

---

14   Viveiros de Castro 2009, p. 133.
15   Deleuze and Guattari 1987, p. 444.
16   Deleuze and Guattari 1987, p. 442.
17   Deleuze and Guattari 1987, p. 237.

tity and hierarchy. This is why becomings pass through the very hierarchies that place men above women, humans above animals, undoing them by challenging the very identity of man and woman, human and animal. The examples of becoming are drawn from the history and mythology of transformations, where humans take on the qualities of animals and vice versa, transformations that exceed imitation or resemblance. Becomings are alliances, but strange alliances that constitute neither resemblance nor identity. The apparatus of capture makes the disparate similar by subjecting them to the same standard and the same rule; in contrast to this becoming makes the similar different, even from itself, undoing all standards and all hierarchies of comparison.

It is in this context, in the distinction between capture/exchange and becoming, that we get a definition of affect. As Deleuze and Guattari write, 'For the affect is not a personal feeling, nor is it a characteristic; it is the effectuation of a power of the pack that throws the self into upheaval and makes it reel'.[18] Affects are tied to becomings, to transformations. If we then wanted to think of affects in terms of an opposition to emotions it is possible to argue that emotions are affects rendered comparable and exchangeable. Thus, we could place affects and emotions alongside the opposition between free action and work, in which the second term is the comparison and capture of the latter. Emotions then are not only more individuated, more discrete and determined, they are comparable and more exchangeable. From this perspective to have an emotion is to have a determinate feeling, sadness, joy, etc., while affects are less discernible feelings than indices of transformation. These discernible emotions constitute a common point of comparison, a common ground of experience between interchangeable subjects. Despite the fact that Spinoza argued that there are as many loves and hates as there are objects to love and hate, and as many lovers and haters, revealing the nominalist multiplicity underlying the oppositions of love and hate, we continue to speak of love and hate, jealousy and envy, as if they were always the same thing, constituting a common ground of comparison and experience. It would also be possible to argue that these two different organisations of feeling refer to two fundamentally different planes: on the first, that of affects, there are only relations of movement, change and transformation, while on the second, that of emotions, there is always a reference to a hidden plane of transcendence. Emotions always seem to refer us back to some transcendent idea of human nature, an idea that is all the more pernicious in remaining entirely hidden.

---

18   Deleuze and Guattari 1987, p. 240.

The opposition between affect and emotion then would refer back to the underlying opposition of Deleuze and Guattari's work, the opposition between immanence and transcendence. Fredric Jameson has criticised Deleuze and Guattari, especially the later Deleuze and Guattari of *A Thousand Plateaus*, for departing from the material analysis of the production of desire for an increasingly moral distinction between concepts such as virtual/actual, immanent/transcendent.[19] However, this opposition is less a stark binary between good and bad terms that one can select or choose, than it is a relation of production and representation, organisation and its capture. It is necessary to see the hierarchy and transcendence that constitutes the apparatus of capture as nothing other than a product of the organisation of immanent relations. Frédéric Lordon and Andre Orlean have coined the term 'immanent transcendence' to characterise the production of the transcendent by the immanent.[20] Their primary point of reference is Spinoza, whose ethics and politics could be understood as an examination of how it is that the organisation of striving produces multiple ideals of transcendence, from the state to God. These are not empty illusions, but actually reorganisations of desire functioning like feedback loops – the points of resonance that Deleuze and Guattari discuss. We organise our lives around these concepts, making them effectively true. The same point could be raised with respect to emotions: once an affect is labeled, recognised, and made a common point of comparison, it functions as an ordering principle for future affects. Affects become the raw material for a socially recognised system of emotions. From this perspective it then becomes even easier to relate these affects to 'ideal' and transcendent modes of causation – the taste of wheat tells us nothing of the conditions that have produced it.

Such a reading of the distinction between emotion and affect corresponds to the shift in the definition and deployment of axioms in the second volume of *Capitalism and Schizophrenia*. In the first volume the emphasis on axioms was on their indifference to meaning and belief as social reproduction was in some sense divorced from the reproduction of the family. Axioms were juxtaposed to both the collective meaning of codes and the private meaning of recoding. The affective tenor of axioms was that of cynicism, of an indifference to meaning and belief, this affective evacuation was coupled with the recoding of various forms of piety and nostalgia. In the second volume, however, the emphasis shifts from an opposition between axioms and codes to one internal to axioms; it is an opposition between the denumerable sets that axioms act on

---

19   Jameson 1997, p. 411.
20   Lordon and Orléan 2008, p. 246.

and manipulate and the nondenumerable sets that exceed them. As Deleuze and Guattari write,

> What characterizes the nondenumerable is neither the set nor its elements; rather, it is the connection, the 'and' produced between elements, between sets, and which belongs to neither, which eludes them and constitutes a line of flight. The axiomatic manipulates only denumerable sets, even infinite ones, whereas the minorities constitute 'fuzzy' nondenumerable, nonaxiomizable sets, in short, 'masses', multiplicities of escape and flux.[21]

The nondenumerable relates to the becomings that exceed capture and subjectifications. Axioms can be added or subtracted for every identity, but cannot contend with the passages and transformations which exceed identity. Affects are the moments of transformation, the increases and decreases of power that pass between the determinable and identifiable emotions. They are preindividuated, to use Simondon's terminology, or ambivalent in Spinoza's sense. Affects are what exceed the defined and denumerable states. However, as such they risk being simply epiphenomenal, vanishing moments of transformation that pass between determinate states.

The opposition of affect and emotion then returns us to what could be considered the question of revolution as understood by Deleuze and Guattari. It is not a matter of consolidating all of these various affects and intensities of change and transformation into a new code or axiom, referring them back to some higher unity of organisation, but of constituting a politics of becoming, a minor politics of transformative possibilities. In *Anti-Oedipus* there was a search for the figure of this transformation, the schizo, the revolutionary etc., while *A Thousand Plateaus* searches for the nomad, the minority, the becomings that pass beneath identities and relations. The overall project remains fundamentally the same. However, there is a difference in that the first book stresses the figural dimension of this rupture, hence the 'schizo', while in the second the schizo not only disappears almost entirely, but the emphasis is on the minority, the becoming, that which exceeds representation and axiomatisation. This difference of focus could be seen as something of an improvement, removing the awkwardness of arguing for something that could be considered pro-schizophrenia. The minor politics of the nondenumerable set avoid such awkward identifications. However, the difference of focus also raises the ques-

---

21   Deleuze and Guattari 1987, p. 470.

tion as to what extent a politics can bypass figures, codes, and emotions alto-gether? Is it possible to constitute a politics of affects that would not require reterritorialisation in new emotions, a new structure of feeling.

4   Affective Consumptions and Productions

The concept of affect, and its attendant concepts and provocations, shifts in the two volumes of *Capitalism and Schizophrenia*. In the first, the genealogy of affect pivots around a central conceptual opposition, that between production and consumption, but this general distinction between production and con-sumption also constitutes a specific genealogy of affects, of the cynicism and piety that constitute the affective composition of capital. In the latter volume the conceptual distinction shifts from production and consumption to becom-ing and its capture, and the genealogy of affects, to an opposition between affects, understood as indices of transformation, and emotions, understood as determined and subject to capture. History gives way to categorical distinc-tions, even a morality of good and bad. This is Jameson's critique.

Rather than read the transitions and transpositions of affect from *Anti-Oedipus* to *A Thousand Plateaus* as a either a linear trajectory of improvement, in which the concept is developed, or denigration, in which original insights are lost, I prefer to read the two different texts as each posing distinct and dif-ferent problems. These different problems can be understood to be a genealogy of affects in the first text, in which each particular epoch or era of social pro-duction can be understood to have a dominant affect, or affects. In this case cynicism and piety, rationalism and sentimentality, can be understood as the particular affective composition of capital, of a mode of production defined by the separation of production and reproduction. (To which I could add, but it really deserves more than a parenthesis, that these two different tasks can be understood to constitute a gendered division of labour, with the gender-ing of cynicism as the masculine affect par excellence, while sentimentality is feminised. This division cuts through culture as well as economy, constitut-ing various genres of entertainment, from cynical anti-heroes of action films to the sentimentality of lifetime movies). There is much to be said for such an understanding of contemporary capital, making it possible to understand not only the current fatalism that defines economics but also the sentimentality that defines contemporary politics. From this perspective political candidates can be understood by precisely how they articulate and embody this combin-ation of cynicism and sentimentality, deferring to the market while posing for the right photo ops, and shedding tears at the right moment. However, such a division also risks being too historicist, too oriented towards a hegemonic structure of feeling. Against this conception *A Thousand Plateaus* provides a necessary corrective. It makes it possible to label the hegemonic structures of feelings as emotions, as recognised, comparable, and public structures of feeling, reserving the term affects for the transformations that pass between and under these states, never being named or conceptualised. It is through these affects that change happens, not just the change of passing from one emotion to another, but becoming, the transformations that disrupt and undo the existing emotional order.

The first offers us a history of affects, a history that situates affects within the divide between axiom and code, the abstractions that govern life and the codings that constitute its experience, while the second posits affects in terms of their untimely becomings that exceed historical determination. Both are required not only to make sense of both the stabilisations and uncertainties of the present moment, but ultimately to transform it. In order to change the present it is necessary to identify both the dominant structures of feeling, the cynicism and sentimentalisms, but also to identify the affects and becomings that pass between them, that constitute a new sensibility dwelling in the heart of the old.

CHAPTER 9

Beyond Enslavement and Subjection: Deviations from Deleuze and Guattari

One of the minor theoretical interventions of *A Thousand Plateaus* is the distinction between social subjection and machinic enslavement. This distinction is minor not in the sense of a 'minor literature' or 'science', a subversion, but in the more mundane sense that it largely retraces and recapitulates distinctions made elsewhere by others. It appears as one of the borrowed conceptual distinction rather than an invention. As Deleuze and Guattari write,

> There is enslavement when human beings themselves are constituent pieces of a machine that they compose among themselves and with other things (animal, tools), under the control and direction of a higher unity. But there is subjection when the higher unity constitutes the human being as a subject linked to a new exterior object, which can be an animal, a tool, or even a machine.[1]

This distinction is given in the plateau titled 'Apparatus of Capture', and it is subordinated to the larger focus of articulating the relation between the state and market. It makes up no more than two pages, and in many senses seems to borrow from its general theoretical milieu of the sixties and seventies. Machinic enslavement would seem to carry with it the entire history of alienation of dehumanisation that makes the individual part of the machine. Social subjection bears traces of Althusser's famous declaration that 'ideology interpellates individuals as subjects', or of the general 'critique of the subject' developed through Althusser and Foucault. Its only innovation, the only point that goes beyond a general citation of concepts that are the general background of Deleuze and Guattari's particular conceptual innovations, is in presenting these concepts less as theoretical alternatives, pitting humanism against posthumanism, than as different aspects of the same machine, the same apparatus of capture. That is perhaps not the only philosophical innovation and transformation; the distinction between enslavement and subjection carries with it a larger series of references, not just the immediate precursors of Althusser and

---

1   Deleuze and Guattari 1987, p. 131.

Foucault but more distant antecedents in Marx and Gilbert Simondon, but its implications exceed the distinction between part and whole to encompass not only the already mentioned division between the state and market, but also the intersection between technology and politics. Far from being a simple distinction, the division between enslavement and subjection opens up a way to think the history of different formations of subjectivity, and the tensions internal to them in their historicity.

1   The Prehistory of Enslavement and Subjection: Simondon and Marx

The distinction between enslavement and subjection is as much a distinction of technology as politics, mapped onto the distinction between tool and machine. As much as the explicit point of reference is Lewis Mumford's designation of the ancient despotic megamachine, the intersection of technology and individuation encompasses a much larger field of problems, drawing together Gilbert Simondon and Karl Marx. Simondon's earliest work on the mode of existence of technical objects examines the relationship between individuation and technology. Technology stands as both the culmination and the disintegration of the individual. The first is the schema of an individual operating on nature, reshaping nature with a tool. The tool is recognised as subordinate to the individual. The second is that of the machine, which is part of a technological system, a system that displaces the mastery of the individual, incorporating individuals and their tools as part of its general functioning.[2] Simondon goes so far as to argue that as long as technological development was primarily the development of new tools and new devices for the individual, the idea of progress was unproblematic; it is only with the invention of the machine, as the perfection of the system displaces the individual's mastery, that progress becomes a question.[3] The tool reaffirms the individual's autonomy, the machine questions it, thus technology only becomes a question with the machine.

In *Capital* Marx considers what he calls the labour process independently 'of any specific social formation'.[4] Marx describes this process as a general schema in which the worker transforms nature, and him or herself, through the mediation of a tool or instrument. This tool or instrument is introduced first through

2   Simondon 1958, p. 103.
3   Simondon 1958, p. 116.
4   Marx 1977, p. 283.

a subordination to nature and its laws, utilising chemical or physical processes, but through the cunning of reason it becomes a promethean instrument of transformation. It is in this context that Marx cites Hegel's description of the cunning of reason at work in the labour process.[5] Labour is the subordination of human activity to natural laws in order to master them, the negation of the negation. As Marx writes, 'Thus nature becomes one of the organs of his activity, which he annexes to his own bodily organs, adding stature to himself in spite of the Bible'.[6] Despite Marx's claim that the basic schema of all production is made up of activity, object, and tool, the chapter on 'Machinery and Large Scale Industry' which examines the automation system in the factory reduces the worker to a 'conscious organ of the machine'. The tool is identified with a Promethean self-transformation, one that transforms man from god's image to a maker of images and things, while the machine is identified with fragmentation and disruption of the unity of the body. This process of fragmentation culminates in Marx's famous passages known as 'The Fragment on Machines' in which the machine becomes the virtuouso, the skilled worker, and the worker has been reduced to nothing other than a watchman over the labour process, a conscious organ that merely oversees the vast network of machines.[7]

Simondon's general history of technology is similar to Marx's understanding of the development from tools, governed by the figure of the tool as instrument wielded by an individual to machines, which reduce man and 'his tools' to a part of the machine, a conscious organ of a greater machinery. Despite this proximity of his understanding of technology with Marx, Simondon argues that alienation needs to be expanded beyond a purely economic meaning.[8] For Simondon alienation is not limited to the question of ownership of the means of production, but includes the entire psychological and social relationship with one's activity.[9] This psychological and social alienation stems from a division that is at the heart of technology, a division between the part, the immediate task, and the ensemble, the totality. The alienation thus follows a division between

---

5   As Hegel writes, 'Reason is as cunning as it is mighty. Its cunning generally consists in the mediating activity which, while it lets objects act upon one another according to their own nature, and wear each other out, executes only its purpose without itself mingling in the process'; Hegel 1991b, p. 284.

6   Marx 1977, p. 285.

7   Marx 1973.

8   As Muriel Combes argues, Simondon rejects Marx based on a purely 'economistic' interpretation of alienation, alienation as loss of property, something which does not fit with the original articulation of the concept in the *Economic and Philosophical Manuscripts of 1844*; Combes 2013, p. 74.

9   Simondon 1958, *p.* 118.

mental and manual labour, between those who grasp the specific elements of the process, and those who grasp the overall ensemble of technology. It is an alienation of both capitalist, or manager, as personification of the process, and of the worker, as personification of the part, the specific use of this or that part of process.[10] For Simondon alienation follows the basic trajectory of western society according to which a basic unity of form and matter, sense and utility, a unity which can be found in the primitive relation with magic, is increasingly differentiated into different spheres, such as technology and religion, following a logic of specialisation. The machine, with its division between conception and execution, is situated at the end point of this process. As the machine separates part from whole, form from matter, and conception and execution, it leaves both sides of the relation partial and incomplete.[11] This fundamental alienation is the alienation of grasping only one part of this intersection, seeing the part without grasping the whole, or understanding the totality without grasping the parts. The worker and the technician are both alienated from the totality of the labour process.[12] As Simondon writes, 'The figure of the unhappy inventor came about at the same time as that of the dehumanised worker; it is its counter-type and it arises from the same cause'.[13]

Simondon's understanding of the alienation of the worker in contemporary production is extended and developed by Bernard Stiegler. Or, more to the point, Stiegler frames the intersection of Marx and Simondon through the concept of 'proletarianisation'. As with Simondon, proletarianisation must be understood broadly, or at least beyond a simply economic sense: it is not the loss of the means of production that defines proletarianisation, but the loss of the knowledge and skill of the worker. For Stiegler the proletarianisation of the worker, the transformation of the worker into labour power, a quantifiable force, is the precursor of the proletarianisation of the consumer, the loss of the knowledge to live (savoir vivre) that transforms the individual into buying power.[14] In each case the recording and automation of knowledge and gestures leads to a loss of individuation. There is no real difference between a mechanised drill press, a microwavable meal, and an app that uses global position systems: or, if there is any difference, it can only be understood as increasing loss of individuation through an expansion of proletarianisation, as the corporeal and affective aspects of individuation are increasingly mechanised.[15]

---

10   Simondon 1958, p. 119.
11   Simondon 1958, p. 250.
12   Chabot 2013, p. 39.
13   Simondon 2009, p. 21.
14   Stiegler 2010, p. 35.
15   Stiegler 2017, p. 28.

Skills, knowledge, and eventually even taste become part of the machine. Just as Simondon extended alienation from the ownership and control of the labour process to its conception and execution, encompassing more of subjectivity, Stiegler extends proletarianisation to cover the general loss of knowledge and skill in an automated consumer society.

If Simondon gives us the general figure of enslavement, of the individual reduced to part of a machine, it is not to naturalise the other extreme, the worker as craftsman. The skilled worker is not the generic and natural norm from which the demands of the machine can be charted. It also must be grasped as a particular mode of individuation, a particular way of incorporating skills, habits, and knowledge from its general milieu to wield a tool. To put it in terms that become much more important in Simondon's latter work, and also function as a point of intersection between Simondon and Marx, the worker, even one with the most rudimentary skills, must be understood as transindividual, as the intersection of collective skills and knowledge and their specific instantiation.[16] While Simondon provides the conditions to theorize the generation of the individual, the way in which the individual-tool relation must be understood as a particular assemblage, a particular relation of subjectivity and technology, it is Marx who makes the connection of individuation and subjection. For Marx, the 'free worker', the individual who sells his or her labor power, must be historicised, framed in contrast to labour relations that proceed it. Most importantly, selling of labour power must be contrasted with slavery, with the extraction of labour power by compulsion. The slave is driven by fear, by the threat of punishment, while the worker is driven by the fear of being replaced. As Marx writes,

> In contrast to the slave, this labour becomes more productive because more intensive, since the slave works only under the spur of external fear but not for his existence which is guaranteed even if it does not belong to him. The free worker, however, is impelled by his wants. The consciousness (or better: the idea) of free self-determination, of liberty, makes a much better worker of one than of the other, as does the related feeling (sense) of responsibility; since he, like any seller of wares, is responsible for the goods he delivers and for the quality which he must provide, he

---

16   As Étienne Balibar writes, 'We must give this thesis its maximum force to understand the conclusions that Marx wants to reach. Not only is labor socialized historically, so that it becomes transindividual. Essentially it always was, insofar as there is no labor without cooperation, even in its most primitive forms, and the isolation of the productive labourer in relation to nature was only ever an appearance'; Balibar 2014, p. 85.

must strive to ensure that he is not driven from the field by other sellers of the same type as himself.[17]

Marx's comments, part of the posthumously published sixth chapter of *Capital*, 'Results of the Immediate Process of Production', have a prophetic dimension, seeming to prefigure later discussions of subjectivity and subjection. One could read any entire history of writings on the subject and subjection, from Althusser's essay on ideology through Foucault's theorisation of the subject up to Frédéric Lordon's concept of the self-motivation of the worker. All these texts and theories echo the theme found here in Marx: internal compulsion is more effective than external force. Subjection is the internalisation of the very forces of compulsion, the point where the division between constraint and freedom breaks down.

Whereas Simondon expands alienation to become not just the alienation of labour, of the worker, from the process of production to alienation of all in the face of technology, Marx offers a contradiction between the technological and ideological trajectory of labour under capital. The technological process is one that moves from the worker as tool user, as master of nature, to the conscious organ of the machine. It is one of machinic enslavement. In contrast to this the social or legal transformation that initiates capitalism is one in which the worker ceases to be a part of the production process, part of the means of production, as in slavery, and becomes the productive subject, the driving force. Ideologically the direction of history is social subjection. The legal autonomy and isolation that Marx placed at the centre of the labour process have only been extended and deepened by the contemporary forces of individualisation. One is responsible for not only the entirety of the labour process, but for one's own history in it. The modern resumé presents a worker whose entire history, including getting downsized, is represented as a series of choices and decisions.[18] One takes responsibility for things that are entirely outside of their control. One could hope for a contradiction here, a variant of what Marx called 'the moving contradiction', not the contradiction between labour as determinant of value (and participation in wages) and its role as productive force, but a contradiction on the side of subjectivity: the subjective component of labour is reduced to a minimum, a conscious organ, while the subjective dimension of responsibility is increased. Marx, however, gives hints to suggest that this is not a contradiction at all, at least one with any explosive force.

---

17   Marx 1977, p. 1031.
18   This point is borne out by the sociological literature on the current labour situation, such as Richard Sennett's *The Corrosion of Character*.

As the worker becomes less and less the central and organising figure of the production process, becoming a conscious organ to a process that encompasses science, technology, and general social knowledge, he or she is less able to see her contribution to production. It appears that it is capital itself that is productive. As Marx writes,

> This entire development of the productive forces of *socialized labor* (in contrast to the more or less isolated labor of individuals), and together with it the *uses of science* (the general product of social development), *in the immediate process of production*, takes the form [stellt sich dar] of the productive power of capital. It does not appear as the productive power of labor, or even of that part of it that is identical with capital. And least of all does it appear as the productive power either of the individual workers or of the workers joined together in the process of production.[19]

The dots are not entirely connected here, and one could argue that much of the recent writing on subjection has been an attempt to connect them in myriad ways, but Marx would seem to suggest that machinic enslavement, the reduction of the worker to a part in a machine, increases subjection. It does so in at least two ways: first, it disconnects production from the worker's capacity and powers, making it appear as a miraculous attribute of capital itself. To connect the dots further, it could be said to increase the worker's subjection before capital itself: the worker appears to be dependent upon capital for a job, for a livelihood, rather than capital being dependent on the worker for its production. The dots, once connected, draw a picture of a worker who increasingly sees him or herself as dependent upon capital, and responsible for his or her fate, and of a capitalist that is identified as not only the creator of wealth but also of jobs, or, in the parlance of our times, a 'job creator'.

2   Returns of Enslavement

In contrast to Simondon's history of increased alienation, Stiegler's proletarianisation, in which the skilled worker with the tool is replaced by the machine, or even Marx's contradictory history of enslavement and subjection, as mechanical fragmentation is coupled with economic isolation, Deleuze and Guattari offer a history that is rectilinear, moving forward only to return to a slightly

19   Marx 1977, p. 1024.

altered beginning. Machinic subjection is both the beginning and endpoint, but it is not the same machinic subjection. As Deleuze and Guattari write, 'It could be said that a small amount of subjectivation took us away from machinic enslavement, but a large amount brings us back to it'.[20] Deleuze and Guattari's claim has to situated against both Deleuze and Guattari's claim of history and temporality in capital, and the general intertwining of the technological and political dimensions of subjection. The question of the passage from enslavement to subjection and back is both a question of the overall historical trajectory of capital and of the point where technology intersects with politics.

The question of temporality and history, like many questions and concepts, shifts somewhat without completely changing from the first to second volume of *Capitalism and Schizophrenia*. Despite the seemingly paradoxical claim that there can only be a universal history of contingency, of encounters and transformations, Deleuze and Guattari present an underlying historical trajectory that passes from a kind of enslavement, to subjection, and back again. Enslavement begins with the ancient despot, and the ancient state, which is a kind of megamachine. Bodies are reduced to parts of machines by being coded, subject to connections and control. As Deleuze and Guattari write,

> The social machine is literally a machine, irrespective of any metaphor, inasmuch as it exhibits an immobile motor and undertakes a variety of interventions: flows are set apart, elements are detached from a chain, and portions of the tasks to be performed are distributed. Coding the flows implies all of these operations.[21]

Coding, as Deleuze and Guattari present, bears on the constituent parts of subjectivity, their preindividual dimensions: a code restricts not the actions of an individual qua individual, but dictates the different parts of bodies, flows and desire, that can and cannot be conjoined. It is machinic avant la lettre in that it subordinates these parts and their flows back to the social machine. The machine, the code and overcode, defines primitive machines and despotism, but is transformed by capitalism. What defines capital for Deleuze and Guattari is not the 'free worker', liberated from slavery, serfdom, and dependence, free to sell his or her labour, but 'decoding', a divestment in the parts of bodies and their places in the social machine – the privatisation of desire. This decoding follows a kind of proletarianisation, in Stiegler's sense, as the memory and knowledge that is put to work is that of machines, not bodies.

---

20   Deleuze and Guattari 1987, p. 458.
21   Deleuze and Guattari 1983, p. 141.

Capitalism's originality resides rather in the fact that the social machine has for its parts technical machines as constant capital attached to the full body of the socius, and no longer men, the latter having become adjacent to the technical machines – whence the fact that inscription no longer bears directly, or at least in theory has no need of bearing directly, on men.[22]

What Deleuze and Guattari refer to as decoding has as its necessary condition and consequence the shift of codes from bodies to machines. This does not mean that the individual, subjectivity, is left entirely out of the equation, free from any social constraint. Capital functions with axioms, not codes: these axioms are abstract and quantitative rather than concrete and qualitative. Axioms establish a relation between a flow of labour, of abstract labour, and a flow of money. Capital reproduces itself not at the level of code, but the axiom; bodies and with it the entire system of desire is privatised. Capital is indifferent to the intimate details of desire '… Your capital or your labor capacity, the rest is not important'.[23]

It is in this privatisation of desire that we can see something akin to social subjection. The private space, the family, is not entirely excluded from social reproduction, but functions paradoxically through its decoding, its disengagement from production. Individuals exist socially, exist in the sphere of production only as abstract quantities, as labour power, buying power, etc., the axioms of the economy: this liberates a private space, a space of consumption, a consumption of social existence. 'Private persons are therefore images of the second order, images of images – that is, *simulacra* that are thus endowed with an aptitude for representing the first-order images of social persons'.[24] Deleuze and Guattari's critique of familialism is not just a critique of the explanatory power of Oedipus and the family within psychoanalysis, but of the general tendency to make the family the matrix of subjectivity. Social subjection is a split in the subject, a division between one's social function, as impersonal as that may be, and the personal, private manner in which it is experienced. Or as Deleuze and Guattari write, using Lacan's terminology, 'The subject of the statement is the social person, and the subject of the enunciation, the private person'.[25] One speaks of the social person, of world leaders, bosses, and revolutionaries, but one does so insofar as they have been reduced to neuroses and

---

22   Deleuze and Guattari 1983, p. 251.
23   Deleuze and Guattari 1983. p. 251.
24   Deleuze and Guattari 1983, p. 264.
25   Deleuze and Guattari 1983, p. 265.

family dramas. What is occluded here is the social dimension: sociality only appears in the functional abstractions of the economy.

Capital must be understood not simply as the process by which 'all that is holy is profaned, and all that is solid melts into air', as a general form of decoding, of abstraction. As much as the destruction of old traditions, especially those having to do with labour and consumption, is integral to the functioning of capital, it is no less important that it revives and sustains old traditions and authorities, traditions and authorities now rendered private and personal. It has to be understood as a dual process. As Deleuze and Guattari write:

> Civilized modern societies are defined by processes of decoding and deterritorialization. But *what they deterritorialize with one hand, they reterritorialize with the other*. These neoterritorialities are often artificial, residual, archaic; but they are archaisms having a perfectly current function, our modern way of 'imbricating', of sectioning off, of reintroducing code fragments, resuscitating old codes, inventing pseudo codes or jargons ... These modern archaisms are extremely complex and varied. Some are mainly folkloric, but they nonetheless represent social and potentially political forces ... Others are enclaves whose archaism is just as capable of nourishing a modern fascism as of freeing a revolutionary charge ... Some of these archaisms take form as if spontaneously in the current of the movement of deterritorialization ... Others are organized and promoted by the state, even though they might turn against the state and cause it serious problems (regionalism, nationalism).[26]

What *Anti-Oedipus* presents is less a progression from enslavement to subjection, or from subjection back to enslavement, than the coexistence of the two. It is necessary to think subjection, the constitution of a private space for desire, a private meaning outside of codes, as itself a kind of enslavement, or a privatisation of enslavement. The supposed liberty of the private desire, of decoding, that allows one to consume the entire world from the privacy of their home, is itself a kind of subjection. We are subjected at home and enslaved at work.

This division, rather than progression, of two different formations of subjectivity is not without its precursors in Marx. In one of the most rhetorically dense passages in *Capital* Marx distinguishes between the hidden abode of production, the site of the exploitation of labour, and what he referred to as the

---

26   Deleuze and Guattari 1983, pp. 257–8.

sphere of circulation, the market or the space of exchange. In the former one is enslaved, or at least that is what Marx will come to argue in *Capital*, made part of the productive force of capital, but in the latter one is subjected, is seen and sees oneself as a free subject. As Marx writes,

> The sphere of circulation or commodity exchange, within whose boundaries the sale and purchase of labour-power goes on, is in fact a very Eden of the innate rights of man. It is the exclusive realm of freedom, equality, and Bentham. Freedom, because both buyer and seller of a commodity, let us say of labour power, are determined by their own free will. They contract as free persons, who are equal before the law ... The only force bringing them together, and putting them into relation with each other, is the selfishness, the gain and the private interest of each.[27]

Maurizzio Lazzarato offers a theoretical expansion of this polemic by drawing together Deleuze and Guattari's concept of major and minor with that of enslavement and subjection. For Deleuze and Guattari the major and minor distinction is less a matter of a simple quantitative valuation, of more or less, than of standard and deviant. The majority is that which is counted as the norm. The wage, the salary, is as much a semiotic, a technique of representation, as it is a remuneration of labour. It counts labour, positing it as socially necessary and productive. To have a wage is to have one's work recognised as productive, as social, as something that can be contested and changed; to be unwaged is to work invisibly. Unstated but nonetheless important in Lazzarato's focus on the wage and representation is the work of Marxist feminists such as Silvia Federici, Mariorosa Dalla Costa, and Selma James, who argue that as much as the wage is at the base of capitalist exploitation, concealing it in the image of full compensation for work performed, it also conceals the unwaged reproductive work of childcare, cleaning, and countless other domestic tasks that have been naturalised as 'women's work'.[28] Subjection is a kind of inclusion, a recognition of labour, and participation through the wage, but it always has as its basis the productive power of enslavement that exceeds it. As Lazzarato writes,

> Capital, therefore, does not simply extort an extension of labour time (the difference between paid human time and human time spent at the work-

---

27   Marx 1977, p. 280.
28   Federici 2012, p. 16.

place), it initiates a process that exploits the difference between subjection and enslavement. For if subjective subjection – the social alienation inherent to a particular job or any social function (worker, unemployed, teacher, etc.) – is always assignable and measurable (the wage appropriate to one's position, the salary appropriate to a social function), the part of machinic enslavement constituting actual production is never assignable nor quantifiable as such.[29]

The wage addresses or interpellates an individual worker, offering an imaginary representation of their social contribution; production, as Marx argued, exploits transindividual productive capacities. Social subjection and machinic enslavement become not two different epochs, or even two different modes of subjection, but two different individuations acting on the same subjects, or processes of subjection, in different ways. The one affects subjectivity and identity insofar as it is signified, represented, and conceptualised, the other at the level of gestures, affects, and actions.[30] 'Machinic enslavement ... refers to non-representational, operational, diagrammatic techniques that function by exploiting partial, modular, and subindividual subjectivities'.[31] Lazzarato is not explicitly concerned with housework, or the unwaged work of the home, but all work that exceeds its capture and representation in a wage, which is to say all work, since work in general is irreducibly collective and social. Workers are subjectified as individual wage earners, even part of the company, but enslaved as collective bodies and transformations.

3 Technologies of Subjection/Enslavement

The changing political valences of subjection and enslavement is only one part of the picture. Social subjection and machinic enslavement are also tied to the history of technology from the tool to the machine. *Anti-Oedipus* offers its own kind of precursor of the argument that 'a large amount of subjectification brings us back to [enslavement]', tying it explicitly to technology. This point is underscored by the literal machine, or device, the television. Deleuze and Guattari make only a few references to television in their writings, and do not have anything like an explicit theory of it as a medium or technology. However, its few appearances in *Anti-Oedipus* and *A Thousand Plateaus* draw together

29   Lazzarato 2014, p. 45.
30   Lazzarato 2014, p. 39.
31   Lazzarato 2015, p. 184.

subjection and technology in a provocative way, constituting a kind of theory through an example. Television appears in *Anti-Oedipus* as a device for the privatisation of the world. '[T]hese images do not initiate a making public of the private so much as a privatization of the public: the whole world unfolds right at home, without one's having to leave the TV screen'. Television appears again in *A Thousand Plateaus* as the example of subjection leading to enslavement.

> For example, one is subjected to TV insofar as one uses and consumes it, in the very particular situation of subject of the statement that more or less mistakes itself for a subject of the enunciation ('you, dear television viewers, who make T.V. what it is ...'); the technical machine is the medium between two subjects. But one is enslaved by TV as a human machine insofar as the television viewers are no longer consumers or users, nor even subjects who supposedly 'make' it, but intrinsic component pieces, 'input' and 'output', feedback or recurrences that are no longer connected to the machine in such a way as to produce it or use it.[32]

Much of the initial definition of Oedipal, privatised, subjectivity is repeated here. There is the split between the subject of the enunciation and the statement, only now it is related to a constitutive misrecognition: one thinks one enunciates, plays a role in the constitution of television, but one is spoken for without ever speaking. This does not mean that one is entirely passive, beneath the 'subjection', the constant appeals and addresses to the subjects of TV land, there is the collection of information. The subjection of the audience masks and makes possible the enslavement of the market.

Deleuze and Guattari's example is drawn from television, which addresses, or interpellates, individuals as subjects because it has reduced them to input and outputs. The television example is both odd and oddly prescient. One can find the same process at work in Amazon and other online sites: the more one is reduced to an algorithm based on one's shopping, the more the recommendations are tailored to one's particular taste and interests. Social subjection increases with machinic enslavement, the more one is reduced to quantifiable data, the more one's experience is personalised and tailored. As Deleuze argued in his strangely prophetic text on control societies, such technologies move beyond enslavement and subjection. As much as enslavement reduced individuals to conscious organs of machines it still put to work the entire body, the

---

32   Deleuze and Guattari 1987, p. 458.

entire individual, even if that individual just became the eye of conveyor belt or supermarket scanner. Machinic enslavement now takes only one aspect of the individual, one's shopping experiences, debt, knowledge, combining that through algorithms with the knowledge or debt of others that are not physically present or known to each other. This is coupled with technologies of subjection that personalise and modulate their appearance for each viewer or subscriber. No one sees the same google results or twitter feed. There is less 'an internet' than multiple internets all personalised. It is only in contemporary technology, in the age of social media, that the picture Deleuze and Guattari draw from television has come true, of individuals reduced to data, to input and outputs, at the level of enslavement at the same moment they are subjected.

If we can roughly map subjection onto the individual and enslavement onto the mass, the collective, we have to confront the fact that contemporary power functions without these terms. As Deleuze writes, 'Individuals become dividuals and masses become samples, data, markets, or "banks"'.[33] Understanding what Deleuze means by this, and what is at stake in it, is perhaps best approached by the second term. How do masses, data, and markets displace 'masses'? It is not by size or scale, since any of these, markets or masses, could be large or small, but the fact that data, markets, and banks never recognise themselves as such. They are never capable of saying 'we', to borrow Stiegler's terminology. Markets, data, and samples function below the level of transindividuation, they are constitutive of neither individual nor collective identity. Machinic enslavement is always situated at the outside of collective identity. As much as it is collective, necessarily involving multiple bodies inserted into multiple technical apparatuses, this collectivity is not explicitly recognised as such, as bodies and minds are put to work along with bodies and minds that are not seen or recognised. The entire concept of the working class, of the proletariat, is an attempt to make this collectivity explicit, a 'for itself' in Hegelian terminology. However, the contemporary technological and economic reorganisation of production makes this impossible. The workers of a factory can say we, but those that are held together by the more tenuous networks of a 'sharing platform' are less capable of sensing and articulating such a connection. This same basic transformation, from unity to dispersion and from representation to function, also affects the other term, the dividual. If the bank or market operates at a level too broad and dispersed to constitute a mass, the dividual operates at a level too minute, too dispersed to constitute an individual. Even consumption or the market of exchange, formerly the sphere of freedom, equality,

---

33   Deleuze 1995, p. 180.

and Bentham, deals less with individuals, subjects of the market, than drives, desires, sensibilities, and moods. Contrary to what is claimed, consumer society is less an individualistic society than a society of drives, affects, and moods, of the control of the preindividual aspects of society.[34] The line between subjection and enslavement no longer passes between individual and society, but between the preindividual and the transindividual, between that which is constitutive of individuality and that which is constitutive of collectivity.[35]

4   Conclusion

Unravelling and then tying together the technological, economic, and political valences of enslavement and subjection might seem antithetical to Deleuze and Guattari's entire philosophy. After all, as Deleuze and Guattari repeatedly argue, the social machine is not a metaphor: the entire language of machines, apparatuses, and assemblages is posited to situate together the technological, the economic, and political dimensions. However, following Guillaume Sibertin-Blanc's Marxist and Althusserian reading of Deleuze and Guattari, it might be productive to see the overdetermination of enslavement and subjection as simultaneously technological, economic, and political.[36] Doing so highlights the point of their convergence. One can see the way in which the intersection of social subjection and enslavement characterises contemporary capitalism, the intersection of social media, financial speculation, and political fragmentation and individuation. However, one can also see the way in which the different aspects of subjection and enslavement diverge from each other as well. The various forms of machinic enslavement that reduce individuals to drives, clicks, and attention risk producing subjects that do not recognise themselves in the narratives of subjection. Recognising the overdetermined nature of machinic enslavement and social subjection means viewing them without teleology or direction. Neither a teleology that goes from subjection to enslavement, as individual tool users are incorporated into machines, as Simondon argued; nor is there a telos from enslavement to subjection, as bodies incorporated into production are increasingly interpellated as autonomous individuals, to take Marx's argument. Nor is it a matter, as Deleuze and Guattari argued, of a paradoxical trajectory in which subjection is both the movement away from, and ultimately towards, enslavement, or of a technological enslavement

---

34   Stiegler 2009, p. 48.
35   Read 2016, p. 215.
36   Sibertin-Blanc 2016, p. 122.

that completely undermines any subjection, as Lazzarato and Stiegler argued. Rather subjection and enslavement intersect at the level of politics, economics, and technology, as individuals become part of machines, of different technologies, and are subjected to different ideologies.

PART 3

Between Marx and Spinoza: Philosophy and Ideology

∵

CHAPTER 10

The *Potentia* of Living Labor: Negri and the Practice of Philosophy

> But only where theory does not deny practice and practice does not
> deny theory is there character, truth, and religion. Spinoza is the
> Moses of modern freethinkers and materialists.
>
> LUDWIG FEUERBACH, *Principles of the Philosophy of the Future*

∴

A cursory survey of the writings of Antonio Negri presents one with an expansive plurality of topics covered. Negri's writing embraces topics from Spinoza's ontology and political philosophy to works on Marx, the history of political thought, globalisation and the changing conditions and politics of labour. This broad survey of topics by one writer is itself remarkable. What is perhaps more provocative, however, is that within these different books on apparently unrelated themes, there appears a series of concepts, or words – *potentia*, living labour, constituent power, and immaterial labour – which seem to connote or designate a series of interrelated problems. These problems could at least be provisionally situated at the intersection of labour and power: the materiality of a creative power that constitutes the world, not through some power of transcendence, but which creates the world by being entirely immanent to it. Thus, it is not simply the breadth of topics covered: ontology, politics, sociology, etc., which makes Negri an impressive, singular – and ultimately challenging – figure in contemporary philosophy and political thought, but the indication that beneath these seemingly disparate researches there is a unity of a philosophical political project.

But what exactly is this unity? It is in answering this question that some of the traditional ways of understanding the intersection of philosophy and politics fall short of the challenge of Negri's thought. One possibility is to understand Negri's thought as developing an ontology of immanence and power, drawn from the weighty tomes of Spinoza, which is then applied to politics and society. On the other extreme, it is possible to understand Negri as a thinker who interprets philosophy through a history of the socio-political transformations of labour. An ontology 'applied' to the messy realities of politics or a historicisation of the fundamental transformations of ontology. While these two interpretations are possible, they miss the point in that they situate the different spheres of inquiry in a relation that is both hierarchical and one-directional: philosophy determines politics or politics determines philosophy. Negri's thought transforms both the philosophy of politics, proposing a new understanding of power and labour, but also a new political philosophy, a new way of doing philosophy, of situating philosophy in relation to politics, economics, and other forms of knowledge.

What this means can best be grasped by a brief comparison with Louis Althusser. As Louis Althusser argued, Marx's writings are not to be understood as a new *philosophy of praxis*, a philosophy that would elevate praxis to the place that previous (idealist) philosophies had elevated reason or knowledge, but a new *practice of philosophy*, a new way of doing philosophy. As a term for analysis, 'philosophical practice' refers less to the concepts produced or positions taken than the particular manner in which each philosopher has of writing, broaching questions, and producing concepts. It is on this level that Marx's radical break can be measured. For Althusser, this new way of doing philosophy was characterised by the extreme heteronomy of philosophy, its determination and transformation by other forms of practice: economic, political, etc. '... [P]ractice is what philosophy, throughout its history, has never been able to incorporate. Practice is that other thing, on the basis of which it is possible not only to knock philosophy off balance, but also to begin to see clearly into the interior of philosophy'.[1] Althusser insists on the fundamental difference between the 'philosophy of praxis' and the 'practice of philosophy', arguing against philosophers such as Antonio Gramsci and Jean-Paul Sartre who saw praxis as not only the central concept of Marx's philosophy, but as a way to restore the rift between philosophy and Marxism, speculation and practice. Negri's position is irreducible to either terms of the opposition, it is best defined as *developing a new philosophy of praxis through a new practice of philosophy*. In other words, a philosophy of praxis, of the constitutive dimension of human activity, cannot simply be developed speculatively, as a pure movement of thought, but must be developed through a continual encounter with its constitutive conditions and limitations, with the materiality of the world. 'Discontinuity and untimeliness are the soul of theoretical practice, just as the crisis is the key to the development of the real'.[2] This is the unity of his

---

1 Althusser 1990a, p. 249.
2 Negri 1996a, p. 53.

thought, a disjunct unity in which philosophical speculation must continually open itself to historicity and materiality, and the challenge that Negri poses to philosophy.

In the following pages I will outline this challenge by focusing on Negri's interpretation of Spinoza and Marx – obviously only small parts of Negri's corpus. In doing so I will outline Negri's philosophy of praxis, *potentia*, living labour, or constituent power, and show how this concept is developed through a passage of discontinuity that passes through politics, metaphysics, and history in order to reassemble them in a forceful new articulation of materialist philosophy.

1   Part One: Pars Destruens – Pars Construens

The gap, or the disjuncture – that is, thought's relationship to praxis – is articulated by Negri through a reading, and a rearticulation of the relation between the destructive, negative, or critical moment of thought (*pars destruens*) and the creative or affirmative moment in a praxis of thinking (*pars construens*) in Spinoza. The relation of a simultaneous destruction and creation, maintained in their paradoxical unity, is the unstable maintenance of thought at the limit of the concept, and at the edge of praxis, or invention. *Pars destruens* is a total destruction of the presuppositions of thought, the received thoughts and ideas. It is through this destruction that thinking can engage with *pars construens*, a creation, or invention, and thus a praxis and poetics without guarantee.[3] Developing a link between the seventeenth-century practice of critical doubt and social practice, Negri writes: 'Doubt is a social practice destructive of things, not simply of spectres and unreal ideas – destructive to the extent that it affirms liberty'.[4] Unlike Descartes, who follows the path of radical doubt to the point that it brings him back to the same place, the same fire, nightclothes, and sheet of paper, Spinoza's critical practice makes it possible to invent. It is a practice, a tension of thinking that risks itself in the creation of the new.[5]

The relation of *pars destruens/pars construens* is not something which Spinoza's thinking or texts directly offer to a casual or passive reading, it

---

3 William Haver has suggested that the conjunction of pars destruens/pars construens, or a doing that necessarily exceeds knowing in the thought of Negri and Hardt, should be understood as a practice of invention (Haver 1997).

4 Negri 1989, p. 160.

5 Negri 1991b, p. xv.

demands a strategy of reading, and an engagement with the limits and divisions of the text. Negri's reading of Spinoza combines a complex conjunction of interpretive practices. Negri investigates both the historical conditions and the textual articulation of Spinoza's writing, but not through the conventional dialectic of historical context and hermeneutically recuperated meaning. Central to Negri's reading is that Spinoza's thought cannot be reduced to a simple reflection of the historical period of its articulation, that in some sense Spinoza's thought is a 'philosophy of the future': but this irreducibility is not a matter of a simple transcendence of those conditions, or Spinoza's 'discovery' of some 'universal' truth. The irreducibility of Spinoza's thought to its conditions is founded on its relationship to what Negri identifies as the 'crisis'.[6] Historically, at the time of Spinoza's writing, the crisis is the tension between the emerging developments of scientific and productive forces, and the organisation of the 'market', as the organising and mediating force of the social.[7] This crisis is identified historically in the recession and wars of the late 1600s, all of which indicate the impossibility of a smooth transition from feudalism to capitalism; that is, the impossibility of subordinating the new productive forces of science and technology to the old values and order. This crisis is more than a precondition for interpreting Spinoza's thought, and thus more than a simple context, for at least two reasons. The first is the complexity of Spinoza's response to this crisis; the manner in which the historical antagonism of productivity and order becomes a problem and a tension internal to Spinoza's project. The second reason is that this 'crisis' is not a totally discrete event limited to the time of Spinoza's writing, but is extended and displaced, in its repetition, to include the present. The relation, division, or even antagonism, between the multiplicity of immanent relations of constitution and production, what Marx called the forces of production, and the mediating orders of law, state, and market, or what Marx called the relations of production, is the crisis without stasis that is history and historicity. The crisis that Spinoza confronts continues to define the present, in that the present is still defined by this tension, by the difficulty of subordinating the new productive forces to the relations of production.

This thought of the crisis frames the various textual tensions and divisions that Negri explores and articulates in his reading of Spinoza. For Negri, Spinoza's text is divided in both its metaphysics and politics between a neo-Platonist tendency toward the affirmation of a transcendent order in the first foundation of the *Ethics*, and a materialist philosophy of constitution as organisation in the second foundation.[8] The development of the relationship *pars*

---

6   Negri 1991b, p. 266.

7   Negri 1991b, p. 20.

8   A note on the distinction between 'order' and 'organization': As Hardt indicates, order of

destruens/pars construens has as its enabling condition this crisis, and the destruction of any transcendent mediation of this crisis, and of transcendence altogether. '... [T]here are in effect two Spinozas, if only we were able to succeed in suppressing and subduing the suggestions or the apologies that erudite history produces, if we were able to situate ourselves on the solid terrain of the critical and historiographic consciousness of our own times, these two Spinozas would come to life in full play'.[9] If the crisis makes possible a reading of the tensions and divisions of Spinoza's text, then Spinoza also makes possible a reading of the crisis; that is, Spinoza makes possible a reinvestigation and a rethinking of the ontological, subjective, and political dimensions of the contradiction between 'relations and forces of production'.[10] Spinoza makes possible an ontological understanding of production: production is not simply relegated to the economic sphere, but becomes the manner in which praxis changes itself and its own conditions. Production becomes the path to liberation.

According to Negri, Spinoza's *Ethics* opens onto a fundamental paradox, a paradox that stems from the absolute affirmation of substance as infinite being, and as the power of existence. The paradox is the tension between two grounds of ontology: two ways of conceiving the relation between unity and multiplicity, or between substance and the modes. 'In Spinoza a decision is never made between two perspectives: the dynamic one, for which substance is a force, and the static one, for which substance is pure linear coordination'.[11] This paradox is at once the central question of any reading of Spinoza in that it poses all of the old questions of the relation between the infinite and the finite, the substance and the modes, or of what Negri calls the organisation of the infinite; and also, at least in Negri's reading, the question of the very grounds of thought and practice. The paradox is the division between order and organisation, between emanation, which proceeds from substance to the modes, and constitution, which proceeds from the modes to substance. The first foundation of the *Ethics* which Negri locates in Parts I and II, is not only the exposition of this paradox, but its partial and incomplete resolution through the mediating order of the

---

being, truth, or society, is a structure which is always above, prior to, and in part exterior to, the material relations it organises. Organisation, meanwhile, is the development of the accidental and immanent relations between various forces and relations (Hardt 1993, p. xv). However, these definitions are only meant to provide the starting point for investigations and developments of the relation between order and organisation on the terrain of metaphysics, politics, etc.

9   Negri 1991b, p. 4.
10   Negri 1991b, p. 223.
11   Negri 1991b, p. 79.

attributes. The attributes, thought and extension, are what the intellect perceives as the essence of substance (EID3). The first foundation tends towards emanation rather than constitution; emanation is not just a relation of priority or degradation between substance, mode, and attribute, but the harmony or linearity of this relation.[12] For Negri another name for this first foundation, displaced to the political register, is 'Utopia', or the preexistent rationality of production and its ordering.[13]

The second foundation, or at least the problem of the second foundation, is developed at the point where the paradox of the mode/substance relation is brought to its extreme point, and thus to the destruction of any pre-given mediation. The second foundation is not simply a question of the resolution of a paradox, but also a refusal of any mediating ground of consciousness, any finalised or pre-given order of being. Negri locates the beginning of this foundation, which is also a destruction, a *pars destruens* of the last remnants of the idealism of emanation, in Spinoza's development of the relationship between power, conatus, and corporeality. This later part of the *Ethics*, which makes up parts III and IV, develop the double exigency of the *pars destruens/pars construens* relation. First, it constitutes the destruction of any ontology as static, concealed, and grounding in the strong sense. This destruction is necessary for any rigorous thought of constitutive power, which is to say, a thought of praxis that is anything other than an actualisation of nature, the forms, the Idea, or some other presupposed ground or foundation. The disjunctive conjunction of *par destruens* of *pars construens* is also a critical engagement with the priority of thought as primary and prior to the body and its activity. These two demands converge in relation to the problem of the attributes, which install the primacy of thought in the order of being.[14] According to Negri the veritable elimination

---

12   Negri 1991b, p. 59.

13   Pierre Macherey has indicated that Negri makes the same mistake as Hegel in interpreting the attributes as the 'mediation' and 'degradation' of substance; such a reading misses the force of Spinoza's concept of substance as 'self-caused' (Macherey 1992, p. 249). While Macherey's reading offers criticism which in some sense cannot be refused, any thorough response (and there is neither time nor space for one here), would have to return to what Negri means by 'crisis' as the starting point for his reading of Spinoza, and the manner in which this crisis is at once political, ontological, and epistemological. The intersection and overlap of the 'first foundation' and the ideology of utopia would already indicate the complexity of ontological and political questions that Negri's reading of Spinoza both presupposes and develops. This complexity, a complexity which is at times presented as a simple homology of attributes and the market, would mean that there are always more than interpretive questions at stake in Negri's reading and refusal of the attributes.

14   As Michael Hardt indicates, the attributes pose a problem for any materialist reading of Spinoza, in that they would seem to necessitate a priority of thought in their very defini-

of the attributes in parts III and IV is part of a destructive and critical movement. *Pars destruens* is the destruction of ontology as a reification of the world as order, and the priority of thought as knowing over doing.[15]

From the opening of the *Ethics*, the exposition of power is aligned with a critical movement of *pars destruens*. Spinoza's exposition of power is both a political critique as well as an ontological transformation. In Part II of the *Ethics* Spinoza distinguishes between God's power as *potentia*, inseparable from its actuality, and the legislative power of *potestas*, which is predicated on the separation between will and intellect (E1IP3S). As Gilles Deleuze writes, Spinoza's development of the concept of power is immediately a political critique. A deconstruction of *potestas* as the analogy of divine and legislative power, is interwoven throughout the appendices and scholia of the *Ethics*: 'One of the basic points of the *Ethics* consists in denying that God has any power (*potestas*) analogous to that of a tyrant, or even an enlightened prince'.[16] Spinoza's critique of the anthropocentric idea of God, God as the supreme legislator of the universe, undoes any argument for authority that would base its legitimacy on such an analogy.[17] There is no kingdom in heaven that would justify the authority of worldly kings. As Deleuze argues, Spinoza's scholia carry out an immediate political critique, rushing ahead of the general ontological argument to draw out the political consequences in a battle with the existing forces.[18] For Negri, Spinoza's idea of power extends beyond its immediate political critique, the image of God, to any attempt to subordinate the productivity of being to a hierarchical order whatsoever, which in part accounts for its relevance. Spinoza is not just a critic of God, or the monarch in the image of God, but also of the state and the ideal of the market. '... [T]he idea of the market is close to the idea of the state. In these two cases the productive cooperation of subjects and their reciprocal vital association are mystified into an organization of value,

---

tion, which makes perception, or thought, the site of the division between thought and extension. As Hardt indicates, Negri's resolution of this problem, which is based on a historical and thematic interruption between the two 'foundations' of the *Ethics*, is not without its difficulties (Hardt 1993).

15 Negri 1989, p. 160.
16 Deleuze 1988b, p. 97.
17 Warren Montag argues that the object of Spinoza's critique is not simply any analogy between God and Kings, but extends to the ideal of the free subject underlying various humanisms and liberalism. 'The God who lies beyond the (material) world and is free to direct it according to his unconditioned will is thus the mirror image of the man who transcends the physical world and governs his own body with absolute mastery, itself a mirror image of God: a vicious theological anthropological circle' (Montag 1999, p. 39).
18 Deleuze 1997b, p. 146.

of the norm, of command; and human association is thus subordinated to the capitalist function of exploitation ...'.[19] Thus, this political critique has as a precondition the development of an immanent ontological organisation that is directly opposed to any transcendental order. As Negri writes:

> *Potentia* as the dynamic and constitutive inherence of the single in the multiplicity, of mind in the body, of freedom in necessity – power against Power – where *potestas* is presented as the subordination of the multiplicity, of the mind, of freedom and of *potentia*.[20]

The denial of any speculative priority to *potestas* (or Power) opens the possibility of a new ground of ontology. It is this new ground which is developed in the 'second foundation' of the *Ethics*, in the material and practical horizon of the modes.

As Negri indicates, the transformation of the 'second foundation' is in the first instance a radical inversion, or destruction of the metaphysics of emanation. It inverts the order of being by developing a 'physics' of the material relations of the modes. This inversion is made possible by the univocity of being, by Spinoza's refusal to maintain any hierarchy between thought and extension, or any teleology or finality to being. 'If God is all, all is God. The difference is important: on one side an idealistic horizon, on the other side a materialistic potentiality'.[21] Univocity and power (*potentia*) are the conditions for an affirmation of singularity and materiality as the only possible ground.[22] Being is only in its multiple and disjoined organisations. As ground, *potentia* constitutes an essentially different terrain from the ground thought as emanation, or of an ontology of transcendence in the first foundation. It is rigorously materialist, in

---

19   Negri 1997, p. 230. For Negri, Spinoza's anomaly, his break with liberal thought, is not simply located in his refusal of the social contract, but more importantly in his refusal of the market. Negri follows C.B. Macpherson's *The Political Theory of Possessive Individualism* in finding the conflict and competition of the market society underlying the idea of a state of nature. From this perspective the sovereign is the necessary force to sustain market relations. As Negri argues, Hobbes is the Marx of the bourgeoisie. Against this ideal, which subordinates production to order, Spinoza traces the immanent organisation of production: it is production, as a collective and social relation, which constitutes the world.

20   Negri 1991b, p. 190.

21   Negri 1991b, p. 64.

22   Negri traces a thread of singularity that begins with the opening definitions of part II of the *Ethics*. These two definitions begin to unfold an ontology of univocity where the 'thing' is defined as an expression of its singular power of acting (EIID3). From these definitions Negri locates a fugitive thread of singularity working through the *Ethics* (Negri 1991b, pp. 60–3).

the sense that acting, the body, force, and organisation are given priority over reflection, universality, and order. There is no original hierarchy of being, no ideal form or predetermined value, from which to judge the different singular expressions of power (*potentia*).

Central to the transformation from the first and second foundation is Spinoza's writing of the *Tractatus Theologico-Politicus*, a work that Negri argues was written in the midst of the *Ethics* as a response to the political and ideological conjuncture. The *Tractatus Theologico-Politicus* transforms the *Ethics* not simply through what it says, its critique of superstition and its interrogation of the force of the imagination, but also in the manner in which it turns Spinoza's attention to the materiality of history. The *Ethics* immediately dispenses with the 'anthropo-theological imaginary', the idea of God as man and man as a kind of God, as being founded on inadequate ideas of power, being, and causality, but the *Treatise* considers the effects this idea had in history. In the *Theologico-Political Treatise* Spinoza interrogates scripture; however, he is not content to simply oppose reason to the imagination of the prophets. Rather, in examining scripture Spinoza finds that as much as prophecy must be considered to be false, since the mind cannot know the future, it is real in that it determines the actions of individuals, becomes the ground for obedience, and ultimately constructs the world. As Spinoza writes, 'the object of knowledge by revelation is nothing other than obedience'.[23] There are of course elements of the rational and libertarian critique of religion in Spinoza's writing, but these become tools in the excavation of what Althusser calls 'the materiality of the existence of ideology'.[24] Spinoza is never content to simply critique what he calls superstition, in a sterile opposition of truth to falsity, or reason to imagination, rather he finds in the imagination, in the language of prophecy and miracles, a force that affects and transforms human society. 'But what seems important here is that this is the first unfolded emergence of the constitutive power of human action'.[25] The obedience that is secured by revelation makes possible the formation of community itself, and, since nothing is more useful to man than man, this community, or society, is the precondition of the development of reason. 'Imaginative activity reaches the level of an ontological statute, certainly not to confirm the truth of prophecy but to consolidate the truth of the world and the positivity, the productivity, and the sociability of human action'.[26] The *Ethics* speculatively affirms that all power is *potentia*, immanent, actual, and

---

23   Spinoza 1998, p. 7.
24   Althusser 1997, p. 10.
25   Negri 1991b, p. 97.
26   Negri 1991b, p. 98.

self-organising, and the *Tractatus Theologico-Politicus* confirms and radicalises this by showing how the idea of *potestas*, of God the legislator, is itself a product of *potentia*, of the power of the human imagination, and that it is this power which effectively makes the world.

The *Tractatus Theologico-Politicus* cannot be separated from the *Ethics* as a work to be classified under the heading of politics, or philology. It transforms the *Ethics*. As Negri writes:

> After the development of such a radical *pars destruens*, after the identi-fication of a solid point of support by which the metaphysical perspect-ive re-opens, the elaboration of the *pars construens* requires a practical moment. The ethics could not be constituted in a project, in the meta-physics of the mode and of reality, if it were not inserted into history, into politics, into the phenomenology of a single and collective life: if it were not to derive new nourishment from that engagement.[27]

This difference, this exposure to historicity and the social, is what the affirm-ation of *potentia*, power in its practical constitutive moment, demands. This displacement, or shift, is not exterior to the relation *pars destruens/pars con-struens*, as its application, nor is it entirely interior, as its speculative founda-tion, but it is the movement where the practice of thinking finds itself intersec-ted with and transformed by its encounter with the materiality and history of the existing world. 'Politics is the metaphysics of the imagination, the meta-physics of the human constitution of reality, the world'.[28] Thus, as much as Negri's work on Spinoza provides the fundamental elements of an ontology, a constitutive ontology that affirms the sociality, collectivity, and productive nature of being, it also underscores the fundamental orientation for the pro-duction of such an ontology – it is an ontology which can only be produced through the displacement, and disjuncture, that exposes thought to its con-stitutive conditions in historical reality.

While the *Theologico-Political Treatise* constitutes a fundamental displace-ment of the problems of the *Ethics*, from order as metaphysical problem to the historicity of the organisation of human desires and beliefs, it does not complete this process. The *Theologico-Political Treatise* does not supplant the *Ethics*. Negri argues that the *Treatise* does not follow through on its most rad-ical insights. It begins with the materiality of the imagination, with the power

27   Negri 1991b, p. 84.
28   Negri 1991b, p. 97.

of constitutive praxis, but it ultimately crashes upon the universals of 'natural right' and the 'natural light of religion', universals which undermine the constitutive process.[29] The contract subordinates the powers of society to a transcendent order and a pre-constituted end, thereby limiting the constitutive process. However, the results of the *Treatise* are fundamentally ambiguous: as much as the contract is introduced as an ordering structure of society, it is modified by the idea of power. As Spinoza writes, 'Nature's right is co-extensive with her power'.[30] This redefinition of right as power fundamentally undermines two of the constitutive dimensions of natural right that philosophy exemplified by the contract, 'the absolute conception of the individual foundation and the absolute conception of the contractual passage'.[31] In place of the absolutely individualistic foundation that paves the way for the absolute authority of the sovereign, Spinoza introduces a new theoretical object, the 'passions of the body social'. Right is coextensive with power: there is no natural state of power nor a final goal, only the historicity of its various organisations. There is thus no transfer of power, no actual passage from *potentia* to *potestas*, there is just the organisation of *potentia*, of the striving (*conatus*), desire (*cupiditas*), and affects of the multitude.[32] It is precisely this organisation that is examined and developed in what Negri calls the 'second foundation' of the *Ethics*, Parts III and IV, which develop the logic and sociability of the passions. This second foundation does not only develop the idea of *conatus* as the essence of each individual (EIIIP7), it also develops the logic of the affects as the determination of this desire. The affects begin with the most immediate, and simple, determinations – pain, pleasure, love and hate – and gradually unfold to encompass the constitutive conditions and constitutive power of subjectivity, which is not an autonomous starting point but is immersed in the power of affects. 'The nexus of composition, complexity, conflictiveness, and dynamism is a continual nexus of successive dislocations that are neither dialectical nor linear but, rather, discontinuous'.[33] Thus, as much as the *Theologico-Political Treatise* disrupts the remnants of a metaphysical order, its provocation that the historicity of desire and affects are constitutive of the world, it demands a renewed ontological speculation. It is not the *Theologico-Political Treatise* or the

---

29   Negri 1991b, p. 108.
30   Spinoza 1998, p. 179.
31   Negri 1991b, p. 109.
32   Étienne Balibar's essay 'Jus-Pactum-Lex: On the Constitution of the Subject in the *Theologico-Political Treatise*' provides the strongest illustration of the overdetermined and hence singular nature of any contract, or any foundation of the state.
33   Negri 1991b, p. 151.

Ethics that makes up the foundational book of constitutive power, but rather the movement, the displacement, from the one to the other. In Negri's book on Spinoza this movement continues to a reading of the *Political Treatise*, thus passing from metaphysics (the *Ethics*) to politics (the *Theological Political Treatise*) only to return to politics (*Political Treatise*), which in turn informs a new metaphysics (the 'multitude' as a concept produced in the interstices of the *Ethics* and the *Political Treatise*), while at the same time stating that 'Spinoza's true politics is his metaphysics'. This statement should be read not as a choice, placing Spinoza's metaphysical works over his political writings, but as a slogan of displacement. Constitutive power as praxis is developed through a practice of philosophy as a continual displacement that moves from metaphysics to politics and back, and this movement continues beyond a reading of Spinoza.

At a crucial point in the *Grundrisse*, Marx insists on the difference, perhaps irreducible, between the appropriation of the world in thought, and a practical material relation to that world.[34] In Negri's reading this difference has as its consequence a continual shifting, or displacement, of the terrain of research, what Marx describes as the difference between research (*Forschung*) and presentation (*Darstellung*).[35] The shift of research is not simply a conceit of the intellectual, the continual rewriting and reorganising of drafts and notes in order to finally perfect that great book, but is a recognition of the limit of thought. As Deleuze famously commented to Foucault, 'Practice is an ensemble of relays from one theoretical point to another, and theory is a relay from one practice to another. No theory can develop without encountering a wall and practice is necessary in order to pierce the wall'.[36] Deleuze's almost canonical remarks on practice are in part based upon his reading of Spinoza. For Deleuze, the first two parts of the *Ethics* are speculative, articulating the common notions of substance and mode according to their specific logic, while the second two are practical, demonstrating how common notions can be constructed from the practices of a singular mode of life. For Negri the displacement from speculation to practice, metaphysics to politics, extends beyond the *Ethics*, encompassing Spinoza's political works. Spinoza's thought moves from ontological speculation to the practical reality of the theological-political imagination, back to an ontological examination of the power of the imagination and affects. The relays that pass from theoretical speculation to practical activity and back again produce the possibility for liberation.

---

34   Marx 1973, p. 101.
35   Marx 1977, p. 102.
36   Deleuze and Foucault 1977, p. 207.

The movement from ontology to politics is a movement that maintains the two in an intimate relation that is never quite one of identity, but never quite separation. The transition between ontology and politics is the movement from the difference between *potestas* and *potentia* as a difference of ontological ground, and the difference between *potestas* and *potentia* as they relate on the social-historical terrain of antagonism and constitution. This shift of terrain involves an apparent inversion of priority between *potestas* and *potentia*; while it is possible to reduce transcendent order to immanent organisation on the terrain of ontological speculation, the social-historical political world seems to resist such a reduction and inversion. The texts of history, and our own daily existence, would continually remind us of the practical and material primacy of constituted or instituted power (*potestas*) over constitutive power (*potentia*).[37] Constitutive power seems blocked at every point by the dead weight of constituted, or instituted, power, by the forces of order of market and state. Yet, as Spinoza's own encounter with the history of religion has demonstrated, *potestas*, even in its extreme form as God's law, must be seen as nothing other than an expression and an application of constitutive power, of *potentia*. The apparent priority of *potestas*, in its worldly form of the capitalist market, must be exposed as the workings of *potentia*, but this can only be done by deepening the ontological and socio-political determinations, by moving from ontology to politics and back again.

2 Part Two: Living Labor

Negri's idea of constitutive power is not developed exclusively through Spinoza, it encompasses several figures, most notably Machiavelli and Marx, making up a tradition that extends beyond Spinoza's texts. As Negri writes in the *Savage Anomaly*, 'In each case Machiavelli, Spinoza and Marx represent in the history of Western thought the irreducible alternative of every conception of the bourgeois mediation of development of every subordination of productive forces to capitalist relations of production'.[38] This tradition and trajectory will take on more importance in Negri's later works, adding more depth and breadth, as the list of names is extended and the specific analyses are developed in such works as *Insurgencies* and *Empire* (co-authored with Michael Hardt). In this regard Negri's work can be productively compared with the work of Deleuze and the

---

37   Hardt 1991, p. xiv.
38   Negri 1991b, p. 141.

later Althusser, both of whom sought to create a 'counter-tradition' of materialist and immanent philosophy, opposed to the dominant tradition of idealism and teleology. There are multiple ways to create a tradition, however, from the inquiry into influences and sources, which would track down 'who read what' with the scrupulous eye of a detective, to the invention of relations and connections.[39] As Jorge Luis Borges wrote with respect to Kafka, 'every writer *creates* his precursors. His work modifies our conception of the past, as it will modify our future'. Thus, every tradition is itself the production and object of a practice of philosophy and must be judged as such.

Negri's particular practice of philosophy is situated towards the second pole, the pole of the invention of a tradition through the development of intersections and connections of concepts. In developing the series 'Machiavelli–Spinoza–Marx' Negri is less interested in the extent to which the different philosophers read each other's works, and more interested in what this intersection makes possible.[40] This is not to suggest that Negri completely overlooks these historical relations of influence. His retrieval of politics and historicity is based on finding the traces of Machiavelli in Spinoza, just as his retrieval of democracy in Marx owes much to Marx's reading of Spinoza. Negri goes beyond the actual connections to develop the intersections that the respective thinkers themselves may have overlooked: intersections and points of contact made manifest by the changes of history. In *Insurgencies* the lineage 'Machiavelli–Spinoza–Marx' is intersected and punctuated by the history of political revolutions, American, French, and Russian, and, in *Empire*, the same philosophical trajectory is intersected with the history of labour, sovereignty, and colonialism. These historical and political events deepen and extend the philosophical connections.

Within this series Marx occupies a fundamentally ambiguous position. First, as it has been argued above, for Negri Spinoza's innovation – the innovation that makes him the 'savage anomaly' – is based on the manner in which he develops an ontology of the forces of production that are not subordinated to any order of the relations of production. Marx thus defines the general political and philosophical problem, the problem of the relationship between pro-

---

39   Negri 2004, p. 61.

40   Negri 2004, p. 61. It is well documented that Spinoza was well acquainted with Machiavelli; Spinoza's treatises on politics bear the unmistakable mark of the latter's thought, a point that Negri does return to several times in *The Savage Anomaly*. With Respect to the connection between Spinoza and Marx see Maximilien Rubel, 'Marx a la rencontre de Spinoza', Alexandre Matheron 'Le Traité Theologico-Politique vu par le jeune Marx', and Albert Igoin 'De l'ellipse de la theorie politique de Spinoza chez le jeune Marx' as well as Marx's handcopied pages of the *Theologico-Political Treatise* in *Cahiers Spinoza* 1 (Summer 1977).

duction and human liberation, through which the revolutionary potential of Spinoza's philosophy can come to light. If Negri's *practice of philosophy* can be at least provisionally described as a discontinuous series of relays between 'metaphysics' and 'politics', gradually unfolding and developing the idea of constitutive power through this continual displacement, it would seem at first glance that the engagement with Marx would fit entirely within the context of 'politics'. In the list of names that constitute the tradition of constitutive power, Marx would be the proper name of that engagement with the practical immersion in the existing historical and political realities of the development of capitalism. Marx provides the socio-political context for the interpretation of Spinoza, and Spinoza transforms this context, redefining production beyond a strictly economic definition to encompass the production of obedience, ideas, and affects. Far from being limited to the side of metaphysics in the transition from politics to metaphysics, Spinoza broadens and redefines the definition of the political. Thus, it is possible to argue that the practice of philosophy that Negri develops does not remain satisfied with static oppositions between politics and metaphysics but continually redefines politics and metaphysics in the passage from one to the other.[41]

Negri's engagement with Marx also encompasses a movement of dislocation from politics and metaphysics that defines and determines the fundamental idea of constituent power. This is especially true for Negri's recent works, the works written in the last decades of the previous century, which explicitly develop the idea of 'constitutive power' from decades of political struggle and theoretical research. The intersection of politics and metaphysics in Marx, the point where metaphysics and politics make contact only to be transformed, is living labour. As Negri writes:

> As long as we follow the political Marx, political revolution and social emancipation are two historical matrices that intersect on the same terrain – the constitutional terrain – but still in an external manner, without a metaphysical logic of this intersection being given ... This necessity

---

41   Once again a useful point of intersection is to be found in Althusser, who defines his particular 'practice of philosophy' against the established divisions between 'politics' and 'metaphysics'. As Althusser writes, 'Of course this conception of philosophy as struggle – and, in the last instance, as class struggle in theory – implied a reversal of the traditional relation between philosophy and politics ... I claimed that it was necessary to get rid of the suspect division between philosophy and politics which at one and the same time treats the political figures as inferior – that is, as non-philosophers or Sunday afternoon philosophers – and also implies that the political positions of philosophers must be sought exclusively in the texts in which they talk about philosophy' (Althusser 1990c, p. 206).

resides at the core of Marx's theory of capital, where living labor appears
as the foundation, and the motor of all production, development, and
innovation. This essential source also animates the center of our investigation. Living labor against dead labor, constituent power against constituted power: this single polarity runs through the whole schema of
Marxist analysis and resolves it in an entirely original theoretical practical totality.[42]

It is in Marx's critique of political economy, in the mature works, often considered to be beyond philosophy, that Marx's idea of living labour is developed.
Negri argues that this concept, or logic, of living labour has a metaphysical or
ontological, rather than simply economic or political, dimension, defining the
productive capacity of human action. Moreover, as the quote above indicates, it
is through this 'metaphysics of living labor', and not the various manifestos and
pronouncements of the young Marx, that Marx's true politics are to be found.
Thus, as with the reading of Spinoza, Negri's reading of Marx extends and develops a philosophy of praxis through a new practice of philosophy. It is a practice
that cuts across the divisions that separate politics from economics, and politics from metaphysical speculation.

As with the case of Spinoza this critical *pars destruens* has an ontological,
political, and interpretive dimension. In this case the interpretive dimension
is turned not towards scripture, but towards Marx's texts, texts that have been
criticised as fixated on the workings of capital as a worldly form of power (*potestas*). These texts must be reinterpreted in order to reveal the power (*potentia*)
of labour. This reinterpretation begins with what is referred to as Mario Tronti's
'autonomist hypothesis'. Tronti's important theoretical discovery was to invert
the dominant interpretation of capitalism. Rather than analyse the structures
and transformations of the capitalist mode of production, Tronti argued that it
is necessary to examine the history and movement of the working class. 'We too
have worked with a concept that puts capitalist development first, and workers second. This is a mistake. And now we have to turn the problem on its head,
reverse the polarity, and start again from the beginning: and the beginning is
the class struggle of the working class'.[43] What Tronti proposed is ultimately a
'Copernican revolution' of sorts, an investigation that takes as its starting point
not capital but the working class in order to examine how capital itself adapts
itself to and is transformed by working-class struggle. The starting point must
be labour and not capital.

---

42   Negri 1999a, p. 33.
43   Tronti 1979, p. 1.

Marx argued that the dual nature of the commodity, as exchange value and use value, necessitated that labour too has a dual nature. In order for commodities to be exchanged as values and quantities, the labour that makes them must be quantitatively interchangeable. The concrete labour of different individuals must be transformed into exchangeable units of labour time; it must be made into abstract labour. As Marx writes, 'let us remember that commodities possess an objective character as values only in so far as they are all expressions of an identical social substance, human labor, that the objective character as values is therefore purely social'.[44] This abstract labour is produced by all of the techniques, from machinery to surveillance on the factory floor, that make labour interchangeable. These two sides of labour are given in the opening pages of *Capital*, and from them it is possible to understand all of *Capital* (not to mention capitalism) as a struggle of capital's tendency to reduce labour to abstract, unskilled, and interchangeable units against the concrete materiality of labouring individuals. In the opposition between 'abstract' and 'concrete' labour, the worker confronts capital, with its tendency to reduce all labourers to interchangeable cogs, as an individual, as a labouring body.

Living labour cuts across the duality of concrete and abstract labor. For the most part Marx's use of the term living labour [*lebendig Arbeit*] plays a rhetorical role in Marx's writing. Rhetorically it informs and underlies an entire metaphorics of life and death which presents the opposition between living labour in the form of the working class, and 'dead labour' as capitalist wealth and machinery, as the opposition between 'life' and 'death'; or, more dramatically, life and the 'living-dead monstrosity of capital'.[45] Beyond this rhetorical function Negri argues that there is a concept, and a metaphysics, of living labour underlying Marx's writing. The concept of living labour crosses the division between concrete and abstract labour; it is their antagonistic articulation.[46] At the same time it cuts across the division that places an individual worker against the collective force of capitalism. From abstract labour, living labour takes its flexibility and indifference: it is the capacity to do any work whatsoever; from concrete labour, it gets its determination and its connection to need. As Marx argues in the *Grundrisse*, living labour can be defined by the fact that the fundamental condition of labour in capital, as poverty, freed from any determinate means of production, is at one and the same time poverty and power.

---

44   Marx 1977, p. 139.
45   Marx 1977, p. 302.
46   Negri 1991a, p. 47.

This living labor, existing as an *abstraction* from these moments of its actual reality (also, not-value); this complete denudation, purely subject-ive existence of labor, stripped of all objectivity. Labor as *absolute poverty*; poverty not as shortage, but as total exclusion of objective wealth ... Labor not as an object, but as activity; not as itself value, but as the *liv-ing source of value* ... Thus, it is not at all contradictory, or, rather, the in-every-way mutually contradictory statements that labor is *absolute poverty as object*, on one side, and is, on the other side, the *general pos-sibility* [*allgemeine Möglichkeit*] of wealth as subject and as activity, are reciprocally determined and follow from the essence of labor, such as it is *presupposed* by capital as its contradiction and as its contradictory being [*gegensätzliches Dasein*], and such as it, in turn, presupposes cap-ital.[47]

Living labour is the possibility for the creation of any value whatsoever. Or, framed in more antagonistic terms, living labour is the situation that the cap-italist mode of production is itself dependent on a powerful, flexible, force of subjectivity that it has not created and cannot control.

As a concept living labour does not appear beyond a few references in the *Grundrisse*. It is for this reason that Negri argued for the superiority of the *Grundrisse* in the 1970s: the *Grundrisse*, Negri argued, is a superior work fuelled by the intense antagonistic force of subjectivity. However, in the years since the publication of *Marx Beyond Marx*, Negri has developed living labour as a perspective that extends beyond that privileged text to all of Marx's corpus and into all of social reality. The challenge in both cases is to unearth the productiv-ity of living labour from the apparent productive power of capital. In capitalism it is not just the individual commodity that is fetishised, concealing the labour and social networks that give it value, but capital itself becomes the ultimate fetish. Wealth appears to generate wealth: the productive power of living labor is everywhere concealed.

For Negri, Marx's analysis of the productive power of living labour and its obscuring by capitalism comes to light in the chapters on 'cooperation' in *Cap-ital*. In the factory a large group of workers are assembled under one roof in order to work together; this collective structure of work produces a surplus above and beyond the individual surplus value. As Marx writes '[T]he special productive power of the combined working day, is under all circumstances, the social productive power of labor, or the productive power of social labor.

47   Marx 1973, pp. 295–6.

This power arises from cooperation itself. When the worker co-operates in a planned way with others, he strips off the fetters of his individuality, and develops the capabilities of his species [*Gattungsvermögen*]'.[48] For Marx 'cooperation' is a basic fact: people working together produce more than individuals working in isolation; however, it is how this fact shapes the historical development of capitalism and the logic of *Capital* which is of interest to Negri. The cooperative power determines the particular power relation of capitalism: as more workers are assembled it becomes more necessary to supervise such workers. 'That a capitalist should command in the field of production is now as indispensable as that a general should command on the field of battle'.[49] At the same time the newly collective workforce also struggles against capital outside of the factory, shortening the working day, and in turn altering the structure of capitalism.[50] As Negri writes: 'The strong result of Marx's analyses of the struggles around the length of the working day and the Factory Acts consists thus in indicating a new constitutive process, not inside but outside the dialectic of capital and situated in the autonomy of cooperation, that is, in the subjectivity of the working class'.[51] Cooperation is not just the fact that a group is more productive than an individual, it is the materiality and facticity of living labour. Cooperation makes possible the struggle over the work which in turn forces a restructuring of the capitalist enterprise. If exploitation cannot be based upon the length of the working day, on absolute surplus value, it must be based upon the intensity of the labour performed, on the relative surplus value made possible by new technologies. 'Every constitution of a new structure is the constitution of antagonism'.[52] At each turn in the restructuring of capital, from the massive factories to high technology production, one does not find the all powerful force (*potestas*) of capital remaking the world in its own image, but the *potentia* of living labour. 'Living social labor takes the place of the capitalist *mise en forme* of the social totality. It becomes the absolute protagonist of history. A radical inversion takes place: all that constituted power codifies, constituent power frees'.[53] The power of living labor does not simply transform the accumulation of capital, it does so in a way that intensifies the cooperative dimension of living labour:

---

48   Marx 1977, p. 447.
49   Marx 1977, p. 448.
50   For more on the relationship between 'cooperation' and the logic of capital see my *The Micropolitics of Capital: Marx and the Prehistory of the Present* (Read 2003).
51   Negri 1999a, p. 262.
52   Negri 1991a, p. 56.
53   Negri 1999a, p. 265.

the transition from absolute to relative surplus value is also a transition in which capital relies more and more on the cooperative associations of labour itself.[54]

From Negri's reading of 'cooperation' it is possible to grasp the full extent of the intersection of the strategy of the autonomist approach to Marx and what has been called Spinoza's strategy of the 'sive'.[55] Spinoza wrote 'Deus sive Natura', God, that is, nature, finding the materialist immanent causality of *potentia* beneath God's law. In Negri it is possible to produce the statement *capital, that is, living labour*. Of course as with Spinoza, such a statement turns against the dominant ideology, and against common sense. During Spinoza's time it appeared that God was the sovereign author of the world, the ultimate justification for all that transpired in it, and in ours it appears that capital itself is productive, producing wealth. As Marx argued in a draft of the sixth chapter of *Capital*, titled 'The Results of the Immediate Process of Production', 'the more labor becomes "socialized", distributed across society, and integrated with the technological conditions of capitalism, the more it appears that it is capital itself which is productive'.[56] This is due in part to machinery and technology, which as fixed capital is nothing less than the objectification of capitalism itself. As Negri argues, this is also due to the fact that as living labour is distributed across society, as all of society comes under the rule of capital, labour paradoxically disappears as it is integrated into all of society. 'As capital develops, the force of associative productive labor increases at such a rate that it begins to become indistinguishable from social activity itself'.[57] Thus, Negri's reading of Marx could be at least provisionally identified as an application of Marx to our modern demagogues and prophets who (falsely) attribute the power of living labour to capital, a reading which

---

54   Here I am briefly referring to not only certain theses advanced by Marx, but also to Negri's socio-historical research, which traces the different forms and figures of living labour from the mass worker to the productive power of immaterial labour. See for example *Revolution Retrieved: Writings on Marx, Keynes, Capitalist Crisis and New Social Subjects, The Politics of Subversion*, and the collective research project, *Le Bassin de Travail Immatériel (BTI) dans la MétropoleParisienne*.

55   On the strategy of the 'sive' see: Tosel 1997, p. 155.

56   As Marx writes: 'This entire development of the productive forces of *socialized labor* (in contrast to the more or less isolated labor of individuals), and together with it the *uses of science* (the general product of social development), *in the immediate process of production*, takes the form [stellt sich dar] of the productive power of capital. It does not appear as the productive power of labor, or even of that part of it that is identical with capital. And least of all does it appear as the productive power either of the individual workers or of the workers joined together in the process of production' (Marx 1977, p. 1024).

57   Negri 1999a, p. 260.

adapts Spinoza's critical *pars destruens* to the illusions and mystifications of classical political economy, orthodox Marxism, and conventional wisdom, all of which see the power (*potestas*) of capital making the world and not the *potentia* of living labor. As Negri argues, the strongest point of convergence between Spinoza and Marx is in how they understand power (*potentia*) to be alienated in its organisation and representation. 'In other words, in the postindustrial age the Spinozian critique of representation of capitalist power corresponds more to the truth than does the analysis of political economy'.[58] Moreover, in both Spinoza and Marx there is a similar passage from metaphysics to politics and back again. While it is possible to locate a formulation of living labour in the *Grundrisse*, and it is possible to even locate the precursor of this idea in the young Marx's use of the term 'species being' (*Gattungswesen*) to describe the metaphysics of human activity, the concept of living labour is sharpened and concretised through a historical examination of the struggle over the working day. The reading of Marx repeats and extends a dimension of the reading of Spinoza: a metaphysical concept requires a passage through the terrain of history in order to become determinate. As much as Negri's reading of Marx applies Spinoza's critique of the mystification of constituent power to labour, and the conflict of labour and capital, it does so in a way that the very problem is itself fundamentally transformed. Marx's critique of political economy is expanded by Spinoza's analysis of the passions and desires of the body politic, just as Spinoza's ontology of *potentia* is developed and determined by the investigation of labor. Negri's reading of Marx continues a strategy of displacement from politics to metaphysics (and back again).

Negri does not limit his reading of living labour to Marx's critique of capital, to the 'mature works' of *Capital* and the *Grundrisse*. Negri's idea of living labour is developed by following a trajectory that cuts through all of Marx's works, from the early writings to the political and polemical pieces and, ultimately, to the critique of political economy. It can even be glimpsed in such early works as *The Contribution to the Critique of Hegel's Philosophy of Right*:

> Democracy is the essence of every political constitution, socialized man under the form of a particular constitution of the state. It stands related to other constitutions as the genus to its species; only here the genus itself appears as existent, and therefore opposed as a particular species to those existents which do not conform to the essence ... Democracy is *human*

---

58   Negri 1997, p. 246.

existence, while in the other political forms man has only *legal* existence. That is the fundamental difference of democracy.[59]

Marx's early understanding of democracy is indebted to Spinoza in that it posits democracy as the essence of every political form; all states are in fact democracies in that they all must rely on the power and imagination of the people. It also develops the problem of constituent power in that it makes the fundamental problem of politics the problem of the 'alienation' of constituent power in some constituted structure or order. For Marx the critique of politics takes its bearing from the critique of religion developed by Feuerbach. 'The immediate task of philosophy, which is in the service of history, is to unmask human self-alienation in its secular form now that it has been unmasked in its sacred form'.[60] The fundamental question of Marx's early works is how to complete the critique of religion. How is it possible to develop an understanding of constituent power, the power of human practice, that is not immediately alienated and betrayed in some structure or institution, in the state or in the market? Negri argues that the solution of this problem arrives somewhat belatedly in living labour, in the critique of political economy, but the force of this concept extends beyond political economy to encompass a new understanding of praxis as such. For Negri, Marx's later writings on political economy which develop the idea of living labour complete and answer the question of democracy and human liberation which preoccupied Marx in his youth. Thus, the cryptic, and often-cited formulation: 'Human anatomy contains a key to the anatomy of the ape', can be understood as a way of making sense of Marx's writing.[61]

In the later works Marx produces the concept of living labour, which is not just the foundation for a critical understanding for a history of capital, but also resolves and completes the questions posed by the young Marx. Living labour is constituent power that does not produce a constitution, a structure that would deprive it of its revolutionary power, but rather continually reinvents new orders and structures – it makes the world immanently from below. This is demonstrated, albeit obliquely, in *Capital* and the *Grundrisse* where it is shown that it is the antagonistic force of living labour that restructures capitalism, pushing it to new levels that socialise and develop the power of labour. Thus, in Negri's reading, Marx's critique of political economy also completes his early demand for a critique of politics, paradoxically finding the solution to political

---

59   Marx 1970a, p. 30.
60   Marx 1970a, p. 132.
61   Marx 1973, p. 105.

problems in breaking down the distinction between politics and economy (the social). 'The abolition of the political as a separate category is nothing but the definitive hegemony of constituent power, of creative free labor. Constituent power does not eliminate the political but makes it live as a category of social interaction, in the entirety of human social relationships and in the density of cooperation'.[62] In the *Theologico-Political Treatise* Spinoza limited the force of constituent power, of *potentia*, by situating it within a contract, by limiting it to a determinate political structure. In order for constituent power to free itself from constituted power, from a state, structure, or constitution, it must be radically open to its process of transformation and self-transformation. The solution of this problem is to be found in overcoming the separation between the social, the power of affects, desires, and bodies, and the political, the structures that organise the body politic. Marx situates constituent power on an immanent and even quotidian horizon, in the day to day practices of living labour, the relations of cooperation and antagonism that make and remake the world.

Living labour is on the one hand entirely indebted to a Spinozistic ontology and concept of politics, but it moves beyond these areas to include and transform the critique of political economy. 'Cooperative living labor produces a social ontology that is constitutive and innovative, a weaving of forms that touch the economic and the political; living labor produces an indistinct mixture of the political and economic that has a creative figure'.[63]

3   Conclusion: A New Practice of Philosophy

The movement that has been traced here, from Negri's encounter with Spinoza to Marx's idea of living labour, could be reversed. It is well known that the actual chronological itinerary of Negri's thought moves from Marx to Spinoza. Negri's interpretation of Spinoza is indebted to a Marxist interpretation of the historical conjuncture within which Spinoza wrote. It is equally possible to read Marx through Spinoza or Spinoza through Marx, and this is the direction that Negri's thought seems to be moving in with works such as *Insurgencies* and recent essays on the concept of the 'multitude'. Negri's return to Spinoza (in the essays collected in *Subversive Spinoza*) and return to Marx (in *Insurgencies*) establishes a relay that does not move in one direction, from Marx to Spinoza

---

62   Negri 1999a, p. 267.
63   Negri 1999a, p. 33.

or Spinoza to Marx, but continually loops back on itself, expanding Marxist problems by way of Spinoza and Spinozist concepts through Marx. This looping effect is not limited to Spinoza and Marx, but expands to include other figures of Negri's tradition such as Machiavelli, Foucault, Deleuze and Guattari, etc. What is clear is that for Negri no figure of philosophy can be limited to a prescribed area within the history of philosophy, politics, metaphysics, and economy – and that every addition to the series would further deepen and transform the idea of constituent power. That is not to suggest, however, that what Negri is proposing is some sort of eclecticism in which every possible theoretical and political perspective can be added. No, what Negri is developing is a practice of philosophy that is adequate to the complexity of the real, in other words, *materialism*.

Materialism has a paradoxical status as philosophy. There is no need to rehearse here all of the various charges levelled against this philosophical position. It is worth noting that one of the strongest statements of the paradoxes of materialism came from Marx himself. As Marx argued in the *Theses on Feuerbach*, most of what is called materialism, in that it begins with the idea of matter, is, despite itself, idealist. As Marx wrote:

> The chief defect of all hitherto existing materialism (that of Feuerbach included) is that the thing, reality, sensuousness, is conceived only in the form of the *object or of contemplation*, but not as *sensuous human activity, practice*, not subjectively. Hence in contradistinction to materialism, the *active* side was developed abstractly by idealism – which of course does not know real sensuous activity as such.[64]

In order to avoid this problem materialism must ground itself on the idea of sensuous human activity as practice. However, this solution poses new problems in that practice is said in multiple senses. There are multiple practices, political, economic, etc. each with their own particular levels of effectivity and materiality. These practices constituted the world and philosophy's place in the world, but philosophy is itself a practice, a practice that can only effect the world insofar as it sees itself determined by it. (Descartes, with his notion of radical doubt, is only the first of a long line of philosophers who, because of their fundamental belief in their transcendence from existing conditions, change nothing, and end up affirming the existing values). 'Being in materialism means conceiving constituent power as determinate practices – both of destruction and of creation. It means confronting the determinate conditions

---

64   Marx 1970b.

and depths of the historical passages'.[65] The movement from metaphysics to politics and from political economy to politics that defines and determines the multiple names of constituent power, *potentia*, living labour, etc. is not simply the gesture of theoretical humility, but is the practice which determines and enriches the concept, demonstrating its efficacy and force in the world. It is only by practising philosophy in its continual displacement and encounter that one can produce an idea of praxis that can change the world.

Finally, it is worth noting that Negri's particular tradition, like that of Deleuze and Althusser, is made up of fundamentally different figures than those of what is generally identified as the continental tradition, a tradition that Negri at times calls negative thought (Kant, Hegel, Nietzsche, Heidegger, etc.), a tradition that has identified the present as an 'end of philosophy'.[66] Thus, to risk hyperbole, it is possible to say that what is at stake in Negri's particular practice of philosophy is nothing less than a reinvention of philosophy, a reinvention of philosophy as a practice of liberation. Thus the challenge of Negri's recasting of the history of philosophy can be framed through a statement applied to Machiavelli, the third, and, in this case, overlooked major thinker in this tradition, 'To think the new in a total absence of its conditions'.[67] The task is not to invent a counter-tradition of philosophy, but to make that tradition the tool for transforming and inventing a new future. As with Spinoza and Marx, this new tradition cannot simply be constructed through the history of philosophy alone, it must encounter the weight of history and the passions and desires of politics.

65   Negri 1999a, p. 266.
66   The difference between these two traditions, which are also and at the same time practices of philosophy, can be traced through a recent discussion between Negri and Jacques Derrida. Commenting on Derrida's attempt to purge Marx of any ontological dimension in *Specters of Marx*, Negri writes, 'Today, exploitation, or, rather, capitalist relations of production, concern a laboring subject amassed in intellectually and cooperative force. A new paradigm; most definitely exploited, yet new – a different power, a new consistency of laboring energy, an accumulation of cooperative energy. This is a new – postdeconstructive – ontology' (Negri 1999b, p. 12). Derrida continues to refuse to use the term 'ontology' but recognises that Negri's ontology, because it passes through history and politics, is perhaps something different than what is traditionally meant by that term. As Derrida writes, 'perhaps the two of us could, from now on, agree to regard the word "ontology" as a shibboleth, which only pretends to mean what the word "ontology" has always meant ... In philosophical company, we could act as if we were still speaking the language of metaphysics or ontology, knowing full well, between us that this was not at all so' (Derrida 1999, p. 261).
67   Negri 1996a, p. 54.

CHAPTER 11

The Order and Connection of Ideas: Theoretical Practice in Macherey's Turn to Spinoza

In the last decades of the twentieth century, many prominent philosophers who were known for their work on Marx turned to Spinoza. These philosophers, such as Gabriel Albiac, Étienne Balibar, Pierre Macherey, Alexandre Matheron, Vittorio Morfino, and Antonio Negri, who represent strands of continental Marxist thought, produced major studies and monographs on the seventeenth-century philosopher. Why this turn to Spinoza? Possibly one might conclude that it was something like a 'consolation of philosophy'. As the turbulent events of the sixties and seventies (May '68 and the Hot Autumn of Italy) faded into memory of a more radical past, these philosophers turned from politics to metaphysics, retreating from a world of political concerns to pure philosophy. However, an examination of the titles and topics of their writings on Spinoza reveal that this is not the case: these philosophers turned to Spinoza not as a retreat from politics or materialism, but rather as an engagement with it. For these philosophers, Spinoza does not represent a turn towards speculation, but rather his work is the condition for a reinvestigation of democracy, revolution, and politics. Implicit in this turn is nothing less than a transformation of Marxist philosophy, which has for the most part dismissed the history of philosophy as ideology, as well as that of the protocols and standards of conventional studies in the history of philosophy, which tend to view with suspicion any turn towards past philosophers to address current issues.

Given the sheer number of volumes and numbers of problems considered, it is problematic to speak of a singular 'turn' to Spinoza. It is more accurate and productive to engage each of these philosopher's discussions of Spinoza individually, to examine specific problems and concepts. For the purpose of my investigation I am interested in looking at the work of Pierre Macherey. He is primarily known in the English-speaking world for *A Theory of Literary Production*, a text that has generally been seen as an application of Althusser's so-called structural Marxism to literary theory. Less well known is Macherey's work in the decades since: work dedicated to the study of Spinoza. In that time he has published *Hegel ou Spinoza* (1979), *Avec Spinoza: études sur la doctrine et l'histoire du spinozisme* (1992), and the five-volume *Introduction à l'Éthique de Spinoza* (1994–8). While the first of these texts, published in 1979, is in part concerned with problems internal to Marxist philosophy, arguing for a reconsideration of Spinoza's critique of teleology as an alternative to Hegelian dialectics, the latter texts are concerned primarily with an explication and examination of the thought of Spinoza. This is especially true of the *Introduction*, which is dedicated to reading Spinoza 'to the letter', discussing each proposition, axiom, and scholium with painstaking dedication to the meaning and sense of Spinoza's writing. As such, it would seem absurd to claim that the project is concerned with problems of Marxist philosophy. Yet, as I will demonstrate, it is through Macherey's close attention to the letter of Spinoza's text that he addresses a problem that is both overlooked and demanded by Marx's philosophy: the problem of the materiality, or effectivity, of philosophy as a kind of practice.

This problem of the 'materiality of philosophy' can be glimpsed in Marx's famous eleventh thesis on Feuerbach: 'The philosophers have only *interpreted* the world, in various ways; the point is to change it'.[1] As critics unendingly point out, this statement was written by someone who continued to interpret the world and continued to write as a philosopher, and who wrote with the intention of changing the world. There was a contradiction between the statement and the practice. This contradiction points to a larger problem in Marx's thought: the problem of the role of thought, of philosophy, in the superstructure – its situation as conditioned by other practices and effecting other practices. Without addressing this problem, Marx's materialism cannot comprehend the world that it aims to transform. Macherey's writing finds in Spinoza's philosophy – specifically in the causality that Spinoza ascribes to thought, the order and connection of ideas – a way of addressing the specific materiality of thought. Thus, despite the modest proposal of Macherey's *Introduction* to Spinoza, what is at stake with such a project is nothing less than a transformation of philosophy's self-conception: from an autonomous and eternal reflection to a situated practice of transformation.

1   Marx: From Ideology to Theoretical Practice

It is possible to argue that, underlying the initial definition of ideology in *The German Ideology*, there is a basic question of the relation between philosophy and its historical conditions – conditions that include, in the last instance, the economy. As Marx argues in that text, the fundamental shortcoming of German Idealism and, with it, all prior philosophy, is its unthought connection with German reality – with the social and material conditions of German

---

1   Marx 1970b, p. 123.

society in the mid-nineteenth century (everything from the French Revolution to the Reformation and the university system) that produced the particular philosophical problems that it treats as universal.[2] Philosophy is unable to address its conditions. As Étienne Balibar wrote in a provocative formulation, 'For Philosophy ideology is the materialist name of its own finitude'.[3] Beneath the banner of 'ideology critique' and the denunciation of philosophy in the name of the 'really existing' conditions, there is a problem that, for the most part, philosophers and Marxism have overlooked; what could be called the 'actuality' of philosophy – the intersection of philosophy with its conditions and effects in history. Such a problem has not been explored or even posed by the more reductive or dogmatic tendencies within Marxism or by much (bourgeois) philosophy after Marx. These intellectual 'camps' were in most respects equally satisfied to keep Marxism and philosophy hermetically sealed from one another. What these divergent camps could perhaps agree on is a rather literal interpretation of the eleventh thesis as Marx's final word on philosophy.

One notable exception to these tendencies is the work of Louis Althusser, much of which could be characterised as an attempt not merely to bridge the gap separating academic philosophy and Marxist politics, but even more to continually interrogate one by means of the other. One of the central concepts of this interrogation is 'theoretical practice'. 'Theoretical practice' is not, as critics claimed, an attempt to glorify theoretical work, declaring it to be a kind of practice. Rather it is the investigation of the work that thinking does, its limitations and its effects. At its most basic level, the very idea of theoretical practice works simultaneously in two opposed directions at once. First, against most of the history of (idealist) philosophy, it declares that philosophy is not an autonomous practice; it is not the sovereign and pure work of a universal mind contemplating the truth. Philosophy is conditioned by other factors, other practices (most notably science, politics and ideology), which pose its questions, concepts, and problems. At the same time, however, the idea of theoretical practice does not dismiss philosophical work as 'mere speculation' or an empty conflict of phrases, as some Marxists have done, but suggests that philosophy has effects. Although they operate at a distance, philosophy's effects are nonetheless quite real on the very practices, politics and ideologies that

---

2   Citing *The German Ideology*, Macherey writes: 'Hence this notion that Marxism was the first to explore: philosophy is not an independent speculative activity, as would be a pure speculation, but is tied to "real" conditions, which are its historical conditions; and this is why, let it be said in passing, there is a history of philosophy, which can be retraced and understood' (Macherey 1998, p. 9).

3   Balibar 2017b, p. 120.

condition it. What Marx offers philosophy is not, Althusser argues, a new philosophy of praxis in which labour would take the place traditionally occupied by reason or mind, but a new practice of philosophy – a new way of 'doing' philosophy. For Althusser, this new way of doing philosophy is characterised by the extreme heteronomy of philosophy, its determination and transformation by other forms of practice: economic, political, and so on. '... [P]ractice is what philosophy, throughout its history, has never been able to incorporate. Practice is that other thing, on the basis of which it is possible not only to knock philosophy off balance, but also to begin to see clearly into the interior of philosophy'.[4] At its most ambitious, the idea of theoretical practice suggests not only a materialist redefinition of philosophy in terms of its conditions and its effects, but the idea that one can only understand the transformative effects of philosophy if one first sees it as conditioned.[5] Such an assertion – that one must begin with constraint and determination in order to understand freedom – puts us close to the spirit, if not the letter, of Spinoza's writing. That is to say that if the general trajectory of Spinoza's thought is to begin with the manner in which we are conditioned to explore the transformation of those conditions, to proceed from bondage to freedom, then this is as true for thinking as it is for acting.

2   Spinoza: Thinking as Production

Despite the influence that we know Spinoza had on his thinking, Althusser did not explicitly refer to Spinoza in the texts that initially posed the problem of 'theoretical practice'. Rather, as with much of Althusser's writing in the 1960s, the points of reference are all drawn from within the confines of the communist tradition: Marx, Lenin, and Mao. Althusser struggled to supplement the works of historical materialism, the thorough analysis of the capitalist mode of production in *Capital*, with dialectical materialism, a theory of Marx's theoretical practice that Marx himself never wrote. In order to understand how philosophy, or theoretical practice, begins from conditions only to transform them, Althusser looks to Marx's description of the general conditions of the labour process. According to Marx, the elements of the labour process are 'purposeful activity, that is work itself, the object on which that work is performed, and the instrument of that work'.[6] What was for Marx a historical invariant covering the

---

4   Althusser 1990c, p. 249.
5   Macherey 1998, p. 32.
6   Marx 1977, p. 284.

complete history of labour, from the crudest possible production to modern machinery, becomes for Althusser the basic dimension of all practice, which starts from determinate conditions that it transforms through the mediation of tools.[7] Based on this schema, theoretical practice works on raw material, the various ideologies, with concepts its tools, in order to produce knowledge, its final product. While this schema outlined the constitutive orientation of any practice it did so only as an analogy, as a metaphor for a concept yet to be produced. What the analogy does not clarify is what precisely theoretical practice and practice in general, or labour, have in common; that is, what makes it possible to use the terms 'practice', 'operation', and 'transformation' to apply to thoughts and concepts without collapsing into mere analogy or homology. The analogy expresses an identity between production and thought, body and mind, but it does not give the ground of this identity. This is where Althusser's adherence to the letter of Marx's text fails him; there is nothing, or at least very little, in Marx's writing that would offer a means to conceptualise the productive dimension of thinking. To characterise this limitation through Althusser's own thoughts on philosophy, it is possible to say that the schema of transformation constitutes something of a metaphor, a phase through which every philosophical system must pass. As Althusser writes, 'In philosophy you can only think through metaphors'.[8] In another context he argues against what he refers to as 'descriptive theory', a theory that superficially grasps a connection between different phenomena without positing the reasons or grounds of the connection. Descriptive theory, like metaphor, is the necessary beginning (and limitation) of any theory.[9] It is possible to say that theoretical practice, or at least the fundamental idea of a connection between the transformation of matter and the transformation of ideas, remains a descriptive theory. The analogy of thinking as a kind of labour or production does not begin with Althusser, or with Marx for that matter. Its history can be traced back to the debates between Descartes and Spinoza on the proper order or method of thinking. Descartes illustrates his 'method' for directing the mind through reference to the linear progression that any physical production must follow.

> Our method in fact resembles the procedures in the mechanical crafts, which have no need of methods other than their own, and which supply their own instructions for making their own tools. If, for example someone wanted to practice one of these crafts – to become a blacksmith,

---

7 Althusser 1969, p. 173.

8 Althusser 1976, p. 140.

9 Althusser 1971b, p. 138.

say, but did not possess any of the tools, he would be forced at first to use a hard stone (or a rough lump of iron) as an anvil, to make a rock do as a hammer ... and to put together other such tools as the need arose. Thus, prepared, he would not immediately attempt to forge swords, helmets or other iron elements for others to use; rather he would first of all make hammers, an anvil, tongs and other tools for his own use. What this example shows is that, since in these preliminary inquiries we have managed to discover only some rough precepts which appear to be innate in our minds rather than the product of any skill, we should not immediately try to use these precepts to settle philosophical disputes or solve mathematical problems.[10]

What is striking about Descartes' use of this analogy is the restriction it places on thought: just as one cannot make swords from simple tools, one should not attempt to address philosophical disputes with the most basic ideas. This caution is not only consistent with Descartes' thought in general, but with the specific way in which he understands human fallibility, the capacity to err. As he argues in the *Meditations on First Philosophy*, the source of error is in the difference between 'will' and 'intellect'; more precisely, the will, because it is free, is always running ahead of the intellect. Method, as Macherey argues, as a rule for the conduct of mind, is a restriction, a negation of this freedom.[11] Method is a necessary condition for truth just as it is the condition for any production.

Spinoza employs an analogy similar to Descartes'. At first glance, the difference appears to be slight. As Spinoza writes in the *Treatise on the Emendation of the Intellect*:

> But just as men, in the beginning, were able to make the easiest things with the tools they were born with (however laboriously and imperfectly), and once these had been made, made other, more difficult things with less labor and more perfectly, and so, proceeding gradually from the simplest works to tools, and from tools to other works and tools, reached the point where they accomplished so many and so difficult things with little labor, in the same way the intellect, by its inborn power, makes intellectual tools for itself, by which it acquires other powers ... until it reaches the pinnacle of wisdom.[12]

---

10   Descartes 1985b, p. 31.
11   Macherey 1979, p. 78.
12   Spinoza 1985, p. 17.

The slight difference which functions as wedge, distancing Spinoza's conception of knowledge from Descartes', is that for Spinoza the initial tools of production, or thought, are not produced by a method, but are given. We have, as Spinoza writes, 'one true idea', and this idea becomes the condition for the production of knowledge. Moreover, it is not the rules but the activity of thought that his analogy underscores. With thoughts, as with the history of tools, crude beginnings become the conditions not for certainty, but for the production of new thoughts and ideas. As Macherey argues, Spinoza's point in this text is not to salvage Descartes' idea of method from its potential critics, but to paradoxically dispense with the instrumental idea of method – that is, method as instrument for arriving at truth – in order to propose a redefinition of thinking as activity and production.[13] Unlike Descartes, who finds in the history of production a linear order and a rule, Spinoza uses the history of material production to stress the necessary but provisional starting point of any process of knowledge production. As Macherey argues, 'The ideas from which we commence in order to arrive at knowledge, are not the innate truths upon which we are able to base, for once and for all, as if on a foundation of stone, an order of reason, but they are the raw material to be worked, which must be profoundly modified in order to ultimately be used in the production of truth'.[14] For Spinoza a method is not something that one begins with, prior and external to the actual act of thinking, but is itself produced in and through the process of thinking. The 'method of thought' is nothing other than the process of its production. 'Method does not precede the development of knowledge which it expresses or reflects'.[15] Thought is not a faculty of reflection, which is free to lose itself or find itself according to this or that method, but is an activity, a process that begins from determinate conditions and produces knowledge.

Spinoza's argument traces the same trajectory as Althusser's idea of the schema of 'theoretical practice'. In each case there are given conditions, a provocation, which the philosopher does not choose, which function as a kind of raw material. This raw material is transformed by an act of thought or reflection. Spinoza's *Theological Political Treatise* illustrates this point by placing the chapter on method, on the interpretation of scripture, as the seventh chapter of the book. In order for Spinoza to make his argument that scripture must be studied as nature is studied, he must first show how the text of scripture is riddled with conflict over its unified meaning. The conflicting interpretations of scripture that lead mankind into strife are both the provocation and raw

---

13   Macherey 1979, p. 60.
14   Macherey 1979, p. 63; my translation.
15   Macherey 1979, p. 56; my translation.

material of Spinoza's method. Spinoza is writing in the midst of this conflict, arguing for freedom to think and write. At the same time, conflict over the 'true' meaning of scripture reveals dispersion, lacunae, and ambiguity where others have insisted on unity and perfection.[16] Thus, when Spinoza declares that 'all knowledge from Scripture must be sought from Scripture alone' as the guiding principle of his method, this rule is not imposed from the outset but demanded by the actual dispersion and disorder of scripture.[17] Spinoza's method is not a transcendental condition of knowledge, but an immanent process. It is the transformation that thought effects as it operates on itself. As with Althusser's schema, however, it remains to be seen how this process, this transformation that begins from given conditions, produces knowledge.

This point of convergence between Althusser and Spinoza, which is also most likely an aspect of the latter's influence on the former, indicates an unexamined point of contact between Spinoza and Marx. It is not just that Spinoza can be understood as a precursor to Marx, through the lines of descent that can be traced through the passages of Spinoza's *Tractatus Theologico-Politicus* that Marx copied into his notebooks, but that Marx's thought, or materialism in general, requires an understanding of the effectivity, the productive dimension, of thought.[18] Without this, without an account of how thought can be considered to be 'material', not in the same sense as a 'paving-stone' or 'rifle', but in terms of its concrete causality, conditions and effects, Marxism or materialism will never shake the adjective 'vulgar'.[19] While this point of intersection was developed, but never entirely thematised, by Althusser, it becomes central to the work of Pierre Macherey, whose magisterial five-volume introduction to Spinoza's *Ethics* has as its subtext an examination of the very idea of thought as a production, through an examination of the causality proper to thought. What Althusser expresses as an analogy, a similarity between thought and production, without giving the ground of the analogy, becomes in Macherey's interpretation of Spinoza grounded through an examination of the ontology of thought and being.

---

16   Montag 1999, p. 13.
17   Spinoza 2001, p. 88.
18   Matheron 1971, p. 161.
19   As Althusser writes: 'Of course, the material existence of the ideology in an apparatus and its practice does not have the same modality as the material existence of a paving-stone or a rifle. But, at the risk of being taken for a Neo-Aristotelian, I shall say that "matter is discussed in many senses" [*la matière se dit en plusieurs sens*], or rather that it exists in different modalities, all rooted in the last instance in "physical" matter' (Althusser 1971b, p. 166).

3   The Order and Connection of Ideas

Macherey argues that while the term *Deus sive Natura* (God that is nature), has been used as shorthand to indicate the explosive force of Spinoza's ontology, stating an absolute identity of creator and creation, the identity of an immanent process, it is possible to indicate his reworking of the very idea of thought through another formula, *'causa seu ratio'* (cause or reason).[20] The relation between causality and reason is articulated first in the *Treatise on the Emendation of the Intellect* in which Spinoza argues 'that true knowledge proceeds from cause to effect'. As with the argument regarding method, Spinoza's immediate adversary here is Descartes. Descartes argues that analysis, which proceeds from the known to the unknown, from effect to cause, is superior to synthesis, which, in proceeding from known to known, has only a pedagogical or ornamental function.[21] As Spinoza writes: 'This is the same as what the ancients said, i.e., that true knowledge proceeds from cause to effect – except that so far as I know they never conceived the soul (as we do here) as acting according to certain laws, like a *spiritual automaton*'.[22] For Spinoza the two ways of thinking are distinguished by the fact that the latter proceeds from cause to effect, following the actual production of things, while the former, in proceeding from effect to cause, often leads to confusion.[23] 'The knowledge of an effect depends on, and involves, knowledge of its cause' (E1A4). The cause is primary not only physically and ontologically but, as Macherey argues, epistemologically as well. For Spinoza the geometric 'method' is neither a guarantee of knowledge, nor a pedagogical tool, but a manner of following the necessary connection of ideas, as one idea produces another.

In Althusser's conception of 'theoretical practice', the connection between matter (production) and ideas (theory) was unthematised, stated and obscured by the analogy of the labour of production. Macherey's reading of Spinoza argues that it is causality that makes it possible to consider thought and matter as a practice. This is how Macherey interprets the famous proposition 7 of part two of the *Ethics*: 'The order and connection of ideas is the same as the order and connection of things [ordo et connexio idem est ac ordo et connexio rerum]'. Proposition seven, like the rest of the *Ethics*, must be read word by word. One of the things that such a reading reveals is that Spinoza does not

---

20   Macherey 1994–8, p. 58.
21   Descartes 1985a, p. 110.
22   Spinoza 1985, p. 37.
23   Macherey 1994–8, p. 17.

discuss an order and connection of ideas and bodies, but of ideas and things (rerum rather than corporum). Moreover, Macherey argues, it is the order and connection that is the same, and this means that ideas, like other things, are determined by other ideas that they in turn affect and determine.[24] Ideas and things have the same order and connection, which is nothing other than a necessary causal relation. Thus, Macherey focuses on the common factor of causality as that which makes ideas and things the same. This is a fundamentally different focus from what has generally been understood as 'parallelism', which suggests the idea that thought and extension constitute two separate but parallel orders – in which there is an idea for every thing and so on, to infinity.

Macherey's understanding of proposition 7 as it unfolds through the rest of the *Ethics* develops a much more complex, nuanced account of causality than is suggested by the image of two parallel lines of ideas and bodies. The two propositions immediately following proposition seven outline the two different ways that ideas can be understood: ideas can be considered formally, that is, as pure ideas, determinations of thought, and as singular, actually existing ideas. With respect to the formal existence of ideas it is possible to say that there is a kind of parallel between the infinite power of thought and existence, a parallel which is founded on identity of power – 'God's actual power of thinking is equal to his actual power of acting' (EIIP7S). In this first sense, taking ideas considered as expressions of the infinite power of thinking and acting, as *natura naturans*, it is possible to speak of a 'parallelism' that is not a relation between two different series, external to and separate from each other, but of the same thing, conceived under different attributes. Ideas must also be considered as singular existing ideas, however – not as they are determined by the infinite power of thought, but as they are determined by their situation in the world. Singular existing ideas have a different causality, they relate not to God as the infinite power of thought, but to an actually existing idea that has caused them, which in turn has been caused by other ideas and so on (EIIP9).[25] It is in relation to this second sense, the infinite series of ideas, that

---

24   Macherey 1994–8, p. 73; Macherey argues that it is necessary to read the proposition word by word, and stresses that *idem* is masculine or neuter; thus, it can only qualify the 'order' or the 'order and connection'.

25   Spinoza restates this distinction in part 5: 'We conceive of things as actual in two ways: either insofar as we conceive of them to exist in relation to a certain time and place, or insofar as we conceive of them to be contained in God and to follow from the necessity of the divine nature. But the things we conceive in this second way as true, or real, we conceive under a species of eternity, and their ideas involve the eternal and infinite essence of God' (EVP29Schol).

the mind can be considered to be a kind of *spiritual automaton*, as a determined series of connections or relations between ideas. As Macherey argues, situating Spinoza's understanding of thought and extension against his contemporaries:

> Unlike Hobbes, for whom there is nothing outside of bodies, and also unlike Descartes, for whom causality applies only to bodies, Spinoza's *causa seu ratio* argues that extension and thought have the same principle of intelligibility while maintaining the specific rules proper to each of their systems [*maintenant la spécificité des lois propres à chacun des ces systèmes*].[26]

The identity of order and connection, of causal relations, does not mean that ideas and things (or bodies) are completely identical or that they are interchangeable. This connection, in which ideas correspond to things, can only be said of ideas formally, or ideas and things as they pertain to the power of infinite intellect. For finite modes of thought, however, ideas and things, concepts and experience, are quite often out of sync. The danger of 'parallelism', as it is often understood, is that it suggests some kind of pre-established harmony between thinking and the world, eclipsing the irreducible heterogeneity of perspectives and ideas, a heterogeneity that Spinoza sought to comprehend and act on.

As Spinoza demonstrates, the causal order of ideas which determines the thought of a specific individual, a causal order which encompasses affects and bodies, does not express a fundamental sameness, but rather accounts for the divergence and differences of actually existing thoughts and points of view. The identity and difference of the order and connection of thoughts and affects explains the difference and diversity of thoughts and ideas: that is, when different individuals with different histories are confronted by the same conditions, the same images or affects, they will draw different connections. As Spinoza illustrates, when confronted with hoof prints in the mud, a farmer will think of planting and a soldier will think of war, according to their fundamentally different experiences, which are nothing more than the way in which the mind has been 'determined to produce an effect [in this case a particular image or general idea] in a certain and determinate manner' (1D7). The same causal order, or the same rule that ideas are caused, is responsible for fundamentally different effects, different ideas. While the order of intellect is 'the same in all men',

---

26   Macherey 1994–8, p. 130, my translation.

the affects and experiences of each person are not (EIIP18S). All thinking is overdetermined, determined in part by the causality of affects and experiences, and determined in part by the causality of ideas and intellect. These intersecting causalities also encompass identity; all thinking obeys the same power and logic of ideas; and difference, every experience, every history of affects, is individuated according to one's history.

4   Will and Intellect

Causality is the common order of ideas and things, minds and bodies, making it possible to speak of thought as a kind of production, as something that produces knowledge from given concepts and experiences. At the same causality, the causes that affect the body and mind, explain divergences and differences of opinion, how the same image can cause different ideas in two different minds. How does the same concept, the same relation – that of cause and effect – explain knowledge and opinion, truth and error? The answer lies in the distinction that Spinoza makes between adequate ideas (which express their cause) and inadequate ideas. As he writes:

> I say expressly that the mind has, not an adequate, but only a confused knowledge, of itself, of its own body, and of external bodies, so long as it perceives things from the common order of Nature, that is, so long as it is determined externally, from fortuitous encounters with things, to regard this or that, and not so long as it is determined internally, from the fact that it regards a number of things at once to understand their agreements, differences, and oppositions.
>   EIIP29Schol

The difference between knowledge and ignorance, as with the difference between freedom and constraint, is not between a causal order (in this case of reason), or the absence of such an order, but between two different orders. 'Inadequate and confused ideas follow with the same necessity as adequate, or clear and distinct ideas' (EIIP36). There is a logic of error just as there is a logic of truth.[27] As Spinoza demonstrates throughout the *Ethics*, and most

---

27   Macherey underscores the fact that there is a fundamental symmetry between EIIP36 and
      EIIP40 ('Whatever ideas follow in the mind from ideas which are adequate in the mind
      are also adequate'). Both propositions establish a causal order between ideas. However
      Macherey indicates that Spinoza uses a different verb in each proposition, *sequi* in the

famously in the appendix to part one, the various illusions of superstition, the belief in God the king, in a universe governed by final causes, or in the explanatory power of 'transcendentals', are not simply illusions, purely negative. They are produced by conditions that range from the basic striving for survival to the limits of the imagination, and finally, to the political struggles and ideologies that benefit from superstition. In every act of thinking, from the most confused to the most adequate, there is a causal connection, just as every action is determined; the only difference is between those which are determined externally and those that are determined internally. Externally caused ideas are subject to the overpowering causality of other things, what Spinoza refers to as 'the common order of nature', while internally caused ideas are subject to the mind's power of reflecting upon things and conceiving of ideas. However, even the very terms 'external' and 'internal' are wholly inadequate to expressing this difference; the scholium only gestures to the problem which is developed and explored throughout the *Ethics* – that is, of the difference between two kinds of necessity: self-caused, free determination, and externally caused, or compelled (EID7).

With respect to thinking, all ideas are in some sense necessary. The difference lies between those that express and comprehend their necessity (thought as *sub specie aeternitatis*) and those that are, in a sense, necessarily ideas of contingency.[28] Which is to say that while inadequate ideas are themselves necessary, produced by a series of conditions, there is a logic and a reason as to why one is compelled to think this or that, while as ideas they are uncertain and vacillate. Hence they are necessary in relation to the order that produces them, but contingent in relation to the mind that conceives or perceives them (EIIP44). Misunderstanding and misinterpretations are themselves produced from determinate conditions and relations, they are 'true errors'.[29] Spinoza demonstrates how the experience of a particular chronological order (meeting Paul in the morning, and so on) produces the idea of contingency or utter chance. Through the constant juxtaposition of the future against the past one is determined to think in terms of contingency, and ultimately, freedom. Inadequate ideas do not comprehend their necessity. '[A] thing is called

---

first and *consequi* in the latter, suggesting that while there may be a 'connection' of inadequate ideas, this connection never constitutes an order (Macherey 1979, p. 299).

28   'We conceive of things as actual in two ways: either insofar as we conceive of them to exist in relation to a certain time and place, or insofar as we conceive of them to be contained in God and to follow from the necessity of the divine nature. But the things we conceive in this second way as true, or real, we conceive under a species of eternity, and their ideas involve the eternal and infinite essence of God' (EVP29Schol).

29   Goldstein 2004, p. 331.

contingent only because of a defect of our knowledge' (EIP33S1). The difference between adequate and inadequate ideas, like the difference between external and internal compulsion in the realm of actions of the body, is not a clean break; it is rather a difference that is continually practised, as one strives to adequately grasp the world.

If adequate and inadequate ideas are necessary, albeit in different senses, then neither truth nor error can be understood to follow from the freedom of the will or intellect. Spinoza's critique of a transcendent faculty of judgment, like his critique of the transcendent idea of a will, famously follows his assertion of determination and necessity. Less famously, however, this argument also follows his critique of so-called universals, those general concepts that reflect the confusion of the imagination, not the mind's power. As Spinoza writes: 'So intellect and will are to this or that idea or to this and that volition as "stone-ness" is to this or that stone or man to Peter or Paul' (EIIP48s). There is no general faculty of the intellect, only this or that concrete idea, just as there is no general faculty of will, only this or that concrete desire. When one posits the idea of a 'will' or 'intellect' existing above and beyond the concrete ideas and volitions, one confuses the multiple instants of an activity, multiple productions, with a potential power. There is no will or intellect that would stand apart from, or behind, actually existing volitions or ideas.

While a similar confusion underlies the idea of a free will and a free intellect, Spinoza's critique does not merely address them as two misguided but distinct abstractions. The fundamental misrecognition, as far as Spinoza is concerned, is not the idea that the will and intellect are faculties, abstract possibilities rather than concrete actions, but their separation. Spinoza argues that ideas are not images reflected on the mind that one can judge, evaluate, and act on afterwards. Ideas contain their own particular causality and determination. To take Spinoza's example, one cannot have a thought of a triangle without also thinking that it has three sides, or that its three angles make up two right angles; the object of thought determines the mind, as a kind of automaton, to think that. One cannot have an idea of a triangle and then choose to deny or affirm that it has three sides and so on; these decisions are determined by the particular causality of the idea, insofar as it is an idea (E1P17S). Spinoza's example, drawn from geometry (philosophy's ideal in terms of clarity and universality since Plato), hits at the centre of this ideal, suggesting that if the abstract figures of geometry can be understood as causes which determine the mind to think, then the same must be true, albeit even more so, with respect to ideas drawn from the arguably more messy world of concrete experiences and desires.[30]

---

30   Macherey 1979, p. 379.

Will and intellect are two different ways of understanding the same thing, the same activity of the mind, working on and within determinate conditions. Thus there is no divide between an infinite will and a finite intellect, as Descartes supposed, or between theoretical reason, which studies the relations of causal necessity determining the perceived world, and practical reason, which deals with the causality of freedom, as Kant argued. Thinking, like acting, does not stand outside the causal nexus that constitutes the world, but is fully immersed within it. To briefly return to Marx, and to the problems sketched out in *The German Ideology*, the separation of philosophy from existence, which is made possible by the division of mental and manual labour, and which in turn makes possible philosophy's leap into a realm of groundless abstraction, is, for Spinoza, an impossibility. For Spinoza there is no consciousness 'other than consciousness of existing practice'; all thinking is situated with respect to ideas, activities, and concepts that condition it.

What has been called Spinoza's 'strategy of the *sive*', from the formulation God, that is Nature (*Deus, sive Natura*), a tendency to break through existing philosophical oppositions by almost inconspicuously making them interchangeable, appears to reach the point of effacing the distinction between will and intellect, theory and practice, blind appetite and conscious desire (Tosel, p. 155). As Spinoza writes 'The mind as far as it can, strives to imagine those things that increase or aid the body's power of acting' (EIIIP12). It is possible to understand this proposition as reducing the mind's activity to what has already been determined by the force of the affects, and the body's desires. Moreover, this thinking is not separate from action, but immediately translates into action (EIIIP28). Thus, it is possible to see the mind as just one link in a causal chain, as the body has been determined so follows the mind. Of course, much of Spinoza's writing on the affects follows this logic, in which the mind is determined by the intersection and imitation of affects. How the mind acts, however, is determined by what it understands, or imagines, to increase the body's power of acting, by what it understands as good or bad. While Spinoza for the most part dismisses the ideas of good and evil as indicating nothing of nature, as effects grasped without their causes, in Part Four of the *Ethics* he argues that these words must be retained with respect to a particular model of life, a particular ideal for which we strive. As Macherey argues, Spinoza distinguishes between a 'spontaneous knowledge of good and evil' which is nothing more than the dim awareness of an affect, and true knowledge of good and evil (EIVP14). The task of liberation is a task of traversing this distinction, a transformation that does not posit a goal 'beyond good and evil', but starts from the spontaneous idea of good and evil and gradually transforms it with knowledge, transforming what is meant by it.[31] The intellect does not separate itself from the will, or mind from desire, but it redefines what is willed and what is desired, acting on its conditions. Human beings still call 'good' whatever they strive for, the difference is that this striving is now a conscious practice and not a blind activity.

5   The Power of the False

Up to this point we have covered the conditions of thought, but what about its effects? How does thinking, or philosophy, transform its conditions? In other words, how is thinking a cause and not just an effect? Spinoza's answer to this can be elucidated by examining the first proposition of part four of the *Ethics*. 'Nothing positive which a false idea has is removed by the presence of the true insofar as it is true' (EIVP1). As Spinoza demonstrates via a favourite example of seventeenth-century philosophy (the apparent motion of the sun), there is nothing in the (adequate) idea of a heliocentric solar system that dispenses with the image of the sun rising in the east. The imaginary image of the sun as a small object circling the earth is not dissipated by the knowledge that things are otherwise. While true or adequate ideas have a particular causality, determine the mind to think (as in the example of the triangle), this causality is not absolute. Knowing the truth, or knowing the right thing to do, does not mean that one always acts accordingly. Human action is marked by that curious pattern of activity that Spinoza describes as 'seeing the better and doing the worse' (EIVP17Schol). True knowledge of the better or the worse (or what increases or diminishes the body's and mind's power) does not necessitate the corresponding actions or even desires. There is a limited power, a limited causality or effectivity, of the true 'insofar as it is true' (*praesenti veri quatenus verum*). As Macherey argues, the formulation of the true 'insofar as it is true' suggests an ineffectual and disembodied conception of truth, an idea of truth that is purely ideal and ineffectual.[32] This would appear contradict Spinoza's argument at the end of part two, which ascribed a certain causality to ideas. This is why Macherey emphasises the qualifying remark 'insofar as it is true': whatever causality, or effectivity, true ideas have, it does not stem from the sovereign power of their truth, but from their particular striving, their particular conatus, which is to say their connections with other ideas.[33] By themselves, true ideas, even those of good and evil, are not capable of dispensing with the illusions of

---

31   Macherey 1997a, p. 23.
32   Macherey 1994–8, p. 61.
33   Macherey 1994–8, p. 60.

the imagination, nor of the desires and fears that overcome the mind. If a true idea overcomes a false idea, an illusion, it is not because it is true, but because of its force as an idea, the intensity with which it is held, and the frequency with which it is reflected upon. In order for the truth, for knowledge and thought, to become effective, to govern one's thought and actions, they must become *actualised* in ideas, actions, and behaviors.

In his often cited essay 'Ideology and Ideological State Apparatuses', Althusser sought to dispense with a particular 'ideology of ideology'. This 'ideology of ideology' is ultimately an idealist understanding of ideology in that it makes ideology to be solely a matter of 'false ideas', thus reducing the political and philosophical problem of ideology to the epistemological problem of truth and error. At first glance, Althusser's problem and Spinoza's problems appear to be entirely different, separated by a transformation of critical vocabularies, the introduction of the term 'ideology', but, more important, by the fact that they have nearly opposite goals. Spinoza is dealing with the limited power of true ideas ('insofar as they are true') and Althusser with ideology, a fundamental misrecognition of the basic conditions of one's existence, what could be called the power of the false. However, the solution they come up with is not only similar but shows Spinoza's subterranean influence on Althusser. As Althusser writes, 'ideology has a material existence'.[34] It exists in rituals, day-to-day practices, and institutions. Spinoza made a similar argument in the Appendix to part one, the text which Warren Montag has pointed out is the concealed point of reference for Althusser.[35] As Spinoza argues, 'superstition', the mutually reinforcing ideas of the individual as free, as a kingdom within a kingdom, and God as transcendental cause, intervening in the world from outside, are ultimately founded on a particular temperament (*ingenium*), on the ignorance of the causes of one's actions and the human tendency to act towards particular ends, which is itself the product of particular habits and practices. Étienne Balibar argues that this account of temperament (*ingenium*), can be supported by the account Spinoza gives of individuality in the *Ethics*.

> By *ingenium*, we should understand a memory whose form has been determined by the individual's experience of life and by his or her various encounters, and which, as a result of the unique way in which it has been constituted, is inscribed both in the mind (or soul) and in the dispositions of the body.[36]

---

34   Althusser 1971b, p. 195.
35   Montag 1995, p. 63.
36   Balibar 1998, p. 29.

However, for Spinoza it is not just ideology, prejudice, or superstition, which is founded on particular habits and practices, but true knowledge as well. This is why liberation from 'servitude', from the powers of the false, is not accomplished once and for all in the act of comprehending the truth, but must itself become a practice, a habit, of organising our thoughts and affects (EVP10S).

As much as Spinoza argues for a radical break that separates the first kind of knowledge (from signs, random experience, and the imagination) from the second (common notions), this break must be put into practice in order for it to have effects (IIP40S2). Spinoza's recognition of the limited effectivity of the true 'insofar as it is true' protects him in advance from what Althusser called 'theoreticism': in his case, the reduction of the historical and political distinction between bourgeois ideology and Marxism to a simple epistemological distinction between 'error' and 'truth'.[37] Extrapolating beyond Althusser's specific situation, it is possible to say that 'theoreticism' replaces the historical and material difference between modes of existence with the stark opposition between error and truth. This makes it possible to see the distance that separates Spinoza from such confidence in knowledge. For Spinoza, just as knowledge emerges from its own process of production, it must also be returned to it, situated with respect to the imagination and the affects. Spinoza does not just criticise 'superstition' but reveals its fundamental conditions and demonstrates a way out, which is a way of living as well as a way of thinking. Knowledge or truth is not a lightning bolt, capable of dispensing with illusion all at once; it is a mode of life. The relation between knowledge and imagination, reason and superstition, or, to use Althusser's terms, science and ideology, is not a break which is accomplished once and for all, but a process, a continual struggle. The rectification of Althusser's philosophy, from the idea of an epistemological break in the 1960s through the self-critique to the idea of philosophy defined as a struggle, or 'class struggle in theory', can thus be understood as a return to Spinoza's fundamental insight regarding the precarious status of knowledge against the tide of superstition and imagination.[38] Philosophy is not defined by its breaks, by errors and illusions that are dispensed with once and for all, but by a continual struggle. As Balibar writes, illustrating this period of Althusser's reworking of the idea of a 'break':

> The radicality of the break between science and ideology, between imaginary and knowledge, is in no way attenuated, and neither as a result

---

37   Althusser 1976, p. 106.
38   Althusser 1990c, p. 206.

is the importance of the 'point of no return' that a first conceptual step always constitutes for knowledge. But the break is put back in a field of forces that continue to act as long as knowledge itself works and progresses, which is to say, to infinity. Every break is at the same time irreversible and precarious, threatened with an impossible return to its ideological prehistory, without which it would not last, it would not progress.[39]

Part four of the Ethics opens with Spinoza's fundamental axiom that every finite thing is ultimately overpowered by something more powerful, a fact that Macherey reminds us applies as much to thoughts, to knowledge, as it does to physical things.[40] Knowledge for Spinoza is not only of this world; it is in it as well. As a finite thing in this world, knowledge must continually struggle to preserve itself, expand itself, against the forces that would overwhelm it.

In Spinoza, recognition of the finite nature of (human) thought takes the form of the following question: How can the power of knowledge be increased against the powers of superstition and the imagination? This is the question that cuts across Spinoza's historical, political, and philosophical writings. In the *Theological-Political Treatise* this actualisation is given a historical dimension, as Spinoza charts the extent to which prophecy and scripture give figure and form to the desire to constitute a community, to the true but often effaced maxim that 'nothing is more useful to man than man' (EIVP35C1). Religion for Spinoza is not simply superstition and illusion; it is a constitutive activity that founds community. Thus, it has a (limited) utility to the project of liberation.[41] In the *Ethics*, there is a more complex and developed account of how truth becomes actualised to become a part of a living and acting life. This response, as it is developed throughout the *Ethics*, intersects with religion (through the intellectual love of God), politics (through common notions), and above all affect (through the idea of a joy that pertains to thinking). These three conditions of liberation intersect, forming the basis of a community, but they are also dealt with separately. As much as Spinoza recognises that knowledge is always a collective project (after all, it is a matter of what he calls 'common notions', demanding at the very least a community that is stable and peaceful enough to allow for contemplation), he also recognises that such a collective project is a difficult undertaking. Moreover, at the time of his writing, it remained a possibility only for the few. Much of Spinoza's *Ethics* is thus concerned with the question as to how an individual can liberate him- or herself against a backdrop

---

39   Balibar 1994a, p. 172.
40   Macherey 1994–8, p. 56.
41   Negri 1991b, p. 98.

of strife and conflict. This could be considered the autobiographical element of the *Ethics* (EIVApp).

6   Philosophy as Operation

As Spinoza argued, if knowledge is to become effective in relation to the affects that constitute much of our day to day striving and existence, it must become invested with affect, it must become saturated with desire. By itself, according to its formal existence, a true idea is powerless to overcome affect and imagination. The true idea must become the object of desire, situated within a practice of recall and repetition, and placed within a community that reinforces it. What is underscored is not only that thinking, the production of knowledge, must be reconsidered in terms of conditions – conditions which are material, imaginary, and political – but also that it is only through a recognition of these conditions that one can grasp its effects. To return to the connections between Spinoza and Marx with which this essay opened, it is possible to glimpse a similar concern regarding what I am calling the actuality of philosophy in Marx's earlier writings. As Marx wrote, in a formulation which has interesting resonances with Spinoza's argument regarding knowledge and affect: '... [M]aterial force must be overthrown by material force; but theory, too, becomes a material force when it has seized the masses'.[42] Althusser argues that Marx's materialism is less a matter of answering a metaphysical question about the ultimate nature of reality, matter over ideas, mind over body, than it is of recognising the fact that philosophy itself is one particular practice, one particular activity, situated by other activities. 'The measure of Marx's materialism is less the materialist content of his theory than the acute, practical consciousness of the conditions, forms and limits within which these ideas can become active'.[43] Marx, like Spinoza, recognised that philosophy was a particular kind of activity, with determinate limits and effects, not the proper name of grasping the totality.

Spinoza's denial of the absolute freedom and effectivity of thought, of the freedom which is generally seen to be the condition of all others and thus the action which is the condition of all other actions, may at first appear to be a greater scandal than Spinoza's denial of free will. Through the perspective of Althusser and Macherey, it is possible to see in this aspect of Spinoza's

---

42   Marx 1970a, p. 137.
43   Althusser 1990a, p. 275.

thought the conditions for a fundamental rethinking of philosophy – a thought of philosophy as practice, or, more precisely, as operation.[44] Moreover, a reconsideration of theoretical practice through a reading of Spinoza makes possible a way of rescuing this concept from its pitfalls. As I stated earlier, this theory remained largely descriptive, stating a similarity between thinking and production without giving the ground of this relation. A brief look at the history of Althusser's thought reveals the limitations of this 'descriptive theory'. In Althusser's writing of the sixties, this descriptive theory of 'theoretical practice' led to the formulation of a general theory of theoretical practice – what Althusser called 'Theoretical Practice' with a capital 'T'. This was the schema of the labour practice, or, more precisely, the materialist dialectic: a general theory of how philosophy works on and within given ideological conditions in order to transform them.[45] Such a theory violates the very conditions that it sets up: at once arguing that all thinking is determined and situated, and then providing a general account of this condition. It is a claim to have unconditioned knowledge of the conditions of all knowledge. This is the impasse of theoreticism. A second and opposed pitfall would be the descent of all thinking into its conditions and causality: there are only historically specific 'theoretical practices', all equally determined by their conditions. In this perspective, thinking would be an activity that is entirely determined by the history of the body and its affects. The limitations of this second pitfall can be seen in Althusser's infamous statement that philosophy 'is class struggle at the level of theory', which reduces thought to politics to the material struggles of forces and bodies.[46] This second pitfall has plagued Marxist denunciations of philosophy as ideology: in their eagerness to reveal the historical conditions of any claim of universality, Marxists lose the very capacity to speak of truth. These two pitfalls, an unjustified universal theory and a unredeemable particularity, plague any attempt to understand philosophy and thinking as historically situated. The only way beyond them is to move beyond a descriptive theory: that is, to theorise the identity and difference of thinking and production, mind and body.

For Macherey, the term that encompasses this situation of philosophy, the word that expresses the identity and difference of thought and matter, philosophy and practice, is 'operation'. Macherey argues that philosophy must be thought as an operation that works within the determinate conditions and constraints of its historical and political conjuncture rather than as an action that

---

44   On Spinoza's critique of the liberal idea of an inalienable (and ineffective) freedom of mind, see Warren Montag's *Bodies, Masses, Power: Spinoza and his Contemporaries*.

45   Althusser 1969, p. 168.

46   Althusser 1990c, p. 206.

starts out from its own free possibility and dictates to the world what principles it should follow. Macherey takes the term 'operation' from a distinction that Spinoza makes in the *Ethics*, a distinction that is lost in most English translations: 'That thing is called free which exists from the necessity of its nature alone and is determined to act by itself alone. But a thing is called necessary, or rather compelled, which is determined by another to exist and to *operate* in a certain and determinate manner' (EID7, translation modified).[47] Macherey suggests the distinction between 'operation' and 'action' in place of the Aristotlean distinction between *praxis* (doing) and *poeisis* (making). In the latter distinction, philosophy was often identified as a kind of action, a kind of doing, an 'inoperative activity' which produces nothing outside of itself and works on nothing other than itself.[48] Macherey argues that this division between praxis and poeisis is extended into the modern era. For example, Kant's ideal of 'practical reason' is free with respect to any determination imposed from the outside. It is practical insofar as it dictates the norms and rules of practice from the space of pure reason. In contrast to this, to define philosophy as an operation is to accept that all philosophy is impure, burdened by concepts and content whose conditions and causality it cannot choose. This constraint is the condition for a production of effects. If philosophy is impure, then every practice insofar as it is forced to question its conditions and effects is potentially philosophical. It is from this perspective, a perspective that also informs his work on Spinoza, that Macherey redefines 'theoretical practice': as situated at the intersection of operations, which always work on determinate conditions and processes:

> 'Theoretical Practice' is not the magical formula that would guarantee that the identity of theory and practice could be given initially: rather, it indicates a process in which operations are produced, inside which theory and practice take shape concurrently, against each other, with each other, in the sense that they are reciprocally put to work, in a movement in which it appears that there is never a pure theory, whose meaning would be limited to its stated results, nor any pure practice, innocent because it would elude the confrontation of its intentions with its effect.[49]

It is only by taking up a position within determinate struggles and conflicts which are not of its choosing that philosophy can have any effect on the world.

---

47   Macherey 1992, p. 72.
48   Macherey 1998, p. 28.
49   Macherey 1998, p. 35.

To preserve the terminological distinction from Spinoza's definition, it is possible to say that all philosophy is an operation striving to become action, striving to transform its conditions.[50] 'As operation, philosophy is practice itself, in
all sectors of its intervention, in so far as it puts back into question the limits
inside which its activities are carried out, and thus discovers the tendentially
unlimited power of its processes'.[51] True knowledge, adequate ideas, have their
limited efficacy insofar as they are true, an efficacy that can be expanded as
knowledge is put back into practice, put to work in its conditions. Just as the
truth is limited in its effectivity, its power, Spinoza demonstrates that the false,
inadequate ideas are in their own way necessary, determined by a causal order
that they do not comprehend. Causality makes it possible to see the connections between truth and error, knowledge and ideology, the way they intersect
and have effects on each other. Rather than choose between a freedom without
effects, as is suggested by certain formulations of the freedom of thought, or
conditions which completely determine what they condition, as in some historicisms or sociological understandings of philosophy, Spinoza makes it possible
to think in terms of a liberty of thought and practice that can only be effected
by working on its conditions.

   Spinoza explicitly thematises this liberty, or liberatory practice, throughout
the *Ethics*. It is in some sense what he means by 'ethics', while simultaneously
demonstrating it. The *Ethics* is a work which situates itself squarely within not
only the dominant philosophical terminology of its time (substance, attribute, mode, etc.), but also its dogmatisms, and from this produces a work which
not only liberates itself from those conditions – becoming something other –
but continues to have effects of liberation in the present. As Macherey argues,
Spinoza's philosophy is eternal not because it transcends its conditions, forming a timeless system, but because its engagement with its history constitutes
a dynamic tension that is stable, capable of producing effects.[52] This is possible because the conditions that Spinoza works from are not monolithic or
uniform. Defining philosophy as an operation does not mean that it is reduced
to a mere effect of its conditions, an epiphenomenon of other more real processes, or even 'its own time comprehended in thought', as Hegel claimed.[53]
This is because every philosophy is overdetermined; every historical period
is made up of multiple practices, which in turn define multiple modes of
thought. The Marxist perspective of Althusser and Macherey makes it possible

---

50   Macherey 1994–8, p. 38.
51   Macherey 1998, p. 36.
52   Macherey 1992, p. 9.
53   Hegel 1991a, p. 21.

to reintroduce contradiction, a contradiction without *telos* or end, to the plurality of knowledges.[54] In Spinoza's case, the seventeenth century was not only defined by religious dogmatism, but also saw the emergence of new forms of knowledge, new material productions, and emerging democratic desires.[55] As Spinoza reflects on the powerful force of superstition at the time of his writing:

> This alone, of course, would have caused the truth to be hidden from the human race to eternity, if mathematics, which is concerned not with ends, but only with the essences and properties of figures, had not shown men another standard of truth. And besides mathematics, we can assign other causes also (which it is unnecessary to enumerate here), which were able to bring it about that men would notice these common prejudices and be led to the true knowledge of things.
>
> EIApp[56]

Spinoza's remark on mathematics, or geometry, not only provides some account for his own use of the geometric method, but also reflects on the historical and social conditions of his writing. There is a tension, even a contradiction, between the perspective of superstition and that of the emerging forms of knowledge associated with mathematics and physics (not to mention 'the other causes' not enumerated, which could be construed to refer to the emerging forms of republican and democratic resistance to monarchical authority), a tension that Spinoza exploits, turning one form of knowledge against the other.[57] His *Ethics* is the work not of a thinker who removed himself

---

54   Althusser 1976, p. 141; The final chapter of Macherey's *Hegel ou Spinoza* (1979) argues that Spinoza offers a nonteleogical dialectic.

55   Negri 1991b, p. 48.

56   Althusser gives this specific discussion of conditions a general formula. As he writes, 'We are able to say that historically philosophy is born from religion, from which it inherits specific questions, which it then converts to the grand themes of philosophy, with all of their different responses: for example the origin or the end of man, of history, and of the world. Nevertheless, I maintain that philosophy is constituted as such, in a rigorous sense, when it encounters the first science: mathematics ... From this moment ... one has to begin to reason in a different manner and on different objects: abstract objects' (Althusser 1994c, p. 49).

57   In a posthumously published manuscript entitled 'Notes sur la philosophie (1967–8)', Althusser presents a generalised schema of philosophy's position vis-à-vis the 'breaks' of science and ideological revolutions of politics. He argues, 'This "overdetermination" of philosophy by these two events obeys the following law: the determination in the last instance of philosophical events by ideological events (the ideological revolutions of the class struggle), determination by scientific events (the breaks) only in the second instance'

from the historical and social conditions of his writing, but of one who transformed those conditions through the very act of his philosophical practice.

As Spinoza writes, 'Man thinks'. This axiom applies not only to philosophers, but to everyone (EIIA2). Thus, philosophy as an activity is determined by and in turn acts on this constitutive plurality of thoughts, which is determined by the constitutive plurality of practices.[58] Thinking is not an action, a practical reason, which founds in its purity and distance from the world the principles that the world should follow, but is an operation, acting within determinate conditions in order to become autonomous, to produce effects of freedom. Liberty is not the absence of necessity, but a transformation of it. Such a formulation, as I have tried to sketch here, would entail nothing less than a transformation of philosophy, a reconsideration of its history, and, more important, a reinvention of its practice.

(Althusser 1995, p. 308; my translation). While Althusser's argument in that manuscript is related to the investigation being pursued here, its schematic and rigid nature gives rise to other problems (See Chapter Three of this volume, The Althusser Effect).

58   Sylvain Lazarus has argued for a fundamental reorientation of political thought based on the axiom that 'everyone thinks' (*les gens pensent*), an argument related to that pursued here (Lazarus 1996, p. 61).

CHAPTER 12

Desire is Man's Very Essence: Spinoza and Hegel as Philosophers of Transindividuality

It is perhaps one of the effects of philosophy's long cold war that the fundamental question of the relationship of individual to society is immediately split into two hostile camps. The first considers the individual to be immediately given; society, or the state, is then nothing other than the sum total of the effects of individual wills, actions, and decisions. Opposed to this idea is the conception of society, culture, or the state as an organic or functional totality, determining and constituting the individuals and subjects it requires. It is with respect to this division, but also against it, that Étienne Balibar has proposed that there is a group of thinkers (they cannot be called a tradition), namely, Spinoza, Hegel, Marx, and Freud, which constitute a transindividual perspective in thinking both the individual and social relations.[1] Even before one arrives at an understanding of what Balibar means by transindividuality, it is possible to understand something of the stakes of his particular intervention. With the exception of Freud, all of the thinkers in the transindividual list, Spinoza, Hegel, and Marx, have generally been considered to be organic or holistic thinkers, thinkers of totality; the only difference then is whether this totality is considered to be the all-encompassing substance, spirit, or capital. All three have been accused at one time or another of denying individuality, dissolving it into nature, history, or the economy. The conceptual field that Balibar intervenes in is thus as asymmetrical as it is dualistic: individualistic conceptions of society and social relations, from social contract theory to neoliberalism, are not only dominant but absolutely hegemonic. Thus even the 'holistic' thinkers have been reborn as individualists. Marxists have produced their own methodological individualism and Spinoza has been interpreted to be a more metaphysical Hobbes, and is even admired by readers of Ayn Rand.[2]

---

1   Balibar 1997, p. 9.
2   The persistence of this individual/collective divide can even be seen in readers of Spinoza, who generally either follow the idea of the conatus, as individual striving, to make Spinoza a thinker of individuality, or follow his critique of mankind as a 'kingdom within a kingdom', to argue for a holistic interpretation. Étienne Balibar has argued in his essay 'Potentia multitudinis, quae una veluti mente ducitur': Spinoza on the Body Politic' that the point of demarcation of these two different perspectives is the passage in the *Political Treatise* where Spinoza writes

Moreover, the condemnation of various forms of holism or organicism, generally grouped under the category of totality, functions as the *bête noire* of various perspectives and disciplines: liberals, postmodernists, and conservatives agree about little else than the fact that the individual is preeminent and anyone who denies its hallowed place is a fascist or Stalinist. This is what it means to refer to 'philosophy's cold war', the presence of the last century's ideological debates beneath the various arguments and interpretations, but our concerns here are less with the cause of these interpretations, the intersection of ideology and argument, than its effects: what such interpretations eclipse, and what it might mean to evade them. The outline of the effects can be seen in Balibar's particular intervention, his particular reorganisation of the history of philosophy. Balibar's intervention cuts a line of demarcation, to borrow Althusser's term, within this opposition: this line is necessarily tilted to one side, engaging with authors generally considered to be writers of the totality, and excavating what an individualistic conception of society necessarily effaces. Balibar's intervention thus seeks to retrieve a thought of relation, of sociality, recasting it not as something opposed to the individual or the social, but as its necessary condition.

The term transindividuality is associated with Gilbert Simondon, who developed it in his posthumously published *Individuation psychique et collective*. In Simondon's work the concept of transindividuality is defined through a critique of the centrality of the individual in the history of philosophy (as well as science). Against the longstanding belief that has defined the process of individuation from the already constituted individual, Simondon presents individuation as a process in which the individual is a phase rather than an absolute starting point (atomism) or ultimate end (hylomorphism). For Simondon the individual is situated with respect to a preindividual milieu, a series of relations that are in a metastable state, not yet individuated but possible conditions for multiple individuations. Individuation is always a realisation and transformation of these relations. Simondon's larger project examines different individuations, physical, biological, psychic, and collective in succession, and it is possible to say that each is problematic, posing problems that must be resolved through subsequent individuations; for example, the biolo-

---

of 'the power of the multitude guided, as it were, by one mind'. Some interpreters, such as Lee Rice, have insisted that such a phrase should not be understood literally, since collectives can never be individuals; while others, such as Antonio Negri and Alexandre Matheron, have insisted on the reality of a collective mind. Balibar pursues a 'critical' interepretation, neither dogmatically individualist nor holist, that is strongly related to his understanding of transindividuality.

gical individuation of humanity, the collection of instincts and habits, makes necessary a psychic individuation, a character or habit that realises these different potentials. The last of these series, and the one that seems to be reserved for human life, is collective individuation, transindividuality. Transindividuality is not some collective which subsumes individuals, but a collectivity that exists only in and through individuation and vice versa: one is individuated through collectivities, through various associations and relations that bring out different possibilities. Transindividuality is only possible through the always incomplete process of individuation, the preindividual milieu that we carry with us. It is because the conditions of our individuation, the affects, habits, and language, never cohere, never fully constitute an individual, that we enter into collectivities. Transindividuality entails a new thought of causality, a new ontology of relations, and a new logic, a new way of understanding definitions, placing Simondon's system in close proximity to Spinoza's immanent causality and Hegel's dialectic. However, my concern here is less with an understanding of Simondon, or even Balibar, than what Simondon's thought proposes for an understanding of Spinoza and Hegel.[3] In this case, Simondon's work, and Balibar's suggestive remarks, functions less as a philosophical text to be considered in its own right than as a provocation, as something that breaks Spinoza and Hegel from the individualist and organicist readings that have subordinated them to the eternal battle between liberalism and its others, communitarianism, communism, and fascism. Thus, in what follows, I would like to examine three questions. First, what might it mean to consider both Hegel and Spinoza as transindividual thinkers? Second, what sort of distinctions might be made on this terrain of transindividuality? And, finally what this might mean for thinking about social relations, and politics.

1   Desire: Between Constitution and Recognition

The unavoidable starting place for any consideration of transindividuality in Hegel and Spinoza is desire. Spinoza's writes, 'Desire is the very essence of man in so far as his essence is conceived as determined to any action from any given

---

3   Simondon is rather dismissive of Spinoza's understanding of the individual, repeating the rather familiar accusation that Spinoza dissolves the individual into a larger pantheistic whole [Simondon 2005, p. 283]. Despite this criticism, Balibar has argued that there is fundamental overlap between Spinoza and Simondon, arguing that the latter offers a 'definition of individuality as transindividuality, or better yet, as a process of transindividual individua(lisa)tion' (Balibar 1996b, pp. 35–46).

affection of itself' (EIIIDI). While this statement is provocative in its own right, read along with the propositions and demonstrations that situate it, Spinoza's formulation is less a basis for a philosophical anthropology than it is a specific modification of a general ontology. Desire is a particular situation of the general striving, the *conatus*, that defines everything (EIIIP6). Everything is a singular expression of striving, but as a finite thing it is also always determined to act in a certain manner. Everything is an individual, but individuality is not understood as something radically separate from relations, but rather as something that is constituted through relations.[4] To rephrase Spinoza's phrase about God as nature: individuality, that is, transindividuality. Transindividuality is an ontology prior to being a thought of social relations. Ontologically we could say that everything is an individual, but this is not an atomism, because individuality is defined as a relation, specifically, a ratio of motion and rest and a capacity to affect and be affected. These relations are themselves part of other individuals, collectivities, and are also composed of other individuals as its parts. The limit case of this is of course nature, on the one hand, and the smallest parts referred to in the Lemmas of Part Two, on the other, but what is truly at stake for Spinoza is everything that transpires in between: the constitution, transformation, and destruction of individuals.[5] The ontological assertion that everything is an individual, defined by its particular striving, does not preclude an understanding of relations; in fact, it makes a thought of them possible: everything is individuated by its own particular history, by what has affected it, by relations. The human condition, the situation of desire, is not qualitatively distinct from this general condition; human bodies (and minds) are more complex than some bodies, due to the number of parts, and thus are capable of entering into more relations, though less complex than others for the same reason. Mankind is not a 'kingdom within a kingdom', but is subject to the same rules that define all of modal existence.

To understand the human condition, the situation of desire, it is necessary to understand how this particular striving that makes up human existence is determined by the affects, imagination, and reason. As Spinoza argues, what we desire is always determined by our history, by a particular determination of our affects and knowledge. Desire is a striving that defines all of humanity, but it does so not in terms of some transcendent goal, some good that everything aims at, but in terms of a multiplicity of aims and desires. As Gilles Deleuze writes, 'fools and the weak, no less than reasonable men and the strong, strive

---

4 Matheron 1969, p. 19.
5 Balibar 1997, p. 17.

to persevere in their being'.[6] What defines this multiplicity is nothing other than the affects, and their history: joy and sadness, the primary affects of the increase and decrease of our power to act and think, are extended onto the various things we take to be their causes into love and hate. Once we apprehend, through habit and repetition, a particular object or individual to be the cause of our joy or sadness, adequately or inadequately, it becomes something that we desire, seek out again, in our fundamental striving. Objects and individuals that we desire, that we love, become the conditions of other loves and hatreds, as we love the things that resemble them or are the causes of their joys and sorrows, in an increasing spiral of conjunctions and connections. We individuate ourselves and are individuated, forming particular tastes and desires, at the same time that we individuate the objects of our desire, our perception or recognition of an object, at least for the first kind of knowledge, which cannot be separated from how it has affected us.[7] Individuation in this context is not limited to what we putatively define as the individual, but includes the individuation of groups, the perception of collective belonging. History and habit defines and differentiates the particular desire, the particular striving, of any individual: individuation is constituted through relations, not in spite of them. What we have in common is not some generic essence, some transcendent faculty, but a particular striving and a complex history. This commonality does not unite us, but radically individuates us into singular strivings: there are as many desires as objects, and as many objects as histories (EIIIP56). Desire is an essence that is singular and relational, rather than universal and foundational.

Striving, *conatus*, is at once a common condition of existence, even a common notion, and in the case of desire, it is also subject to the specific situation of the human condition. This specificity includes, as we have seen, the complex proportion of motion and rest that defines the human body, a complexity that makes memory and habit possible, but it also includes the particular condition of the intellect ('man thinks') and with this the particular problem of adequate and inadequate ideas of our desires. Human striving is situated between appetite and desire. Spinoza defines desire as 'appetite together with consciousness

---

6   Deleuze, 1990b, p. 261.

7   With respect to collectivity Spinoza writes the following, 'If someone has been affected by joy or sadness by someone of a class, or nation, different from his own, and this joy or sadness is accompanied by the idea of that person as its cause, under the universal name of the class or nation, he will love or hate, not only that person, but everyone of the same class or nation' (EIIIP46). Thus, there is a constitution of collectivity along with a constitution of self. Moreover, Laurent Bove has argued that since objects are often perceived as objects of love or hate, the constitution of self is the constitution of the object world (Bove 1996, p. 50). There is a transindividual individuation of self, collectivity, and objects.

of the appetite' (EIIIP9S). The order and connection of desire and appetite are the same, desire is simply the same appetite rendered conscious. It is possible to pose the question as to what kind of difference consciousness makes here: what does it mean to be conscious of our appetites? More to the point, what does it mean to suggest that we have appetites that we are not conscious of? Such questions return us to the heart of Spinoza's philosophy, to the difference and identity of the order and connection of thought and things, not just at the level of ontology but as a general problem of human existence. If we work from the prior assertion regarding desire as always already constituted, organised by habits and past impressions, then it is possible to see subjectivity, for lack of a better word, as framed not only by active and passive affects, but also between those appetites that exceed its consciousness, and those that are conscious, recognized as its desires. Spinoza's central point is to reverse the order of consciousness and desire, to argue that we do not desire something because it is good, but call it good because we desire it. This is what Alexandre Matheron refers to as Spinoza's antifinalism, which is summed up as follows, 'we neither strive for, nor will, neither want, nor desire anything because we judge it to be good; on the contrary, we judge something to be good because we strive for it, will it, want it, and desire it' (EIIIP9S).[8] The telos, the final cause of our desires, has to be situated back into the network of efficient causes, the conditions which make it so the baby desires milk, and ultimately back into the immanent cause, to nature considered as the infinity of productive relations.[9]

Far from being an assertion of some isolated, atomistic, individual, Spinoza's assertion that desire is man's very essence is an affirmation of the always singular, always relational, aspect of human existence: our desires, our essences, are thus distinct, and always produced by and productive of the series of encounters between different desires. However, the relation between these desires, in that it passes through the passions and appetite, is not always recognised as such: just as we freely think that we desire what we desire, we also think that we do so in isolation and separation. We see ourselves as a kingdom within a kingdom, not only separate, but autonomous. As Spinoza remarks in the Appendix to Part One, we are ignorant of the causes of things, but 'conscious of our appetite', to which we should add that one of the things that we are ignorant of is the cause of our own appetite, the practices and relations that constitute its ground.[10] In Spinoza's thought there is a connection between the transindividual basis of desire and the opacity of the self. It is because we do not

---

8   Matheron 1969, p. 84.
9   Bove 1996, p. 42.
10   Fischbach 2005, p. 64.

adequately grasp the transindividual conditions of our desire that we believe ourselves to be free, to truly desire what we desire, and it is because we believe ourselves to be free that we do not adequately grasp the transindividual conditions.[11] It is here that we can perhaps turn to Hegel, knowing that the conflict between the two philosophers is not between the individual and the relational, but between differences within the transindividual.

For Hegel, as for Spinoza, there is a strong link between desire, consciousness, and the human condition. Hegel begins the section of the *Phenomenology of Spirit* on 'Self-Consciousness' with the assertion that 'Self-consciousness is desire in general'. There is a shift from the previous section, which dealt with the problem of consciousness, of the coming to know the world, figured alternately as sense-certainty, the thing, and force, to the self. These dialectical progressions each mark a process away from things taken in their immediacy and self-identity towards the constitutive dimension of relationality.[12] These different figures of consciousness, as much as they reveal more of the world, moving beyond the immediacy of empiricism to an understanding of forces and relations, do not provide an awareness of self-consciousness, an understanding of self. The progression from consciousness to self-consciousness is not just a shift of object, it is a fundamental and progressive shift of orientation: with the movement from consciousness to self-consciousness we enter into 'the native realm of truth'.[13] The object and subject of knowledge become the same. This is fundamentally different from Spinoza, for whom the problems of consciousness with respect to desire, of adequately grasping our mind and body, are not fundamentally different from the problem of the first kind of knowledge in general, of knowledge from the disorder of experience. This is because human desire is not radically different from the *conatus*, from the striving that defines everything: it is only different insofar as the human body and mind are capable of more relations, capable of memory and habit. However, even this difference between Hegel and Spinoza, a difference which will have profound effects for each philosopher's understanding of the human, of philosophical anthropology, is situated on a similar plane, that of the opacity of the immediate: in each case the starting point of everyday consciousness is as much a source of illusion as knowledge.

As with Spinoza, Hegel's discussion of desire begins with a fundamental division that defines the relation between desire and consciousness. Only in this case, the primary difference is not between appetite and desire, but different

---

11   Ibid., p. 96.
12   Jameson 2010, p. 17.
13   Hegel 1977, ¶167.

kinds of desire. Desire for food and water, for those things that make up our necessary survival, constitute a kind of self-consciousness, an awareness of living. This awareness is fleeting and tied up with an object that constantly poses its independence: thirst and hunger reassert themselves to be conquered again. Desire directed at such objects loses by winning: it negates the objects, but in doing so it fails to learn anything of itself other than as something living; or, as Hegel puts it, absolute immediacy is absolute mediation. With such objects, self-consciousness is aware of itself as something that desires, as something that lives, experiencing hunger and thirst, but these desires do not arrive at what would be called self-consciousness in and of itself, they do not express the indetermination and freedom that constitutes human existence. This leads to Hegel's well-known formulation that desire must be a desire for another desire, for another self-consciousness. As Hegel writes, 'self-consciousness achieves its satisfaction only in another self-consciousness'.[14] This leads to the most well known section of Hegel's *Phenomenology*, the dialectic of lordship and bondage, a passage so layered in commentary that it becomes difficult to read at all, let alone interpret anew. Nonetheless, it is from this passage that Hegel introduces the fundamental idea of recognition, which constitutes Hegel's specific thought of transindividuality.

One way to approach this problem of recognition is to wrest it from Hegel's text, with its combination of necessary and contingent progressions, and to situate it on the larger terrain of philosophical problems. Recognition is in part a response to the post-Kantian problem of self-knowledge: Kant decimated the assertion of the transparency of the Cartesian subject through the parallogisms of pure reason, which made it impossible to maintain a pure and rational transparency of the self. Recognition provides another way to self-knowledge, one that is immediately intertwined with a political problem: the trick is to square the circle, to reconcile autonomy with the opacity of the self.[15] (It is worth noting, following the discussion of the opacity of desire in Spinoza above, how alien Spinoza's thought is to this problem: Spinoza already arrived at what Fischbach calls 'the secondarity of the conscience of self' without the need of the Kantian critique of the paralogisms of pure reason). At the root of Hegel's reflection on recognition is the idea that self-consciousness is radically different from consciousness of objects, things in the world. As Kojève writes, 'Contemplation reveals the object, not the subject'.[16] This is in part the task that Hegel's essay on 'Lordship and Bondage' takes on, passing through a reflection

---

14   Ibid., ¶175.
15   Williams 2000, p. 34.
16   Kojève 1969, p. 3.

on violence, work, death, and struggle in a dense passage that provides the matrix for nearly every possible philosophical anthropology.

Hegel's passage considers the various possibilities of recognition, its constitutive ambiguities, in which recognition always passes through misrecognition. Once we pass the initial condition, where the struggle for recognition manifests itself in mutual annihilation, these possibilities manifest themselves first as their extremes, as master and slave: 'one being only recognized, the other only recognizing'. These positions do not just constitute two extremes on the pole of recognition, but are immediately situated in the specific dialectic of the *Phenomenology* in which what appears to be true ultimately undoes itself. The master, who is recognised without recognising in turn, ultimately is a slave: while the slave, who recognises without being recognised, is ultimately a master. The ideal here is mutual recognition, but we do not arrive at this ideal without passing through the disruption of the fear of death and the formative activity of work. The slave overcomes the limit of his or her position, recognising without being recognised. It is this tension between an idealist anthropology of recognition and a materialist anthropology of work that has made this passage the inspiration for both Fukuyama and Kojève, for an identity politics of recognition and a revolutionary politics of transformation.[17] Without engaging all of those possible interpretations, it is possible to argue the actual exposition of this passage undermines its humanist beginnings: at the outset, Hegel argued that there is a fundamental division between desire satisfied by objects and the desire for recognition, a division which underscores the intersubjective rather than transindividual conditions of subjectivity. However, in the dialectical reversal of this passage, the point where the master is revealed to be a slave, and vice versa, the reversal turns as much on the relation to the object as to the relation to the other: the master is a slave, not just because he is recognised by one whom he cannot recognise, but because his relation to the object is as a pure object of desire, absolute mediation in its immediacy, while the slave works on the object. As Hegel writes, 'Work, on the other hand, is desire held in check, fleetingness staved off; in other words, work forms and shapes the thing'.[18] This work coupled with the fear of death proves to be another direction for recognition, at least in part: the slave is not recognised, but comes to recognise him or herself through a world that is the product of labour. Labour constitutes another basis for recognition. What is more important to Hegel is less the sharp division between the desire for recognition (what

---

17   Jameson 2010, p. 89.
18   Hegel 1977, ¶195.

we might want to call intersubjectivity), and the relation with things, than the fundamental negation of one's determinate condition: to be recognised is to be seen as something more than this determinate existence, a point that can be arrived at through the instability of fear and the determination of work.[19]

What then is the difference between Hegel and Spinoza when it comes to the question of desire and transindividuality? It is not that Spinoza posits desire as a fundamental assertion of self, as a striving unaffected by others, and that Hegel situates that desire within a general struggle for recognition. Such a division, which places Hegel and Spinoza on opposite sides of the holist/individualist split, would seem to miss their fundamental overlap. For both Spinoza and Hegel, subjectivity is always already relational: individuality cannot be separated from transindividuality. We might say that the difference is still framed by this term 'recognition', which is in some sense absent from Spinoza's thought. Spinoza's understanding of desire, of a desire that is always determined and situated, is in some sense predicated on a fundamental misrecognition. We do not recognise the conditions of our desire, taking it as original and given. This is not the same as the misrecognition that Hegel places as the basis of his dialectic of master and slave: a misrecognition of the other that is always capable of recognition, and carries it as its imminent possibility. Thus it would be wrong to consider Spinoza to be the philosopher of misrecognition that could be juxtaposed to the philosopher of recognition, even though Spinoza gives the former a much more constitutive role in experience. (One could say that the misrecognition is experience for Spinoza, if by experience we mean the first kind of knowledge). If only because Spinoza does not present us with a *telos* from misrecogniton to recognition, desire is radically indifferent from the affects that determine it: the passage from inadequate to adequate ideas is not a dialectic from the in itself to the for itself, but a much more conflictual and uncertain process.

The question remains as how best to contrast Spinoza and Hegel with respect to transindividuality. Returning to Balibar's use of Simondon's terminology, we could say that the difference between Hegel and Spinoza is not just between an immanent and dialectical conception of transindividuality, but between a conception of transindividuality in which the connection with the preindividual is emphasised and a conception in which the transindividual is dominated by intersubjectivity.[20] In Spinoza's conception of desire, desire is

---

19   Williams 2000, p. 66.
20   For Simondon, intersubjectivity fundamentally occludes transindividuality: the relation between already constituted individuals conceals precisely what is at stake in transindividuality, which is the intersection between that which is prior to the individual, the

always relational, always framed by the affects and history, but this relation is less a relation between individuals, between individuals already constituted, than it is a relation between the affects that constitute individuals. When one individual loves what another loves, or hates something that appears to cause pain to an object of love, the relation is less one of recognition between individual and individual, than it is a relation between the transindividual conditions of individuation. The same is true of reason, which is constituted by the common notions. To grasp something adequately is to think in common, to have the same thoughts as others who comprehend.[21] Spinoza's relations are less between constituted individuals, than between the constitutive conditions of individuation, the affects and common notions that pass between individuals, making possible their different relations. As much as recognition constitutes subjectivity for Hegel, making possible the different subjective positions, it does so through individuals who are already constituted: it is an intersubjective relation between individuals who remain in some sense individuated even if they are not recognised as fully human. However, this is not unambiguously the case: as much as Hegel's dialectic of recognition and misrecognition passes through individuals, who may or may not recognise each other, it is also framed by a series of relations – to objects, affects (primarily desire and fear), and practices that exceed the purely intersubjective, most notably work. Hegel's dialectic is itself split between two versions of recognition: the first passes entirely through individuals, through intersubjectivity, while the second is framed by the relation between the subject and the material world.

Recognition has become the watchword, not so much of an interpretation of Hegel, but of an orientation in politics that takes Hegel as its starting point.[22] However, the phrase 'politics of recognition' eclipses as much as it clarifies, since it is not clear that we are dealing with only one form of recognition. With respect to the 'master/slave' dialectic, it would already appear that one divides into two: the dialectic of recognition is split between an intersubjective recognition of subject by subject, master by slave, and the slave's recognition of self in the externalisation of labor.[23] These two dialectics, one of recognition and the other of externalisation, continue through Hegel's thought. Work remains a fundamentally transindividual relation for Hegel, constituting both individual subjects, through the labour of discipline, and social relations,

---

     preindividual relations, and that which exceeds it, the transindividual. Between these two
     relations, the individual is only a phase. (Simondon 2005, p. 317)

21   Balibar 1997, p. 23.
22   The central text on recognition is Alex Honneth's *The Struggle for Recognition*.
23   Jameson 2010, p. 57.

through the interconnection of need. It almost goes without saying that recognition remains the fundamental theme of Hegel's political philosophy. It is worth noting, however, that this is less and less the recognition of self by the other, a relation between individuals, as it is the recognition of the individual in the social institutions and structures that realise its freedom, and are its intimate conditions. Recognition in Hegel is not intersubjectivity, or at least it is not just intersubjectivity, it is also the recognition of self through practices (the individual recognises its transformative conditions), and the recognition of individuality through and in its constitutive institutions. Thus, to recast the opposition between Spinoza and Hegel, which will be explored in the following section: for Spinoza, individuation is always framed in the intersection of the preindividual and transindividual, while for Hegel it is framed between the individual, or intersubjective, and the transindividual.

2   The Politics of Transindividuality

Hegel and Spinoza's understanding of the relational constitution of subjectivity through desire situates them on the same terrain in terms of what could be referred to as their political ontology. This terrain is defined negatively by their distance from any individualist ontology that would reduce the political to a rational choice of isolated subjects, as in social contract theory. The criticism of social contract theory is quite explicit in Hegel, who not only critiques it as incomplete knowledge, but accounts for its genesis in the practices of civil society. It is no less trenchant in Spinoza, who as much as he offers a contract in the *Tractatus Theologico-Politicus* overdetermines it with the affective constitution of social relations. More important than this shared negative terrain is a shared positive terrain that can be defined as the following: for both Spinoza and Hegel, the constitution of the state, of politics, cannot be separated from the constitution of subjectivity; a constitution that is, as we have been trying to demonstrate here, transindividual: determining both individuality and collectivity. The state constitutes subjects, through its various institutions, but at the same time, these subjects, collective and individual, constitute these institutions, through desire, through striving and struggle. This constitution can just as easily take the form of destruction, of contradiction and conflict, which destroys institutions. The objective for both Spinoza and Hegel is to constitute a state, a political structure that will not restrict individual freedom but realise it, in order to overcome on the terrain of politics the antinomy of the individual and society. What I would like to explore in this section is how this political project resituates and reshuffles the different articulation of the transindividual in Hegel and Spinoza's understanding of desire.

The specific project of Spinoza and Hegel's philosophy, which defines their points of contact and differences, is how they understand the interrelation of the constitution of individualities, collective and individual, by the state and social relations, and the constitution of the state, of collectivity, by individualities. Which is to say the specific way in which they comprehend the politics of transindividuality. The locus of this constitution, transformation, and destruction are the various institutions that Hegel and Spinoza examine: Hegel in the well known breakdown of family, civil society, and the state in the *Philosophy of Right*; and Spinoza in the less well known, but equally important, examination of the singular case of the institution of Hebrew theocracy in the *Tractatus Theologico-Politicus*. These institutions, for lack of a better word, constitute transindividual relations, the site where desire is both constructed and undone, where reason intersects with imagination, recognition with misrecognition.

What I have referred to above as the negative and affirmative dimensions, the critique of individuality as a starting point, and the development of another thought of social relations, intersect with respect to the the autonomous self-willing individual. In fundamentally different ways, Spinoza and Hegel not only eschew the ontology of the individual, the spontaneous philosophy of social contract theory and civil society, but account for the genesis of such an idea in a particular representation of social relations, a particular misrecognition of these conditions – in Hegel's terminology, or, in Spinoza's, an inadequate idea. Thus, Spinoza and Hegel could be considered critical transindividual thinkers. The model of criticism I am referring to here is less Kant's transcendental critique than it is Marx's critique of German Idealism in *The German Ideology*. In that text, Marx does not just denounce Idealism, declaring it to be false, but demonstrates how, through the material process of history, it comes to appear that 'consciousness determines life'.[24] Thus, it is not enough to simply denounce the limitations of an individualistic understanding of social relations and propose an alternate ontology of transindividuality, to resort to a sterile opposition of true to false: rather, it is necessary to explain how the latter paradoxically constitutes the former. How, through transindividuality, people come to see themselves as a kingdom within a kingdom, and posit society as nothing other than the sum total of self-interested competitive relations. In their respective critical engagements with the spontaneous philosophy of 'possessive individualism', with Hobbesian social contract theory and classical

---

24   Read 2003, p. 64.

economics, we can begin to see the differences of their accounts of the politics of transindividuality.

In something of a reversal of the chronological order, I would like to begin with Hegel's critique of the individualism of civil society. Hegel's discussion of civil society in the *Philosophy of Right* is oriented towards two fundamental tasks: first, civil society is the negative moment, the moment of understanding, which breaks up the immediate identity of the family; second, it is also Hegel's incorporation of the perspectives of political economy, which are seen as both valid in their attempt to understand the systematic nature of individual actions and limited in constructing society from precisely those individual actions.[25] The passage on civil society has the same starting point as the passage on 'Self-Consciousness' in the *Phenomenology*, namely need, and it has the same ending point, namely recognition, but it passes through the institutions of the market rather than through the narrative of struggle. As needs, and the possibility of meeting them, multiply through the work of civil society (the drive to profit and exploit others), they necessary become more conscious, intelligent, and free. 'The social moment accordingly contains the aspect of liberation, because the strict natural necessity of need is concealed and man's relation is to his own opinion, which is universal, and to a necessity imposed by himself alone, instead of simply to an external necessity, to inner contingency, and to arbitrariness'.[26] Civil society, the system of market-based relations, is an education of desire, traversing the same terrain as the *Phenomenology*. The movement is from immediacy and particularity to universality. Except now recognition passes through the consumption of things. In choosing from the variety of goods available on the market, rather than what is given, determined by the contingency of place, one necessarily chooses according to social criteria, the recognition of others. Labour follows the same fundamental logic, moving from immediacy and particularity to mediation and universality through socialisation and technology: as I am forced to work with others, and with the forces of machines, my work loses its one-sided and rough character to become universal. Both consumption and work overcome the immediate particularity of individuality, the isolated self-interest of civil society, but they do so in opposed ways. They are both transindividual individuations, the one pushed towards individuality, the other towards interchangeability: consumption is the moment of individuation, of differentiation, the particular in the universal, while labour is the moment of discipline, the universal in the particular.

---

25   Hegel 1991a, p. 227.
26   Ibid., p. 230.

There is still a contradiction between consumption and production, but it is not the stark contradiction between the emptiness of the master's desire and the realisation of the slave through labour. It is no longer the difference of two different conceptual personae, of master and slave, but two different transindividual individuations in civil society.[27] What remains the same, linking this passage with its predecessor in the *Phenomenology*, is that misrecognition is given only to pass necessarily into recognition. Here, misrecognition concerns individuality, the subject of civil society sees him or herself as autonomous and sees others merely as means. The education of universality ultimately undoes this perspective. As much as work and consumption educate particularity, as institutions, the market and labour remain all too subject to the contingencies of early capitalist existence. These contingencies manifest themselves in the contamination of commodities, the 'buyer beware' attitude of the market, and in the uncertainty of the labour situation itself, as the perfection of the division of labour makes every form of work, every trade, unstable. The self-interested individual must ultimately recognise itself in the structures and institutions of the state. It must consciously will the universal, rather than simply see it as means to its particular end. Civil society passes into the state.

Hegel presents civil society as both the genesis of the isolated individual, and its overcoming through the education of desire and the discipline of labour. Hegel recognises the limited nature of this perspective for both society and the individual, and argues that social contract theory is nothing other than an attempt to construct the state out of this limited perspective, presenting itself as a purely instrumental relation, as nothing more than the effect of individual wills. Despite this critical recognition, civil society remains merely a moment in the transition from family to the State. As with the dialectic of master and slave, misrecognition is only posited to be overcome: it exists only as the dim outline of an eventual recognition. We can call this teleology, and repeat this well-known criticism of Hegel, but following the investigation of transindividuality above, we could argue that this relates to a limited conception of the transindividual, dominated by intersubjectivity and the opposition between recognition and misrecognition, a point that will stand out in contrast with Spinoza.

In contrast to Hegel's engagement with individualism through the texts and practices of political economy, Spinoza's engagement begins with the terrain of religion in the Appendix to Part One of the *Ethics*. The Appendix would appear to describe a general, even universal, condition of the limits of mankind's knowledge regarding the world, and the unavoidable fictions of the free subject

---

27   Jameson 2010, p. 112.

and anthropocentric God. However, commentators such as Matheron, Bove, and Balibar have focused on the overlooked distinction that Spinoza makes in that text between prejudice and superstition. Prejudice is the opacity of the immediate, the awareness of our desires without their conditions, that leads us to project the *telos* of desire unto the universe itself, to see some intentionality, even a mysterious one, behind the random events of the world. Superstition is an attempt to organise this spontaneous philosophy, assigning it a determinate and shared set of symbols and meanings through a set of practices.[28] As we have argued above, the history that constitutes desire is radically singular, shaped by the encounters that make up one's life. Superstition is an attempt to organise these singular encounters into a collective memory, a collective desire, by restricting and regulating practices and symbols. It is an attempt to create habit, a character, at the collective level.[29] As Spinoza writes, '... nature creates individuals, not nations, and it is only difference of language, of laws, and of established customs that divides individuals into nations'.[30] Superstition is the constitution of community on the grounds of the imagination. Thus, as much as the Appendix describes something of the general human condition, it does so less as a universal essence than as a flexible schema. It provides the general conditions that different forms of superstition, different religions (and we can add, ideologies) will realise: namely, the *telos* of individual striving, the search for a meaning in the complexity of the world. As Spinoza writes, 'the multitude has no ruler more potent than superstition'.[31]

Tracing the distinction between prejudice and superstition, between the originary opacity of existence (the tendency to see oneself as a 'kingdom within a kingdom'), and the kingdoms that are constructed on such unstable grounds, makes it possible to extract a politics from Spinoza's ontology. Or, more to the point, it connects the transindividual conception of individuality of the *Ethics* with the examination of political institutions in the *Theological-Political Treatise*. However, this connection is framed through the rather singular case of the ancient Hebrew state. The State is perhaps the most powerful example

---

28   Bove 1996, p. 179.
29   Étienne Balibar has focused on the word 'ingenium', translated as nature or temperament, to argue for the link between individual and collective memory. 'By ingenium, we should understand a memory whose form has been determined by the individual's experience of life and by his or her various encounters, and which, as a result of the unique way in which it has been constituted, is inscribed both in the mind (or soul) and in the dispositions of the body' (Balibar 1998, p. 29). The task of politics, at least in theocracy, is to constitute an ingenium, a memory, for the collective body.
30   Spinoza 2001, p. 200.
31   Ibid., p. 2.

of the constitution of national and individual identity through the practices and rituals of religion. The quotidian dimensions of the ancient Hebraic law, dictating meals, harvest times, and basic details of comportment, articulated together the nature and character of the individual with that of the nation. As Spinoza writes, 'to men so habituated to it obedience must have appeared no longer as bondage, but as freedom'.[32] As powerful as this reduction of the individual to the collective is, it remains a singular case, dependent on the sacred covenant between God and Moses. Theocracy remains a limit case in the assessment of political constitutions, not just because it is dependent upon a singular and unrepeatable event, but also because the absolute identity of self and state, freedom and obedience, is difficult to maintain given the singular nature of desire.[33] An irreducible aspect of theocracy remains, however, through the various themes of selection and symbolic participation that define almost every nation as 'one nation under God'.[34]

Hegel and Spinoza each offer a critical account of individualism, of the isolated autonomous subject that much political thought, not to mention contemporary common sense, takes to be a natural given. This account is critical in that it exposes the transindividual conditions of this perspective. For Hegel it is rooted in the practices and relations of civil society, which isolate individuals while relating them behind their backs. For Spinoza, these practices are primarily religious, the rituals and practices that produce the imaginary of an autonomous individual, anthropocentric God, and chosen community. This difference is less one of philosophical and political position, a fundamental argument about the centrality of economy or religion, base or superstructure, than it is a difference of historical moment, the difference of over one hundred and fifty years, from the dominance of religion to that of civil society and capital. Which does not mean that there are not overlaps and points of contact. Matheron has suggested that Spinoza's general remark about the communication of affects, the constitution of objects through desire, and the critique of finalism, provide a basis for an understanding of economic alienation.[35] What is money, but the universal object of love, an object that imposes its finality over other particular strivings. This somewhat anachronistic and underdeveloped critique is useful in underscoring an important difference between Spinoza and Hegel. As critical as Hegel is of civil society, or its atomistic perspective, it remains for him a moment, a moment that will pass as individuality recognises

---

32   Ibid., p. 199.
33   Ibid., p. 3.
34   Balibar 1996c, p. 200.
35   Matheron 1969, p. 122.

the necessity of the state. Misrecognition necessarily passes to recognition. For Spinoza, however, there is no such progression. The imagination, whether it be of God or money, the universal object of desire, is as much a part of human existence as reason. There is no *telos*, no necessary progression from an inadequate conception of one's connections and relations to an adequate one. Instead, there is a necessary ambivalence between the transindividual dimensions of desire and rationality.[36] For both Hegel and Spinoza, the opposition is not between individual and community, with either one occupying the position of the true or correct political position, as in versions of individualism or communitarianism, but between two different regimes of the transindividual, one of which confronts the individual as a hostile condition and the other which is grasped adequately, or recognised, in Hegel's terminology. Their difference lies in part in how they understand this transformation.

3   Conclusions

Hegel's transindividual critique provides an account of the structures and institutions that produce the isolated and individual perspective: civil society, which is to say capital, produces a world in which the individual sees him or herself as isolated, relating to others only through competition. This production, like the slave's status, is no sooner given as it is overcome, as the conditions for its production (in this case the interconnected world of work and desire), prove to be the conditions of its dialectical overcoming. In contrast to this, Spinoza presents a critical perspective in which recognition and misrecogntion, or, in more properly Spinozist terms, reason and imagination, are mutually constitutive, mutually intertwining, despite Spinoza's suggestive remarks regarding theocracy as a particular practice, a particular constitution of subjectivity, which could be extended to an understanding of the various institutions which produce the perspective of a kingdom within a kingdom. In general, however, Spinoza sees individuation as a natural given, a product of the necessarily fragmentary and partial nature of initial knowledge. It is possible to say that each supplements the other: Hegel offers sociohistorical specificity, arguing that family, civil society, and the state must be seen as transindividual conditions, while Spinoza presents what could be called, following Macherey, a non-teleological dialectic in which superstition and knowledge, imagination and reason, are posited as mutually constitutive conditions of collectivity and

---

36   Balibar 1998, p. 88.

individuality. However, as I have suggested, their differences with respect to the basic problem of transindividuality, the emphasis on the preindividual as constitutive of the individuation of desire versus a transindividual constitution of self more oriented around the central ideal of recognition, would make this difficult. Rather, it is possible to see a definite problem and a provocation emerge between their two perspectives on the transindividual: if transindividuality includes as one of its modalities a fundamental opacity of its very conditions, the perspective of the isolated individual, and if this inadequacy is seen as constitutive rather than a premise that will be necessarily overcome, as imagination, as something more than the vanishing presupposition of reason, then it can only be overcome politically, by a transformation of the transindividual conditions that constitute it.

CHAPTER 13

The Order and Connection of Ideology is the Same as the Order and Connection of Exploitation: Or, Towards a Bestiary of the Capitalist Imagination

Of all of the various attempts to define and clarify the recent turn to Spinoza, perhaps the most provocative is offered by Antonio Negri: '... in the postindustrial age the Spinozian critique of representation of capitalist power corresponds more to the truth than does the analysis of political economy'.[1] Negri's formulation is provocative not just in that it suggests a critique of capitalist power which is not grounded by (the Marxist) critique of political economy, but in that it suggests a need to counter capital not just at the level of the economy, but at the level of its representation of power. Capital needs to be countered at the level of ideas as much as social relations. Negri's provocation has perhaps been answered by two contemporary neo-Spinozist writers, Frédéric Lordon and Yves Citton, the former of whom has developed a Spinozist critique of political economy while the latter has pioneered an analysis of the representations of power.

Read together, Lordon and Citton's work can be understood as a response to two fundamentally different questions. The first is a question integral to both Marx and Spinoza: how to understand the relation between the order and connection of things and ideas – base and superstructure – in terms of their identity, causal relations, and difference? Spinoza and Marx offer two very different formulations and answers to this question. It is precisely their difference that brings them together. Spinoza offers a non-reductive immanence to Marx's hierarchy, while Marx's thought offers to historically situate and place the eternal order of being and thinking. Thus if the first question is ontological, encompassing different perspectives throughout time, to a fundamental and unchanging question about the relation of minds and bodies, things and ideas, the second question is more contemporary, more conjunctural, brought about by changes in economic and political structure. How can the current economic and political transformations – neoliberalism, the crisis, austerity – be understood and transformed by looking at the intersections of material conditions, ideas, and imagination? Several writers have underscored the manner in which

---

1 Negri 1997, p. 246.

neoliberalism is perhaps best understood as a change of political imagination as much as social relations, a question that has become all the more pressing after the current crash, as the neoliberal imagination continues to structure responses and policy.[2] Answering these two questions together, or examining the ontological by means of the conjunctural and vice versa, in turn answers a third question, why turn to Spinoza today as a way of understanding social and political life.

Lordon and Citton's projects intersect in the most recent wave of neo-Spinozist scholarship. Their project is unified in the sense that it is turned specifically to considering the question of the relationship of Spinoza's thought to a theory of social relations, or even the social sciences, as can be seen in their jointly edited *Spinoza et les science sociales*. At the core of this project is a turn – not so much to Spinoza's critique of the imaginary, as it was with Louis Althusser's account of ideology, or his ontology, as in Antonio Negri's account of constituent power – but to Spinoza's anthropology (if it can be called that) as it encompasses desire, affects, and the imagination. For both Lordon and Citton it is the conatus, the striving underlying every existence, that makes possible a new thought of social relations.[3] This striving, this desire, as much as it defines 'man's very essence', is irreducibly singular – we each strive in different ways – but the direction and orientation of this striving is shaped by affects and the history of encounters. Spinoza's conatus overcomes the dualism between holistic and individualistic accounts of social relations, starting with neither the society nor the individual but the relations that are their mutual constitution. At the same time, their projects are divided according to their different disciplinary focus. Lordon has most persistently examined the extent to which Spinoza's anthropology of desire could address the fundamental questions of motive and interest underlying economic thought in works such as *Capitalisme, désir, et servitude: Marx and Spinoza* (published in English as *Willing Slaves of Capital: Spinoza and Marx on Desire*) and *La Société des Affects: Pour un structuralisme des passions*, while Citton has turned his attention to the way in which our actions and desires are structured by narratives and ideology in *Mythocratie: Storytelling et Imaginaire de Gauche* and related works. It is by reading Lordon and Citton together that we can return not only to Spinoza's fundamental insight regarding the order and connection of things and ideas, understanding the challenge of thinking beyond the division of idealism and materialism, but forward as well, towards the question of the relationship of base and superstructure in contemporary society.

---

2 Mirowski 2013, p. 1.
3 Citton and Lordon 2008, p. 27.

1   **Lordon: Economy of Affects/Affective Economy**

Lordon's approach to Spinoza is framed by two questions or problems; the first is from Marx while the second is from the social sciences in general. With respect to the first, Lordon argues that the Spinoza/Marx relation should be considered less one of influence of the latter on the former, than of Spinoza answering a question that Marx had formulated but could not answer. That question is the fundamental question of reproduction, of why it is that workers continue to come to work every day, subjecting themselves to exploitation. Or, to pose the question in Spinoza's terms, why do workers struggle for exploitation as if it were liberation? Lordon argues that Spinoza is more suited to answer this question than Marx; at the centre of Spinoza's anthropology is an account of how the very striving in preserving one's being can be structured and restructured by social relations, most notably the affects.[4] Affects animate individual desires, providing its love and hates, but they are in turn determined by the history of relations. The response to the specific question posed by Marxism, that of the continued participation of workers in their exploitation, then relates to a larger problem, a problem which is as foundational to the social sciences as it is to philosophy: the question of how to reconcile individual intentions and social structures. As Lordon argues, this question has become especially pressing as of late in social sciences as the structuralist turn of recent years has been met with a call to the return of the concept of individual agency.[5]

What Lordon argues that Spinoza offers is an 'energetic structuralism', one that does not oppose structure to striving, the richness of affective life to the forms of institutions, but posits the intersection of striving with affects, individuality with social relations.[6] As much as Spinoza makes desire 'man's very essence', it no less important that he unmoors desire from every *telos*, every end, even from the idea of survival. Individuals strive, but what they strive for is defined by their histories, by the causal relations that affect and determine them. One person may strive for alcohol, another for knowledge, but this is only because a series of encounters, a series of affects of joy and sadness, have determined them to seek these things as sources of joy. The desire that is man's very essence is intransitive, lacking an object; its becoming-transitive is the process of not just individual biography and economic history, but is, more importantly, the site of their intersection.[7] The relational basis of the

---

4   Lordon 2014, p. x.
5   Lordon 2013, p. 18.
6   Lordon 2001, p. 10.
7   Lordon 2001, p. 11.

conatus includes, in Lordon's interpretation, not just the immediately present others and their affective composition, but the past strivings that structure and determine institutions.[8] The striving of the conatus must be historicised. The things that we strive for, those that we call good, such as money, which Spinoza argues 'occupies the mind of the multitude more than anything else', have as their necessary precondition not only the encounters that frame our imagination, but the destruction of other objects, other relations. As with the example of money, it is not only because money has been associated with personal pleasures – a child's first allowance and the pedagogy of consumption – but the entire sphere of social goods, that it becomes an object of desire.

Historicising Spinoza starts with the fundamental capitalist relation in which workers separated from the means of production must sell their labour in order to earn money. As Marx argues, this relation is itself the product of a process of separation from the means of production called 'primitive accumulation'. For Lordon the separation of workers from the means of production is viewed less as a loss, an alienation, than a fundamental reorientation of striving, of the conatus.[9] There is an indifference to the activity itself, the goals of the particular activity are stripped of their meaning, their particular orientations of good and bad, perfect and imperfect. As much as we might affectively attach ourselves to any particular job, any particular task, developing our potential and relations, becoming the cause of our joy, this is secondary to the desire – and need – for money. At the level of affect and desire, it is the object, the money earned, that matters. There is thus an affective split at the core of the labour process between the activity and its results.

Reading Spinoza through primitive accumulation (and vice versa) has two effects. First, it reveals the falsity of any justification of capitalism that rests on some anthropology of interest or competition. There is no basic greed or fundamental competitive impulse functioning as the anthropological basis of capitalism. Absolutely asocial self-interest would not drive people to work every day, but drive them to simply grab what they wanted. Going to work every day to earn money is less an expression of some fundamental drive of competition than an effect of the political and social organization of labour. The striving to persevere in capitalism is already structured by the separation from the means of production and the wage relation.[10] The recognition that all striving, even that of basic self interest, is already structured, then opens up the question of

<hr>

8   Lordon 2012, p. 67.
9   Weeks 2011, p. 43.
10   Lordon 2006, p. 75.

the structuring of all striving, of all the myriad ways of working that are instituted in capitalism. What we could call the affective composition of labour is how much joy is sought in the activity of labour itself, or how much is sought in terms of the accumulation it makes possible, at any given time. This shift between activity and object is complicated by (and is both cause and effect of) the changing relations of hope and fear in a given historical moment.

Lordon offers a sketch of this history of the affective composition of labour, beginning in primitive accumulation and continuing in terms of the shift between Fordism and Post-Fordism. The first period, that of Fordism, is defined by its intersecting transformations of both the separation of activity from value and the affective investment of consumption. Labour is simplified and fragmented, stripped of its pleasures and mastery. This is the work of the assembly line. But at the same time, the sphere of consumption is expanded. Ford's famous 'five dollar day' increased the spending power of consumers.[11] The affective composition of Fordism could be described as a fundamental reorganisation of conatus, of striving, away from labour, from activity, and towards consumption. The worker's activity is fragmented, made part of a whole that exceeds it, becoming as much passivity as activity. The sadness of work, its exhaustion, is compensated for with the joys of consumption. This transformation from an affective investment in work to an affective investment in consumption could also be described as a shift from active joy, joy in one's capacity to act, to passive joy, a joy that is passively received (or consumed). Passive joyful affects are those that increase our power of acting, while remaining outside of our control. The pleasures of consumption, of consumerism, can be understood as passive joys, they promise some increase of our power, of our joys and strivings, but what they can never give, what can never be sold is the very capacity to actively produce new pleasures. As Pascal Sévérac has argued, the real threat to becoming active stems not from the sad affects, the angers and hatreds that always express a lessening of our capacity to act, but the passive joys. Passive joys placate us, giving us a sense of an increase of power, but this increase is passively endured rather than actively produced.[12] Consumerism remains the very model of a passive joy, as the pleasures of consumption are passive in the face of manufacture and marketing which mould and shape them.

The Fordist compromise can thus be distinguished from later, post-Fordist, articulations of affects, transformations that can also be described through a transformation of work and consumption. Broadly speaking, these transform-

---

11   Lordon 2014, p. 29.
12   Sévérac 2005, p. 333.

ations can initially be described by a dismantling of the security and stability of work. The Fordist compromise carried with it a dimension of stability, brought about by collective bargaining and the centrality of the contract.[13] Post-Fordism, as it is defined by Lordon, is first and foremost a transformation of the norms and structures that organise and structure action. As such, it is fundamentally asymmetrical: workers are exposed to more and more risk, while capitalists, specifically those concerned with financial capital, are liberated from the classical risks of investment.[14] This loss of security for the worker fundamentally changes the affective dimension of money. It is no longer an object of hope, the possible means of realising one's desires, but becomes that which wards off fear. Money becomes part of the desire for security, the only possible security: one's skills, one's actions, will have no value in the future, but money always will.[15] One could understand this shift from Fordism to Post-Fordism as a shift from a regime of hope (tinged with fear) to a regime of fear (tinged with hope). Hope and fear cannot be separated, but that does not mean that a given affective composition is not defined more by one than the other. Thus, it could be argued that the concept of 'precarity' is best understood as an affective concept. It is less of a matter of some objective shift in the status of security than it is a shift in how work and security is perceived.[16] If precarity can be used to adequately describe contemporary economic life, it is less because everyone is working under some kind of temporary or part-time contract (although these have become significant), than it is because a constant sense of insecurity infuses every work situation.[17] Precarity affects even stable employment through its technological transformation; it is always possible to be working or at least in touch with work, and a generalised anxiety infuses all of work, as more indirect measures of productivity replace the quotas of the assembly line.[18] Work is further abstracted, not just from its object, but from the activity itself, as the activity loses any internal standard from which it can be judged. Generalised insecurity, constant contact, and the uncertainty of evaluation define the post-Fordist economy of fear.

Lordon does not completely identify post-Fordism with fear. The imperative of post-Fordism is not, as it was with Fordism, to devalue work in favour of consumption, but to turn work itself into an object of desire. Work becomes

13   Lordon 2002, p. 70.
14   Citton 2012b, p. 68.
15   Lordon 2014, p. 24.
16   Berlant 2011, p. 201.
17   Southwood 2011, p. 16.
18   Berardi 2009, p. 32.

the terrain for desire, for affective realisation. As Pierre Dardot and Christian Laval argue, the constitution of the neoliberal subject could be defined as a revalorisation of insecurity and risk into opportunity and chance.[19] Insecurity is rebranded as opportunity. Or, as Lordon argues, neoliberalism could be defined as the maximum colinearisation of individual and institutional striving: the individual becomes a microcosm of the economic system, 'a company of one', realising one's own potential. Corporate life and individual life are subject to the exact same rules, and can be explained in the same way. Thus, rather than see neoliberal society as an open and innovative society, Lordon insists that it is an economic order which tolerates minimal difference between institution and individual, remaking all of affective life in the model of ceaseless maximisation of profit, of networking and self-transformation.

Lordon's presentation of history is schematic, perhaps overly so; in a recent book, *La Société des Affects*, he augments this schema by turning to two of the final propositions of Part Three of *Ethics*. In those final passages Spinoza argues that there are as many loves and hates 'as there are species of objects by which we are affected' (EIIIP56) and that 'each affect of each individual differs from the affect of another as much as the essence of one from the essence of the other' (EIIIP57). The multiple objects, and multiple strivings, constitute the basis for multiple affective compositions, each one ambivalent and shifting, as the same object is both the object of love and hate, and the same individual comes to hate what they once loved. Rereading these propositions back into the schematic history of different affective modes of production does not dispense with the latter, shattering it into a pure multiplicity where a thousand flowers bloom. Rather, these differences, variations of love and hate, must be understood as variations on a dominant theme. As Lordon argues, there will always be kind bosses and interesting jobs, but these differences and deviations are ultimately just different expressions of the same fundamental relation. The nicest boss in the world cannot fundamentally alter the fundamental structure of labour conditions; the affective engagement at the level of individual intent does nothing to alter the basic relation with the activity and object.[20] This affective veneer, the work of human relations, is not inconsequential: as much as it has a role in motivating individual workers, the real work it does is in producing the appearance of difference, a society of individual actions rather than persistent structures. Much of the quotidian criticism of work, or of capitalism in general, focuses on the differences: we complain about this boss, or

---

19   Dardot and Laval 2014, p. 276.
20   Lordon 2013, p. 94.

protest this big corporation for being particularly offensive, but do not address the fundamental relation of exploitation or the profit motive which exceeds the different ways in which it is instantiated. The plurality, a plurality dictated by what Spinoza would call the order of nature, the different ways in which things have affected us, takes precedence over the perception of common relations.

The emphasis on plurality, on a superficial difference of employer or corporation, underneath which lies a fundamental sameness of structure, is not London's only reference to the symbolic dimension of contemporary capitalism, the manner in which it determines not just the object of desire and the activity of the conatus, but its fundamental sense and orientation. Lordon defines this orientation as symbolic violence:

> Symbolic violence consists then properly speaking in the production of a double imaginary, the imaginary fulfilment, which makes the humble joys assigned to the dominated appear sufficient, and the imaginary of powerlessness, which convinces them to renounce any greater ones to which they might aspire.[21]

Consumer society offers images of the plentitude of desire, defining all of the various goods, while the labour market delimits the possibility of what can be done, delimiting the very contours of activity. As much as the conatus is structured by the fundamental condition of capitalism, by the commodification of goods, and the structure of the labour relation, this structure is necessarily 'personalised', experienced in singular ways, which is to say that it becomes a biography, a narrative.

2   Citton: Politics of Myth/Myth of Politics

The idea that narrative, biography, functions as a necessary supplement to the articulation of the conatus raises its own set of questions. Any narrative of individual striving necessarily encompasses biographical and social dimensions; it is made up of both individual experiences and cultural inheritances. Narrative, like the conatus, is the point of intersection of the individual and the collective, or, in a word – transindividual.[22] It is precisely this transindividual dimension of the imagination that is at the centre of Citton's investigation into

21   Lordon 2014, p. 110 [Translation slightly modified].
22   Citton 2010, p. 30.

'mythocracy'. At the core of Citton's concept of mythocracy is a reexamination of both the imagination of power, the way that political theories represent
and imagine power, and the power of the imagination, the role of the imagination in political and social existence. As Citton argues, this new imagination
of power has its foundation in Spinoza's assertion 'that we neither strive for,
nor will, neither want nor desire anything because we judge it to be good; on
the contrary we judge something to be good because we strive for it, will it,
want it or desire it' (EIIIP9S). As we have seen, this reorientation of desire does
not so much constitute a Copernican revolution back to the self, but explodes
it into a universe of causal connections and an eternity of relations. Citton
argues that this assertion radically undermines any attempt to make desire the
degree zero of autonomy, and to make the will of individuals the foundation
of politics.[23] Desires must be understood as produced. Spinoza's attentiveness
to the production and historicity of desire becomes even more timely in an
age in which the conditions for producing desire, for constituting new affects,
have only increased and multiplied. The mixture of democracy, consumer society, and marketing that defines contemporary society demands that we move
beyond thinking in terms of repression and consent as the basis for politics.
It is necessary to theorise the forms of 'soft power' that produce and constitute desires and consent.[24] Rather than simply assume that what the 'people'
want is good, it is increasingly important to examine the political and economic
conditions that structure desire, determining why we want what we want. Far
from being a relic from some sort of pre-democratic age, Spinoza's basic question as to why people fight for servitude as if it were salvation becomes all the
more pressing in contemporary politics. Spinoza escapes the binary of absolute freedom or total domination, making it possible to grasp the relations, the
determinations, the conducts and the actions that constitute the actual relations of power.[25]

Whereas Lordon turns his attention to the role of economic transformations
in determining the orientation and organisation of striving, Citton focuses on
the role that the imagination, myth, and narrative play in orienting and being
oriented by desire. Despite this difference of object, there is a fundamentally
shared method. Narratives like institutions only function in and through the
strivings that animate them and are oriented by them. Narratives only work if
they capture individual hopes, fears, and desires. Narratives do not just capture existing hopes and desires, but constitute them, defining our desire and

---

23   Citton 2006, p. 14.
24   Citton 2010, p. 11.
25   Citton 2010, p. 62.

capacity to act. The stories we learn shape and form our desires. The division between the initial affects that are captured and captivated by stories, and the latter striving shaped by narratives, is only heuristic. Reality is much more causally complex. We do not enter into the world with 'natural' strivings, untouched by narrative and myth, only to then have them channelled by the fictions we consume. Our desires, our loves and hates, are already shaped by narratives, by scripts inherited through television and books. We enter into a world already scripted, and, as Spinoza argues in his definition of the first kind of knowledge, our life is defined as much by signs and images as things experienced.[26]

The stories that we tell, the narratives that we weave, shape and inform our affects and imagination, which in turn shape and inform our actions. As Spinoza argues, what we imagine we are capable of in turn limits our capacities. It is possible that we over-estimate ourselves, but underestimation is almost impossible: '[Man] really cannot do what he images he cannot do'. (EIIIDXXVIIIE). The corollary of this is not necessarily true: we cannot do everything that we imagine. But imagining that something is possible is a precondition for action. To which Citton adds that the scenarios that we imagine, the stories and narratives that we consume, inform our understanding of reality, not in the sense that we confuse fiction with reality, but that the basic relations that underlie our fictions shape our understanding of reality. It is not that we confuse fiction with reality, believing everything that we see, but that the fundamental elements of every narrative – events, actions, and transformations – become the very way that we make sense of reality. Fiction exists in a permanent relation of metalepsis with reality, as figures and relations from one constantly inform the other.[27] Narrative is a way of prefiguring acting, and the very conditions of individual and collective transformation. Case in point: themes of individualism and individual responsibility are less particular narratives, particular works of fiction, than 'meta-scenes', underlying many stories, crisscrossing multiple narratives, all the various versions of hero's journeys and 'chosen ones', and spilling into individual and political life.[28] Meta-scenes, the general conditions of every narrative, are the constitutions and solidification of

---

26   Citton's point on this comes close to Bernard Stiegler's argument regarding primary, secondary, and tertiary retentions. Stiegler's conceptual vocabulary is drawn from Husserl rather than Spinoza, but that does not keep him from making a similar point. For Stiegler, retentions and memories shape protentions or future experience. The increasing prevalence of tertiary retentions, of inherited memories through television and mass media, eventually programmes and designs memory. (Citton 2010, p. 79)

27   Citton 2010, p. 86.

28   Citton 2012a, p. 128.

power, the manner in which it acts on actions. They are the *potestas* that organises and orients *potentia*. This power increases as the conditions for the production and dissemination of narratives, of scenes and meta-scenes, belongs to a few monopolies. These monopolies are both material and symbolic, controlling both the presses and the conditions and dissemination of the characters and stories that are figures of collective love and admiration.[29]

The imagination would seem to be forever relegated to subjection, to a subjection that increases in our contemporary society of the spectacle. However, Spinoza argues that we have the power of ordering and connecting the affections of the body according to the order of the intellect (EVP10). The mind cannot determine the body, but it can shape and form other connections. As Citton writes,

> The particular power of humanity (and the linchpin of our emancipation) is thus located in our faculty to reorder differently the images, the thoughts, the affects, the desires and the beliefs that are associated in our mind, the phrases that come out of our mouths, and the movements that emanate from our bodies.[30]

It is necessary to not only see passivity and activity crisscrossing the individual and collective imagination, but, more importantly, to see that the increasing collective dimension of our imagination, the tendency to think and experience the world in and through narratives which are disseminated across multiple bodies and minds, is a condition for both activity and passivity. It is because we are determined, subject to the dissemination of affects and imagination across multiple bodies and minds, that we also have the capacity to act, affecting and determining other bodies and minds. A truly individual, and idiosyncratic imagination, locked in its own references and associations, would be incapable of communicating. Rather than to immediately associate collectivity with passivity and the individual with activity, it is necessary to think of the passive and active dimension of both collective and individual imagination. As Citton argues, mythocracy is both the condition of our subjection and our liberation. If, as Spinoza argued, we can reorder our affects according to the intellect, then the creation of new narratives is the creation of new ways of feeling and imagining the world, which is in turn the creation of new ways of acting in it.

---

29   Citton 2010, p. 143.
30   Citton 2010, p. 75 (my translation).

Citton's mythocracy follows the same basic order and connection as Lordon's energetic structuralism, arguing that narratives, like institutions, are made by the very desires and strivings that they organise. Despite this similarity of method, which is nothing other than the basic condition of the conatus, of desire that is as much determined by what it imagines as how it can act, the question remains of the real relations between activity and imagination, economy and mythocracy.

3   Conclusion: The Order and Connection of Exploitation and Ideology

As much as both economic colinearisation – the transformation of striving – and narrative meta-scenarisation – the transformation of the imagination – can be theorised through the same relations, in each case it is a matter of the determination of the conatus, striving, of the order of actions and of ideas. The question remains as to how to link together both the economic order of activities and objects, and the ideological order of narratives and imagination. Of course they intersect all the time, and must necessarily do so. The economic order of colinearisation of desire, an order that increasingly ties the striving and desire of the individual with that of the capitalist system, cannot function without its corresponding narratives and mythocracy. This mythocracy has as its founding condition the idea of individual autonomy and responsibility. The contemporary order supplements this orientation with narratives of individual success and failure. There is no capitalist orientation of desire without its cast of Horatio Algers or their modern infomercial-hawking equivalents, of hardworking individuals who have made it rich. Images of individual success and transformation reflect and control our spontaneous ideology of autonomy and independence, effectively reinforcing it. Such figures not only constitute objects of envy and desire, figures to emulate, but they also inform how we make sense of the very transformations that are possible, turning our attention away from structural conditions and collective efforts and towards individual striving. If individual success constitutes one side of the capitalist mythocracy, then its no less necessary corollary is the figure of the lazy or irresponsible worker, the welfare queen, or public worker.[31] Failure must be individualised as well. The 'welfare-queen' is the reverse of the entrepreneurial subject: she is one who has failed to mobilise her abilities and talents, relying on others for

---

31   Citton 2010, p. 68.

her very existence. The economic imaginary has as its extremes not the worker and capitalist, but the independent individual, or the entrepreneur who creates opportunities and new conditions, and the individual that fails to work hard, to take risks, and becomes dependent. It thus functions as an allegory of the extremes of autonomy and dependence. The myths of individual success and failure, informed and shaped by other myths of nation and race, orient our loves and hates, while simultaneously occluding the actual causal relations that determine our existence.

Thus as much as it is possible, even necessary, to posit the intersection of the structuring of desire and imagination, such an assertion does not in itself articulate the ground of their intersection and causality. How does the change of economic relations affect and determine the relations of myths and interpretation, and vice versa. A clue is perhaps offered by Spinoza's critique of superstition, which argued that material uncertainty alters and transforms the very capacity to make sense of the world. As Spinoza writes of humanity's tendency for superstition, 'If men were able to exercise complete control over all their circumstances, or if continuous good fortune where always their lot, they would never be prey to superstition'.[32] While Spinoza's *Ethics* insists on the absolute identity of the order and connection of ideas and things as two different ways of grasping the same thing, Spinoza's political writings argue for a causality in which the anxieties and fears of material life transform the interpretation of the world. Fear and hope drive us to see meaning and intention where there is no intention, transforming causes into signs. Thus, it is possible to ask if Spinoza's understanding of superstition can be transposed to the world of economic relations and political myths.

Is there a similar causal connection between economic uncertainty, the fears of precarity that Lordon analyses, and the myths of individual action and agency that Citton argues constitute our economic world? Does economic uncertainty and fear give rise to superstitious narratives of individual guilt and blame? Would this explain why such narratives have only increased rather than diminished in the years of the economic recession?[33] There is some suggestion of this possibility offered by Jennifer Silva in her book, *Coming Up Short: Working Class Adulthood in an Age of Uncertainty*. Silva's work is less theoretical than ethnographic, studying the lives of working-class individuals whose path is not anything like the conventional life of career and family. As she describes this general transition:

---

32   Spinoza 1998, p. 1.
33   Mirowski 2013, p. 155.

At its core, this emerging working-class adult self is characterized by low expectations of work, wariness toward romantic commitment widespread of social institutions, profound isolation from others, and an overriding focus on their emotions and psychic health. Rather than turn to politics to address the obstacles standing in the way of a secure adult life, the majority of the men and women I interview crafted deeply *personal* coming of age stories, grounding their adult identities in recovering from their painful pasts – whether additional childhood abuse, family trauma, or abandonment and forging an emancipated, transformed and adult self.[34]

As Silva argues, in a manner that is oddly proximate to such neo-Spinozists, what drives this transformation of life away from public action to private action is a mood economy, in which the only possible payoff is the infinite work on the self. This 'mood economy' can be understood as a particular transformation of the affective composition of labour, one that valorises neither the activity of work nor the objects of consumption, but makes self-transformation the only valued activity. In that sense, it is the interiorisation of the limited prospects of austerity society. Thus to complete Lordon's schema of different affective compositions, we could argue that the affective composition of austerity displaces the affective investment of the work of finding work in neoliberalism, the work of networking, with an affective investment in the infinite work on the self. Such a composition of the striving is difficult to realise or imagine without an entire transformation of the imagination of the sense and capacity of individual action. The modern regime of responsibility simultaneously elevates the self, making one responsible for all of the various forms of hardship and difficulty one has endured, while denigrating the individual's capacity to act: all energies are turned inward, towards self-improvement. Self-improvement is less a specific narrative as it is a kind of meta-scenarisation, underlying multiple genres and forms of fiction, daytime, television, and political narratives. The correlation of an individual economy of self-improvement and an imaginary of individual responsibility does not yet prove any sort of causation. It is difficult to understand which came first, diminishing prospects of rewarding work or even consumption, or the various ideologies and spiritualities of the individual self and the infinite task of its improvement.

The intersection of economy and mythocracy is not utter determination. There are other possibilities for organising strivings in an economy of dwind-

---

34   Silva 2013, p. 11.

ling job prospects and security. There are also other possible ways to imagine, to organise the affects, ones that draw less and less on the individual as focal point and target, but develop the commonalities and conditions for action. The political movements aimed against austerity, from Occupy Wall Street to the organisations against student debt, have perhaps had success more at the level of constituting different imaginations and gestures than at the level of organisation. It is not that we act differently – at least not yet, still returning to the same jobs and actions, the same labour relations and pleasures of consumer society – but that we have at least begun to organise our thoughts and affects differently, as new terms, such as the 99%, become the focus of our attention and desire, and, with these, a new sensibility, a new experience of the present.

To argue that the existing correlations between the order of the economy and that of ideology are not necessary is to pose the question of relation in a different way, in terms of difference and transformation rather than correlation. How is it possible to construct other imaginaries? Other economic relations? The perspective pursued here breaks strongly with two classical answers to these questions. Given that every economy, every orientation of striving, is sustained by an imaginary (with its corresponding characters and conditions for acting), a purely economic change, a change of the mode of production, is impossible. Similarly, any change of the imagination without a corresponding change of economic relations would crash against the fact that every economy is also a series of practices that ground and determine a particular way of interpreting the world. Neither the economy nor ideology can be the site of transformation in itself. This connection between the order of bodies and ideas does not mean that everyone is forever locked in the same actions and thoughts. Rather it suggests that every transformation must be a transformation of both thoughts, a reorganising of ways of thinking, of imagination, and actions, of practices and relations. This transformation begins with a transformation of narrative, of myth, and not a transition from myth to knowledge. This is because there is, as Spinoza argues, a limited efficacy of the true insofar as it is true: knowledge alone is incapable of seizing minds and bodies, of eliciting interest and desire. Transformation must be imagined before it is known. In order to transform the world it is necessary to see that transformation is possible, to move beyond the world in its 'givenness', recognising the forces and limitations that constitute it as such.[35] Humanity cannot do what it cannot imagine that it can do.

---

35   Lordon 2014, p. 140.

The order of collective, political liberation follows the same general structure of personal liberation outlined in the *Ethics*: it is a spiral in which new orders of thoughts and relations condition new orders of practices and vice versa, each turn in the spiral reinforcing itself and expanding to affect others. This transformation is as much a transformation of the imagination as it is the world, and is necessarily one before it can be the other. This is what is at stake in every revolutionary transformation.

CHAPTER 14

Conscienta Sive Ideologia: The Spontaneity of Ideology

In *On Universals: Constructing and Deconstructing Community*, Étienne Balibar writes the following provocative statement: 'Conscientia sive ideologia' (Consciousness, that is ideology).[1] Balibar's formulation is derived from Spinoza, from his famous *Deus sive natura* (God, that is nature), his strategy of the sive in which philosophical oppositions are overcome with the assertion of their paradoxical identity. Here the strategy is applied to Marx, specifically to the theorisation of ideology from *The German Ideology* and after. It is at once a Spinozist in-joke and a provocation: the strategy of the 'sive' does not just identify two terms, but challenges an entire system of thought that necessary relies on such oppositions. Between the joke and the provocation is the work of Louis Althusser, not just because Althusser was both a Spinozist and a Marxist, but because Althusser's various formulations of ideology, formulations indebted to both Spinoza and Marx, continually thought ideology in both its spontaneity and its universality, framing it as coexistent with experience and consciousness. Such an assertion, as with all strategies of the sive, raises as many difficulties and questions as it resolves. These questions hinge on the way in which the concept of ideology is caught between universality and specificity, structural condition and particular content, or, ultimately, between necessity and contingency, an integral element of experience or a particular effect of a given social formation. The closer ideology gets to being coextensive with consciousness, the more it loses its socio-historical specificity, becoming something like a constitutive error of experience, or antinomy of thought. The extension of the epistemic register is not without its effects on politics, since if ideology is coextensive with consciousness then what possibilities are there for radical critique and change? The opposite pole is no less fraught with difficulties. Ideologies considered in terms of their specific content and concepts, as bourgeois, capitalist, or neoliberal, raise the question of their conditions of production and dissemination, at worst collapsing into a kind a conspiracy. Ideology is caught between the poles of necessity and contingency, form and content, and structure and history.

---

1 Balibar 2020b, p. 29.

In what follows I intend to trace some of Althusser's attempts to think through what could be called the spontaneity of ideology, beginning with how the concept is developed through a reading of Marx and Spinoza together, continuing through Althusser's own attempts to think through the relation between practice and abstraction, and, ultimately, turning to the lingering effects of Althusser's formulation of 'spontaneous ideology' in Pierre Macherey's concept of infra-ideology and Étienne Balibar's work on universalisation. The assertion, or hypothesis underlying this essay, is that it is only by paradoxically thinking ideology as both material, grounded in practices, and ideal, constituting the form and basis for thought, that it is possible to shift the concept from its polemical use to become a critical tool for analysis.

1   Between Marx and Spinoza

Althusser's influential 'Ideology and Ideological State Apparatus', a text which reshaped the concept of ideology, makes only one reference to Spinoza. As Althusser writes, 'The accusation of being in ideology only applies to others, never to oneself (unless one is really a Spinozist or a Marxist, which, in this matter, is to be exactly the same thing.)'[2] Althusser does not expand upon what it would mean to be aware that one is in ideology, instead crediting Spinoza with discovering the moebius strip of ideology, of its status of having no outside, of being completely coextensive with thought, while simultaneously being nothing but outside with respect to reality. Despite the scant references to Spinoza it could be argued that Althusser structures his entire essay on ideology around the Appendix to Part One of Spinoza's *Ethics*. Both texts argue that ideology is nothing other than an anthropocentric conception of the universe, one that places human desires and agency at the centre. As Althusser writes later, describing the theoretical structure, or apparatus of the appendix:

> The imagination is (1) to put the (human) subject at the center and origin of every perception, of every action, of every object, and of every meaning, but (2) to reverse in this way the real order of things, since the real order *is explained* ... solely by the determination of causes, which the subjectivity of the imagination explains everything by means of ends, by the subjective illusion of the ends of its desire and its expectations. This is, strictly speaking, to *reverse* the order of the world, to make it walk, as

---

2   Althusser 2014b, p. 265.

Hegel and Marx will say, *on its head*. It is put work, as Spinoza superbly said, an entire *'apparatus'* ... *an apparatus of reversal of causes into ends*.[3]

Ideology, or the imagination, is the reversal of causes into ends, an apparatus of reversal. Here we see two themes that are integral to and repeated in Althusser's account of ideology. First, there is the subject as the interpretive grid, or matrix, the tendency to make ends and intention the basis of intelligibility. The subject is the spontaneous ideology of its own foundation. Second, this spontaneity must be understood as itself an effect, as the product of apparatus, of a material production. It is an effect that appears as natural, ultimately becoming a cause.

In Spinoza's Appendix what Althusser posits as an apparatus appears less a structure then a simple fact of finite human existence. The imagination, or as Spinoza labels it, prejudice, has a foundation that is less political, or social, than anthropological. Its primary condition is that we are born 'ignorant of the causes of things ... and conscious of our appetite'. Ignorance of causes and consciousness of appetite becomes the basis for a universe grasped in terms of intentions and actions undertaken towards an end. Igorance constitutes a kind of knowledge, or at least passes itself off as one. Spinoza defines this initial ignorance of the causes of things, including our desire, prejudice (praejudicia) while the latter, ignorance as it is reinforced by its social dimension, by a doctrine of ignorance and a practice of belief, is dubbed superstition (supersitio).[4] Prejudice is transformed into superstition once the social dimension enters this horizon of ignorance and desire, once this belief in final causes becomes not just the basis of an individual perspective but takes on a social significance, tied to human relations and domination. The priority is less a temporal one than a logical one. It is not that anyone is ever born into a world of singular prejudice, a world without history, without signs and interpretations, left to interpret the world on their own. We enter into a world of superstition, of organised beliefs and norms, because we are prone to superstition. For Spinoza it is the collective noun 'man' rather than the individual noun 'I' that thinks, and this collective condition defines superstition as well. We are always already in superstition, influenced by signs and interpretations. This collective condition has as its condition of possibility individual finitude, the awareness of desire and ignorance of causes that is the first kind of knowledge. The apparatus of superstitions

---

3   Althusser 1997, p. 6.
4   As Pierre Macherey argues, the Appendix can be understood as something of a practical demonstration of the implications of EIIP36: 'Inadequate and confused ideas follow with the same necessity as adequate or clear and distinct ideas'. Macherey 1998a, p. 206.

seizes or makes use of a condition that, for lack of a better word, can be considered anthropological, foundational to humanity.

Given Althusser's attempt to posit an apparatus in the Appendix to Part One of the *Ethics*, it is striking that he does not turn to a text that is similar both in terms of its specific argumentative structure as wells as its placement in a text's theoretical development. I am referring here to 'the commodity fetishism' section of *Capital*, Volume I. In his preface to a French edition Althusser infamously advised readers to put Part One of *Capital* aside, advising them to turn first to the more immediate and concrete struggles over the working day, and his own theoretical writing suggests he took heed of that advice, never returning to Marx's writing on commodity fetishism.[5] In doing so he perhaps overlooked the proximity of this text to Spinoza's Appendix. These texts are not just similar in their placement, as polemical and critical philosophical interventions at the end of a philosophical argument. They are also both in some sense preemptive; in Spinoza's *Ethics* the discussion of the illusions of consciousness come before the development of the mind and affects in subsequent books, while in Marx the discussion of fetishism introduces, as something of a thought experiment, the concept of the mode of production, or at least of different manners of producing, including that of the 'free association of producers'. The preemptive nature of these texts is a necessary corollary of the disruptive nature of their theses. Spinoza does not just undermine the anthropomorphic god, but shows how this conception of god stems from our own anthropocentric conception of the universe, a conception that is the product of the consciousness of desire and the ignorance of the causes of things. Spinoza's Appendix does not just complete and illustrate the conception of god as the immanent cause, developed in Part One of the *Ethics*, revealing the way in which immanent causality subverts all notions of teleology and intentionality on the part of God, but confronts a common sense that is common precisely because it is a product of humanity's practical engagement with the world. The Appendix retroactively explains why Part One is so difficult to accept by getting ahead of itself, confronting the persistent illusions of God and the universe with a philosophical anthropology that Spinoza will develop in subsequent sections of the *Ethics*. Similarly Marx's section on 'commodity fetishism' confronts directly the tenacity of the image of the objectivity of value, the idea that value is not a social relation but an attribute of commodities, by gesturing ahead to problems and concepts yet to be developed, problems having to do with the connection between social relations and forms of thought. Both Spinoza's

---

5   Althusser 1971, p. 81.

Appendix and section on 'commodity fetishism' are situated as the polemical conclusion to a theoretical argument, and the anticipation of the evocation of practice, of action.

Marx and Spinoza converge not just in terms of their specific rhetorical strategy, the preliminary and polemical nature of their texts, but on a central philosophical point, the limits of knowledge and the primacy of practice.[6] In Marx's terms 'Life is not determined by consciousness, but consciousness by life'.[7] For Spinoza the primacy of practice, of the natural conditions of bodies and affects, is as much a matter of limitation as determination: he refers to this as the limited efficacy of the true insofar as it is true.[8] True knowledge cannot change or alter illusions or superstitions without being put into practice, without being materialised in bodies and desires. Marx and Spinoza both turn to optics to argue for the determination of thought and experience. The limit of the true insofar as it is true is the inability for knowledge to alter how we are affected, how we imagine the world. '... When the rays of the sun, falling on the surface of the water, are reflected to our eyes, we imagine it as if it were in the water, even if we know its true place'.[9] Or, as Marx describes the illusion internal to vision, 'In the same way the light from an object is perceived by us not as the subjective excitation of our optic nerve, but as the objective form of something outside the eye itself'.[10] As Althusser's interpretation makes clear the 'limited efficacy of the true insofar as it is true' has as its corollary the primacy of practice to thought, of the apparatus to its concept. Thus, as much as Althusser avoids the letter of commodity fetishism, he remains close to its fundamental spirit, to an understanding of the way in which a material relation, a practice, is prior to and productive of a particular way of thinking.

Étienne Balibar raises the question why Althusser eschews the section on commodity fetishism given its proximity to his own conception of an apparatus.[11] It is the concept of fetishism, rather than of ideology, that seems best suited to grasp an apparatus that produces a particular imaginary spontaneously as an effect of a particular practical relation. In his short book on Marx, Balibar argues that ideology and fetishism are best understood not as variants of the generic problem of subjection, but as two fundamentally different

---

6   Fischbach 2005, p. 88.
7   Marx and Engels 1970, p. 47.
8   Spinoza EIVP1.
9   Spinoza EIV P1Schol.
10   Marx 1977, p. 165.
11   Balibar 2020b, p. 37.

modalities of subjection.[12] The former is tied to the state, to state apparatuses, the other is tied to the market. As Balibar argues, Marx's model of fetishism, especially as it unfolds in *Capital*, culminates not just in commodities that are imbued with value but with subjects that necessarily conduct themselves in the same way with respect to the market. The link between the two, between subject and object, is labour power. Balibar's reading of *Capital* takes a detour through George Lukàcs' concept of reification. As Lukács writes, '*Subjectively* – where the market economy has been fully developed – a man's activity becomes estranged from himself, it turns into a commodity which, subject to the non-human objectivity of the natural laws of society, must go its own way independently of man just like any consumer article'.[13] The way the world appears necessarily turns back onto the subject itself, as their labour becomes another commodity. In contrast to this image of subjection emerging from a particular practice, or apparatus, Althusser turns to the theological dimension of the Appendix, the image of God or a Subject (with a capital S) as the necessary condition of ideological interpellation. As Balibar writes,

> A subject interpellated by an authority that speaks in the name of the universal, or an individual who *imagines* being interpellated by such a law or authority (which is basically the mechanism Althusser describes), becomes ipso facto a member of the *community* governed by that law.[14]

Much has been made of Althusser's scene, the scene of interpellation, so much so that the figure and its various interpretations, various restagings and reexaminations of the scene of hailing, have eclipsed its conceptual basis. It functions more as a parable than an illustration. For Balibar it is not a matter of interpreting the primal scene of interpellation, but of grasping what makes such a scene necessary. Ideology is irreducible to fetishism because it is a different universal, a different figure of the universal, not the universal of the market of interchangeable and indifferent subjects of labour power but the universal of subjects constituted in and through their subjection to a form of authority. This is the irreducible theocratic element of every state, the transcendent imaginary instance that is simultaneously the cause and the effect of the immanent organisations.[15]

---

12   Balibar 1995, p. 78.
13   Lukács 1971, p. 87.
14   Balibar 2020, p. 37.
15   Balibar 1997, p. 197.

Althusser's 'Ideology and Ideological State Apparatuses' can thus be understood to be situated between Spinoza's Appendix and Marx's 'commodity fetishism'. It is formulated at the point of their postulated intersection, the point where practices and relations produce a particular consciousness and representation of the social order, but the differences are no less important. Spinoza's prejudice is as much the effect of a particular human finitude, anthropological, as it is the effect of a particular apparatus. In contrast to this, Marx's writing on value and the commodity fetish suggest that it is humanity itself, or at least its image, that is a product of the exchangability of labour. As Marx writes,

> For a society of commodity producers, whose general social relation of production consists in the fact that they treat their products as commodities, hence as values, and in this material [*sachlich*] form bring their individual, private labors into relation with each other as homogenous human labor, Christianity with its religious cult of man in the abstract, more particularly in its bourgeois development, i.e. in Protestantism, Deism, etc. is the most fitting form of religion.[16]

Whereas Marx's writing on fetishism stresses equality and interchangeability as the spontaneous ideology of market relations, Spinoza's appendix argues that the spontaneous philosophy of prejudice sets up a hierarchy between the subject, interpellated as free, and God as the subject behind the mystery of the universe. Following Balibar, we can understood these two spontaneous philosophies, or two mode of subjections, as roughly corresponding to market and state, to relations of exchange in which equality is posited, and to relations of hierarchy in which political belonging is always tied to subjection to a higher authority.

The tension between the two subjections is also a tension between the basis of the spontaneous ideology. As much as Marx uses the metaphor of optics to describe the irreducibility of appearance to knowledge, implying the fetishism is almost a fact of life, it is clear that fetishism stems from social relations, from the isolation of producers from each other and abstract labour. It is a social effect and not a product of human finitude. In contrast to this, Spinoza gives us a spontaneous philosophy situated between prejudice, understood as the natural ignorance of causes and awareness of desire, and superstition as the organisation of this ignorance into a system of belief. However, as much as it is possible to find an anthropological dimension to Spinoza's spontan-

16   Marx 1977, p. 1972.

eous philosophy, this anthropology is less a statement of humanity's original fallen, and ignorant, nature, than of social relations as the organisation of both imagination and knowledge. That we are born ignorant of causes is less important than the way that ignorance is organised in order to become the basis of politics. The spontaneity of ideology is a concept that emerges in the intersection of Spinoza and Marx, between anthropological finitude and the opacity of social relations. Spontaneous ideology as a concept and a problem is situated between market and state, equality and subjection, between an immediacy of illusion that is anthropological and the mediation that is the effect of social relations.

2   Between Spontaneity and Practice

Althusser's remarks on Spinoza and ideology are neither the first, not last words on spontaneous ideology. The concept and word gets its most lengthy formulation in Althusser's course on *Philosophy and the Spontaneous Philosophy of Scientists* from 1967, and continues to be developed throughout the late sixties and early seventies. The concept is situated between the development of a theory of ideology, a theory that gets its most lengthy treatment in the text on reproduction, and a series of more pedagogical interventions on the very place of philosophy. These pedagogical interventions are in some sense doubly displaced, as they are written from the outside of philosophy, by a Marxist intervening in philosophy, even as they are delivered to those who are outside of philosophy, to scientists and activists. It is perhaps because of this that the dominant question of these texts is not to do with the philosophical sources of Althusser's concept of ideology, but rather the relation between ideology and practice, or practices.

In the course for scientists 'spontaneous ideology' is defined initially as the particular conception that arises from a particular practice. There is a spontaneous philosophy to every practice, scientist, philosopher, writer, etc.; all have a particular conception that stems from their particular practice. Spontaneity is the immediate determination of thought by a particular practice or action. Its immediacy is the effect of relations and mediations that are obscured. As Pierre Macherey writes, 'The spontaneous is never but spontaneous in scare quotes, that is to say a false spontaneity which is in reality the result of a manipulation, an artifice, an editing'.[17] As much as the spontaneous ideology reflects the

---

17   Macherey 2009, p. 16.

primacy of practice to thought, it is not Althusser's last word on ideology, nor is it the determining condition. As Althusser writes,

> Their own ideology, the spontaneous ideology of their practice (their ideology of science or the arts) does not depend solely on their own practice: it depends mainly and in the last instance on the dominant ideological system of the society in which they live. Ultimately, it is this ideological system especially that governs the very forms of their ideology of science and of the arts. What seems to happen before their eyes happens, in reality, behind their backs.[18]

The relation between the two ideologies can be considered a variation of that between prejudice and superstition, between the generic ground of any ideology as emerging from the finite nature of a specific practice and its limitations and an ideological system that organises and subsumes spontaneous ideologies in order to reproduce the relations of production. Spontaneity is thus shifted away from anthropology, from a specific human nature and human finitude, to the basic ideas and conceptions tied to a specific practice. Spontaneity is not an effect of the fundamental finitude of human nature, but of the fact that every practice carries with it its own conceptual dimension, produces its own theory. This is what separates the worst architect from the best of bees, to cite Marx.[19] As much as this spontaneous ideology has a certain immediacy, tied as it is to a particular practice, it is ultimately not determined by this practice. The spontaneous ideology is determined in the last instance by the dominant ideology. The determination by the dominant ideology is also the primacy of the totality, the mode of production to each specific practice.

The question remains as to how to grasp this intersection, how to understand how the various spontaneous ideologies, tied as they are to specific practices, from science to the arts, not only intersect with this dominant ideology, but are determined by it. In the complete manuscript of *Sur la Reproduction* (Published as *On the Reproduction of Capitalism*), Althusser moves beyond the essay's focus on the school as the dominant ideological state apparatus to focus on the centrality of the legal/moral ideology, and in doing so redefines both the spontaneity and dominance of this ideology. As Althusser argues, law as a system of obligation requires a supplement in order to guarantee subjection. There is no law compelling people to obey the law, and even if there were, such

---

18   Althusser 1990b, p. 95.
19   Marx 1977, p. 284.

a law would require an additional law, and so on, in an infinite regress. 'Law is a formal, systematized, non-contradictory, (tendentially) comprehensive system that cannot exist by itself'.[20] Of course obedience could always be guaranteed by the police, by repression, but this is not sufficient. Law, and legal obedience, functions by a supplement. As Althusser goes on to write, 'Legal ideology plus the little supplement of moral ideology'.[21] Althusser then sets up what could be considered a system of supplements, law is supplemented by legal ideology, legal ideology by moral ideology. All of which reinforce and intersect around the same idea of individuality, responsibility, and morality. Each practice, from law, to legal ideology, to morality, requires an additional practice or discourse in order to sustain itself. While such an assertion is well in line with Althusser's thesis that Ideological State Apparatuses function by ideology, in other word reproduce existing relations of production without repression or violence, it is at odds with his earlier identification of the school, and education, as the dominant ideological state apparatus. An assertion which Althusser admits was influenced by the centrality of the university in the events of May 1968 in Paris.

In a manuscript written five years later, *Initiation à la philosophe pour les non-philosophes*, Althusser returns to the question of legal ideology, only now it is framed less as supplement to the law than an a mediation between state and morality. In this later text, it is precisely the legal ideology's ability to mediate between the state and the law, morality and the law, and religion and the law that makes it all pervasive.[22] Thus to risk stitching together these two texts with one of Althusser's own concepts, we could say that it is less a matter of the way a particular ideology, or ideological apparatus is determined as dominant, as in the case of education, than of the overdetermination of ideology. The legal ideology's centrality is defined by its intersection with, as a supplement and an intermediary for, other discourses, practices, and ideology. It is less the foundational ideology that makes all others possible than the point where all other ideologies converge and transform each other. The practical mediations of the legal ideology are doubled by its theoretical mediations. The legal ideology of individual responsibility can easily shift from original sin to the work ethic, from Eden to the state of nature. On the terrain of ideas, the legal idea of the individual offers a reconciliation of the abstract and concrete, functioning in multiple discourses while simultaneously appearing to be grounded in concrete reality.

---

20   Althusser 2014b, p. 68.
21   Althusser 2014b, p. 68.
22   Althusser 2014a, p. 357.

Althusser's repeated returns to the question of legal ideology in the seventies can be understood as an attempt to reconcile two aspects of ideology grasped so far, the primacy of practice, of the apparatus, and the role of ideology in reproducing the relations of production; in other words, the spontaneous and the dominant. Legal or moral ideology is spontaneous because its central concepts, the responsible subject, the universality of the law, are articulated through a variety of practices. For Althusser the most significant of these practices is the labour contract, the contract that represents the sale of labour as the exchange of a commodity for its price. One could expand this to include the other quotidian practices of legal responsibility and individuality, the various forms signed and contracts entered into over the course of the day. The spontaneity of the legal ideology is everywhere, intersecting with the spontaneous ideology of the market and the state. Legal ideology is also dominant, not just in the sense that it is central to capitalist society, but because the isolated and responsible legal individual is the necessary condition of the reproduction of class relations. It is where the dominant ideas become the ideas of domination.

Legal ideology can be understood as the intersection of the spontaneous and the dominant ideology, an articulation that itself borrows from the divides of superstition and prejudice, of practice and doctrine, in the case of Spinoza, and of subordinate and dominant class, in the case of Marx. These divisions which neither entirely coincide, nor entirely diverge, are the necessary, but not sufficient conditions for developing the intersection between the spontaneous and dominant ideology. The dominant must contain, must encompass in some way the immediate spontaneous ideologies, or experiences of the dominanated, so in some way the dominant ideology is that of the ruled, not the ruling class; at the same time, however, the dominant ideology must organise and interpret the various experiences of different practices, of different spontaneous ideologies, turning them towards the necessary goal of reproduction: the dominant ideology is the ideology of the dominant class. This conflict between dominant and subordinate, ruling and ruled class, constitutes the basis of the theoretical debates within ideology, debates between its popular, or, in Balibar's terms, Machiavellian dimension, which makes the ruler appear to be of the people, and its dominant, or Marxist dimension, in which the ideas of the ruling class are disseminated. As Balibar writes, 'I shall take the liberty of advancing the following interpretation: domination by an established order does indeed rest, as Marx argued after Hegel, on the ideological universalization of its principles. But contrary to what Marx believed the dominant ideas cannot be those of the dominant class. They have to be those of the dominated ...'[23] What Balibar

---

23   Balibar 2002c, p. 7.

identifies as the Marxist – ruling ideas are ideas of the ruling class – or Machiavellian – the ruler must appear to be of the people – moment, opens up a problem at the heart of ideology as to how dominant and dominated coexist in the same doctrine. In each case ideology is the universalisation of specific spontaneous ideologies, the only difference is whether the universalisation in question is brought from above or below, from the dominant or ruling ideology or from the spontaneous and dominated. This difference is also the basis for many political interventions within the field of ideology itself: populism and various forms of elitism, of the constitution of technical and economic elites, are nothing but the practical variant of the prior theoretical positions, or vice versa.

As much as it is possible to map the various theoretical conceptions and practical interventions in ideology along the poles of spontaneous and dominant, it would be false to assume that there is only one spontaneous ideology. There are as many spontaneous ideologies as there are practices. It is not just that the scientist, artist, and philosopher have their own specific spontaneous ideologies, but that even the fundamental relation of selling one's labour power is itself made up of multiple ideologies. As Althusser enumerates the different spontaneous ideologies of the wage relation,

> This ideology that 'makes the workers go' comprises the following basic elements, which are so many illusions and impostures, yet 'are successful' as long as the workers' class struggle does not combat them: 1) the bourgeois legal illusion according to which 'labor is paid for at its value'; 2) the corresponding legal-moral ideology which has it that one must 'respect one's labor contract' and, through it, the enterprise's house rules and regulations; 3) the technicist-economist ideology which has it that 'there must, after all, be different jobs within the division of labor' and such-and-such individuals to fill them. This ideology does a great deal more to make workers 'go' than repression does.[24]

As much as the legal ideology plays a central role, passing transversally between the spontaneous ideology of the wage and the contract and the reproduction of the relations of production, it is not the only spontaneous ideology, it is also coupled with the spontaneous ideology of technology, of the division of labour. One could even argue that the spontaneous legal ideology is split in two, torn between its legal and economic dimension, between the legal ideas

---

24   Althusser 2014b, p. 42.

of order and responsibility and the economic ideas of fair and equal exchange, between dimensions closer to the state and to the market, to return to our earlier distinction. One could hazard a guess, but it would just have to be a guess given that we are dealing with Althusser's drafts and unfinished projects, that the different aspects of these different ideologies, come into play in different work situations, one more fitting with service workers, another for engineers and mechanics, or in different moments of struggle. The tension between the spontaneous ideology and dominant ideology is then, like the corresponding concept of dominant and subordinate mode of production, a conceptual distinction that lends itself less to an overarching logic than a conjunctural analysis. It can perhaps only be thought in terms of the concrete analysis of a concrete situation.

3   Ideology after Ideology

At this point, and somewhat by way of a conclusion, I would like to look at the way in which the problems left in the wake of Althuser's conceptualisation of spontaneous ideology persist in the work of Pierre Macherey and Étienne Balibar. In different ways both Macherey and Balibar return to the spontaneity of ideology, the way in which ideology is less a doctrine, a set of beliefs and ideals, than the determination of thought by a practice. Here the problem is precisely how to think that determination of ideas by practices, the order and connection of practices and ideas, without lapsing into reflection or simple linear causal determination. The split between the spontaneous ideology and the larger ideology makes it possible to think both the identity and difference of the spontaneous ideology and the general problem of ideology. The second problem concerns the relation between the dominant ideology and dominated ideologies, especially insofar as the latter is not just a singular spontaneous ideology, but encompasses multiple ideologies, tied to different practices. This is a problem of the intersection of universalisation and domination, as it has been explored by Étienne Balibar.

With respect to the former, as much as Macherey's *Le Sujet des Normes* constitutes a return to the problem of ideology, even returning to Althusser's essay on Ideological State Apparatuses, it is also written as a response to the critiques of the very concept of ideology that followed in its wake. Critiques only alluded to so far here. The most important of these to the development of the concept of infra-ideology are historical as much as they are theoretical, the claim that contemporary society functions through forms of power that are more direct, more immediate, and thus less in need of conceptual grounding than ideology.

Ideology, a dominant ideology, the great narratives of nation taught in schools or moral tales of the law and morality, seem quaint and archaic in a society governed less by overarching ideals than market imperatives. Macherey's point of reference here is Michel Foucault's argument that contemporary society, the society of discipline or biopower, functions through norms rather than ideology. Norms are understood to be more operative than interpretive, delineating what needs to be done rather than what must be believed. As Macherey writes, what he calls infra-ideology is an 'ideology which intervenes insidiously in advance and from below, and which does not need, in order to have effects, to be formulated or represented, to pass through the relay of signification'.[25] That infra-ideology does not require signification does not mean that it functions without signs or words, but that these signs and words indicate less something to believed than something to be done.

What Macherey focuses on in the concept of infra-ideology is not only that it is functional, but that it is profoundly flexible because it is all-encompassing. Productivity can be understood as a paradigmatic example of an infra-ideology. It is free of any ground or larger rationale in part because it is its own rationale. Precisely because productivity is not tied to any particular goal or direction makes it possible to apply it to every goal or action. The flexibility of infra-ideology can be understood as an extension of Althusser's assertion that ideology has no outside; now the interiority of infra-ideology is no longer maintained by the figure of the subject, the interpellation of individuals as subjects, but by the ubiquity and flexibility of its operative term and field. Infra-ideology defines less the perspective taken by an individual subject, or individual, than an omnipresent way in which reality appears, a kind of spontaneous metaphysics, a metaphysics produced not in thought but in the central practical matter of capital, the transformation of labour power into profit.[26] As Macherey writes,

> From this point of view, we could say that when the capitalist occupies himself with his workers' labor-power, which he has acquired the right to employ in exchange for a wage, treating it as a 'productive power' whose productivity he intends to increase in order to produce relative surplus value – he practices metaphysics not in a theoretical but in a practical way. He practices this peculiar sort of metaphysics not during his leisure time, as a distraction or mental exercise, as he would a crossword puzzle, but throughout the entire working day dedicated to production. By open-

---

25   Macherey 2014, p. 302.
26   Macherey 2014, p. 348.

ing up his company to notions such as 'power', 'capacity' and 'causation', he thereby makes them a reality, realizing these fictions, these products of the mind, which he then employs with daunting efficacy. In this way, with payrolls and charts of organizational tasks at hand, he shows, better than a philosopher's abstract proofs, that the work of metaphysics could not be more material, provided that one knows how to put it to good use in introducing it into the factory. One could, incidentally, derive from this a new and caustic definition of metaphysics: in this rather specific context, it boils down to a mechanism for profit-making, which is no small matter. This means that, amongst other inventions that have changed the course of history, capitalism has found the means, the procedure, the 'trick' enabling it to put abstract concepts into practice – the hallmark of its 'genius'.[27]

Macherey's concept of infra-ideology can be understood as a radical expansion of spontaneous philosophy, the point where it becomes a kind of spontaneous metaphysics, a metaphysics that is all the more intractable, inescapable, by not being uttered as such. Productivity is less a specific ideology than a general imperative.

Macherey's infra-ideology can also be understood as a spontaneous ideology without a dominant ideology, or without the point of transition to a dominant ideology. Or, more to the point, it can be considered to be the spontaneous ideology as dominant ideology, as an ideology which becomes dominant without ever ceasing to function in its spontaneity, in its immediate connection with the practical dimension of daily life, especially as the practical dimension is no longer a specific practice or field of inquiry, as in Althusser's examination of science, but the more generalised practice of wage labour. Infra-ideology universalises these conditions without referring to them as a transcendent condition. The maximum point of its extension is also its limit. This limit can be framed in multiple senses. First, there is a question of the necessity of reproduction. Can an infra-ideology, an ideology of maximum extension but minimum signification, be the necessary and sufficient ground of social reproduction? Does it require that additional transcendent dimension, the Subject capital S, that functioned as the ultimate ground of ideological interpellation. This can be understood to be Althusser's question in the essay on ideological state apparatuses. To which we could add the question raised by the complete edition of *Sur la reproduction*, how does infra-ideology contend with the plurality of

27   Macherey 2015.

spontaneous ideologies? This question becomes all the more pressing in light of the rift between Spinoza and Marx, between what could be called ideology of the state and a fetishism of the market. If these constitute two different spontaneous ideologies, drawn from two different practices, market relations and state law, with different dominant ideologies, different universalisations, then how is it possible to grasp their specific articulations and conflict?

Balibar has argued that the relationship between the spontaneous ideologies of the market and the state should be understood as a conflict of universalisation. As much as Spinoza and Marx have theorised the irreducible particularity at the heart of every universal, the particular striving or class position that elevates and obscures itself in the constitution of the universal, they do not pose the problem of the conflict between universals. As Balibar argues with the aid of Hegel, the conflict between the spontaneous ideology of the market and the ideology of the state, between commodity exchange and law, is not a conflict between the particular and the universal, but a conflict within two different universals or universalisations.[28] The first, the universalisation of the market, of exchange relations, is best described as infra-ideology, as a universalisation that passes behind the back of the individuals involved, appearing less as a specific doctrine or even an interpellation of subjectivity, than as a generic set of values and ideals, productivity and utility, that are both ubiquitous and without ground. The second, the ideology of the state, of the nation, also has its quotidian practices that constitute the ground of its spontaneous ideology. These include the spontaneous legal ideology that Althusser refers to but extend beyond it, especially as the state is embodied in traditions and norms that make it a nation. As Balibar argues, the nation and the state are also produced and reproduced by the various practices and rituals attached to the learning and transmission of a language and even those that govern the passage of life and death.[29] The education apparatus is only the particular site of the production of a memory and tradition that constitutes the nation. The nation takes on certain aspects of the sacred. These two spontaneous ideologies, or spontaneous grounds of ideologies, are different not just in terms of the practices that ground them, but in terms of the very conceptualisation. The infra-ideology of the market simultaneously falls short of and exceeds an ideological doctrine, to remain either just below conceptualisation or above it, becoming a kind of spontaneous metaphysics. This does not mean that it cannot be rendered explicit and conceptualised as such: one way to grasp the

---

28   Balibar 2020b, p. 22.
29   Balibar 2004, p. 20.

intellectual products of neoliberalism, from homo economicus to the selfish gene, is as an attempt to make an ideology of the infra-ideology of market relations. It stands in sharp contrast to the ideology of the state, which is inseperable from both its transcendent moment and its embodiment in traditions and norms. Nature makes no nations, which is why nationalism must create its memory and tradition as the basis for its spontaneous ideology. The two ideologies are different in terms of their ground, that which they are spontaneous ideologies of, but also in terms of their articulations: capital is more axiomatic than code, less in need of hearts and minds than bodies, while the state necessarily constitutes individuals as subjects and collectives as nations. We can understand these differences in terms of fetishism and ideology, market and state, or in terms of the difference between Spinoza and Marx, insofar as the former asserted that every superstition necessarily has its hierarchy, its division between humanity and god, nation and subject, while the latter posits an ideology of interchangeable subjects of labour power. As much as it is possible to return these differences to one overarching dualism or split, thematised in terms of either philosopher, Spinoza or Marx, or state or market, it is possible to argue that these multiple points of demarcation, and tension, divisions between the spontaneous ideology and the dominant ideology, between the different spontaneous ideologies, and different dominant ideologies, are constitutive of the very concept of ideology

4   The Future of an Illusion

By way of a conclusion it seems useful to think of this itinerary, back to Spinoza and Marx, and through Althusser to Macherey and Balibar, as less a lesson in genealogy, and more of an attempt to think a concept, in this case ideology, or the spontaneity of ideology, along with its tendencies and tensions. It is as much a matter of the way in which the concept does not cohere, caught in tension between anthropological and historical justifications, between the various spontaneous ideologies and the dominant ideology, as it is seeing the elements of the constitution of the concept. These fissures and fault lines are not just the gestures of a theoretical modesty, of the conflicted and incomplete nature of any philosophical system: they are also the points of intervention for theoretical and political practice. The concept of 'spontaneous ideology' reveals both the strength and limits of ideology. On the one hand it demonstrates that ideology is like a second nature, so thoroughly wedded to our practical comportments that it appears as nature. It accounts for the immediacy of ideology. While on the other it demonstrates the fault lines of ideology, the gap that separates the spontaneous philosophy from its practices, the spontaneous philosophies from each other, and all from their universalisation in the dominant ideology. The tension of the concepts development, the gap that separates Spinoza's superstition from Marx's fetishism, is in the end the basis of new lines of demarcation. What appears as necessary, the existing articulation of ideology, must be grasped as overdetermined and contingent. This, and not the sterile declaration of truth, is what it means to intervene philosophically in ideology.

PART 4

Returns of Philosophical Anthropology: New Subjections/New Transformations

∴

A Genealogy of Homo-Economicus: Neoliberalism and the Production of Subjectivity

In the opening pages of David Harvey's *A Brief History of Neoliberalism* we find the following statement: 'Neoliberalism ... has pervasive effects on ways of thought to the point where it has become incorporated into the common-sense way many of us interpret, live in, and understand the world'.[1] While Harvey's book presents a great deal of research on neoliberalism, presenting its origins in such academic institutions as the 'Chicago School', its spread in the initial experiments in Chile, and its return to the countries of its origin through the regimes of Reagan and Thatcher, as well as its effects on China and the rest of the world, the actual process by which it became hegemonic, to the point of becoming common sense, is not examined. While it might be wrong to look for philosophy in a work which is primarily a work of history, a 'brief' history at that, aimed at shedding light on the current conjuncture, it is worth pointing out this lacuna since it intersects with a commonly accepted idea about 'neoliberalism', that it is as much a transformation in ideology as it is a transformation of ideology. Neoliberalism, in the texts that have critically confronted it, is generally understood as not just a new ideology, but a transformation of ideology in terms of its conditions and effects. In terms of its conditions, it is an ideology that is generated not from the state, or from a dominant class, but from the quotidian experience of buying and selling commodities from the market, which is then extended across other social spaces, 'the marketplace of ideas', to become an image of society. Secondly, it is an ideology that refers not only to the political realm, to an ideal of the state, but to the entirety of human existence. It claims to present not an ideal, but a reality; human nature. As Fredric Jameson writes, summing up this connection and the challenge it poses: '"The market is in human nature" is the proposition that cannot be allowed to stand unchallenged; in my opinion, it is the most crucial terrain of ideological struggle in our time'.[2]

A critical examination of neoliberalism must address this transformation of its discursive deployment, as a new understanding of human nature and

---

1 Harvey 2005, p. 3.
2 Jameson 1991, p. 263.

social existence rather than a political programme. Thus it is not enough to contrast neoliberalism as a political programme, analysing its policies in terms of success or failure. An examination of neoliberalism entails a reexamination of the fundamental problematic of ideology, the intersection of power, concepts, modes of existence and subjectivity. It is in confronting neoliberalism that the seemingly abstract debates of the last thirty years, debates between poststructuralists such as Michel Foucault and neo-Marxists such as Antonio Negri about the nature of power and the relation between 'ideologies' or 'discourses' and material existence, cease to be abstract doctrines and become concrete ways of comprehending and transforming the present. Foucault's lectures on neoliberalism do not only extend his own critical project into new areas, they also serve to demonstrate the importance of grasping the present by examining the way in which the truth and subjectivity are produced.

1   Homo Economicus: The Subject of Neoliberalism

The nexus between the production of a particular conception of human nature, a particular formation of subjectivity, and a particular political ideology, a particular way of thinking about politics, is at the centre of Michel Foucault's research. As much as Foucault characterised his own project as studying '... the different modes by which, in our culture, human beings are made subjects', this process has always intersected with regimes of power/knowledge.[3] Thus, it would appear that Foucault's work takes up exactly what writers on neoliberalism find to be so vexing: the manner in which neoliberalism is not just a manner of governing states or economies, but is intimately tied to the government of the individual, to a particular manner of living. However, it is well known that Foucault's research primarily views this relation from ancient Greece through the nineteenth century, leaving modern developments such as neoliberalism unaddressed. While this is the general pattern of Foucault's work, in the late seventies he devoted a year of his lectures at the Collège de France to the topic of neoliberalism. These lectures, published as *The Birth of Biopolitics*, are something of an anomaly in part because of this shift into the late twentieth century and also because, unlike other lecture courses, at least those that have been published in recent years on 'abnormals', 'psychiatric power' and 'the hermeneutics of the subject', the material from these lectures never made it into Foucault's published works.

---

3   Foucault 1982, p. 208.

In order to frame Foucault's analysis it is useful to begin with how he sees the distinction between liberalism and neoliberalism. For Foucault, this difference has to do with the different ways in which they each focus on economic activity. Classical liberalism focused on exchange, on what Adam Smith called mankind's tendency to 'barter, truck, and exchange'. It naturalised the market as a system with its own rationality, its own interest, and its own specific efficiency, arguing ultimately for its superior efficiency as a distributor of goods and services. The market became a space of autonomy that had to be carved out of the state through the unconditional right of private property. What Foucault stresses in his understanding, is the way in which the market becomes more than just a specific institution or practice to the point where it has become the basis for a reinterpretation and thus a critique of state power. Classical liberalism makes exchange the general matrix of society. It establishes a homology: just as relations in the marketplace can be understood as an exchange of certain freedoms for a set of rights and liberties.[4] Neoliberalism, according to Foucault, extends the process of making economic activity a general matrix of social and political relations, but it takes as its focus not exchange but competition.[5] What the two forms of liberalism, the 'classical' and 'neo-', share, according to Foucault, is a general idea of 'homo economicus', that is, the way in which they place a particular 'anthropology' of man as an economic subject at the basis of politics. What changes is the emphasis from an anthropology of exchange to one of competition. The shift from exchange to competition has profound effects: while exchange was considered to be natural, competition is understood by the neo-liberals of the twentieth century to be an artificial relation that must be protected against the tendency for markets to form monopolies and interventions by the state. Competition necessitates a constant intervention on the part of the state, not in relation to the market, but in relation to the conditions of the market.[6]

What is more important for us is the way in which this shift in 'anthropology' from 'homo economicus' as an exchanging creature to a competitive creature, or rather as a creature whose tendency to compete must be fostered, entails a general shift in the way in which human beings make themselves and are

---

4   As Foucault writes on this point: 'The combination of the savage and exchange is, I think, basic to juridical thought, and not only to eighteenth century theories of right – we constantly find the savage exchange couple from the eighteenth century theory of right to the anthropology of the nineteenth and twentieth centuries. In both the juridical thought of the eighteenth century and the anthropology of the nineteenth and twentieth centuries the savage is essentially a man who exchanges'. (Foucault 2003 p. 194).

5   Foucault 2008, p. 12.

6   Foucault 2008, p. 139.

made subjects. First, neoliberalism entails a massive expansion of the field and scope of economics. Foucault cites Gary Becker on this point: 'Economics is the science which studies human behavior as relationship between ends and scarce means which have alternate uses'.[7] Everything for which human beings attempt to realise their ends, from marriage, to crime, to expenditures on children, can be understood 'economically' according to a particular calculation of cost for benefit. Secondly, this entails a massive redefinition of 'labour' and the 'worker'. The worker has become 'human capital'. Salary or wages become the revenue that is earned on an initial investment, an investment in one's skills or abilities. Any activity that increases the capacity to earn income, to achieve satisfaction, even migration, the crossing of borders from one country to another, is an investment in human capital. Of course a large portion of 'human capital', one's body, brains, and genetic material, not to mention race or class, is simply given and cannot be improved. Foucault argues that this natural limit is something that exists to be overcome through technologies; from plastic surgery to possible genetic engineering that make it possible to transform one's initial investment. As Foucault writes summarising this point of view: 'Homo economicus is an entrepreneur, an entrepreneur of himself'.[8]

Foucault's object in his analysis is not to bemoan this as a victory for capitalist ideology, the point at which the 'ruling ideas' have truly become the ideas of the 'ruling class', so much so that everyone from a minimum wage employee to a c.e.o. considers themselves to be entrepreneurs. Nor is his task to critique the fundamental increase of the scope of economic rationality in neo-liberal economics: the assertion that economics is coextensive with all of society, all of rationality, and that it is economics 'all the way down'. Rather, Foucault takes the neo-liberal ideal to be a new regime of truth, and a new way in which people are made subjects: homo economicus is fundamentally a different subject, structured by different motivations and governed by different principles, than homo juridicus, or the legal subject of the state. Neoliberalism constitutes a new mode of 'governmentality', a manner, or a mentality, in which people are governed and govern themselves. The operative terms of this governmentality are no longer rights and laws but interest, investment and competition. Whereas rights exist to be exchanged, and are in some sense constituted through the original exchange of the social contract, interest is irreducible and inalienable, it cannot be exchanged. The state channels flows of interest and desire by making desirable activities inexpensive and undesirable activities costly, counting on the fact that subjects calculate their interests. As

7   Foucault 2008, p. 235.
8   Foucault, 2008, p. 226.

a form of governmentality, neoliberalism would seem paradoxically to govern without governing; that is, in order to function its subjects must have a great deal of freedom to act – to choose between competing strategies.

> The new governmental reason needs freedom; therefore, the new art of government consumes freedom. It must produce it, it must organize it. The new art of government therefore appears as the management of freedom, not in the sense of the imperative: 'be free', with the immediate contradiction that this imperative may contain … [T]he liberalism we can describe as the art of government formed in the eighteenth century entails at its heart a productive/destructive relationship with freedom. Liberalism must produce freedom, but this very act entails the establishment of limitations, controls, forms of coercion, and obligations relying on threats, etcetera.[9]

These freedoms, the freedoms of the market, are not the outside of politics, of governmentality, as its limit, but rather are an integral element of its strategy. As a mode of governmentality, neoliberalism operates on interests, desires, and aspirations rather than through rights and obligations; it does not directly mark the body, as sovereign power, or even curtail actions, as disciplinary power; rather, it acts on the conditions of actions. Thus, neoliberal governmentality follows a general trajectory of intensification. This trajectory follows a fundamental paradox; as power becomes less restrictive, less corporeal, it also becomes more intense, saturating the field of actions, and possible actions.[10]

Foucault limits his discussion of neoliberalism to its major theoretical texts and paradigms, following its initial formulation in post-war Germany through to its most comprehensive version in the Chicago School. Whereas Foucault's early analyses are often remembered for their analysis of practical documents, the description of the panopticon or the practice of the confessional, the lectures on 'neoliberalism' predominantly follow the major theoretical discussions. This is in some sense a limitation of the lecture course format, or at least a reflection that this material was never developed into a full study. Any analysis that is faithful to the spirit and not just the letter of Foucault's text would

---

9   Foucault 2008, p. 63.
10 Jeffrey Nealon has developed the logic of intensification in Foucault, arguing that this can be seen in the transition from disciplinary power to biopower; the former operates through specific sites and identities, while the latter operates on sexuality, which is diffuse throughout society, coextensive with subjectivity (Nealon 2008, p. 46). A similar point could be raised with respect to neoliberalism.

focus on its existence as a practice and not just a theory diffused throughout the economy, state, and society. As Thomas Lemke argues, neoliberalism is a political project that attempts to create a social reality that it suggests already exists, stating that competition is the basis of social relations while fostering those same relations.[11] The contemporary trend away from long-term labour contracts, towards temporary and part-time labour, is not only an effective economic strategy, freeing corporations from contracts and the expensive commitments of health care and other benefits, it is an effective strategy of subjectification as well. It encourages workers to see themselves not as 'workers' in a political sense, who have something to gain through solidarity and collective organisation, but as 'companies of one'. They become individuals for whom every action, from taking courses on a new computer software application to having their teeth whitened, can be considered an investment in human capital. As Eric Alliez and Michel Feher write: 'Corporations' massive recourse to subcontracting plays a fundamental role in this to the extent that it turns the workers' desire for independence ... into a "business spirit" that meets capital's growing need for satellites'.[12] Neoliberalism is not simply an ideology in the pejorative sense of the term, or a belief that one could elect to have or not have, but is itself produced by strategies, tactics, and policies that create subjects of interest, locked in competition.

Because Foucault brackets what could be considered the 'ideological' dimension of neoliberalism, its connection with the global hegemony of not only capitalism, but specifically a new regime of capitalist accumulation, his lectures have little to say about its historical conditions. Foucault links the original articulation of neoliberalism to a particular reaction to Nazi Germany. As Foucault argues, the original neo-liberals, the 'Ordo-liberals', considered Nazi Germany not to be an effect of capitalism, but the most extreme version of what is opposed to capitalism and the market – planning. While Foucault's analysis captures the particular 'fear of the state' that underlies neoliberalism, its belief that any planning, any intervention against competition, is tantamount to totalitarianism, it does not account for the dominance of neoliberalism in the present, specifically its dominance as a particular 'technology of the self', a particular mode of subjection. At the same time, Foucault offers the possibility of a different understanding of the history of neoliberalism when he argues that neoliberalism, or the neo-liberal subject as homo economicus, or homo entrepreneur, emerges to address a particular lacunae in liberal economic thought,

---

11   Lemke 2002, p. 60.
12   Alliez and Feher 1986, p. 349.

namely labour. In this sense neoliberalism rushes to fill the same void, the same gap that Marx attempted to fill, without reference to Marx, and with very different results.[13] Marx and neo-liberals agree that although classical economic theory examined the sphere of exchange, the market, it failed to enter the 'hidden abode of production', examining how capital is produced. Of course the agreement ends there, because what Marx and neo-liberals find in labour is fundamentally different: for Marx labour is the sphere of exploitation while for the neo-liberals, as we have seen, labour is no sooner introduced as a problem than the difference between labour and capital is effaced through the theory of 'human capital'.[14] Neoliberalism scrambles and exchanges the terms of opposition between 'worker' and 'capitalist'. To quote Étienne Balibar, 'The capitalist is defined as worker, as an "entrepreneur"; the worker, as the bearer of a capacity, of a human capital'.[15] Labour is no longer limited to the specific sites of the factory or the workplace, but is any activity that works towards desired ends. The terms 'labour' and 'human capital' intersect, overcoming in terminology their longstanding opposition; the former becomes the activity and the latter becomes the effects of the activity, its history. From this intersection the discourse of the economy becomes an entire way of life, a common sense in which every action – crime, marriage, higher education and so on – can be charted according to a calculus of maximum output for minimum expenditure; it can be seen an investment. Thus situating Marx and neoliberalism with respect to a similar problem makes it possible to grasp something of the politics of neoliberalism, which through a generalisation of the idea of the 'entrepreneur', 'investment' and 'risk' beyond the realm of finance capital to every quotidian relation, effaces the very fact of exploitation. Neoliberalism can be considered

---

13   Foucault, 2008, p. 221.

14   In *The Birth of Biopolitics* Foucault argues that Marx filled this void with an 'anthropology' of labour. This is similar to the critique that Foucault develops in 'Truth and Juridical Forms,' in which he argues that Marx posited labour as the 'concrete essence of man'. As Foucault writes: 'So I don't think we can simply accept the traditional Marxist analysis, which assumes that, labor being man's concrete essence, the capitalist system is what transforms labor into profit, into hyperprofit or surplus value. The fact is capitalism penetrates much more deeply into our existence. That system, as it was established in the nineteenth century, was obliged to elaborate a set of political techniques, techniques of power, by which man was tied to something like labor – a set of techniques by which people's bodies and time would become labor power and labor time so as to be effectively used and thereby transformed into hyper profit' (Foucault 2000, 86). This idea, of 'capillary power relations' that turn man into a subject of labour, is an idea which Foucault sometimes develops as a critique and at other times attributes to Marx; see for example 'Les Mailles du pouvoir' and less explicitly *Discipline and Punish*.

15   Balibar 1994, p. 53.

a particular version of 'capitalism without capitalism', a way of maintaining not only private property but the existing distribution of wealth in capitalism while simultaneously doing away with the antagonism and social insecurity of capitalism, in this case paradoxically by extending capitalism, at least its symbols, terms, and logic, to all of society. The opposition between capitalist and worker has been effaced not by a transformation of the mode of production, a new organisation of the production and distribution of wealth, but by the mode of subjection, a new production of subjectivity. Thus, neoliberalism entails a very specific extension of the economy across all of society; it is not, as Marx argued, because everything rests on an economic base (at least in the last instance) that the effects of the economy are extended across of all of society, rather it is an economic perspective, that of the market, that becomes coextensive with all of society. As Christian Laval argues, all actions are seen to conform to the fundamental economic ideas of self-interest, of greatest benefit for least possible cost. It is not the structure of the economy that is extended across society but the subject of economic thinking, its implicit anthropology.[16]

2   Resisting the Present: Towards a Criticism of Neoliberalism

Neoliberalism is thus a 'restoration' not only of class power, of capitalism as the only possible economic system, it is a restoration of capitalism as synonymous with rationality. Thus, the question remains, why now, or at least why over the last thirty years has capitalism taken this neo-liberal turn? If Foucault's invocation of the spectre of Nazi Germany is insufficient to account for the specific historical formation of capitalism, the opposition to Marx does little to help clarify the dominance of neoliberalism now. Somewhat paradoxically this question can be at least partially answered by looking at one of the few points of intersection between Marx and neoliberalism.

In the *Grundrisse*, Marx does not use the term 'human capital', but fixed capital, a term generally used to refer to machinery, factories, and other investments in the means of production to refer to the subjectivity, the subjective powers of the worker. In general Marx understood the progression of capital to be a process by which the skills, knowledge, and know-how of workers were gradually incorporated into machinery, into fixed capital, reducing the labourer to an unskilled and ultimately replaceable cog in a machine. This is 'proletarianisation', the process by which capitalism produces its gravediggers in a

---

16   Laval 2007, p. 17.

class of impoverished workers who have nothing to lose but their chains. In the *Grundrisse*, however, Marx addresses a fundamentally different possibility, capital's exploitation of not just the physical powers of the body, but the general social knowledge spread throughout society and embodied in each individual. This is what Marx refers to as the 'general intellect' – the diffused social knowledge of society. This knowledge, the capacity to use various languages, protocols, and symbolic systems, is largely produced outside of work. As Marx writes: 'The saving of labor time is equal to an increase of free time, i.e. time for the full development of the individual, which in turn reacts back upon the productive power of labor as itself the greatest productive power. From the standpoint of the direct production process it can be regarded as the production of fixed capital, this fixed capital being man himself'.[17] Marx's deviation from the standard terminology of his own corpus, terminology that designates the worker as labour power (or living labour), the machine or factory as fixed capital, and money as circulating capital, is ultimately revealing. It reveals something of a future that Marx could barely envision, a future that has become our present: the real subsumption of society by capital. This subsumption involves not only the formation of what Marx referred to as a specifically capitalist mode of production, but also the incorporation of all subjective potential, the capacity to communicate, to feel, to create, to think, into productive powers for capital. Capital no longer simply exploits labour, understood as the physical capacity to transform objects, but puts to work the capacities to create and communicate that traverse social relations. It is possible to say that with real subsumption capital has no outside, there is no relationship that cannot be transformed into a commodity, but at the same time capital is nothing but outside, production takes place outside of the factory and the firm, in various social relationships. Because of this fundamental displacement subjectivity becomes paramount, subjectivity itself becomes productive and it is this same subjectivity that must be controlled.

For Antonio Negri there is a direct relationship between real subsumption as a transformation of the capitalist mode of production and neoliberalism as a transformation of the presentation of capitalism. It is not simply that neoliberalism works to efface the fundamental division between worker and capitalist, between wages and capital, through the production of neo-liberal subjectivity. After all, this opposition, this antagonism, has preexisted neoliberalism by centuries. Neoliberalism is a discourse and practice that is aimed to curtail the powers of labour that are distributed across all of society – at the exact

---

17   Marx, 1973: 712.

moment in which all of social existence becomes labour, or potential labour, neoliberalism constructs the image of a society of capitalists, of entrepreneurs. As production moves from the closed space of the factory to become distributed across all of social space, encompassing all spheres of cultural and social existence, neoliberalism presents an image of society as a market, effacing production altogether.[18] This underscores the difference between neoliberalism as a form of power and the disciplinary power at work in the closed spaces of the factory. If disciplinary power worked by confining and fixing bodies to the production apparatuses, neoliberal power works by dispersing bodies and individuals through privatisation and isolation. Deregulation, the central term and political strategy of neoliberalism, is not the absence of governing, or regulating, but a form of governing through isolation and dispersion.[19] As more and more wealth is produced by the collective social powers of society, neoliberalism presents us with an image of society made up of self-interested individuals. For Negri, neoliberalism and the idea of human capital is a misrepresentation of the productive powers of society. 'The only problem is that extreme liberalization of the economy reveals its opposite, namely that the social and productive environment is not made up of atomized individuals ... the real environment is made up of collective individuals'.[20] In Negri's analysis, the relation between neoliberalism and real subsumption takes on the characteristics of a Manichean opposition. We are all workers or we are all capitalists: either view society as an extension of labour across all social spheres, from the factory to the school to the home, and across all aspects of human existence, from the work of the hands to the mind, or view society as a logic of competition and investment that encompasses all human relationships. While Negri's presentation has an advantage over Foucault's lectures in that it grasps the historical formation of neoliberalism against the backdrop of a specific transformation of capital, in some sense following Foucault's tendency to present disciplinary power and biopower against the backdrop of specific changes in the economic organisation of society, it does so by almost casting neoliberalism as an ideology in the pejorative sense of the term. It would appear that for Negri real subsumption is the truth of society, and neoliberalism is only a misrepresentation of that truth. As Thomas Lemke has argued, Foucault's idea of governmentality is argued against such a division that posits actual material reality on one side and its ideological misrepresentation on the other. A governmentality is a particular mentality, a particular manner of governing, that is actualised

---

18   Hardt and Negri 1994, 226.
19   Negri 1989, p. 99.
20   Negri, 1989, p. 2006.

in habits, perceptions, and subjectivity. Governmentality situates actions and conceptions on the same plane of immanence.[21] Which is to say that any criticism of neoliberalism as governmentality must not focus on its errors, on its myopic conception of social existence, but on its particular production of truth. For Foucault, we have to take seriously the manner in which the fundamental understanding of individuals as governed by interest and competition is not just an ideology that can be refused and debunked, but is an intimate part of how our lives and subjectivity are structured.

Despite Negri's tendency to lapse back into an opposition between labour and ideology, his object raises important questions echoed by other critics of neoliberalism. What is lost in neoliberalism is the critical distance opened up between different spheres and representations of subjectivity, not only the difference between work and the market, as in Marxism, but also the difference between the citizen and the economic subject, as in classical liberalism. All of these differences are effaced as one relation; that of economic self-interest, or competition, replaces the multiple spaces and relations of worker, citizen, and economic subject of consumption. To put the problem in Foucault's terms, what has disappeared in neoliberalism is the tactical polyvalence of discourse; everything is framed in terms of interests, freedoms and risks.[22] As Wendy Brown argues, one can survey the quotidian effects or practices of governmentality in the manner in which individualised/market-based solutions appear in lieu of collective political solutions: gated communities for concerns about security and safety; bottled water for concerns about water purity; and private schools (or vouchers) for failing public schools, all of which offer the opportunity for individuals to opt out rather than address political problems.[23] Privatisation is not just neoliberalism's strategy for dealing with the public sector, what David Harvey calls accumulation by dispossession, but a consistent element of its particular form of governmentality, its ethos: everything becomes privatised, institutions, structures, issues, and problems that used to constitute the public.[24] It is privatisation all the way down. For Brown, neoliberalism entails a massive de-democratisation, as terms such as the public good, rights and debate, no longer have any meaning. 'The model neoliberal citizen is one who strategizes for her or himself among various social, political, and economic options, not one who strives with others to alter or organize these options'.[25]

---

21   Lemke, 2002, p. 54.
22   Foucault 1978, p. 101.
23   Brown 2006, p. 704.
24   Harvey 2005, p. 154.
25   Brown, 2005, p. 43.

Thus, while it is possible to argue that neoliberalism is a more flexible, open form of power as opposed to the closed spaces of disciplines, a form of power that operates on freedoms, on a constitutive multiplicity, it is in some sense all the more closed in that as a form of governmentality, as a political rationality, it is without an outside. It does not encounter any tension with a competing logic of worker or citizen, with a different articulation of subjectivity. States, corporations, individuals are all governed by the same logic, that of interest and competition.

Foucault's development, albeit partial, of an account of neoliberalism as governmentality has as its major advantage a clarification of the terrain on which neoliberalism can be countered. It is not enough to simply oppose neoliberalism as ideology, revealing the truth of social existence that it misses, or to enumerate its various failings as policy. Rather any opposition to neoliberalism must take seriously its effectiveness, the manner in which it has transformed work subjectivity and social relationships. As Foucault argues, neoliberalism operates less on actions, directly curtailing them, than on the condition and effects of actions, on the sense of possibility. The reigning ideal of interest and the calculations of cost and benefit do not so much limit what one can do – neoliberal thinkers are famously indifferent to prescriptive ideals, examining the illegal drug trade as a more or less rational investment – but limit the sense of what is possible. Specifically the ideal of the fundamentally self-interested individual curtails any collective transformation of the conditions of existence. It is not that such actions are not prohibited, restricted by the dictates of a sovereign or the structures of disciplinary power; they are not seen as possible, closed off by a society made up of self-interested individuals. It is perhaps no accident that one of the most famous political implementers of neoliberal reforms, Margaret Thatcher, used the slogan 'there is no alternative', legitimating neoliberalism based on the stark absence of possibilities. Similarly, and as part of a belated response to the former Prime Minister, it is also perhaps no accident that the slogan of the famous Seattle protests against the IMF and World Bank was 'another world is possible', and it is very often the sense of a possibility of not only another world, but of another way of organising politics that is remembered, the image of turtles and teamsters marching hand and hand, when those protests are referred to.[26] It is also this sense of possibility that the present seems to be lacking; it is difficult to imagine let alone enact a future other than a future dominated by interest and the destructive vicissitudes of competition. A political response to neoliberalism must meet it on its terrain, that of the production of subjectivity, freedom and possibility.

26   Lazzarato 2004, 19.

CHAPTER 16

Abstract Materialism: Sohn-Rethel and the Task of a Materialist Philosophy Today

Materialism has always been the bastard step-son of philosophy. Its very position is paradoxical, if not impossible. It must use concepts and arguments to conceptualise and argue against the primacy of concepts and argument. This perennial problem is even worse today. If Marx was in some sense the most sophisticated materialist philosopher, elevating the material beyond the brute materiality of the body, to locate the material in the reality of production and the conflicted terrain of social relations, then one could argue that even this version of materialism is in jeopardy today. The economy, the last instance of materialist philosophy after Marx, can no longer be identified with the machines and noise of the factory; it has, it has been said, become digital, immaterial. What then remains of materialism when the economy has become ideal, determined more and more by the idealist category par excellence, speculation, and even labour has been declared immaterial, intersecting with beliefs and desires? At least the beginning of a response can be found in the seemingly paradoxical concept of 'real abstraction'. This term, introduced by Marx, takes on a central importance in the work of Alfred Sohn-Rethel, where it is no longer a methodological postulate, but the cornerstone of a philosophy that seeks to understand the material basis of abstraction and its effects on society, thought, and consciousness.

As important as this idea of real abstraction is for an understanding of Marx's philosophy, and its specific rupture with idealist philosophy, it is perhaps more useful for navigating the increasingly abstract terrain of contemporary capitalism. To follow a remark by Fredric Jameson, any attempt to understand the problem of abstraction must take into consideration the structural and qualitatively distinct abstractions of contemporary capitalism.[1] Thus our interest here is not limited to a consideration of the real abstraction as a heuristic device clarifying Marx's specific intervention in the field of philosophy, but also includes the real abstraction as a framing device for thinking about the history and contradictions of contemporary capitalism.

---

1   Jameson 1998, p. 143.

1   Marx: From Philosophy as Abstraction to Real Abstraction

What exactly is meant by materialism? This question becomes particularly pressing in terms of the pairing of materialism and abstraction, but is no less a question with respect to Marx's writing. As a general definition of material-ism in Marx's philosophy we could start with the overturning of the priority of the relationship between life and thought in *The German Ideology*. As Marx writes, 'Life is not determined by consciousness, but consciousness by life'.[2] Marx's inversion of the priority between thought and life in that text seems inadequate to grasp the materiality of abstraction, as it is organised around a stark opposition between the concrete and abstract, between the abstractions of philosophy of the concrete experience of real life. A point of clarification is offered by the first of the 'Theses on Feuerbach', which offers a more nuanced, even dialectical statement of the relation between materialism and idealism. That thesis is perhaps most well known for its definition of praxis, but what is less frequently addressed is the manner in which it states a fundamental contradiction, if not paradox, integral to Marx's definition of materialism. As long as materialism takes as its model the material object, such as the body, it will remain secretly idealist, because this object will always be an object for contemplation. Idealism, on the other hand, and Marx is thinking primarily of idealism after Kant, German Idealism, is secretly materialist; that is, as long as it is concerned primarily with activity.[3] The rest of the theses follow this line: developing a materialist philosophy that is not so much opposed to idealism, but drawn from it, claiming its defining characteristic of activity and prac-tical, rather than simply contemplative, reason. It is what Étienne Balibar refers to as a 'materialism without matter'.[4] This can be seen in the infamous sixth thesis: Marx does not so much oppose the idea of a human essence as make it the produce of social relations, simultaneously moving against the idea of a human essence, and situating it on the terrain of social relations. The concept of relation itself is the lynchpin, the point of transition between the ideal and the material, essence and appearance. The history of philosophy has vacillated between two positions: in the first, relations are thought to be entirely mental, or extrinsic; while in the second, relations are real, intrinsic.[5] One could argue, following Balibar, that what we find in Marx is a third position, one that pos-its the real as relation. This is one way of understanding not just the infamous

---

2   Marx and Engels 1970, p. 47.
3   Balibar 1995, p. 25.
4   Balibar 1995, p. 23.
5   Morfino p. 105.

sixth thesis on Feuerbach, but the early work on ideology, in which the opposite of ideology is not the truth found in this or that instance of society, but in
the totality of social relations.[6]

All this becomes much more complex if one shifts from Marx's early critique of philosophy to the critique of political economy. Marx's engagement
with philosophy, at least the philosophy of post-Hegelian German Idealism,
was always two-pronged: demonstrating that it failed to account for its material
conditions, while simultaneously appropriating something of its fundamental
orientation to produce a materialism of activity, transformation, and relations.
Marx's strategy of critical reading must necessarily shift when confronting
political economy, which cannot be said to fail to consider its material conditions since it directly intervenes in them. Marx is of course most famous for
arguing that the categories of political economy 'are forms of thought expressing with social validity the conditions and relations of a definite, historically
determined mode of production'.[7] It is from this assertion that we get the well
known Marxist imperative to 'always historicise', to always consider the historical conditions of any given concept or situation. It is perhaps less well known,
however, that Marx often expressed the difference between his understanding of political economy and bourgeois political economy as one which hinged
on the status of abstraction itself: for Marx abstract labour and surplus value
are the fundamental points of distinction between his account and the bourgeois account of capitalism.[8] Marx's understanding of capital hinges on the
understanding of the abstractions, labour considered indifferent to its material situation and surplus value considered independent of this or that manner
of generating surplus; these abstractions considered in terms of their concrete
and material conditions and effects.

These two dimensions of Marx's critique of political economy, history and
abstraction, converge in Marx's '1857 Introduction', which give methodological
centrality to the idea of abstraction. Marx argues that while it would appear
to make the most sense to begin any discussion of political economy with the
population, as an irreducibly concrete point of reference, the population, considered independently of the relations and divisions that constitute it, is an
abstraction. Marx argues that the categories of abstract labour, labour indifferent to its conditions, is more accurate, not in spite of its abstraction, but
precisely because of its abstraction, an abstraction that is itself a product of history. Abstract categories such as labour, labour considered independent of the

---

6   Balibar 1994, p. 92.
7   Marx 1977, p. 324.
8   Marx and Engels 1955, 186.

various attributes, which would seem to be valid to all societies, only become 'true in practice' in the most advanced social relations. As Marx writes: 'The simplest abstraction, then, which modern economics places at the head of its discussions and which expresses an immeasurably ancient relation valid in all forms of society, nevertheless achieves practical truth as an abstraction only as a category of the most modern society'.[9] Marx's statement reflects not only a break with any historicism, at least any historicisms predicated on the linear progression from the simple to more complex social formations, but a thorough transformation of the notion of abstraction. Abstract labour is not simply a valid category for capitalist society, a concept that can be applied to it, but it is practically true, experienced in practice. This is a point made even stronger in *Capital*: abstract labour becomes a practical reality when the social and technological conditions exist to make the labour of disparate and distinct individuals interchangeable.[10] As Marx writes in *Capital*, 'it is a process that goes on behind men's backs', a point that is illustrated by the effects of a transformation of the technological conditions of labour in one part of the world on the value of labour across the globe. This is a fundamentally different sense of abstraction, not the abstraction of a mind operating on some irreducibly concrete experience, but an abstraction produced by the interrelation of multiple concrete relations, relations that exceed the consciousness of the individual.

2   From Real Abstraction to Social Synthesis

With this survey of the problems of identifying materialism in the writings of Marx, we can now turn to Sohn-Rethel's use of the concept of real abstraction. Sohn-Rethel's understanding of real abstraction takes as its starting point Marx's presentation of the commodity form in the opening of *Capital*. Sohn-Rethel reads these passages to extract a thought of the practical constitution of abstraction. Contrary to what one might expect, however, it is not drawn from Marx's distinction between concrete and abstract labour. For Sohn-Rethel use value and exchange value are each related to particular activities, the activities of exchange and use, each of which has its own specific logics and relations to the object in question. What Sohn-Rethel stresses is that in the act of a commodity exchange one may be focused on the concrete qualities of the commodity, its use value, but act as if its quantitative exchange value really

9   Marx 1973 p. 104.
10   Read 2003, p. 69.

mattered; it is this after all that governs exchange. 'It is the action of exchange, and the action alone that is abstract. The consciousness and the action of the people part company in exchange and go different ways'.[11] This is the scandal that Marx's thought represents for philosophy: it is not just that 'consciousness is determined by life' in terms of the content and concepts that make up ideology, but that the very form of thought, abstraction, is determined by practice. Marx's assertion that 'life determines consciousness' remains trivially true unless it becomes a matter of the form of thought itself.[12]

Sohn-Rethel's examination of the connection between the form of thought and practice is not focused on labour, even abstract labour, but on the division between two fundamental practical activities: exchange and use. Sohn-Rethel takes his bearings from Marx's radical separation of exchange from use, exchange value contains 'not an atom of use'; for Sohn-Rethel it is less a matter of what constitutes the basis for value than the constitution of two different spheres, one defined by the practical matters of use, the other by abstraction. 'The concept of property is itself only a conceptualization of the factual necessity of keeping use and exchange separated'.[13] Despite the fact that this abstraction takes place practically in the sphere of the market, it is still a practice, defined by spatial and material relations. As much as it takes place within a particular place and time, it abstracts from them, effacing them: use values exist in a particular place and time, but exchange values are free from the effects of space and time, as is money. It is this abstraction that makes possible the specific abstractions of capitalist thought: abstractions that have as their defining characteristic the purely quantitative unit of space and time. The defining characteristic of money and the commodity form is to be a pure abstraction, pure quantity without quality, and this pure abstraction exists in the practice of commodity exchange before it exists in thought. Practice is primary to thought, but practice is less labour as some kind of metabolic relation with nature than second nature: the relations of exchange and the division between exchange and use that constitutes the form of social activity. The abstractions of economics, its tendency to speak of 'widgets', to deal with the commodity in its abstraction from use, from what the commodity is, is something that made 'its way from reality into the textbooks', and not the other way around.[14] It is a reflection of a society ruled by abstractions.[15]

---

11   Sohn-Rethel 1978, p. 26.
12   Sohn-Rethel 1978, p. 8.
13   Sohn-Rethel 1978, p. 40.
14   Marx 1973, p. 90.
15   Marx 1973 p. 164.

Sohn-Rethel's focus on exchange rather than labour as the activity constitutive of thought may seem strange, undermining Marx's fundamental assertion that society is best understood from the mode of production, not distribution.[16] Sohn-Rethel does not so much dispense with labour, but justifies his selection through a theory of social relations, what he calls a social synthesis. Sohn-Rethel's idea of a social synthesis is an attempt to answer the question as to how society coheres, holds itself together: in other words, why is there society rather than nothing? This problem becomes particularly difficult in a society defined by the competition of isolated individuals. As Sohn-Rethel writes: 'How does society hold together when production is carried out independently by private producers, and all forms of previous production in common have broken asunder?'[17] The answer is the social synthesis, and the particular form that this synthesis takes in capitalist society. Basically, a capitalist society is held together through the abstract concepts of value, and the abstraction that it makes possible, despite the fact that physically, at the level of labouring bodies and the accumulation of use values, it remains distinct. We labour in isolation and consume in the privacy of our home, but the condition of both this production and consumption is the totality of relations constitutive of exchange value. Sohn-Rethel refers to this as a society of appropriation, in which society is socialised at the level of appropriation, or exchange. It is a society unified in the head, despite its isolation in the labouring or consuming body. Labour, the metabolic relation with nature, is dominated by exchange: second nature dominates first nature. A society of appropriation is distinct from a society of production: the latter would imply not only different social relations, but different forms of thought, no longer predicated on the radical divide between the physical object and abstract unit.

Sohn-Rethel's social synthesis is ultimately not just a theory of how society holds together, but how thought holds together as well. As Sohn-Rethel writes, 'forms of thought and forms of society have one thing in common. They are both forms'.[18] A social synthesis expresses this identity of thinking and society. Thus, it constitutes another blow to the claims of idealist thought, if not philosophy itself: it is not just that the abstraction is primarily practical rather than conceptual, but that thought is not the attribute of an individual consciousness: it is a social process through and through. 'Nothing that a single commodity-owner might undertake on his own could give rise to this abstraction, no more than a hammock could play its part when attached to

---

16   Postone 1996 p. 178.
17   Sohn-Rethel 1978, p. 29.
18   Sohn-Rethel 1978, p. 17.

one pole only'.[19] Exchange is a relation, and the abstractions that it constitutes and sustain it have a necessary collective, or rather transindividual, status, as something that exists in relation.[20] Their transindividual status is necessary, even fundamental, to their socially synthetic function. If in commodity exchange the action and consciousness of individuals goes separate ways, then this separation is also a separation between a social synthesis and an individuated perception.

3   The Real Abstraction of Subjectivity

The two materialist theses that I outlined at the beginning, the primacy of practice and the primacy of social relations, become in Sohn-Rethel's work an emphasis on the primacy of exchange as an activity constitutive of thought and society as a social synthesis. These concepts converge in the idea of real abstraction: abstractions that are lived prior to being thought, and are social before being individual. Or, put differently, thought is irreducibly social because it is irredeemably practical, structured by practice. Having defined the basic contours of Sohn-Rethel's materialist philosophy, we can now return to the initial question as to the question of materiality today.

The final chapter of *Intellectual and Manual Labour* lays out a particular interpretation of Marx's methodology. As Sohn-Rethel argues, Marx's central works were always a critique of political economy, rather than a direct exposition of capitalist reality: materiality is always approached through a particular form of thought.[21] This suggests that philosophical texts can always be interrogated against the present at the same time that they make such an interrogation possible. We can then ask, where do we stand with this concept of real abstraction today: what does it make possible, and what are its limitations? First, there is the way in which it posits a particular split in the intellect. The intellect is immediately social: the fundamental conceptual schemas of thought are produced by social relations, but this sociality is lived differently than it is constituted. The schema of the intellect is social, but unconsciously so; consciously the focus is on the specific qualities of the commodity in question. This is the division between use value and exchange value, only now it explains the gen-

---

19   Sohn-Rethel 1978, p. 69.
20   I use the term transindividual here following the work of Gilbert Simondon to mean that which both exceeds the individual and is the condition for individuation. For more on the term see *The Politics of Transindividuality*.
21   Sohn-Rethel 1978, p. 195.

esis of thought, not value. 'Nothing could be wrapped in greater secrecy than the truth that the independence of the intellect is owed to its original social character'.[22] Sohn-Rethel's assertion could be used to make sense of Marx's formulation in the *Grundrisse* of the fundamental paradox of capitalist social existence:

> Only in the eighteenth century, in 'civil society', do the various forms of social connectedness confront the individual as a mere means towards his private purposes, as external necessity. But the epoch which produces this standpoint, that of the isolated individual, is also precisely that of the hitherto most developed social (from this standpoint, general) relations.[23]

Only now these developed relations do not just concern the interconnected relations of civil society, but the relations constitutive of thought. To cast it into a different conceptual vocabulary, Sohn-Rethel's thought is rigorously transindividual, in that the individual, even the solipsistic individual, acting in competitive isolation or fulfilling its own independent desires on the market, is an effect and condition of social relations, relations that exceed its comprehension precisely because they are relations.[24]

  For Sohn-Rethel the contradiction of the social forces of production and the isolated relations of production passes into the interior of thought itself: the form of thought is irreducibly social, partaking in the real abstractions that define the conceptual space of pure quantity, but its contents are irredeemably individual, even solipsistic, as consciousness focuses on the specific qualities of the commodity in question. This is perhaps Sohn-Rethel's unique take on the central contradiction between forces and relations of production; only now this contradiction passes into the interior of subjectivity itself, between work and consumption. Sohn-Rethel's analysis of the real abstraction draws a picture of consciousness that is split between a practical immersion in the transindividual real abstractions and a solipsistic consciousness, practically relational and yet isolated in thought. Sohn-Rethel is largely concerned with the epistemic rather than subjective, or psychological aspects of this shift, its relation to thought in general rather than the individual's consciousness. However, many of the readers of Sohn-Rethel have pursued this direction, reading his real abstraction less as a criticism of epistemology than as a description of

---

22   Sohn-Rethel 1978, p. 77.
23   Marx 1973, 223.
24   Sohn-Rethel, 1978, p. 69.

subjectivity in capitalism. It is beyond the scope of this essay, but it is well documented that Theodor Adorno corresponded with Sohn-Rethel for several years, and shared a similar interest in the connections between the commodity form and the form of thought. This is most clearly demonstrated in the homology that Adorno sets up between the commodity form and the concept as two different instance of formal identity.[25] The commodity form and the concept both function by equalising disparate content, subsuming it under formal identity. In *Minima Moralia*, moreover, Adorno offers a sketch that roughly matches Sohn-Rethel's split between sociality and isolation. As Adorno writes:

> The intellectual, particularly when philosophically inclined, is cut off from practical life: revulsion from it has driven him to concern himself with so-called things of the mind. But material practice is not only the pre-condition of his existence, it is basic to the world which he criticizes in his work. If he knows nothing of this basis he shoots into thin air ... [H]e hypostatizes as an absolute his intellect which was only formed through contact with economic reality and abstract exchange relations, and which can become intellect solely by reflecting on its own conditions.[26]

Adorno's diagnosis here is a negative one: the less the intellectual thinks of economic reality, the more she thinks in line with it, perpetuating the ideal of consciousness separate from material reality; however, if she turns towards economic reality she risks losing the autonomy necessary to criticise it. 'Intellectual business is helped, by the isolation of intellect from business, to become a comfortable ideology'. The idea is that the social relations are reproduced not so much in a given content, such as ideology, or even in a given form, but in the constant split between form and content.[27] Slavoj Žižek focuses on precisely this split, finding in it the constitutive conditions of cynicism, which is the subjective attitude proper to this split, to a life caught between a radical split between ideas and actions.[28] Practically we act as if the different commodities and disparate labours are interchangeable, exchange value, but at the level of consciousness we are focused on the concrete and isolated qualities, use values.

Despite the resonances that this particular version of contradiction may have, resonances that extend Marx's remarks about the isolated individual

---

25   Adorno 1992, p. 146 and Jameson 1990, p. 23.
26   Adorno 1974, p. 132.
27   Sohn-Rethel, p. 15.
28   Žižek 1989, p. 31.

emerging in the most developed relations into an age of a globalised consumer society, they also reveal Sohn-Rethel's dependence on a particular social and technical division of labour. The dominance of labour by the social synthesis of appropriation culminates in the Taylorist labour process; a process that Sohn-Rethel identifies with the dominance of labour by not only the demand for more productivity, but also by a knowledge framed by the abstract space and time of F.W. Taylor's time and motion studies.[29] The labour of a singular body is forced into the abstract quantities of productivity, abstract quantities that necessarily pre-exist it. Sohn-Rethel's analysis follows the historical trajectory developed in Marx's *Capital*. The transition from handicrafts to large-scale industry is not just a technical reorganisation of work, but a fundamental restructuring according to a new principle: work is no longer organised around the knowledge and actions of the worker, but according to the demands of the commodity form. Automation is the physical materialisation of this transformation. As much as automation reduces labour to a simple function of space and time, it also extends and maximises the socialisation of the abstract intellect. As Sohn-Rethel writes, 'Automation amounts to the socialization of the human labour power which, in certain aspects, it surpasses in its scope of capability, range of action, its speed, reliability and precision, though only in a restricted and set specialization'.[30] This sociality is no longer simply the socialisation of real abstractions in the form of thought, the abstract space and time that constitute the basis of scientific thought; with automation these abstractions are materialised, passing through bodies and machines, even if they only intersect with the minimal dimension of labour. As Marx writes, 'it is no longer necessary for the individual himself to put his hand to the object; it is sufficient for him to be an organ of the collective labourer, and to perform one of its subordinate functions'.[31]

At this point Sohn-Rethel's argument duplicates Marx's argument in the so-called 'Fragment on Machines' in the *Grundrisse*, despite the fact that he does not draw from this subsequently influential text. In this text, as in *Capital*, Marx identifies the emergence of machinery with the destruction of skill as the basis for production. While a tool is always dependent on the virtuosity of the worker, the incorporation of knowledge into the machine in terms of its design and ability to mimic and duplicate activities that were performed by workers makes it so the machine itself is the 'virtuoso'. As the skill, technical know-how, and

29   Sohn-Rethel p. 149.
30   Sohn-Rethel p. 176.
31   Marx 1977, p. 644.

science is made into a physical attribute of the machine, it is no longer necessary for the worker to physically embody the skill and knowledge necessary for
production. 'The science which compels the inanimate limbs of the machinery,
by their construction, to act purposefully, as an automaton, does not exist in the
worker's consciousness but rather acts upon him through the machine as an
alien power, as the power of the machine itself'.[32] The description in the fragment is the culmination of the domination of the hand by the head. The real
abstractions of money and the commodity form, abstract quantity and time
and space, have become incorporated in a machine, as a general social knowledge. Marx refers to this social knowledge as the general intellect:

> Nature builds no machines, no locomotives, railways, electric telegraphs,
> self-acting mules etc. These are the products of human industry; nat-
> ural material transformed into organs of the human will over nature, or
> of human participation in nature. They are *organs of the human brain,
> created by the human hand*; the power of knowledge objectified [*verge-
> genständlichte Wissenskraft*]. The development of fixed capital indicates
> to what degree general social knowledge has become a *direct force of pro-
> duction*, and to what degree, hence, the conditions of the process of social
> life itself have come under the control of the general intellect and been
> transformed in accordance with it.[33]

For Marx and Sohn-Rethel the rise of knowledge and machinery in the production process necessitates a reduction of the role of labour, labour is nothing
but a miserable residue, a conscious organ overseeing the powers of generalised intellectual activity.

For Paolo Virno the 'general intellect' represents less a fundamental continuity with the organisation of the labour process by the real abstraction, the
dominance of appropriation over production, than a fundamental mutation of
the real abstraction itself. Virno's interpretation begins from an examination of
the relevance of the general intellect for understanding contemporary production; the ability of the concept, and the prophetic vision of the future it entails,
to match up to the present. Marx's 'Fragment' presents capitalism as a moving
self-contradiction, but this is not the contradiction of the working class with
nothing to lose but their chains, a contradiction of complete proletarianisation
that can only lead to the expropriation of the expropriators. In the 'Fragment',

---

32   Marx 1973, p. 693.
33   Marx 1973, p. 706.

the opposite takes place, capital dies of socialisation, socialised knowledge as a productive force. As Marx writes, 'Capital itself is the moving contradiction, [in] that it presses to reduce labour time to a minimum, while it posits labour time, on the other side, as sole measure and source of wealth'.[34] Capital annuls labour as the source of wealth, while maintaining it as the measure of value.

As Virno remarks, the first thing that one has to consider in reading this description of capital's death by automation is 'the full factual realization of the tendency described ... without any emancipatory – or merely conflictual – reversal'.[35] Nearly everything about the fragment has come true except the crisis of labour and the undermining of capital. This does not lead to tossing the analysis out, to yet another rejection of Marx based on a supposed prophecy which failed to come to pass, but a fundamental question: how is it that capitalism has overcome its own basis, overcoming labour power as the basis of wealth, without this resulting in revolution or even conflict? Virno argues that this can be answered by a simple modification of the definition of the general intellect, a simple correction to take into consideration what Marx failed to see. 'Marx thus neglects the way in which the general intellect manifests itself as living labour'.[36] The social knowledge that enters into the centre of the production process is not just materialised in machines and technology, but in skill, talent, aptitude, and habits.[37] This radically redefines the nature of general intellect, and its machines, which are no longer just machines in the literal sense, but protocols and programmes for production. For Virno, 'The general intellect includes the epistemic models that structure social communication'.[38] This entails a fundamental transformation of the nature of the real abstraction.

The shift in the nature of the real abstraction has to do with their relation to production. For Sohn-Rethel the central distinction is between two different social syntheses: a logic of production and a logic of appropriation. In the first, production is the socially synthetic moment, relating the different labouring activities and use values in their heterogeneity and plurality. In the second, logic of appropriation, the real abstractions of the commodity and money relate and bring together the different, disparate, and disjointed labours under the domination of the real abstraction of the commodity form. With respect to the second, to the logic of appropriation, this real abstraction dominates production, but it does so externally, imposing a quantitative demand and a formal

---

34   Marx 1973, p. 706.
35   Virno 1996b p. 267.
36   Virno 2007a p. 5.
37   Read 2003, p. 121.
38   Virno 1996a p. 22.

structure on the labouring process. Virno understands the transformation from labour to the general intellect as the operative real abstraction to be a fundamental transformation of precisely this exteriority. As Virno writes:

> Whereas money, the 'universal equivalent' itself incarnates in its independent existence the commensurability of products, jobs, and subjects, the general intellect instead stabilizes the analytic premises of every type of practice. Models of social knowledge do not equate the various activities of labour, but rather present themselves as the 'immediate forces of production.'[39]

The general intellect does not regulate production, it does not stand over labour, as in the case of Taylorism, and the rule of abstract science. Rather, the general intellect migrates into the centre of production, becoming part of labour itself, determining its production. The real abstractions of Sohn-Rethel's analysis, what we could call the real abstractions of formal subsumption, emphasise just that, form. Money and the commodity form operate first and foremost by rendering different objects, different bodies, and different activities interchangeable. As much as this equality, this eden of 'freedom, equality, and Bentham', is, as Marx famously argued, underwritten and undermined by the fundamental inequality and asymmetry of the capital/labour relation, these real abstractions produce a kind of 'socially necessary semblance'.[40] The real abstractions of formal interchangeability, money and the commodity, thus cut into two directions: on the one hand, they subordinate labour, the work of this specific hand to the abstract intellect; on the other hand, the image of equality and interchangeability that they produce haunts capitalism, threatening to become a claim for equality in general.[41] The shift from money and the commodity as the real abstraction to the general intellect entails a profound shift in the social semblance. The general intellect is defined by the absolute incommensurability between different forms of knowledge and operative paradigms. 'The models of social knowledge are not units of measurement; instead, they constitute the premise for operative heterogeneous possibilities ... They do not equalize anything; instead, they act as premise to every type of action'.[42] Not only is their no equivalence, no possible ground of comparison between these different forms of knowledge, but

---

39   Virno 1996a p. 23.
40   Virno 2007b p. 42.
41   Keenan p. 118.
42   Virno 2004, p. 87.

any given individual passes through multiple paradigms, multiple conceptual apparatuses, in a given life or even day.

The migration of the real abstraction into the centre of production fundamentally alters the relationship between thought and existence. Sohn-Rethel's real abstractions were practised more than they were thought. They make possible the abstractions of science, of a particular conception of science predicated on abstract quantitative space and time, but they are not properly thought, at least in the moment of exchange; as we have seen, 'the action and the consciousness of people goes separate ways'. With respect to production, to labour itself, these abstractions are imposed from the outside, forming the measure and standard that subordinates labour to the logic of appropriation. The shift from the formal real abstraction to the general intellect, which could be called a *real* real abstraction, if that was not too awkward, is also a fundamental shift in this relation as well. The difference is not one of interiority, of subjectivisation, this was already at stake in Sohn-Rethel's description, in which what was interiorised was the split between form and content lived as a kind of cynicism, but of the priority between abstract and concrete. As Virno writes:

> Innumerable conceptual constructions, embodied in as many techniques, procedures, and regulations, orient the gaze and serve as the premises of any operation whatsoever. Direct perception and the most spontaneous action come last. This is the historical situation that comes about once the split between hand and mind manifests its irreversibility; when the autonomy of abstract intellect conditions and regulates the social productive process, on the whole and in every one of its singular aspects.[43]

The various formations of knowledge, the various paradigms, programs and cultural literacies, are not simply imposed on the production process from the outside, but become internal to it, they are its raw material and means of production. This migration of the real abstractions into the productive process is not without its effects at the level of subjectivity, as a certain relation between life and concept is reversed. Marx's famous formula of materialist philosophy has been reversed: consciousness now determines life, only it is not the consciousness dreamed of by the philosophers, but a consciousness that is itself produced, circulated and consumed by the productive process.

---

43   Virno 2001 p. 171.

These fundamental shifts of the real abstraction from the formal abstractions of money and the commodity to the general intellect have profound effects for subjectivity. Unlike Sohn-Rethel, who is primarily interested in epistemology, despite making some interesting and suggestive remarks about the real abstraction and a split in subjectivity between the collective form and individual perception, Virno, like Adorno and Žižek, is explicitly concerned with the intersection of the real abstraction and subjectivity. As he writes, 'If we fail to perceive the points of identity between labour practices and modes of life, we will comprehend nothing of the changes taking place in present-day production and misunderstand a great deal about the forms of contemporary culture'.[44] The mode of life, the emotional tonality, which corresponds to this shift in the general intellect, is a rise of cynicism and opportunism. Rather than see these particular modes of subjectivity as simple ethical failings, or effects of the defeat of the left, cynicism and opportunism have to be understood as stemming from the transformation of the real abstraction. The shift from a real abstraction predicated on formal equality to an abstraction predicated on difference, produces a world without grounds for comparison. It is not just that the different paradigms, rules, and forms of knowledge are incomparable, incapable of being directly related, but that due to the extreme precariousness of labour conditions, any individual worker will pass from one operative form of knowledge to another multiple times in the course of a lifetime. The precariousness and incommensurability of these different productive paradigms leads to a cynicism. This is not the basic disconnect between thought and action that Adorno and Žižek had located in the real abstractions of formal subsumption, but a cynicism based on the incommensurability of thought itself.[45] 'Cynics recognize, in the particular context in which they operate, both the preeminent role played by certain cognitive premises as well as the simultaneous absence of real equivalences'.[46] Despite the fundamental difference between this cynicism, predicated on the productive dimension of conceptual thought, and the cynicism of formal subsumption, predicated on a disconnect between thought and action, they connect on the same point: the isolation of the individual. As Virno argues, the cynic constitutes a kind of atrophy of the traits of the metaphysical subject: autonomy, transcendence, and intentionality return not as metaphysical givens, but as the products of a particular

---

44   Virno 1996a p. 14.
45   See 'The Age of Cynicism: Deleuze and Guattari on the Production of Subjectivity in Capitalism', this volume.
46   Virno 2004 p. 88.

economic transformation.[47] As with Marx's initial thesis on Feuerbach, idealism proves to be much more materialist than it would first appear.[48]

4   The Problem of Measure

The problem of equivalence, its disappearance in the face of incommensurable productive paradigms, is not simply a problem for ethical tonality and subjectivity. The problem of measure is central to contemporary capitalism and any resistance to it. Marx's initial coining of the term general intellect was framed by a crisis of value, by the productivity of social knowledge not subject to the measure of wage labour. Virno's updating of the concept, making the general intellect not just substance, internalised in machines, but subject, part of labour power, does not so much resolve the problem as exacerbate it. Much of what constitutes the productive capacity of the general intellect, knowledge, information, and communication is produced off the clock, outside of the sphere of production. As Virno argues, the general intellect can be understood as the migration of precisely those capacities and actions that were defined by being excluded from the realm of work into the production process: the capacity to communicate, not to mention idle talk and curiosity.[49] This tendency of the general intellect to bring the outside of work into the productive process culminates in Virno assertion that the general intellect is less a matter of this or that skill or knowledge than the generic capacity. 'The general intellect is nothing but the *intellect in general*'.[50] What is put to work are the general capacities of the intellect, the capacities to learn new tasks, which are the generic capacities of humanity. These included language and intellect, the old stand-bys of philosophical anthropology, only in this context they are considered less as faculties than as potentials, as capacities to learn new forms of communication and habits. What Virno stresses is that the productive process comes to include anthropogenesis as such, the very formation of the human which is always a deficit of formation since humanity is defined by a capacity to take on new habits.[51] It is at this point, the point when all of humanity, all social activity, becomes part of the productive process, and does so precisely as a potential, as something lacking definition, that it becomes very difficult to subject the process to any measure.

---

47   Virno 1996a p. 24.
48   Virno 2001 p. 172.
49   Virno 1996a p. 16.
50   Virno 2004 p. 66.
51   Virno 2004 p. 63.

The question of measure is a question of the social synthesis: what form of social synthesis corresponds to the transformation of the real abstraction from the formal abstraction of money and the commodity form to the general intellect as the real abstraction? This is a question of the political and economic dimension of the transformation from formal to real subsumption, something that Virno's investigation of the immediate coincidence of economic forms and subjectivity does not address. At this point it is then useful to turn back to Sohn-Rehel, to the social synthesis as a particular social organisation of and through the real abstraction. To say that there is a new social synthesis does not mean that money or labour have disappeared from social reality. As Sohn-Rethel's conceptual articulation suggests, a logic of appropriation does not dispense with a logic of production; but it does annul the specific relations of production. The primary action of mankind's metabolic relation with nature is subordinated to the second nature of abstract forms. While Sohn-Rethel's formulation is perhaps all too schematic, suggesting an absolute rupture where a conflicted and complex (even dialectical) transition is perhaps more appropriate, it is possible to argue that in any given historical moment a particular social synthesis is hegemonic.[52] Moreover, Sohn-Rethel already recognised an increasing trend towards the socialisation of production, a socialisation that cannot be a return to a synthesis of production, even during the time of his writing. The productive capacities of the general intellect, of general social knowledge, require a new social synthesis, a new manner of capturing the diffuse and shifting productive capacities of the general intellect. Such a synthesis would not dispense with the equivalences of the real abstraction, but these equivalences would be secondary to the differential articulation of different forms of knowledge and social connection.

Two models have suggested themselves as new social synthesis: rent and finance capital. Thinkers such as David Harvey and Matteo Pasquinelli have suggested the return of rent in contemporary capitalism, despite the tendency to think of rent as an antiquated, feudal form of accumulation. Rent of space, the rent of metropolitan areas, is precisely a way of capturing the diffuse social creativity of subjectivity. It is a way of capturing, which is to say of profiting from, the creativity of subjectivity produced outside of the networks of capital. As Pasquinelli writes, 'The general value of rent is indeed produced by the

---

52   Michael Hardt and Antonio Negri argue that just as Marx argued that factory labour was in some sense hegemonic during the writing of *Capital*, reshaping other productive practices even if it was a quantitatively small part of the overall production process, immaterial labour is now hegemonic. Hardt and Negri 2004, p. 109.

whole social subjectivity, what is called the multitude'.[53] The revival of rent to understand exploitation does not just refer to social space, rather it is argued that there is a dimension of rent in multiple commodities. Rent is at work whenever collective subjective relations, desire and attention, relations that are not subject to the measure of labour, produce value. Just as in the case of social space this rent is based on a differential distribution of energies and attention. The emphasis on difference also defines the second figure that suggests itself for the social synthesis: finance capital. In Michael Hardt and Antonio Negri's *Commonwealth* they write, 'Finance capital is an enormous engine of abstraction that simultaneous represents and mystifies the common as if reflecting it in a distorted mirror'.[54] (The common could be understood to be roughly synonymous with Virno's definition of the general intellect as a diffuse potentiality). Like rent, finance capital follows the flows of attention and imagination. Investing is determined by a general assessment of the viability of a brand or product, a viability that has no ground other than that of belief and desires. As with rent, what matters is the temporal difference, that differential that places one ahead of the general trend, or gets one out before the whole thing crashes down. It is not that the real abstractions of money and the commodity form have been destroyed, just displaced by the differential speculations on the general intellect. The real abstractions of the commodity form are the conditions of the latter, which are layered over it as different abstractions, different modalities of value. As Pasquinelli writes:

> The total value of a commodity is produced by the material labour plus the cognitive labour plus the symbolic value brought by the public. The first is easily described according to the basic coordinates of wage labour and profit. The second is the value of knowledge embodied in design and intellectual property (patents, copyrights, trademarks). The third refers to the value of the brand produced by the attention economy of publics, mass media, and advertisement.[55]

The different aspects of the commodity constitute different dimensions of the social synthesis, different real abstractions, from the commodity form to the general intellect and beyond to the economies of attention and speculation.

Sohn-Rethel's concept of the real abstraction expanded our understanding of the fundamental contradiction at the heart of capitalism: the real abstrac-

53   Pasquinelli 2008, p. 136.
54   Hardt and Negri 2009 p. 153.
55   Pasquinelli 2008, p. 138.

tion revealed how the contradiction between capital and labour, extended into the field of knowledge and subjectivity. It is not simply that knowledge, scientific knowledge, is shown to be conditioned by the commodity form, and thus immediately implicated in the relations of production, but this knowledge was itself already divided with respect to the thinking subject: it had a practical basis that is social or collective and a conceptual understanding that is isolated or fragmented. Virno's concept of cynicism extended this contradiction to reveal how an increased socialisation, increased tendency to put to work collectivity and knowledge, leads to the fragmentation of cynical and incommensurable subjectivity. In each case the contradiction is also a potential antagonism. The real abstractions of formal subsumption, money and the commodity form, produced an image of equality and relation as much as they perpetuated inequality and isolation. What remains to be developed, at both the level of theory and practice, is an understanding of the antagonisms of the new real abstractions. How can they be wrested away from the social synthesis of finance capital to constitute a new social antagonism? As Sohn-Rethel and Virno suggest, doing so means puncturing the veil of cynicism and recognising the relation, the sociality, in what first appears to be isolation and separation. Grasping the rift between the social constitution and asocial perception of this constitution is the task of a materialist philosophy, overcoming it is the task of a communist politics.

CHAPTER 17

The Production of Subjectivity: From Transindividuality to the Commons

The current conjuncture is marked by a fundamental impasse in terms of how to engage the question of politics. This is in part due to the fact that the various figures through which one engages with politics – the citizen, worker, or militant – have become exhausted of their meaning; the citizen has been replaced by the interest group, the worker by the investor in his or her own human capital, and the militant by the terrorist. As Alain Badiou writes:

> This political subject has gone under various names. He used to be referred to as a 'citizen', certainly not in the sense of the elector or town councilor, but in the sense of the Jacobin of 1793. He used to be called 'professional revolutionary'. He used to be called 'grassroots militant'. We seem to be living in a time when his name is suspended, a time when we must find a new name for him.[1]

Rather than work in the direction that Badiou supposes, finding a new name for the political subject, I would like to focus in this essay on the 'production of subjectivity'. The 'production of subjectivity' is the way in which human beings are constituted as subjects, through structures of language and power; such a philosophical perspective is often seen as tantamount to a denial of political agency altogether, to the assertion that everything is an effect of power, that agency and action cannot exist. What I would like to propose is that far from being a theoretical dead end for politics the production of subjectivity is the condition for its renewal. It is only by examining the way in which subjectivity is produced that it is possible to understand how subjectivity might be produced otherwise, ultimately transforming itself, turning a passive condition into an active process. The connection between production and politics that lies at the root of the Marxist project remains as valid as ever, but production needs to be understood in the broadest sense, not just as work, the efforts on the factory floor, but in terms of the myriad ways in which actions, habits, and language produce effects, including effects on subjectivity, ways of perceiving, understanding, and relating to the world.

---

1 Badiou, 2005, p. 102.

As a philosophical perspective, or line of inquiry, 'the production of subjectivity' is fundamentally disorientating, primarily because it forces us to treat something that, in liberal individualistic society, is generally considered to be originary, the subject or individual, as produced, the cause and origin of actions as an effect of prior productions. The perspective cuts through the established binaries of philosophical thought, mingling effects with causes, material conditions with interior states, and objects with subjects. As an initial gesture of orientation I propose that the production of subjectivity can at least be provisionally defined along two axes that it cuts across: that of base and superstructure and that of structure and subject. Rather than understand the work of Marx through the oft-cited figure of base and superstructure, in which the production of things and the reproduction of subjectivity are each given their place and degree of effectivity according to a hierarchical structure, it is perhaps more interesting to view his work through the intersection of a mode of production and a mode of subjection. This assertion gets its textual support through the multiple places where Marx addresses the prehistory of capitalism, the breakdown of feudalism and previous modes of production. It is not enough for capitalism to constitute itself economically, to exploit the flows of wealth and labour, but it must constitute itself subjectively as well, develop the desires and habits necessary for it to perpetuate itself.[2] As Marx writes: 'The advance of capitalist production develops a working class which by education [*Erziehung*], tradition, and habit [*Gewohneit*] looks upon the requirements of that mode of production as self evident natural laws'.[3] Thus the production of subjectivity demands that two facets of social reality, that of the constitution of ideas and desires and that of the production of things, must be thought of not as hierarchically structured with respect to each other, but fully immanent, taking place at the same time, and within the same sites. This is not to say, however, that the 'production of subjectivity' is a pure subjection; subjectivity is not simply an effect of the economic structure, without its own specific causality and effects, effects that are even antagonistic to the demands of the economic structure. This combination of subjection and subjectivity can be understood by focusing on the two senses of the phrase 'the production of subjectivity', as the simultaneous non-identity of the manner in which subjectivity is *produced* and the manner in which subjectivity is *productive*, not just in terms of value or wealth, but in terms of its general capacity to produce effects. The subject is in some sense an effect of the structure, but it is never just an effect of

---

2   Both of these axes are developed at greater length in my *The Micro-Politics of Capital: Marx and the Prehistory of Capitalism*.

3   Marx 1977, p. 899.

the structure. This can be seen to make up the antagonistic logic of Marx's *Capital*, from the discussion of the labour process to the struggle over the working day: at each step the subjects that capital produces, through training, education, and habit, produce a surplus of subjectivity, of desires and needs, that struggle against the very site of their constitution.

1   From *Gattungswesen* to Transindividuality

I have recapped these two aspects somewhat briefly only to introduce two other problems introduced by the production of subjectivity: namely, the relation of the individual to society and political subjectification. It is in relation to these problems that we see the difficulty of this orientation, its challenge to the existing ways of thinking, and its promise, its capacity to reorient thought. These problems, that of a social ontology and politics, would at first glance appear to be not only distinct but distant from each other: the first being speculative and the second practical. However, they are inseparable, linked by the difficulty of imagining and envisioning forms of collectivity: a task that requires the creation of new modes of thought and the destruction of an individualistic ontology. (The burden of this individualist ontology has weighed down theories of the production and constitution of subjectivity: imagining the production of subjectivity as an individualistic project of aesthetic self-fashioning or ironic distance from the conditions of production). Starting from the production of subjectivity means that first the subject, the individual, must be seen as produced, as an effect, thus the individual cannot be privileged as a given, as the irreducible basis of ontology, epistemology, and politics. Furthermore, maintaining both senses of the genitive, that is the simultaneous non-identity of the way in which subjectivity is productive and produced, means that the subject can also not simply be seen simply as an effect of society. Thus, the two ways of understanding the relation between the individual and society, either starting from individuals as a given and understanding society as nothing more that the sum total of individuals, or, starting from society and seeing individuals as nothing more than effects of a larger structure, are barred from the outset. As Étienne Balibar has argued, these two conceptions, which could be named individualism and holism (or organicism), constitute much of the thought of the problem of society and the individual in Western philosophy.[4] Thus, the political problem and the ontological problem prove to be, if not the same, then at

---

4   Balibar 1997b, p. 6.

least similar; in each case it is a matter of thinking beyond the opposition of the individual and society, of moving beyond these starting points to grasp the productive nexus from which both individualities and collectivities emerge.

Marx's thought occasionally attempts to break with both of these options. I say occasionally because despite the fact that we could argue that Marx's implied social ontology is consistently opposed to both a methodological individualism and a holism of the organic or functionalist variety, Marx only explicitly argues against these perspectives on those occasional moments where he reflects on his fundamental philosophical orientation. As Marx writes, critiquing the isolated individual that classical economic thought places at its foundation, 'The human being is in the most literal sense a political animal, not merely a gregarious animal, but an animal which can individuate itself only in the midst of society'.[5] As we will clarify below, what is essential about this point is that the alternative between the individual and the collective is rejected: individuation is an unavoidably social process. More fundamentally, it could be argued the core of Marx's critique of political economy, from the early texts on alienation to *Capital*, is the idea that capital exploits not just individuals, but the collective conditions of subjectivity, what Marx referred to as species-being [*Gattungswesen*]. However, for reasons that are more historical than philosophical, Marx considered this generic essence to be first and foremost one of labour, and labour understood specifically as the production of things through the work of the body and hands. Labour is inescapably collective, in part because it encompasses the biological basis of subjectivity; it is related to our common condition of biological necessity. Labour is not simply an anthropological constant, defining man's metabolic relation with nature, however; it encompasses skills, tools, and knowledge that are the products of history and social relations. Labour is mankind's inescapable relation with nature and its constitution of a second, or inorganic, nature. Labour constitutes and is constituted by habits, practices, and operational schema that traverse individuals, making up a social relation and a shared reservoir of knowledge. Labour is not just a passively shared condition, that of need, but it actively places us in relation, to work is to work in relation to others. Marx's clearest statement regarding capitalism's exploitation of the collective conditions of subjectivity is in the chapter in *Capital* on cooperation. As Marx argues, when a large number of people are assembled in one place, such as a factory, the sum total of their productive activity exceeds that of the work of the same number of isolated individuals. As Marx writes, 'When the worker co-operates in a

---

5   Marx, 1973, p. 84 (translation modified).

planned way with others, he strips off the fetters of his individuality, and develops the capabilities of this species'.[6] Exploitation is not of the individual, the alienation of what is unique and proper to the individual, but is the appropriation of that which is improper to the individual, and only exists in relation.

Despite the fact that Marx places this exploitation of the collective conditions of subjectivity at the centre of *Capital*, he does not theoretically develop its conditions. Marx is in many respects quite nominalist regarding the cause of this social surplus, the reason why a group working together is necessarily greater than the sum of its parts. As Marx writes:

> Whether the combined working day, in a given case, acquires this increased productivity because it heightens the mechanical force of labour, or extends its sphere of action over a greater space, or contracts the field of production relatively to the scale of production, or at the critical moment sets large masses of labour to work, or excited rivalry between individuals and raises their animal spirits, or impresses on the similar operations carried on by a number of men the stamp of continuity and many-sidedness, or performs different operations simultaneously, or economizes the means of production by use in common ... whichever of these is the cause of the increase, the special productive power of the combined working day, is, under all circumstances, the social productive power of labour, or the productive power of social labour. This power arises from cooperation itself. When the worker co-operates in a planned way with others, he strips off the fetters of his individuality, and develops the capabilities of this species [*Gattungsvermögen*].[7]

Marx enumerates all of the possible causes, from animal spirits to mass conformity, remaining equally open and equally indifferent to the various causes of cooperation. For Marx it is enough to say that man is a social animal, and leave it at that. Which is not to say that Marx remains completely silent as to the basis of collective existence. In his more speculative or theoretical moments, Marx also refers to the inorganic nature, or body, as the basis of subjectivity. In the first instance, and in keeping with the generic aspect of species being, this inorganic body is nature itself, nature considered in its totality: the animal interacts with a specific part of nature, its ecosystem, while man interacts with nature in its entirety, materially and aesthetically.[8] In later writings Marx uses the term

---

6   Marx 1977, p. 447.

7   Ibid. p. 447.

8   Marx 1964, p. 112.

inorganic body to stress that these preconditions are not simply given, but are produced. The inorganic body of man includes second nature, habits, tools, and structures – everything that functions as the precondition of productive activity. Thus the inorganic body is situated at the point of indistinction between nature and history.[9] Moreover, these conditions are not just physical in the form of tools and natural conditions but encompass the mental preconditions of production as well. Or, more to the point, every tool is indissociable from habits, ways of acting and comporting oneself. Thus, if an irreducible mental component accompanies all labour, separating 'the worst architect from the best of bees', this mental component is irreducibly collective as well, composed of shared knowledge embodied in habits and practices.[10]

In different but related ways, Balibar and Paolo Virno have suggested the term transindividuality, to name and conceptualise what Marx designates with such borrowed concepts as 'species-being' and the 'inorganic body'. The term is drawn from the work of Gilbert Simondon, who interrogates the privilege that Western thought has ascribed to the principle of individuation.[11] For Simondon individuation has to be grasped as a process, in which the individual is neither the ultimate end nor absolute beginning, but a continual effect of an activity. There are multiple and successive individuations, physical, biological, psychic, and collective, each resolving the problems posed by the others, and transforming the fundamental terms of the relation. At the basis of Simondon's understanding is a fundamental fact of existence that Marx indicates (and Virno underscores): the very things that form the core and basis of our individuality, our subjectivity, sensations, language, and habits, by definition cannot be unique to us as individuals.[12] These elements can only be described as preindividual, as the preconditions of subjectivity. In some sense they do not even exist, at least as individual things; instead they make up a metastable condition, a flux of possibilities. Virno, following Simondon, outlines three different level of preindividual singularities; the sensations and drives that make up the biological basis of subjectivity, language which constitutes its psychic and collective relations, and the productive relations, which constitute the historical articulation of the preindividual.[13] The clearest example of what is at stake in designating these different activities and relations as preindividual can be seen by looking at the specific example of language. Language is trans-

---

9   Fischbach 2005, p. 56.
10   Marx 1977, p. 284.
11   Simondon 2005, p. 23.
12   Virno 2003, p. 137.
13   Virno 2004, p. 77.

individual; there is, it is often said, no such thing as a private language, but it is also fundamentally preindividual, language is not made up of individual things, words, but of differential relations. Virno follows Saussure in defining language as a system of relations, but stresses that this should be seen as constituting language's fundamental insubstantiality, its metastability, rather than its structure.[14] Language is not the statement or the system, but the metastable system of relations between the two: every utterance presupposes a system of differences as the condition of its articulation, but every system is constantly being transformed by the utterances that traverse it. Thus, to follow the example of language, preindividual singularities exist as a differentially articulated set of relations, or possible relations: they are metastable. These preconditions are not simply the raw material of subjectivity, they are not completely transformed into a subject, but persist as unresolved potential along with the subject.[15] There is always more to us than our putative identity as individuals, and it is only because of this that anything like collectivity, like social relations, is possible.[16] The two concepts central to Simondon's ontology, or ontogenesis, preindividual and transindividual, are strictly complementary: it is because the individual is only a process, an individuation of a metastable field of preindividual difference, that it is possible to think of the transindividual as something other than a collection of individuals.

From this perspective it is fundamentally incorrect to posit something like 'society' and the 'individual' as two separate entities, the relation of which is a problem. For Simondon transindividuality is not something that stands above the individual, rather it is nothing other than articulation of the individual. Individuals are individuals of the collective, of particular social relations and structures, just as collectives are nothing other than a reflection of the individuals that constitute them. Transindividuality is not the relation between two constituted terms, between the individual and society, but is a relation of relations, encompassing the individual's relation to itself, the process of its psychic individuation, as well as the relation amongst individuals, and the relation between different collectivities.[17] Transindividuality is in many respects an articulation of the preindividual, as the habits, language, affects, and perceptions form the basis of a shared culture. Individuals are individuated in relation to a specific language or cultural backdrop, not language or culture in general.[18] Transindividuality, the common, is, as Virno argues, 'historico-natural':

---

14   Virno 2008, p. 50.
15   Simondon 2005, p. 310.
16   Simondon 2005, p. 298.
17   Combes 2013, p. 25.
18   Stiegler 2009, p. 5.

historical because a given language, a given set of habits, or culture is itself the historical and contingent effect of various transformations and developments, but this history does not change the fact that language, habits, productive relations are constitutive of humanity as such.[19] The production of subjectivity, and its corollary concepts such as transindividuality and preindividual, entails not just a rethinking of that antinomy of the individual and the collective, but a new ontology and logic of thinking about the subject. The subject is a 'social individual', not just in the sense that he or she lives within society, but in the sense that individuality can only be articulated, can only be produced, within society.[20]

2   From Transindividuality to the Common

The transformation of capital can be viewed as an increasing incorporation or subsumption of the production of subjectivity into capital, in terms of both the preindividual conditions and transindividual relations. Capital begins with formal subsumption, with labour power, which is initially taken as is, according to its traditional structure of technological and social development, but as capitalism develops it transforms this basic relation, transforming the habits that link knowledge and work. In place of the organically developed habits which connect the work of the hand with that of the head, capitalism interjects the combined knowledge of society, externalised in machines and internalised in concepts, habits, and ways of thinking. At this point capital no longer simply exploits labour, extracting its surplus, but fundamentally alters its technical and social conditions, as it subsumes all of society. Subsumption in this case crosses both sides of market relations, encompassing labour, which comes to involve the work of language, the mind, and the affects, and the commodity form. If sensations, language, and habits or knowledge constitute the preindividual backdrop of subjectivity, then it has to be acknowledged that much of what we sense, discuss, and do, comes to us in the form of commodities. It is from this perspective that we can grasp the ontological dimension of the first sentence of *Capital*, 'The wealth of societies in which the capitalist mode

---

19   Paolo Virno 2008, p. 48.
20   'In this transformation [the worker] is neither the direct human labour he himself performs, not the time during which he works, but rather the appropriation of his own general productive power, his understanding of nature and his mastery over it by virtue of his presence as a social body – it is in a word, the development of the social individual which appears as the great foundation-stone of production and of wealth' (Marx 1973, p. 705).

of production prevails appears as an immense collection of commodities', by inverting it: whatever appears does so as a commodity.[21] This transformation of what appears has effects on subjectivity, as Marx reminds us, production not only creates an object for the subject, but a subject for the object.[22] Under commodity production, the production of private property, this entails a massive reduction of the sense of an object: 'Private property has made us so stupid and one-sided that an object is only ours when we have it ...'[23] The real subsumption of subjectivity by capital is articulated by two different productions of subjectivity, each defined by different economic sectors: in terms of production, there is a movement away from work as a solitary enterprise, the labour of a craftsman, whose individual effort organises the labour process, to work that engages the knowledge and desire of humanity in general, while at the same time, on the side of consumption, there is a reduction of the world to what can be possessed, owned, viewed in the comfort of one's home – a massive privatisation of desire.

Real subsumption is an increased exploitation of the transindividual and commodification of the preindividual. This division between production and consumption defines to some extent the paradox of social existence under contemporary capitalism: never have human beings been more social in their existence, but more individualised, privatised, in the apprehension of their existence. On the one hand, the simplest action from making a meal to writing an essay engages the labour of individuals around the world, materialised in commodities, habits, and machines, while on the other, there is a tendency to transform everything, every social relation, into something that can be purchased as a commodity. In the *Grundrisse* Marx offers perhaps the most succinct definition of the paradox of this relation of individual and collective in the early stages of capitalism. As he writes,

> Only in the eighteenth century, in 'civil society', do the various forms of social connectedness confront the individual as a mere means towards his private purposes, as external necessity. But the epoch which produces this standpoint, that of the isolated individual, is also precisely that of the hitherto most developed social (from this standpoint, general) relations.[24]

---

21   Marx 1977, p. 126.
22   Marx 1973, p. 92.
23   Marx 1964, p. 139.
24   Marx 1973, pg. 223.

Both tendencies have only increased since the eighteenth century, as we have become simultaneously more connected and disconnected. The materialisation of collective intelligence in machines produces new effects of isolation – 'individualizing social actors in their separate automobiles and in front of separate video screens'.[25] Transindividual relations, the cooperation of multiple minds, bodies, and machines produce individuated and isolated perceptions.

As Bernard Stiegler is quick to point out, one would be incorrect to identify these technologies, and the habits of isolation and separation they imply, with an 'individualistic society'. Stiegler utilises Simondon's conception of transindividuality as a relation constitutive of the individual and the collective to diagnose modern technology that allows for neither.[26] The isolation of people watching television, confronting the frustrations of the morning commute, or surfing the internet, is not that of individuals, singular points of difference within a collective, but a serialised repetition of the same. In each case, perception or consciousness is structured by the same object, the television programme, roadway design, or search engine, but in such a way that can never form the basis of a 'we' of collectivity.[27] There is no commonality, no collectivity, constituted by the different individuals watching the same programme, the different cars on the same roadway, or the different 'hits' to the same website: the other people encountered in such contexts are at best measured quantitatively, having effects only in terms of their number, at worst they are engaged with competitively, as obstacles to my goals and intentions.

From this thumbnail description of the current conjuncture it is possible to specify what is meant by the politics of the production of subjectivity. Politics bears directly on the preindividual and transindividual conditions of subjectivity, it is a matter of their distribution, presentation, and articulation. These conditions make up what could be called 'the commons'. The commons is a term that has become the focus of a great deal of political and philosophical discussion in recent years. At first glance this might seem odd, since the term initially applied to commonly held pastures and land, conditions that have been all but eradicated in most of the world. However, the commons can also be understood to refer not just to the conditions necessary for supporting material existence, but subjectivity as well.[28] What is at stake then in the struggle over the various commons, such as the knowledge commons and the digital commons, is

25   Hardt and Negri 2000, p. 322.
26   Stiegler 2008, p. 61.
27   Stiegler 2009, p. 48.
28   Negri 2003, p. 215.

a struggle precisely over the forces and relations which produce subjectivity as much as wealth and value. As we have seen, in capitalism the common is divided, split between labour, which is reified in machines and structures, and consumption, which reduces it to a private object that is passively consumed. The political task must in some sense be one of the actualisation or manifestation of the common. The problem is how to make the common, the transindividual and preindividual conditions of subjectivity, something other than the inchoate backdrop of experience, to make it something actively grasped, so that subjects can transform their conditions rather than simply be formed by them. To butcher a phrase from Hegel, it is necessary to think transindividuality as subject, rather than as substance. It is a matter of bringing the background, the plurality underlying language, sensation, and knowledge, into the foreground: transforming a passive condition into an actual production. The politics of the production of subjectivity is a question of the relation between a subject and the conditions of its production. It is a matter of producing and transforming the very relations that produce us.

It is possible to interpret this political project as a matter of constituting a collective form of subjectivity against an individualised and isolated existence. This is often the tenor that this struggle takes in Marx; it is a struggle of the two productions of subjectivity. The market, or consumption, which produces not only a world as property, but individuals as possessors or consumers, whose relations are governed according to the fictions of 'freedom, equality, and Bentham', and the factory, which produces and exploits a transindividual collectivity. While Marx's general argument against 'egoistic' man of civil society captures something essential about the social ontology underlying political economy and liberal political thought, it lapses into the interminable binary of the individual versus society. Which is to say that it makes it appear as if one could simply choose 'individuality' or 'collectivity' as an ethical value of individualism or solidarity. However, things are not that simple. It is not enough to oppose the collective to the individual, representing the good and the bad form of subjectification respectively. First because, as I have argued, ontologically the individual, the subject, is nothing other than a modification of preindividual conditions and transindividual relations. As Marx argued in the *Grundrisse*, it is necessary to think the 'isolated individual' as social, as the product and condition of a particular society: there is no opposition between the individual and the collective, just different articulations of transindividuality, different productions of subjectivity. There is a second more complex objection to such an opposition: equating the transindividual with the collective, with some ideal of solidarity, assumes that the former can be represented. Marx's early criticism of the state in *The German Ideology* articulated a gap between the conditions productive of subjectivity and the representation of those conditions. The state is an 'illusory communal life' based upon real ties of flesh and blood, language, and the division of labour.[29] This rift between the conditions that are productive of subjectivity and the representation of those conditions is grounded on the connection between transindividuality and subjectivity. The relations that make up transindividuality are nothing more than preindividual conditions in a metastable state, a flux that is simultaneously productive and produced. (For example we could say that 'a language' as much as it is the condition for any articulation, any style, is simultaneously being transformed by various jargons and slang.) Along these lines Simondon makes a distinction between society and community: a society is metastable, criss-crossed by individuations, while a community is closed, static.[30] A community makes its specific conditions of belonging, its specific values or norms, the conditions of belonging as such. The representation of the transindividuality – in that it makes specific qualities or attributes, a language, cultural practices, or values, stand in for the collectivity – as such closes it, makes it a community and not a society.

If the transindividual cannot be represented, how can it be actualised? Answering such a question entails not only examining the link between politics and representation, but also refining the very vocabulary we use to discuss social relations and their materialisation in objects and structures. Virno argues that Simondon's ontology makes possible a redefinition of the fundamental, but often vague and undefined, Marxist concepts of alienation, reification, and fetishisation. As Virno argues:

> Reification is what I call the process through which preindividual reality becomes an external thing, a *res* that appears as a manifest phenomenon, a set of public institutions. By alienation I understand the situation in which the preindividual remains an internal component of the subject but one that the subject is unable to command. The preindividual reality that remains implicit, like a presupposition that conditions us but that we are unable to grasp, is alienated.[31]

Virno's argument is in part based on a revalorisation of reification, reification is the externalisation of the preindividual, its articulation into a series of things, structures, and machines. The central point is that the 'thing' in this

---

29   Marx 1970, p. 53.
30   Simondon 1989, p. 259.
31   Virno 2006, p. 38.

case bears with it the relation and it is public, or at least potentially so, and thus exposed to the possibility of transformation and rearticulation. Virno's fundamental example, or provocation, remains the 'general intellect', Marx's term for the collective knowledge that is at once internalised in machines and dissipated across social space in the form of knowledges, habits, and ways of acting.[32] In this instance the social dimension is inespacable and cannot be eradicated. This is fundamentally distinct from fetishisation in which the qualities and attributes of social existence are attributed to a thing, echoing Marx's classic formula that the social relation between men takes the form of a relation between things. 'Fetishism means assigning to something – for example to money – characteristics that belong to the human mind (sociality, capacity for abstraction and communication, etc.)'[33] Thus, Virno returns the fetish to Marx's earliest arguments about money, in which 'money is the alienated ability of mankind'.[34] Whatever quality or attribute I may lack, intelligence, attractiveness, strength, etc., can be purchased. Money scrambles the preindividual singularities, the fundamental elements of subjectivity, transforming them into things that can be purchased. Marx's assertion of the 'ontological' power of money intersects with Simondon's notion of ontogenesis. It is thus no accident that Marx's essay on the power of money in bourgeois society ends with a discussion of the individual: the world of money is juxtaposed to that of the irreplaceable individual, in which social qualities can only be exchanged for their similar qualities – if you want to be loved you must be capable of love, and so on. 'Every one of your relations to man and to nature must be a *specific expression*, corresponding to the object of your will, of your *real individual life*'.[35]

Returning to the paradox of modern existence addressed above, the socialised isolation, or what I referred to as the simultaneous exploitation of the transindividual and commodification of the preindividual, it is possible to argue that this relation constitutes a new sort of alienation, provided that by alienation we follow Virno in transforming our understanding of what this term means. Alienation, at least in the way that it has been understood as a generic watchword of various versions of Hegelian-Marxism, has been understood as a loss of self, a loss of subjectivity to the object. As such, the concept often uncritically reproduces the very individualistic ontology that Marx's writing is mobilised against. However, as we have already indicated, it is not clear that

---

32   Virno 2008, p. 41.
33   Virno 2006, p. 40.
34   Marx 1964, p. 104.
35   Ibid., p. 105.

Marx necessarily understood the concept in this way; alienation is not just loss of object, and control of activity, it is also alienation from species-being [*Gattungswesen*] from mankind's universal nature, what could be referred to as the preindividual and transindividual components of subjectivity. Alienation is not so much the loss of the subject in the object, but the loss of objectivity for the subject, the loss of the relation to its conditions.[36] As Virno argues, alienation is a separation from the conditions of the production of subjectivity; it is not a loss of what is most unique and personal but a loss of connection to what is most generic and shared. The commodification of the preindividual is such an alienation due to the fact that the basic components of our subjectivity, language, habits, perceptions, come to us in a prepackaged from, as things which can only be passively consumed. The milieu of our existence, preindividual and transindividual, becomes something we are passively subjected to, something consumed, not something that we can act on or transform, a condition that cannot be conditioned.

If alienation best describes the commodification of the preindividual, or vice versa, then what could best describe the exploitation of the transindividual? Answering this question is difficult because it cuts through the distinction that Virno makes between fetishism and reification as two ways of presenting the transindividual. Fetishism and reification both deal with the relationship between sociality and things, things that are not opposed to subjectivity, to the constitution of the individual, but are its condition. With the fetish the thing stands in for the relation; money is nothing other than the concretisation of desires, it is thus able to stand in for various social attributes and relations. As Marx writes of money, 'The individual carries his social power, as well as his bond with society, in his pocket'.[37] While in reification the thing is the relation – the network of machines that constitute the general intellect cannot exist apart from the relations – the thing is that which relates rather than standing in for the relation. Virno's generalisation of the problem of fetishisation makes it possible to return to Marx's critique of the state, which is primarily a critique of the representation of collectivity, of sociality itself, through a seemingly extraneous detour: Gilles Deleuze and Fèlix Guattari's reworking of Marx's critique of capital. Deleuze and Guattari, in their inventive reading of Marx, have generalised this critique of the state into an examination of the way in which every society represents its historical conditions. In every mode of production, in every production of subjectivity, there is an unproductive

---

36   Fischbach 2005, p. 14.
37   Marx 1973. p. 157.

element, a representation of the social order itself, what Deleuze and Guattari call a full body, that appropriates the social forces of production. It is an effect that appears as a cause. As Deleuze and Guattari write:

> ... the forms of social production, like those of desiring production, involve an unengendered non-productive attitude, an element of anti-production coupled with the process, a full body that functions as a *socius*. This socius may be the body of the earth, that of the tyrant, or capital. This is the body that Marx is referring to when he says that it is not the product of labour, but rather appears as its natural or divine presuppositions. In fact, it does not restrict itself merely to opposing productive forces in and of themselves. It falls back on [*il se rabat sur*] all production, constituting a surface over which the forces and agents of production are distributed, thereby appropriating for itself all surplus production and arrogating to itself both the whole and the parts of the process, which now seem to emanate from it as a quasi-cause.[38]

Deleuze and Guattari's concept of the socius expands upon Marx's idea of the inorganic body; it each case it is a matter of the preconditions of production, the material, intellectual, and social conditions that appear as given. Deleuze and Guattari stress the historical nature of this relation; the inorganic body, the socius is not just the natural world, but encompasses those conditions of production, institutions, habits, and ways of being that constitute a kind of second nature. The historically produced conditions of production, the technical and social conditions, including the political structure, appear as something given rather than produced, as divine preconditions. This full body constitutes a particular representation of community, based on a condition of belonging: the lines of filiation or descent that determine a clan; custom and tradition that defines a culture; or language and birth that constitutes a nation. Society itself exists as a fetish, or rather it is fetishised to the extent that what is produced from social relations, such as the power of the despot or capital itself, appears to be the cause of production, rather than its effect. As Deleuze writes, 'The natural object of social consciousness or common sense with regard to the recognition of value is the fetish'.[39] To speak of society as a thing and not a relation, as something given and not produced, is to be under the sway of fetishism.

---

38   Deleuze and Guattari 1983, p. 10.
39   Deleuze 1994, p. 208.

In this series of full bodies capital functions as something of an exception. As Marx argues in the *Grundrisse*, capitalism is fundamentally different from all previous modes of production because in it production is not subordinated to the reproduction of a particular mode of existence. Whereas in the previous modes of production, production, the creation of wealth, was always subordinated to reproduction, to the maintenance of particular structures of authority, particular forms of subjectivity, in capital wealth is subordinated only to itself, to the production of more wealth. As Marx writes: 'In bourgeois economics – and in the epoch of production to which it corresponds – this complete working-out of the human content appears as a complete emptying out, this universal objectification as total alienation, and the tearing down of all limited, one-sided aims as sacrifice of the human end-in-itself to an entirely external end'.[40] To place this back in the terms of Simondon, the fetish is no longer a particular community, a particular condition of social belonging, but it becomes a society organised around an abstract object, money, or capital itself. As we have seen, money is nothing other than the alienation of human potential; it is everything human beings can do, everything human beings can desire, represented in the form of an object, a universal equivalent that is nothing other than the materialisation of this abstract power itself. There is thus a connection between fetishisation and alienation, between the separation from the constitutive conditions, and their projection onto an object. As Marx writes, 'All the powers of labour project themselves as powers of capital, just as all the value-forms of the commodity do as forms of money'.[41] This tendency increases with the real subsumption of society; the more production is distributed across society, the more collective it becomes, the more it appears as if capital itself is productive.

In order to understand capital it is necessary to retreat to the misty realm of fetishism, but it is also necessary to understand how capital fundamentally transforms this relation – there is a fundamental difference between the fetishisation of the despot and the fetishisation of commodities. In the first instance the object in question represents the productive powers of society, the despot stands as a precondition of the labours of society, while in the second the object does not so much represent these powers, giving them a concrete instance, something to believe in, as it operates through them. Money does not represent anything, or rather what it represents is only pure abstract potential, it is the capacity to buy anything, to become anything, social power in the abstract. The

---

40   Marx 1973, p. 488.
41   Marx 1977, p. 756.

axioms of capital refer less to beliefs than to what needs to be done. Deleuze and Guattari express this difference, between the representational and functional full body, as a difference between code and axioms. Codes set up a relation between actions and desires, actions and perceptions, 'relations between flows', in Deleuze and Guattari's terms. To draw on the social ontology that we have been developing here, we could say that codes are a particular articulation of the preindividual conditions for subjectivity, a particular organisation of the transindividual that delimits a community. What is essential is that these codes, in attaching themselves to a particular full body, ascribe a particular meaning to these practices, situating them within a religion, a nation, a culture, a way of life. Codes can be thought of as tradition, or prescriptions and rules bearing on the production and distribution of goods, prestige, and desire. As such they are inseparable from a particular relation to the past – a relation of repetition. This is fundamentally distinct from axioms. Axioms have no 'meaning', they set up relations between differential flows, between purely abstract quantities, the most important of which are the flows of money and abstractive subjective potential, otherwise understood as labour power. As Deleuze and Guattari write: '*your capital or your labour capacity*, the rest is not important ...'[42] Axioms do not repeat or venerate the past, but are fundamentally flexible, it is always possible to add new axioms to the system, to open more markets. What is at stake in Deleuze and Guattari's distinction between code are two different ways of understanding the constitution of social relations. Codes constitute a meaningful totality, a community, while axioms are functional rather than meaningful, making up a society ruled by abstractions. In each case, codes or axioms, the productive powers of mankind, the transindividual is fetishised, transformed into the attribute of an object. However, there is a fundamental difference, the pre-capitalist object, the full body subject to the domination of a code, is more restrictive, tying the transindividual to a particular condition of belonging, a tradition, a tribe, a nation; while the full body of capital is fundamentally open, the productive power of social relations appears, but appears as the attribute of a paradoxically abstract object, money or capital.

Deleuze and Guattari's understanding of codes and axioms (and the relational social ontology they imply) brings us close to Marx's fundamental dialectical point with respect to capitalism: that in capitalism the fundamentally productive power of mankind, of transindividuality, comes close to appearing as such. Capital strips away the illusions that masked exploitation under religious or political guises. As Marx famously wrote in *The Communist Manifesto*:

---

42   Deleuze and Guattari 1983, p. 251.

> Constant revolutionizing of production, uninterrupted disturbance of all
> social conditions, everlasting uncertainty and agitation distinguish the
> bourgeois epoch from all earlier ones. All fixed, fast frozen relations, with
> their train of ancient and venerable prejudices and opinions, are swept
> away, all new-formed ones become antiquated before they can ossify. All
> that is solid melts into air, all that is holy is profaned, and man is at last
> compelled to face with sober senses his real condition of life and his rela-
> tions with his kind.[43]

Capital, in its ceaseless revolutionising of the conditions of production, exposes
the produced nature of sociality as such. In Alain Badiou's terminology, capital
constitutes a desacralization of the social bond.[44] Deleuze and Guattari add
to this process something that Marx did not grasp in his identification of capitalism with ceaseless modernisation: the production of new territories, new
islands and representations of belonging. What once existed as code, as an
object of collective belief and evaluation, as a full body, is reborn as a private
object. The religions, cultures, and practices of the world are reborn as private
objects of consumption: all the world's cultures and all the world's beliefs can
be enjoyed in the privacy of one's own home, Buddhism, Native American Spir-
ituality, etc., As Deleuze and Guattari argue, capitalism is 'a motley painting of
everything that has ever been believed'.[45] These private beliefs are made possible by the fact that society is reproduced and regulated through the axioms
of the market and not the codes of culture. In some sense they are not just
rendered possible by the market, but necessary as well: one could argue, as
Stiegler does, that the loss of a transindividual culture leads to a search for
meaning in the private realm, in the artificial territories of various spiritual
beliefs and desires. The axioms of the market produce the commodity, which
is by definition cut off from, and conceals, its constitutive conditions, masking
the labour in its production (this is one aspect of Marx's definition of commodity fetishism). Once they are separated from their different codes, and cultures,
there is no contradiction between the different cultures, beliefs, values and
ideals occupying the same space of the market. As Peter Sloterdijk illustrates
the materialisation of this indifference:

> The best prep school for *Capital* – would it not consist in watching televi-
> sion several hours a day, looking through several newspapers and maga-

---

43   Marx and Engels 1978, p. 476.
44   Badiou 1999, p. 56.
45   Deleuze and Guattari 1983, p. 34.

zines the remaining hours, and continuously listening to the radio? ... We live in a world that brings things into false equations, produces false sameness of form and false sameness of values (pseudoequivalences) between everything and everyone, and thereby also achieves an intellectual disintegration and indifference in which people lose the ability to distinguish correct from false, important from unimportant, productive from destructive – because they are used to taking the one for the other.[46]

The world, or at least the question of its meaning, becomes a private affair, all the while the world is actually governed by abstract and meaningless flows. Deleuze and Guattari's argument is not, however, that subjectivity is entirely produced in the private realm. It is not a matter of subjectivity simply being produced by the commodity, by the fragments of code and desire left over from every religion and culture: it is the split between these private codes and the axioms of the market that produces and reproduces subjectivity.[47] The latter cannot be called public, since the axioms of capital are by definition cut off from the general problem of meaning, and thus public contestation and debate, taking on the appearance of 'quasi-natural laws' (another aspect of 'commodity fetishism'), becoming what Virno refers to as 'publicness without public sphere'.[48] Transindividuality is fetishised, made to appear in the form of the abstract and indifferent quantities of money, which transforms it into an impersonal force. The impersonality of this force, its abstraction from other practices and norms, makes possible the proliferation of a series of private objects, commodified desires. The market cannot be called a 'we', because there is no way to identify with the impersonal force of its structural laws, but nor can the commodity be identified with the 'I' of the individual, since it remains prepackaged, inaccessible, and alienating. The things that we buy to consume in the privacy of our home are never properly ours, because they demand first and foremost a subordination to the market as a condition of individuation (a condition that becomes true, or more true, as commodities are the conditions of our image and ideal.)[49]

From this perspective we can grasp the full extent of the third of Virno's redefinitions: reification. Transindividuality is reified when it becomes a public thing. Virno's example of this, as we have seen, is Marx's concept of the 'general intellect', the collective powers of intelligence, distributed across the machines

---

46   Sloterdijk 1988, p. 314.
47   Deleuze and Guattari 1983, p. 264.
48   Virno 2004, p. 40.
49   Stiegler 2008, p. 118.

and subjects of social space which contemporary production depends upon. Like money, or capital, 'the general intellect' embodies the collective powers of society, but it does so in a fundamentally different way, rather than being displaced onto an object, such as money. With the general intellect the collective powers of society are articulated through a series of objects and relations, the machines, knowledge, and habits that make up the productive relations of society. In adopting the term from Marx, Virno has insisted that the general intellect should be understood not just as intelligence incorporated in machines, the steam engines or telegraphs of Marx's day or the computers of ours, but as the generic intelligence embodied in subjectivity, the habits and knowledges that make up the preindividual conditions of subjectivity. Thus, one of the defining characteristics of the general intellect is that the rules and norms which govern collective life are constantly being rewritten and transformed, as new codes, new knowledges, and new styles, are produced, exposing the contingency and artificiality of public existence. This contingency cuts both ways. First, it disengages transindividuality from a fixed object, from a repetition of the past, it becomes a pure differential force. Second, it unmoors human activity from any norm, from any criteria, including that of exchange value. As much as money can be denounced as a fetish, as an alienation of human activity and powers, as a real abstraction it still imposes an equivalent on the disparate activities and practices: equal must be exchanged for equal. As Marx wrote in *Capital*, one of the fundamental riddles of capitalism is how it produces inequality, namely surplus value, in a market in which equal is exchanged for equal. The answer to this riddle is of course labour power, and the division between production and consumption, the market and the factory. Despite this inequality, capital, the capital of formal subsumption, cannot dispense with the image of equality, with the general exchangeability and commensurability of labour. As the general intellect moves to the front of the production process, and the contingency and groundlessness of rules and operating procedures becomes dominant, the standard of equality disappears. This gives rise to a fundamentally ambivalent situation. As Virno writes:

> When the fundamental abilities of the human being (thought, language, self-reflection, the capacity for learning) come to the forefront, the situation can take on a disquieting and oppressive appearance; or it can even give way to a *non-governmental* public sphere, far from the myths and rituals of sovereignty.[50]

---

50   Ibid., p. 40.

This disquieting and oppressive appearance refers first of all to new possibilities of exploitation. The work of real subsumption, work that utilises capacities to think, create, and interact, is not isolated in time or space, making exploitation coextensive with existence. Exploitation is no longer organised around the abstract entities of labour and money, but encompasses all of existence. More to the point, it refers to a breakdown of both collectivity and individuality, the combination of fetishisation and alienation. The market, what Deleuze and Guattari refer to as the axioms of capital, becomes the new fetish of transindividuality; it is a form of transindividuality, of collectivity, that produces and presupposes alienation. It does not allow for the possibility of constituting an individuation through the collective, it does not exist as a 'we', but only as a series of quasi-natural laws, from which the 'they' emerges as the hostile backdrop of individual actions. Competition is a paradoxical form of individuation in that it produces individuals who are all the more alike in that they see themselves as absolutely opposed to each other, locked into bitter struggle.[51] At the same time, the collective production of norms of knowledge and action makes possible a new politics, one that liberates the collective from the various full bodies that attempt to represent it, what Virno calls a non-governmental public sphere, but what we have called here 'the common'. The reification of transindividuality, its physical instantiation in practices, machines, and habits, makes possible a new understanding of collectivity, not as an amorphous mass to be represented, but as a multitude that acts and cannot be separated from its acting. This collectivity, this multitude, already exists in the 'hidden abode of production', in the increasingly socialised and collective forces of labour power, but its activity, and potentiality, is more or less invisible, concealed by the fetishisation of peoples and the alienation of individuals.[52] It is a matter of articulating this common, the unrepresentable transindividual collectivity, against the conditions and practices that conceal it. We see the shine and sparkle of the commodities that we purchase, and we see the economic forces that structure and tear apart our existence, but do not see the social relations, transindividuality, that underlie these commodities and the laws of the economy.[53]

The political question is not a matter of looking for 'the subject' capable of transforming the existing political conditions, something that could play the role of the proletariat, the gravedigger of the existing society. Rather, in turning

51   Stiegler 2009, p. 49.

52   Virno 2004, p. 24.

53   Massimo De Angelis has underscored the manner in which the capitalist economy, which is centred on competition, must obscure the cooperative relations that are necessary to its very existence. De Angelis 2007, p. 64.

our attention to the production of subjectivity, to the preindividual conditions and transindividual relations that constitute subjectivity, it is possible to recognise the subjections that make up the present, the fetishisation of mankind's abstract transformative potential in the form of money, and the alienation of subjectivity in the commodities that make up our daily existence. The market constitutes a short circuit of transindividuality, creating individuals as primarily passive consumers of an alienated existence and a public that appears only in the form of a fetishised market. At the same time, however, it is also possible to see in the present conditions of the production of subjectivity lines of liberation, namely the possibility of a public that is no longer constituted around a fetishised full body, of the nation, state, or market, but is open to its own innovation and productive transformation. The production of subjectivity is not simply synonymous with subjection, with the way in which individuals are produced by the system, nor is it a force of eruption, a revolutionary force; rather, it is a method by which the fault lines between subjection and liberation can be traced.

Man is a Werewolf to Man: *Capital* and the Limits of Political Anthropology

Long after the 'humanist controversy' came and went, and lingering into the age of posthumanism, the question of Marx's philosophical anthropology lingers. There are immediate reasons for this, tied to contemporary ideology. Neo-liberalism's theoretical battle against Marxism has often claimed the terrain of human nature rather than history and social relations. One could argue that this story began long before neoliberalism, with Adam Smith's famous declaration of mankind's tendency to 'barter, truck, and exchange', but it has been extended and developed into theories of human nature which make the calculation of costs and benefits the entirety of thinking, willing, and desiring. Humanity becomes human capital, and the attempt to maximise benefits and minimise costs becomes the exemplary matrix of every possible action. The debate between capitalism and communism is often reduced to a debate between competition and cooperation, or egoism or altruism, as defining aspects of human nature, as if we never left Political Philosophy 101. Such a debate does a disservice to Marx, who had little to say about some supposed altruistic nature and much to say about the historical and social conditions of capitalism. One could say that it changes the question to an irreducibly academic debate – human nature remains a question than can never be finally answered – but it is precisely this turn towards human nature that reflects its particular brand of 'capitalist realism'.[1] The appeals to human nature take the existing attitudes and comportments of capitalism, competition and self-interest, attitudes and comportments that can be generally understood to be products of capitalist relations, and presents them as a cause. Neoliberalism, like liberal apologetics for capitalism that preceded it, gets its strength not from a theory of human nature articulated in philosophical texts but from a concrete experience of buying and selling, of what Marx called 'the sphere of exchange'. Or, more to the point, neoliberalism in the broad sense of the term does so, since it is a culture revolution in which the quotidian experiences of work and consumption, especially work which is increasingly individuated and precarious, generate an idea of human nature as their after-image. An effect appears as

---

1   Fisher 2009, p. 7.

a cause.[2] Opposed to this neoliberal claim of human nature, we have not only the anti-humanist claim that 'humanity' is always an effect of power and discourse, but the attempt to dispense with the human altogether, situating it in post-human natural and technological processes that exceed it. Finally, there is the opposite interest in the human in the return of philosophical anthropology in the works of Étienne Balibar, Paolo Virno, and Bernard Stiegler.

Thus it is necessary to return to the question of the human in Marx, its place in the critique of political economy, not to restage the debates of 'humanist Marxism', but to confront the current theoretical conjuncture, a conjuncture that can be provisionally defined in terms of the dominant, neoliberal humanism, the emergent, post-humanism, and the residual, anti-humanism. It is necessary to ask the question again: how does *Capital* make sense, not of human nature, but of what could be broadly defined as the humanity of workers and capital? Or put differently, if Marx does not espouse some ideal of humanity as essentially cooperative, as something other than competiton, then what is the philosophical anthropology at work in *Capital*? Or asked differently, how does *Capital* articulate the limits of an anthropological understanding of the economy?

1 Homo Laborans Revisited

Beyond the facile reduction of Marx to a moralism of cooperation and communal living, the other most persistent, and more reputable, myth of Marx's philosophical anthropology is that he considered the essence of humanity to be labour. This is a recurring theme in criticisms of Marx from Heidegger to Baudrillard. Its central thesis, gleaned in many ways from a reading of Marx's 1844 manuscripts, is that labour defines the essence of humanity, defining its particular essence and activity. This definition posits a somewhat novel definition of the human essence, defining this essence as an activity, as transformation of world and self, a second nature and not a fixed and eternal nature.[3] The problem of applying this critique to *Capital* is that it overlooks the focus and reduction of that text, dedicated as it is to 'the critique of political economy'. The centrality of labour as an activity in *Capital* follows capital itself: just as

---

2 As Fredric Jameson writes, summing up this connection and the challenge it poses, 'The market is in human nature' is the proposition that cannot be allowed to stand unchallenged; in my opinion, it is the most crucial terrain of ideological struggle in our time' (Jameson 1991, p. 263).

3 Fischbach 2002, p. 162.

capital confronts us as an 'immense accumulation of commodities', it also confronts us as an immense reinterpretation of human activity as labour. This is not to say that labour is addressed by Marx as something entirely historical and contingent, having no bearing on the essence of humanity; it is precisely the connection of the historical and the anthropological, the contingent and the necessary, that is central to Marx's investigation. Labour is not an expression of some essence of humanity, but its organisation cannot be separated from the question of human existence.

Capital, it is well known, begins with an examination of the dual nature of the commodity, as use value and exchange value, a dual nature which in turn stems from the dual nature of labour as abstract and concrete. The fact that labour functions as a corollary to the much more central analysis of the commodity form has often led to its specific tensions and problems being overlooked. Concrete and abstract labour are the conceptual corollaries of exchange value and use value, the first is defined by concrete particularity and the second is defined by abstract equivalence. As much as the former serves as the necessary corollary of the latter, in some cases as both condition and effect, this should not obscure the particular innovation of the concept of abstract labour, and the specific problems of the conjunction of abstract and concrete labour.

As with the commodity, there is no immediate mystery to concrete labour; it is the specific work of weaving, tailoring, forging, and so on, the specific work of an individual undertaking a specific task. As much as this concept seems self-evident, like something from a children's book dividing a village into butcher, baker, candlestick maker, there are a few riddles concealed in this concept. As with use value, the emphasis is on the concrete particularity of labour. My labour, your labour, is then absolutely interchangeable with that of others. It is possible to then see concrete labour as something irreducibly specific, as being not only the specific task of a specific individual, but also the singularity of a given moment. As with use value, it is hard to comprehend how something so singular can be exchanged at all; this is of course the riddle that *Capital* opens with, an attempt to think the ground of that which is taken for granted.[4] Concrete labour is only one side of the labour process; however, its concrete specificity is also confronted with its abstract generality. The idea that labour is the source of value is, after all, not Marx's discovery: it can be found in Smith and Ricardo. What is unique to Marx, or what Marx gives himself credit for, is the dual nature of labour, abstract and concrete, which is 'the secret to the

---

4   On this point see Henry 1982.

whole critical conception'.[5] Given that abstract labour is the solution to the riddle of commodity exchange, explaining how it is that commodities of different qualities and uses can be treated as equivalent, the question of its own condition of possibility is particularly important. Marx would seem to offer two reasons. First, Marx offers what could be considered an anthropological ground of abstract labour, arguing that the different forms of labour have as their common denominator the fact that they are produced by different human beings. As Marx writes,

> If we leave aside the determinate quality of productive activity, and therefore the useful character of the labour, what remains is its quality of being an expenditure of human labour-power. Tailoring and weaving, although they are qualitatively different productive activities, are both a productive expenditure of human brains, muscles, nerves, hands, etc. and in this sense both human labour. They are merely two different forms of the expenditure of human labour.[6]

This assertion of a natural, human basis of abstract labour, of a communality, is contradicted, or at least put in tension with, Marx's assertion that the abstract nature of labour is not an anthropological given but a social process. It is the very fact that labour is exchanged, is treated as interchangeable, that provides its abstract commonality. Its common basis is not to be found in the recesses of the human body, but in the social relations themselves. As Marx writes in the same section, 'However, let us remember that commodities possess an objective character as values only in so far as they are all expressions of an identical social substance, human labor, that the objective character as values is therefore purely social'.[7] Marx seems to vacillate between a kind of nominalism and realism of abstract labour, placing the abstract quality alternately in the biological identity of humanity as a species or the social relations of a capitalist society. This apparent ambivalence brings to mind the Sixth Thesis on Feuerbach, which stated that the 'human essence is no abstraction inherent in each single individual. In its reality it is the ensemble of social relations'.[8] The Sixth Thesis states as a principle what *Capital* presents as a tension: the human essence, the very identity of humanity right down to biology and the body itself, exists only in and through the historical articulation of social rela-

---

5 Marx and Engels 1955, p. 186.
6 Marx 1977, p. 134.
7 Marx 1977, p. 138.
8 Marx 1970 p. 122.

tions.[9] Abstract labour, and with it abstract humanity, did not exist prior to the social relations of wage labour. As Marx indicates, the effect of this transformation extend well beyond the restricted domain of an economy, to encompass religion,

> For a society of commodity producers, whose general social relation of production consists in the fact that they treat their products as commodities, hence as values, and in this material [*sachlich*] form bring their individual, private labors into relation with each other as homogenous human labor, Christianity with its religious cult of man in the abstract, more particularly in its bourgeois development, i.e. in Protestantism, Deism, etc. is the most fitting form of religion.[10]

One could read Marx here as completing Feuerbach's project. It is not enough to reduce theology to anthropology, to find the figure of humanity beneath the projection of god; one must recognise that there is no humanity as such, there are only specific social relations which produce and reproduce a given figure of humanity. God, especially that of Deism and Protestantism, is not the product of some general longing of humanity, but of the particular society organised by the abstraction of wage labour. Other societies, other mode of productions, produce different ideas of humanity and God.

The question is not one of completing Feuerbach's critique, but of grasping a human essence that exists in and through its social relations. Paolo Virno has developed the philosophical anthropology behind such a concept of humanity, choosing the term 'natural historical' to characterise exactly this aspect of capitalism. Taking inspiration from the philosophical anthropology developed by such writers an Arnold Gehlen, Virno begins from the premise of a humanity that must be understood as undetermined and open to the world, as lacking in instincts that delineate a particular response to a particular aspect of the world.[11] This does not mean that human beings are entirely outside of biology or nature, existing as something defined entirely by history and contingency, but that the biological capacities that define humanity, the capacity for speech, for forming habits, as well as the need for clothes and other forms of artifice to survive, exist only insofar as they are actualised in specific historical situations. Language is a generic capacity, as is the need to wear some sort of clothing, but this generic capacity can only be realised in specific historical formations,

---

9   Balibar 2017b, p. 153.
10   Marx 1977, p. 172.
11   Gehlen 1988, p. 24.

in specific social relations. Human nature is not something that stands apart from history, it is not some kind of constant, but a set of general capacities that are actualised in specific historical situations.[12]

This general condition is transformed in contemporary capitalism. Capitalism is not just another historically specific actualisation of the generic possibilities of humanity but a putting to work of this abstract human potential itself. The generic equivalence of labour power is the generic indifference of humanity. 'Meta-history irrupts into ordinary history in the none-too-sublime guise of labour-power'.[13] Virno's first formulation, that of abstract human potential, as the biological basis for labour power, is a formulation more or less corresponding to formal subsumption, to the early stage of capital in which all that is altered is the formal relationship of wage labour, the worker selling his or her labour power rather than producing for use or the selling of goods. At this stage, the technological and social composition of labour remains unchanged. Exploitation is the exploitation of absolute surplus value, the exploitation of the difference between the time spent reproducing the costs of labour, necessary labour, and the surplus produced. For Virno real subsumption has to be understood as not just a transformation of this economic relation, as capital restructures the technological and social conditions of labour shifting exploitation from the quantitative expansion of the working day to its qualitative intensification, but also a fundamental alteration of the anthropological basis of labour power. In real subsumption it is not just that one sells one's capacity to do work, a capacity that always remains distinct from its actualisations; what is sold, what is put to work, is nothing other than the very capacity to develop new capacities. What contemporary capitalism puts to work are not just actualised potentials, not this or that habit, but the very potential to create habits itself. As Virno stresses with respect to the 'general intellect', the socialised knowledge that has become a productive force, this intellect is not the specific knowledge of the sciences or computer programming, but the very capacity to learn and create. 'General intellect should not necessarily mean the aggregate of the knowledge acquired by the species, but the faculty of thinking; potential as such, not its countless particular realizations. The general intellect is nothing but the intellect in general'.[14] Contemporary capitalism, the capital-

---

12   Virno 2015b, p. 174.
13   Virno 2015a, p. 162.
14   Virno 2004, p. 66. The term 'general intellect' is drawn from 'the fragment on Machines' in
      Marx's *Grundrisse*. As Marx writes, 'Nature builds no machines, no locomotives, railways,
      electric telegraphs, self-acting mules etc. These are the products of human industry; natural material transformed into organs of the human will over nature, or of human particip-

ism of services, precarity and mobility, is not just one historical articulation of the actualisation of the natural capacity to learn and develop habits, but is, in some sense, the exploitation of this very capacity as capacity. What capital puts to work is not this or that specific manifestation of human nature, but human nature, humanity as potentiality, itself.

> Human nature returns to the centre of attention not because we are finally dealing with biology rather than history, but because the biological prerogatives of the human animal have acquired undeniable historical relevance in the current productive process.[15]

Previous societies, even earlier stages of capital, were grounded upon the production and reproduction of a particular set of habits, concepts, and comportments, but with capitalism, all that is solid melts into air, and what comes to light is not this or that habit, but the very capacity of gaining (and losing) them. 'Precarity and nomadism lay bare at the social level the ceaseless and omnilateral pressure of a world that is never an environment'.[16] Capital is a fundamental short circuit of the anthropological condition: if all previous societies have resolved the potential to speak, understand, and act into an actual language, specific forms of knowledge and a set of habits, contemporary capitalism turns to that potential itself, making it manifest and productive, without ever solidifying into a set of habits, a second nature, or a world. All that is solid melts into air.

Virno's trajectory is one of the increasing becoming abstract of labour power, as capital begins to appropriate more and more of the generic capacities underlying labour power. Capital not only puts to work abstract humanity, but anthropogenesis itself. One has to wonder about what remains of concrete labour in this increasing becoming abstract of labour. As much as contemporary work can be understood as an actualisation of the generic capacities of humanity, it still is actualised in a specific individual's endeavour. The paradoxical actualisation of the virtual, the selling of labour power as the potential to not only work but communicate and interact, still manifests itself in particular actions

---

ation in nature. They are *organs of the human brain, created by the human hand*; the power of knowledge objectified. The development of fixed capital indicates to what degree general social knowledge has become a *direct force of production*, and to what degree, hence, the conditions of the process of social life itself have come under the control of the general intellect and been transformed in accordance with it' (Marx 1973, p. 706).

15   Virno 2009, p. 142.
16   Ibid., p. 143.

and over the course of a particular work day. For Virno the concreteness of this becoming abstract is manifest in two different phenomena. First, there is the general problem of capitalist historicity, that unlike all previous modes of production, capital appears to be not just a specific actualisation of this generic potential, a specific language, custom, set of habits, etc., but the actualisation of potential itself. This creates a particular mystification, a particular appearance in which capital appears as human nature.

> When capitalism appropriates an anthropological requisite like the potential to produce, the accent can fall either on the contextualized ways in which the appropriation takes place, or on the indeterminate character of this requisite, pertaining to any epoch or society. The second emphasis points to the 'bourgeois narrow-mindedness, which regards the capitalist forms of production of production as absolute forms – hence as eternal, natural forms of production'. It is the concept of labour-power that explains the spread of a state of mind (little matter where it be melancholic of euphoric) inspired by the 'end of history'.[17]

While Virno's exploitation of abstraction offers an interesting answer to the question of 'capitalist realism', the inability to think or imagine beyond capitalism, it approaches this question primarily from the perspective of historical consciousness, of a general awareness or failure to think historicity. From a more individuated, or subjective dimension, we could ask how does the increasing tendency of anthropogenesis, of the becoming human of the labour process constitute a particular mode of the production of subjectivity? Virno offers two responses to this question. First, he expands the definition of alienation to encompass a loss of not only one's productive activity but the entirety of social relations. 'Nobody is as poor as those who see their own relation to the presence of others, that is to say, their own communicative faculty, their own possession of a language, reduced to wage labor'.[18] Against this generalised alienation Virno also charts a more affirmative version of this experience in the changing contours of the term 'professionalism'. Whereas the term used to be associated with a specific set of highly trained expertise, a kind of personalisation of the general intellect as forms of knowledge, it has increasingly become associated with an attitude, a subjective comportment. Job postings increasingly demand a professional demeanour and attitude, an attitude

---

17   Virno 2015a, p. 173.
18   Virno 2004, p. 63.

that is more associated with a way of being in the world than any claim on specific knowledge. 'Professionality on the other hand is seen as a subjective property, a form of know-how inseparable from the individual person; it is a sum of knowledges, experiences, attitudes, and a certain sensibility'. Alienation and professionalism, the impoverishment of experience and a generalised opportunism, constitute two sides of contemporary experience; they are the basis of its ambiguity. The present appears as both utter impoverishment and total potential, existence is precarious but everything seems possible.

Virno's emphasis on the ambiguity of contemporary work, caught as it were between the alienation of anthropogenesis, the transformation of the most basic human capacities of language and interaction into commodities, and professionalisation, the valorisation of a subjectivity that is both engaged and abstract, capable of applying itself to diverse situations, returns us to a hidden subjective dimension of the split between concrete and abstract labour. As much as concrete and abstract labour can be understood as corresponding to two different sides of the commodity, use value and exchange value, they also can be understood as corresponding to two different subjective comportments and evaluations. One can identify concrete labour with the specific task and job at hand, especially as that work becomes not just a particular task, but a subjective position, being a butcher, baker, or candlestick maker, and abstract labour with the general task of being employed, of being a part of capital. Concrete and abstract labour then constitute not just two sides of the labour process, always in tension, but two sides of subjectification. What Virno charts is a generalised becoming abstract of the labour process as the identification with a concrete task necessarily gives way to the identification with the labour process itself. In a similar manner Frédéric Lordon has argued that the contemporary labour process is defined by a subjectification of abstract labour. The ideal subject of contemporary labour is the entrepreneur, someone who does not identify with any particular activity or enterprise, but with the very possibility of being employed and engaged in labour.[19] If formal subsumption can be understood as the devalorisation of concrete labour – where specific activities cease to be performed on the basis of their use or use value – then real subsumption can be understood as the revalorisation of abstract labour; it is subjectivity as abstract labour.

---

19   Lordon 2014, p. 87.

2   The Hidden Abode of the Post-Human

As much as it is possible to see a figure of humanity, of a generic humanity, appear alongside abstract labour, this is not the entirety of the connection between labour and the human. It cannot be because in some sense abstract labour is labour viewed from the perspective of exchange, of the market. Labour is only viewed as abstract and interchangeable from the perspective of the labour market. Marx's assertion of the connection between abstract labour and abstract humanity appears in the section on the fetish of commodities. It thus appears in the section in which Marx is discussing the non-appearance of abstract labour as labour. The commodity appears to have value, exchange value, as one of its physical attributes, and it is alongside this appearance that the general idea of humanity appears as something of an afterthought. Or, to be more precise, as much as abstract labour appears it would seem to appear on the labour market, mediated through ideological forms such as religion and law which present it as the generic idea of humanity, while its economic role is obscured by the fetish of the commodity. That the assertion of the connection of humanity and labour is articulated in the section on the commodity could give credit to the idea of humanity itself as a kind of fetish, albeit an ambiguous one. One could argue, as Marx does in *The Communist Manifesto*, that abstract humanity is not just an idea, but is itself a practice, as capital overcomes the division between nations and even differences 'of age and sex', as all become instruments of labour.[20] The icy waters of calculation drown out all particularity in the universality of exploitation. However, this is not to say that this universal is without its positive effects: as a real abstraction it carries with it the after-image of a kind of universality, a universality integral to the very notion of the working class. As much as the worker, the subjectification of abstract labour, can be considered to be ambiguously imposed between exploitation and universality, in order to move beyond this ambiguous appearance it is necessary to move beyond exchange into production, into the hidden abode of production. This ambiguity is only deepened by not just its proximity to the fetish, but its structural homology. Like the fetish character of the commodity, abstract labour necessarily obscures the conditions of its emergence. These conditions include the truly non-universal conditions of housework, reproductive labour, and the racial and sexual division of labour.[21] As Marxist-Feminists as well as the different currents of black Marxism have underscored,

---

20   Marx and Engels 1978, p. 479.
21   Federici 2012, p. 16.

not only does capital emerge from the uneven and combined development of unwaged reproductive labour and slave labour, but this uneven and combined condition is the necessary precondition of its emergence.[22] It is not just that abstract labour is incomplete and partial, not actually reflecting a true universal, but that the conditions of its non-universality, the persistence of a gender division between housework and other forms of labour, are its necessary conditions. The figure of the worker, of abstract labour, is necessarily incomplete.

Moving beyond this ambiguity entails moving beyond the sphere of exchange, even the exchange of labour power, to enter into the hidden abode of production. Here we are confronted with another contradiction, not that between the natural and social basis for abstract labour, or even the contradiction between the universality of the image of the worker and the particularity of its history, but between the generic idea of labour and its specific history. Part Three of *Capital* Volume I, the first section on the labour process, begins with a generic discussion of labour 'independent of any specific social formation'.[23] Marx then outlines a general schema of labour, of any labour process, as consisting of 'purposeful activity, that is work itself', the object upon which such activity is undertaken, and the instrument of that undertaking. Even at this general, and even anthropological stage, Marx's schema includes the kernel of a historical element. Work is not just a transformation of the external world, of nature, but it is simultaneously a transformation of the worker's own nature. It is at once a static schema and a matrix for historical transformation. Nonetheless, it is still striking to see, in the subsequent sections that deal with the specifically capitalist mode of production, with large scale industry and cooperation, that Marx writes 'Capital now sets the worker to work, not with a manual tool, but with a machine that itself handles the tools'.[24] This displacement of the initial schema culminates in the worker's reduction to nothing other than 'conscious organ of the machine', an eye overseeing a process that he or she neither initiates nor comprehends. This fragmentation and reduction of the body to a part, an organ in a larger machine, is not just limited to the body, the hand or the eye, but it crosses the Cartesian divide, becoming an aspect of the mind as well. Mental operations can be subject to the same repetition and fragmentation.[25] It is in this context that we get a very different account of the general intellect, not the abstract intellect of anthropogenetic potential, but the ossified and fragmented intellect. This is how Marx writes about the

22   Alliez and Lazzarato 2016, p. 54.

23   Marx 1977, p. 283.

24   Marx 1977, p. 509.

25   Guéry and Deleule 2014, p. 120.

general intellect in his correspondence for *The New York Daily Tribune* '... the progressive division of labour has, to a certain extent, emasculated the general intellect of the middle-class men by the circumscription of all their energies and mental faculties within the narrow spheres of their mercantile, industrial and professional concerns'.[26] What begins with a Promethean schema of the transformation of nature and humanity ends in humanity's destruction and fragmentation.

Once again we are confronted with a contradiction of sorts. This is not the contradiction between use value and exchange value, abstract labour and concrete labour that sets a dialectic in motion, but a contradiction that is not explicitly thematised by Marx (or Marxism), like the apparent contradiction between the biological and social basis of abstract labour. As with the abstract labour discussed above, it is perhaps necessary to interpret this contradiction in the most generous way possible, to read it for what it might articulate rather than simply as a failing on Marx's part. What it articulates, and puts to work, is in some sense the opposite, perhaps even dialectical opposite, of Marx's concept of abstract labour as the 'ensemble of social relations'. If the ensemble of social relations can constitute an anthropological figure, defining humanity as first a universal figure of labour, and then the manifestation of its anthropogenesis, it can also constitute its destruction, its reduction to organs and parts of a productive process. The former makes it possible to grasp what is at stake in the latter. It is not just that the worker is reduced to the conscious organ of the machine during the hours of work in a kind of dead-end job, but this destruction is the destruction of the knowledge and integrity constitutive of humanity. Not the exploitation of anthropogenesis, but its destruction. As Bernard Stiegler argues, the reduction of the worker to a conscious organ of the machine can be understood as an extension of proletarianisation to the point of the destruction of the very constitution of individual subjectivity.[27] As Balibar describes this anthropological destruction:

> This process of autonomization-intellectualization-materialization of 'knowledge' determines more and more the exercise of the 'property rights' and thereby individuality. But at the same time it renders more and more uncertain the identity of proprietors, the identity of the 'subject' of property. Then we are no longer dealing merely with a mechanism of division of human nature that practically contradicts the requirement

---

26   Marx 1861.
27   Stiegler 2010, p. 40.

of freedom and equality. Instead we are dealing with a dissolution of political individuality.[28]

This is something other than the division of mental and manual labour. In part
because the very idea of a worker reduced to a conscious organ suggests that
this deskilling cuts transversally across this division, the mind like the hand can
be subject to the same reduction, the same repetition of an activity. In each case
the minimal constitution of subjectivity, or anthropogenesis, is undermined
by the deskilling of labour. Labour which is first presented as the elevation and
self-transformation of the human becomes its destruction. The social ensemble
must be grasped as the simultaneous destruction and elevation of the very conditions of humanity, elevating some to their absolute potential, to the becoming of potential, while others are reduced to the destruction of their potential.

Of course Marx considered such an anthropological division in his earliest
writing on *Capital*. In the *1844 Manuscripts* Marx writes the following:

> *Political economy conceals the estrangement inherent in the nature of*
> *labour by not considering the* direct *relationship between the* worker
> (labour) *and production.* It is true that labour produces for the rich won-
> derful things – but for the worker it produces privation. It produces
> palaces – but for the worker, hovels. It produces beauty – but for the
> worker, deformity. It replaces labor by machines, but it throws one section
> of the workers back into barbarous types of labor and it turns the other
> section into a machine. It produces intelligence – but for the worker, stu-
> pidity, cretinism.[29]

It is worth asking how Marx's argument in *Capital* (as well as *The Grundrisse*)
differs from this early assertion. First of all, the condition is transformed, it is
no longer property, private property, as the single cause, but the entirety of
economic and technical conditions of labour. It has been transformed from
determination to overdetermination. Second, the terms of opposition are more
complex, and multiple, the division is not between workers and the rich, but
is internal to the productive process itself. Even within the supposedly unified
group of workers of the general intellect there is a division between the ossified
organs and generic capacity. This division does not map neatly onto any division of class or wage status: as Virno argues, it is often the poorly compensated

---

28   Balibar 1994, p. 58.
29   Marx 1964, p. 110.

worker of the service industry that has to contend with the most uncertainty, novelty, and contingency, putting to work the generic capacity of language and creation. Against this we could contrast the worker in a highly specialised form of knowledge, the university professor, copywriter, and lawyer, who repeats the same intellectual formulas. However, even this contrast fails to capture the way in which one can find the same processes, the same reduction and expansion of human capacities at work in the same individual, the same society. To paraphrase Balibar, at the exact moment that the world becomes unified economically, it becomes violently divided anthropologically.[30]

3   Living Labour and Undead Exploitation

The combined and uneven destruction of the worker cannot be simply opposed to some enrichment of the capitalist. It is not a simple inversion where the poverty of one is the enrichment of the other. In fact, any attempt to produce a figure of the bourgeois, of the capitalist, in capital would come up short. This is another effect of the centrality of labour, of beginning from the perspective of labour: those who do not labour are simply left to the margins and blank spaces. The capitalist appears as 'moneybags' as the bearer of a function of capital. There is one notable exception to this, and that is the chapter on the working day.

The chapter on the working day has a particular status in the structure of *Capital*. It offers the most detailed discussion of conditions of the working class in England, so much so that it at times seems like Marx's attempt to offer his own version of Engels's book of that name. However, it is not without its own reflection on the anthropology of capital, on the conception of human nature that is put to work by the capitalist. This anthropology is foregrounded by the general logic of conflict between capitalist and worker, a logic inscribed in the very status of labour power as a commodity. As Marx writes,

> On the other hand, the peculiar nature of the commodity sold implies a limit to its consumption by the purchaser, and the worker maintains his right as a seller when he wishes to reduce the working day to a particular normal length. There is here therefore an antinomy, of right against

30   The passage in Balibar is 'At the moment at which humankind becomes economically and, to some extent, culturally "united", it is violently divided "biopolitically"' (Balibar 2004, p. 130).

right, both equally bearing the seal of the law of exchange. Between equal rights, force decides.[31]

It is in relation to this general logic of forces – a conflict that, as Marx stresses, exceeds any other limits, moral, and natural – that Marx sardonically notes 'Accordingly to the anthropology of the capitalists, the age of children ended at 10 or at the outside, 11'. The 'anthropology of capitalists' is one in which the only factor of humanity that registers is its capacity to be put to work. It is an anthropology without sleep, childhood, and even food, in which humanity is nothing other than exploitable labour power. This anthropology is not produced speculatively, but is manufactured in the factories.[32]

If one shifts the genitive from the 'anthropology of the capitalist' to an examination of the Marx's understanding of the particular humanity of the capitalist, the matter is just as striking. Marx adopts the voice of the worker, addressing the capitalist as follows, 'You may be a model citizen, perhaps a member of the R.S.P.C.A. [Royal Society for the Prevention of Cruelty to Animals], and you may be in the odour of sanctity as well; but the thing you represent when you come face to face with me has no heart in its breast'.[33] Marx's infamous methodological claim that he would treat individuals as merely 'bearers' of economic relations receives its justification. Capitalism itself is indifferent to the motivations and intentions of the capitalist. Just as the capitalist is indifferent to the humanity of the worker, capitalism is indifferent to the humanity of the capitalist. 'As a capitalist, he is only capital personified'. Between equal abstractions, force decides. However, Marx goes further than this point. It is in the chapter on the working day that Marx makes his famous remark that the capitalist is 'vampire like, living only by sucking living labour'. It is not just that capitalism is indifferent to the humanity of the worker: it is actively hostile to it, inhabiting it like some kind of monster. It is not just the vampire that Marx invokes, but also the Werewolf, another monster that inhabits humanity with an insatiable desire. Capital appears as a motley collection of every folktale and monster movie.

The chapter on the working day offers a striking combination of not only ethnographic detail, but political struggle; it is the only chapter of *Capital* in which the working class appears as an active subject, struggling for the ten hour bill in England, a general logic of forces, and a polemical phantasmagoria of monsters. The combination of these dimensions could be read in moralising tone,

31   Marx 1977, p. 344.
32   Macherey 2015.
33   Marx 1977, p. 343.

the heroic working class confronts the monster that is capital, or they could be understood as another chapter in the generation and constitution of anthropology in *Capital*. First, it extends the destruction of subjectivity from the worker to the capitalist. The worker is reduced to a conscious organ of the machine, while the capitalist becomes the personification of a ceaseless desire for surplus value that exceeds it. The class struggle is not a struggle between different classes of individuals, but a struggle that cuts through the very constitution of humanity.

4   Conclusion

Where does the examination of the anthropology of labour and its limits in and around *Capital* leave us? It is possible to sketch out two possible conclusions. First, if the grand philosophical debate of human nature is framed between Thomas Hobbes' assertion that 'man is a wolf to man' on one side, that humanity is locked in a vicious competition which can only be contained but never ultimately cancelled by the state, and Spinoza's 'man is a god to man' on the other, the idea that nothing is more useful to human life than the combined effort of humanity, then Marx offers a third formulation, 'man is a werewolf to man'. This third position is the assertion that human conflict and sociability have less to do with some natural basis for antagonism or cooperation, than the extent to which humanity itself is thoroughly transformed by its constitutive practices and relations, becoming something other. With the added caveat that there is no human nature outside of this process of transformation and possession: the human essence is nothing other than the ensemble of social relations, including those that make it ultimately hostile to itself. The human world is a world of the commodity form, abstract labour, the general intellect, and conscious organs, a world of gods and monsters.

Second, and perhaps more importantly, Marx's investigation of the constitution and destruction of humanity through labour reveals that the question cannot be a matter of being for or against the human. Nor is it a matter of declaring the current age to be the bold era of the posthuman. We have always been posthuman, the very idea of humanity is inseparable from its social ensemble, from its organisation and destruction. What Marx suggests is another series of questions, it is not a matter of being for or against an essence, or declaring an essence to be surpassed, but of understanding how this essence is produced and organised. Moreover, it then becomes a matter of transforming practices in order to maximise the conditions of liberation and cooperation, to make it more of a world of gods than monsters. That is the revolutionary project.

CHAPTER 19

The 'Other Scene' of Political Anthropology: Between Transindividuality and Equaliberty

The political thought of Étienne Balibar is framed between transindividuality and equaliberty. These terms frame much of Balibar's writing on politics, citizenship, race, and philosophy in recent decades yet they do not have the same status. One is borrowed, a citation from Gilbert Simondon, while the other is Balibar's neologism, a word that combines equality and liberty. The first is situated with respect to Balibar's investigations in the history of philosophy, constituting a tradition of Spinoza, Hegel, and Marx, while the second is deployed in Balibar's investigations of the intersection of race, nation, and class in contemporary politics. One term refers to a question of political anthropology, or even ontology, an articulation of the fundamental problems of individual and collective, while the other is framed between the relation between equality and liberty, rights and freedoms, in the history of political practice. The points of overlap are just as salient as their differences. Transindividuality and equaliberty challenge conventional, which is to say both philosophical and ideological, notions of the individual and society, collectivity and individuality. The point, however, is not that these terms are the same, referring to identical terms and questions, nor that they are rigorously distinct, referring to different fields of inquiry – specifically social ontology and politics – but that the differences and relations might itself be a way of articulating what are some of the most pressing questions in contemporary philosophy, not just the relation between the individual and collective, but the relation between ontology and politics. The relation between transindividuality and equaliberty defines not just a field of political questions on citizenship, civility, the nation, and race, but defines a particular philosophical practice, a particular way of engaging in in political problems.

1   Transindividuality Chez Balibar

The term transindividuality is drawn from the work of Gilbert Simondon, most specifically the posthumously published *L'individuation psychique et collective*. As much as Balibar acknowledges this as the source of the term, his own development of the concept is drawn more from the work of Spinoza, or more specifically Spinoza as initially read by Alexandre Matheron in *Individu et communauté chez Spinoza*. For Balibar the overlap between Matheron and Simondon's work constitutes a particular kind of coevolution in the history of philosophy; Matheron could not have been aware of Simondon's thesis, and, for his part, Simondon tends to see Spinoza as not so much a transindividual thinker as as thinker who dissolves the individual into the larger totality of God or nature, losing any individuation whatsoever.[1] In contrast to this, Matheron insists that what Spinoza presents is both an ontology and politics in which the standard oppositions between the individual and the totality no longer hold. Each individual thing is defined by its particular striving, its particular conatus, but its particular conatus only exists and is oriented in and through its affects, encounters, and relations.[2] Everything is at once rigorously individual and collective. This irreducibility at the level of ontology is doubled at the level of ethics and politics, as Matheron demonstrates the task of Spinoza's *Ethics* is to demonstrate that 'nothing is more useful to man than man', that the opposition between egoism and altruism, between the pursuit of self-interest and the good of the community, is an illusion generated by inadequate ideas and distorted ambitions.[3] The individual and the collective are not opposed, or reducible to one another, but most be thought in their mutual irreducibility.

It is from this point, from the mutual irreducibility of the individual to the collective or the collective to the individual, that Balibar constructs his lineage of transindividual thinkers; a list that encompasses Spinoza, Hegel, Marx, and (sometimes even) Freud.[4] The thinkers on this list have an uneven status in Balibar's thought; Spinoza and Marx have been the subject of both (short) monographs and essays and interventions, while Hegel has recently appeared in several essays, and Freud often only appears conjoined with other thinkers. Taking this publication history as something of a guide it is possible to argue that the two principal thinkers of Balibar's conception of transindividuality are Spinoza and Marx. Or, more to the point, transindividuality is a concept that Balibar develops according to a transversal logic that passes through the different systems and conjunctures of Spinoza and Marx. This itinerary is not one of influence or lineage between the philosophers under consideration, but constitutes different problems and questions within Balibar's examination of transindividuality. (As I will argue below, Hegel represents a different problem

---

1 Balibar 1996, p. 37.
2 Matheron 1969, p. 19.
3 Matheron 1969, p. 274.
4 Balibar 2017b, p. 121.

for Balibar, one associated with equaliberty, or more specifically, the relation between equaliberty and transindividuality.)

Spinoza's definite statement of transindividuality is 'desire is man's very essence'. As Balibar argues, such a formulation redefines the nature of not only humanity, defining a philosophical anthropology, but the very problem of essence. 'The metaphysical notion of essence has thus undergone a profound change; instead of referring to a class or a genus, it now refers to the singularity of individuals'.[5] Everything that exists, exists in terms of its singular striving, but this singular striving, is, as Matheron asserted, nothing outside of the relations that affect it. Transindividuality is ultimately not just a way of bypassing the oppositions of individual and collective, but of thinking a new figure of causality. Causality in the sense that the old opposition between external and internal causes, between being affected and having effects, must be dispensed with in order to understand everything, every striving, as simultaneously a cause and an effect, as a conatus and the affects that orient it. Transindividuality means that any opposition between social causes and individual desires necessarily collapses, the individual exists in and through its relations, and these relations only exist insofar as they are individuated in specific strivings. Thus the very formulation repeats the idea of structural causality, of a cause which exists in and through its effect, and as with structural causality it is less a matter of a transcendent ontological assertion, a claim that would remain the same for all times and places, than a general structure that can only be actualised in specific situations and problems. The combination of external and internal causes, of singular desires and shared affects, can only be thought in and through their specific articulation, their specific character, what Balibar calls, following Spinoza, *ingenium*. *Ingenium*, which is translated as nature or character, is the word that Spinoza uses to refer to both the specific character, or comportment, of an individual, and the specific nature of a city, or polis. It is through this specific ingenium that it is possible to think both the stability and transformation of a given individual's desires and a given collectivity.[6]

That Balibar finds a turn towards relational and historical specificity at the heart of Spinoza's ontology, at the core of a philosophy often summarised as *sub specie aeternitatis*, is perhaps surprising, but it also explains why Balibar turns to Marx to develop and expand the concept of transindividuality. At the level of propositions, the definitive statement of Marx's transindividual thought is the sixth of the *Theses on Feuerbach*, or, more specifically, Marx's statement

5   Balibar 1997b, p. 5.
6   Balibar 1997b, p. 185.

that 'the human essence is no abstraction inherent in each single individual. In its reality it is the ensemble of social relations'.[7] Once again it is a question of essence, essence now framed less in terms of the singularity of its manifestation, the desire that underlies every individual, but the relational nature of its articulation.[8] Balibar emphasises that Marx uses the French word *ensemble*, stressing the non-totalisable nature of the relations that constitute and affect this essence. Spinoza and Marx represent twin assaults on the most common-place nature of a philosophical anthropology, of a human essence that is both universal, a shared essence, and transcendent, existing prior to and outside of its relations. In its place there is the necessity to think both the singularity and relational dimension of this supposed essence, to think it as transindividual. The human essence is singular, but this singularity is nothing other than the way in which it intersects with determinate relations.

Marx's thought of transindividuality is not limited to the uncharacteristic-ally speculative moment of the *Theses on Feuerbach* but continues through his critique of political economy in *Capital*. Transindividuality is the under theor-ised and unnamed concept underlying Marx's more prosaic examinations of the relations of capitalist exploitation. As Marx writes in the Chapter on 'co-operation', '... [T]he special productive power of the combined working day, is under all circumstances, the social productive power of labour, or the product-ive power of social labour. This power arises from cooperation itself. When the worker co-operates in a planned way with others, he strips off the fetters of his individuality, and develops the capabilities of this species [*Gattungsvermö-gen*]'.[9] In this passage the capacity of the species, or species being, appears less as that which is alienated by selling one's labour than as that which is put to work by capital. Capital does just not exploit individual labour power under-stood as the physical or mental expenditure of this or that individual; it exploits the collective labour of not only those gathered in the factory or workshop, but also the collective inheritance of language, skill, and knowledge embodied in any individual's productive labour. As Balibar writes,

> We must give this thesis its maximum force to understand the conclu-sions that Marx wants to reach; not only is labor socialized historically, so that it becomes transindividual. Essentially it always was, insofar as there is no labor without cooperation, even in its most primitive forms, and the

---

7   Marx 1970b, p. 144.
8   Balibar 2017, p. 130.
9   Marx 1977, p. 441.

isolation of the productive labourer in relation to nature was only ever an appearance.[10]

Marx then represents one of the most important reversals of possessive individualism, contesting the equation between individuality, labour, and possession. Labour is irreducibly collective and individual: in a word, it is transindividual.

Spinoza and Marx would each seem to represent two different theses of transindividuality. With Spinoza there is the assertion of an irreducible minimum of individuation at the heart of any collective process. As Spinoza argues in the *Tractatus Theologico-Politicus*, individuals cannot alienate or give away their rights to the sovereign; right, which is to say power, remains an irreducible aspect of individual striving. Individuals cannot suppress their striving, histories, and encounters.[11] If Spinoza asserts the irreducible minimum of the individual in the collective then Marx can be understood to assert the irreducible minimum of the collective in the individual. Labour as well as language and thought are all irreducibly collective. The skills that we use and the language that we speak are collective products. The opposition, or contradiction, on this point is solely heuristic or relative. Spinoza's assertion of the irreducible minimum of the individual has as its corollary the irreducibly relational, or collective nature, of this individual striving. Desire is always oriented, determined by the affects and encounters that shape it. In a similar manner Marx's materialism demands that the collective nature of the labour has as its necessary corollary the singular, embodied performance of this labour. It is always a singular body and mind that is put to work, and it is the kernel of living labour that constitutes the limit of capitalist exploitation. The minimum of the individual cannot be separated from its communication and relation, just as the minimum of the collective cannot be separated from its singular embodiment in the labouring body or thinking mind.[12] We might put to work the combined 'general intellect' of mankind, but we always do so with our head and hands and in our particular finite time. The two theses of transindividuality, the irreducibility of the collective in the individual and the individual in the collective, are not only each present in each transindividual thinker, but are the necessary corollary of each other.

The salient difference between Marx and Spinoza is not that the first is more collectivist and the second is more individualistic. That would negate the very

---

10   Balibar 2014, p. 85.
11   Balibar 2015, p. 11.
12   Ibid.

premise of transindividuality. Nor is it a difference of philosophical speculation and concrete analysis: Spinoza's conjunctural analysis of religion and politics is as important for transindividuality as Marx's philosophical anthropology. If they differ, and complement each other, it has to do with the way that the relation between politics and economics is framed in each. As Balibar writes,

> It would be easy to conclude that Marx is basically unaware of the 'other scene' of politics, the scene of communitarian affiliation, and therefore unaware of symbolic violence as well (although he names it or has bequeathed us with the word ideology, one of the aptest names for it); and to conclude that Spinoza, for his part, basically ignores the irreducible level of economic antagonism (doubtless because, at the economic level, where conatus can perhaps be conceived of as a 'productive force', Spinoza is basically an optimist and a utilitarian).[13]

Marx is then the thinker of economic exploitation, with little to say about the conflict over symbolic identities, while Spinoza is the thinker of the ambiguity of political identities, with little to say about exploitation. As much as this is perhaps true, it does not entirely address the way in which their thought can be articulated with respect to these problems (as Balibar's parenthetical statement reveals). It is a matter of tendencies rather than divisions.

It is at this point that we confront the ambiguity of transindividuality as a politics. As much as Spinoza recognised the irreducible singular striving of the individual as a limit that tyrannical powers would have to confront, he also understood that the strength of superstition, which is to say ideology, is to incorporate, or interpellate, the individual. Superstition, by which Spinoza means religion, begins from the fact that men are 'conscious of their appetites, and ignorant of the causes of things'. As Balibar demonstrates politics, political authority, continues this interpellation. This is the ultimate significance of the contract for the history of politics; it is an ideology that constructs the state as something individually chosen or willed. Hence the continued importance of Spinoza's critique of theocracy: theocracy is not just a state founded on religious authority, but a state founded upon imaginary participation of the individual in the collective through the act of consent.[14] In a similar manner Marx's analysis of commodity fetishism demonstrates the manner in which the irreducible collective, or social nature, of production appears first as the value

---

13   Balibar 2015, p. 12.
14   Balibar 1997a, p. 193.

of commodities, and ultimately as the productive power of capital.[15] The terms could be reversed here as well: an ideological or imaginary dimension of collectivity can be found in Spinoza, in the community founded upon imagined identifications, just as an imaginary or ideological dimension of individuality can be found in Marx, in the market relations of isolated individuals. We can find in Spinoza an analysis of the way in which the irreducibly collective nature of striving constitutes both the basis of not only rational agreement, 'nothing is more useful to man than man', but also imaginary identification, the entire affective economy of ambition and envy. For Marx there is also an analysis of the way in which capital, specifically the market, appears as a regime of 'freedom, equality, and Bentham', as the very realisation of individual aspiration and desire. What Balibar writes of Spinoza, that 'Sociability is ... the unity of a real agreement and an imaginary ambivalence, both of which have real effects', can be understood to apply not only to both Spinoza and Marx, but to transindividuality in general.[16] 'One divides into two' with respect to transindividuality, in that both the irreducibly individual nature of the collective and the irreducibly collective nature of the individual have their imaginary (or symbolic) and real dimensions. Individual identity and collective belonging are each both symbolic and real, affective and rational. Balibar's work on the intersecting nature of race, class, and nation (all of which must be understood as transindividual) is a matter of working through this intersection of imaginary identification and real agreement in historically specific cases.

2   The Incomplete History of Equaliberty

There is an unmistakable overlap between transindividuality and equaliberty. What the former does with the anthropological, or ontological, postulates of the individual and the collective, the latter does with the political articulations of individual and collective through such concepts as rights, citizenship, and nation. Their conceptual overlap can thus be seen in their objects of criticism; each of the terms is critically positioned against a persistent binary or opposition that posits the relation between the collective and the individual as necessarily a zero sum game, as a choice between the individual or the collective. Equality has often been understood, especially since the Cold War, as the demand of the collective, while liberty has been understood as the rights

---

15   Balibar 2017a, p. 191.
16   Balibar 1998, p. 88.

of the individuality. Equaliberty, like transindividuality, must ultimately posit the irreducibility of the individual to the collective and the collective to the individual. This conceptual overlap is doubled by the fact that many transindividual thinkers, including Spinoza and Marx, have as their political ideal a realisation of the individual in the collective and the collective in the individual (to borrow a Hegelian phrasing).[17] The transindividual ontology is completed and realised in a political ideal that seeks the realisation of the individual in the collective, in other words, equaliberty.

Despite this overlap of problems and terms Balibar does not develop equaliberty on the same philosophical terrain as transindividuality, nor does he refer to the same figures. As we have seen above, transindividuality is grounded on the ontology and political thought of Spinoza and Marx (to name two), or, more precisely, the point where politics and ontology intersect. The points of reference for equaliberty, however, are primarily political and historical. Equaliberty is not developed through an ontological examination, but through political transformations and historical experience. As Balibar writes:

> ... if it is absolutely true that equality is practically identical to liberty, this means that it is materially impossible for it to be otherwise – in other words, it means that they are necessarily always contradicted together. This thesis is itself to be interpreted in extension: equality and freedom are contradicted in exactly the same conditions, in the same situation, because there is no example of conditions that supress or repress freedom that do not suppress or limit – that is, do not abolish – equality, and vice versa. I am not afraid of being contradicted here by the history of capitalist exploitation, which by negating the equality proclaimed in the labor contract ends up in the practical negation of freedom of speech and expression, or by the history of socialist regimes that, by suppressing public freedoms, end up constituting a society of privileges and reinforced inequalities.[18]

Balibar turns the cannons of cold war ideology against themselves by arguing that it is history itself that demonstrates the impossibility of liberty without equality, the Western Ideal, or equality without liberty, its Soviet counterpart. The American ideal of liberty without equality is contradicted by the various liberties, from speech to participation in the political process, that are effect-

---

17   Balibar 2015, p. 138.
18   Balibar 2014, p. 49.

ively annulled by massive inequality of material resources. Freedom of speech without access to the very material conditions of being heard effectively annuls itself, just as the equality of state socialism is annulled by the differences that set party members apart from non-party members. As Balibar writes,

> There are no examples of restrictions or suppressions of freedoms without social inequalities, nor of inequalities without restrictions or suppressions of freedoms, be it only to put down resistance, even if there are degrees, secondary tensions, phases of unstable equilibrium, and compromise situations in which exploitation and domination are not homogeneously distributed across all individuals.[19]

Cold War ideology was framed in terms of a choice between liberty or equality, understood as competing political ideals; the history of the same period posits the impossibility of separating equality and liberty. The separation between equality and liberty is also the separation between economics and politics, between economic equality (coupled with political repression) or political liberty (coupled with economic inequality). Thus, the proposition of equaliberty is aimed as much against the divide between economics and politics, the idea that economic transformations do not effect political relations and vice versa, as it is against that between freedom and equality, the individual and collective.

Balibar's turn toward history, towards the historical evidence of the Cold War, does not entirely dispense with philosophical work. Equaliberty is not a fact of nature, some law of the universe that dictates that equality must always accompany liberty and vice versa. This is not a positivism in which the facts of history trump conceptual analysis, but an examination of the institution and transformation of political ideas in and through political practices. The efficacy of equaliberty stems from a particular institutionalisation of politics and humanity, a particular political anthropology. The initial point of reference for this institution is the 'Declaration of the Rights of Man and Citizen'; the historical institution of the identity of man and citizen, humanity and the right to politics. Balibar's assertion contests Marx's famous reading of this Declaration in 'On the Jewish Question', which argued that 'man' was ultimately bourgeois man, the private citizen of market existence, and the conjunction 'and' ultimately reduced all rights of the citizen to man, to an isolated, self-interested, and private existence.[20] As Balibar argues, 'Reread the *Declaration* and you will

---

19   Ibid.
20   Marx 1978a, p. 45.

see that there is in reality no gap between the rights of man and the rights of the citizen, no difference in content: they are exactly the same'.[21] This proclamation constitutes something of an event, a transformation of the terms of politics. As such it is shaped by both what precedes it, and as Balibar argues the French Revolution was simultaneously a revolution against tyranny and inequality, against the absolute powers of the king and the entrenched inequalities of feudal society. Like Marx, Balibar argues that the revolution is shaped by his conditions, but these conditions do not restrict it, leave it at the status of merely political emancipation, but shape its particular political transformation understood as a universal right to politics. At the level of political anthropology it is a break with the ancient conception of politics, in which citizenship, political belonging, had to be qualified, equality was only for equals, which meant that slaves, women, children even manual workers were excluded from political life because of their ties to natural hierarchy and necessity. In the ancient period '... [T]he concept of the citizen is subordinated to anthropological differences'.[22] This institutes a new era of political thought and practice, one that is less the decisive transformation of politics than an era riddled with its own contradictions and tensions. The history of equaliberty, the struggle against the separation of equality and liberty, is the history of the various tensions of this relation as they are worked out and displaced through multiple identities and institutions. It is a history in which the identity of citizen and man are driven beyond any anthropological limitation, any qualification by nation, race, or gender.

The citation of the historical evidence of equaliberty is thus understood as the intersection between institutions and insurrection. For Balibar the citizen instituted by this revolution is split between its constitutive dimension and its insurrectionary dimension. It is at the basis of state authority, but it is so only in its capacity to constantly contest this authority, to revolt once again. Equaliberty is thus a thoroughly historical or historicised concept, which is to say that not only does it unfold over history, and constitute the basis for making sense of a particular history, but it can only unfold historically. 'This is why citizenship is historically engaged in an uninterrupted process of the extension, deepening, and adaptation of norms'.[23] This history has two defining moments. The first is the attempt to reconcile the tension between equality and liberty, between social and political existence, through a third term, through a concept of fraternity, understood as either social citizenship or in terms of

---

21   Balibar 2014, p. 44.
22   Balibar 1994, p. 59.
23   Balibar 2014, p. 123.

property, or self-possession, understood as the only viable equality and the basis of liberty.[24] These two ideals and institutions represent the two dominant ways, ways that could be distinguished as left and right, of stabilising equality and liberty, either through the institution of fraternity through social citizenship that encompasses some ideal of equality under its basic liberties, or the protection and guarantee of property as means to reconcile liberty and the equal right to prosperity.

It is the same intersection of social and politics, economic and political transformations that threatens the very identity of man and citizen, of humanity and political participation. This is the second moment, the unravelling of fraternity or property as the mediation of the tensions between equality and liberty. On the side of fraternity, there is the division of man, of humanity, into the sexes, plural, not just men and women but the myriad identities and relations that do not neatly fit into such a division. On the side of property, there is the fundamental transformation of property to encompass 'intellectual property', a transformation that affects not only the social conditions of labour but also the political conditions of participation. These transformations challenge equaliberty not just in that they disrupt the identity of man and citizen, suggesting new inequalities irreducible to ancient exclusions, but in the sense that any solution to these transformations exceeds what is conventionally understood as equality or liberty. The inequalities and exclusions of sexual difference cannot be resolved by a simple appeal to equality, nor can the intellectual property be resolved by the free access to information.

The history of equaliberty, or equaliberty as an understanding of the history of modern politics, then returns us to the concept of transindividuality. Its limits, sexual difference and intellectual difference, are nothing other than radical challenges to the very conditions and possibility of the citizen as a form of political transindividuation. As such these limits remind us that political individuation is itself situated among other individuations, the individuations of social reproduction and the labour process. Sexual difference reminds us that identity, even the most intimate and naturalised, is always framed in relation with others, is always transindividual.[25] The politicisation of sexual difference can be considered an extension of the initial identification of man and citizen, extending it beyond its gendered exclusion to eventually problematise the very concept of human nature, or human individuality, underlying politics, revealing the gendered and thus non-neutral nature of any politics in the name of

24   Balibar 2014, p. 53.
25   Balibar 2002, p. 27.

man. Intellectual difference relates less to the internal transformations of citizenship than to the division between politics and economics. What Balibar refers to as intellectual difference returns us to Marx's understanding of the transindividual nature of labour, reminding us, as Marx did in *Capital*, that this anthropological fact is not without its divisions, most notably the division between mental and manual labour, divisions that are extenuated by the radical transformation brought about by the capitalist subsumption of labour. Capital increasingly transforms man from the wielder of tools into nothing other than a conscious organ of the machine, making skill and knowledge part of the machine rather than the worker. This has profound effects for the constitution of individuation. As Balibar writes,

> This process of autonomization-intellectualization-materialization of 'knowledge' determines more and more the exercise of the 'property rights' and thereby individuality. But at the same time it renders more and more uncertain the identity of proprietors, the identity of the 'subject' of property. Then we are no longer dealing merely with a mechanism of division of human nature that practically contradicts the requirement of freedom and equality. Instead we are dealing with a dissolution of political individuality.[26]

Sexual difference and intellectual difference challenge the very identity of man and citizen, of citizenship as a transindividual individuation. This is not a return to the ancient inequalities of exclusion, although the incomplete and uneven development of transindividuation means that it is never free of such inequalities; as Balibar argues, the 'current conjuncture' carries with it elements of the ancient, modern, and postmodern transindividuation.[27] Sexual difference and intellectual difference challenge equaliberty, the constitution of the citizen, in a different manner than such ancient exclusions in that their very resolution demands a redefinition of both equality and liberty. Sexual difference cannot be resolved by a simple appeal to equality, nor can the transformations of intellectual difference, the materialisation and transformation of knowledge, be resolved by a simple appeal to liberty, to the freedom of information (or information 'wanting to be free'). Sexual difference and intellectual difference challenge equaliberty, not simply by introducing hitherto unimagined inequalities and dominations, but because their emancipatory transformation

---

26   Balibar 1994, p. 58.
27   Balibar 1994, p. 59.

will necessarily involve new concepts and practices of equality and freedom, challenging both terms in the conjunction.

3   Conclusion: Dialectics of the Other Scene

The relation between the concepts of transindividuality and equaliberty is conflictual and uneven. Transindividuality would seem to be the necessary ontological postulate underlying equaliberty. As such it is a necessary but not sufficient condition, as equaliberty is the institutionalisation and 'becoming explicit' of transindividuality. At the same time, the broad meaning of transindividuality, the ensemble of relations it encompasses, political, economic, and technical, would constantly threaten equaliberty as a particular political institutionalisation of transindividuality. One the one hand, equaliberty completes transindividuality, while, on the other, transindividuality threatens equaliberty.

One way to resolve this tension would be to posit politics as a necessarily becoming equaliberty of transindividuality. In which the task of politics would be a matter of proceeding from an inadequate to adequate idea of transindividuality, to use Spinoza's terminology. We are always already transindividual, constituted even in our isolated, egocentric, and ambitious relations through our encounters and relations, but there is a fundamental difference between the transindividual identity that sees itself as isolated, separate, or even hostile to society, and one that recognises its constitutive relations with others, and recognises itself in those relations. One could argue that such a transformation underlies Spinoza's politics in the shift from the inadequate ideas of ambition to the adequate ideas of mankind's common usefulness to each other. Spinoza's politics are thus in some sense a politics of communication, of a transformation of how people understand and think about their constitutive relations.[28] It is also possible to argue that Marx's, or at least Marxist, politics are shaped by a fundamental epistemological transformation, a different understanding of social relations in the passage from ideology to class consciousness (or science). 'The true society of individuals can only exist in their effective socialization'.[29] Politics in Marx and Spinoza is both a transformation of social relations and a transformation of the understanding of those relations, a transformation of base and superstructure, the order and connection of things and ideas.

---

28   Balibar 1998, p. 98.
29   Balibar 2014, p. 85.

Politics as a recognition of the transindividual takes on a much more explicit form in Hegel. This is perhaps why Balibar turns his attention to Hegel, specifically the *Phenomenology of Spirit* in *Citizen Subject*. Balibar examines two of Hegel's statements, each of which could be understood as formulations of the transindividual, 'Ich das Wir, und Wir, das Ich ist' or 'I that is We and We that is I', and 'das Tun aller und Jeder' or 'The work of all and each'.[30] As such these formulations constitute a particular moment in the becoming subject of substance, of the becoming universal of the common, the point at which spirit, the constitutive historical and relational aspects of subjectivity, is explicitly recognised. There are two limitations to this absolute identity of the individual in the collective, of the we that is an I and the work of all and each. First, as Balibar argues, there is a fundamental problem as to whether any specific community, any given social relation can ultimately realise transindividuality as such. There is a fundamental and eternal difference between the common, transindividuality as the very condition of individual and collective life, and the universal, the recognition and institutionalisation of that common life.[31] This difference cannot be transcended or sublimated. There is no community of the community, no social relation that corresponds to absolute knowledge; the closer specific social formations come to realising the very idea of such a community, the more they universalise their own particular articulation of the common, the more they expose their particular and contingent basis.[32] The conditions of this limit are given in the two formulations of spirit, one that posits it as a social relation of recognition, as a universality, in the I that is We, and the other as a task, an activity, a common project, in the task for all and each. One splits into two, in that any community, any social relation, is always at once common and universal, an activity, a practice, and its representation and recognition. Or, put in the terms we are examining here, transindividuality is the condition of equaliberty but neither reducible to it, nor completely resolved into it.

---

30 Balibar 2017a, p. 158.
31 Balibar 2017a, p. 165.
32 Balibar 2017a, p. 163. Balibar's position here is in many senses similar to Jameson's, who also stresses the social and non-totalisable nature of spirit. As Jameson writes, 'Yes, Spirit is the collective, but we must not call it that, owing to the reification of language, owing to the positivities of the philosophical terms or names themselves, which restore precisely that empirical common-sense ideology it was the very vocation of the dialectic to destroy in the first place. To name the social is to make it over into a thing or an empirical entity, just as to celebrate its objectivity in the face of idealistic subjectivism is to reestablish the old subject-object opposition which was to have been done away with' (Jameson 2010, p. 13).

If we turn our attention to Hegel's *Philosophy of Right* it becomes clear that it is not just a matter of the individual recognising itself in its transindividual conditions, the I that is We, or acting in relation to the common, the work of all and each, but of both at once, of an individual constituted in and through different political individuations. As Balibar writes,

> The Hegelian political subject is thus citizen and burgher [bourgeois] at the same time, a 'man without qualities', and a 'man with qualities', these qualities being at once subjective and objective, that is, dispositions (*habitus*) and properties (*proprietas*). The state thus conceived, however, has two faces; we should perhaps go so far as to say that it divides into two, that it contains *two communities in one*.[33]

This division is in turn split, as private life is torn between civil society and the family, between individual self-interest and substantial belonging. The politics that Hegel proposes in *The Philosophy of Right* is one of the destruction and constitution of different overlapping transindividual individuations, family, civil society, and state.[34]

Returning now to the problem of the relation between transindividuality and equaliberty from this perspective, it is possible to see equaliberty, the ideal of the citizen, as one transindividual individuation. It is perpetually threatened by not only its own limits, the limits ascribed to citizenship demarcated by national borders and other forms of belonging, but by its external conditions, by economic and political transformations, as well as familial relation.[35] These economic and familial transindividual individuations differ from Hegel's in two substantial ways. First, following the later works of Marx, 'civil society', or the economy, is not one transindividual individuation, that of ego-centric self-interest, that can simply be opposed to the universal individuation of the citizen or state, but is itself split between market-based isolated subjectivity and working concepts of solidarity. The economic does not have a univocal individuation, but is itself split between its symbolisation in competition or cooperation, the market or the labour process. As Balibar remarks of the contemporary neoliberal symbolisation, demonstrating the flexibility of this symbolisation, 'The capitalist is defined as a worker, as an "entrepreneur"; the worker, as the bearer of a capacity, of a "human capital"'.[36] To which we must

---

33   Balibar 2015, p. 112.
34   Balibar 2015, p. 113.
35   Carré 2014, p. 30.
36   Balibar 1994, p. 52.

add a third individuation, the loss of individuation and transindividuation through the technological and social fragmentation of the labouring body and subjectivity.[37] As much as this last transformation can be understood to be a product of the contemporary reorganisation of the labour process, Balibar has always argued that Marx's concept of class politics was always divided between the proletariat understood as a class and the process of precarisation and fragmentation of workers.[38] The proletariat was always both a political identity and the capitalist undermining of the collective unity and individual security necessary to constitute any identity. The fundamental point being that there is no institution or practice, economic, political, or social, that univocally constitutes a determinate transindividual individuation; each must pass through the other scene of symbolic identifications and subjections. Second, whereas Hegel could posit a linear progression through the various institutions, family, civil society, and the state, culminating in the recognition of universality, such a progression seems difficult to maintain today. This is both a theoretical and historical point. As Balibar argues, Marx's writing from the early critiques of Hegel to *Capital* interrupted Hegel's linear progression from particularity to universality.[39] Commodity fetishism is one name of this interruption, of the way in which the individual is interrupted in its progress from isolation to transindividuality, the recognition of the constitutive and necessary nature of collective relations. Rather than recognising oneself in the constitutive relations of transindividuality, these relations are fetishised, made into qualities of the commodity. Such a progression is also called into question by the historical experience of the twentieth century, which far from being one of the dissolution of violent particularity into universality, has been marked by the return of various forms of violent exclusion, of pre-modern limitations of the universality of the citizen.[40] Hegel's historical optimism, in which particularity is elevated to universality, violence to a new legal order, is one of the causalities of the long twentieth century.

Equaliberty, the universalisation of man and citizen, is thus a fragile and precarious constitution of the political. It is only one transindividual individuation among others, situated amongst different practices and relations that

---

37   The destruction of individuation brought about by the transformations of the labour process has become the central focus of the work of Bernard Stiegler (Stiegler 2017, p. 201).
      For how this conception of the short-circuit of transindividuation relates to the work of
      Balibar see Read 2015.
38   Balibar 1994, p. 127.
39   Balibar 2017b, p. 146.
40   Balibar 2015, p. 49.

both extend and threaten it. Politics are rare. The corollary of this is provocation that perhaps goes beyond Balibar's formulation. There is no reason to necessarily limit equaliberty to the citizen, to the instituted sphere of the state; there are practices of equaliberty that can be extended in and through the sites of production and social reproduction, transforming work and the family. As much as the citizen is threatened by other transindividual individuations, or by the destruction of individuation through the labour process, the fact that all identities, all subjects, are constituted transindividuality means that there is not one relation, one identity, that cannot be extended, or transformed by equaliberty. The intersection of equality and liberty can be articulated with the labour process, the family, or social relations, transforming them and being transformed in the process. As Yves Citton writes:

> Equaliberty is a matter of pressures, multiple, complex and often contradictory dynamics in which we must try to intervene to increase the share of real freedom enjoyed by all, limiting the tensions and distortions introduced by entrenched inequalities in which one only benefits at the expense of others.[41]

It is not a matter of returning to the citizen, or mourning its loss, but of constituting equaliberty in multiple relations, making it a part of the transindividual individuations that traverse political, economic, and social life.

---

41   Citton 2012, p. 107. My translation.

CHAPTER 20

Anthropocene and Anthropogenesis: Philosophical Anthropology and the Ends of Man

'Humanity', 'man', or 'anthropos' is once again a topic of discussion. Having somehow outlived its erasure as lines in the sand, as well as the proclamations of the post-human epoch, humanity has returned with a vengeance. The first point of return, and the most prominent, is in the push to label the current geological epoch the 'Anthropocene', an epoch in which the defining characteristic is humanity's effect on the environment: plants, animals, water, atmosphere, even the very bedrock have been transformed by agriculture, industry, and transportation. The concept or term Anthropocene has moved beyond the small circle of geologists who coined it to become an object of not only multiple disciplines, but politics as well. It might seem odd to identify the Anthropocene with the return of humanity, since anthropos, man, is primarily named as placeholder. The emphasis is on humanity's effect on the natural world, not on humanity as such, on humanity's putative essence. In contrast to this the second return to the anthropos is explicitly about the question of the human, of its particular anthropogenesis, or constitution; I am referring to the work of Paolo Virno. The recent works of Paolo Virno have taken up the question of human nature and its connection to politics. This turn is not a return to the designation of a human essence outside of history, but an understanding of the way in which the human is constituted, and constitutes itself, in and through specific institutions and practices. Such a turn is not without its precedents in the post-autonomist tradition; Antonio Negri and Michael Hardt wrote in *Empire* of a 'humanism after the death of man', in which 'humanity' is defined less as an essence than as an activity, a practice. Beyond this, a broader return to a political, or political economic, anthropology can be found in the work of Étienne Balibar and Bernard Stiegler. What, if anything, is the relationship between these two different invocations of the 'human', besides their appearing at the same time in different theoretical discourses? What do they have in common beyond a particular challenge to an old consensus that dictated that there is no humanity, no human nature as such, just different social constructions? Why is humanity, or human nature, returning at this point, and what does this return have to say about our need to rethink the contours of nature and society? Or, put more provocatively, why might the Anthropocene demand a reinterrogation of anthropogenesis, of the constitution of the human, and vice versa?

1   Prehistory of the Anthropocene

There are as many dates to mark the beginning of the Anthropocene as there are concepts of it; precisely when it begins already says something about how it is conceptualised. The question of periodising the Anthropocene raises the question of the anthropos, of humanity, albeit obliquely. If it is traced back to such events as the 'Megafauna Extinction' that wiped out the mastodon, giant sloth, and other creatures, then it is hard not to trace to something in humanity, some madness, driving us beyond territory and limit, but if it begins with the 'industrial revolution' then it is possible to call it the Capitalocene.[1] The question of when the Anthropocene begins is also a question of what it is, or what it is the effect of; if it begins with the megafauna extinction at the beginning of the Holocene, under radically different social and technical conditions, then it becomes possible, perhaps even necessary, to understand the Anthropocene as something that began with humanity as a species. In such a case, as in Kolbert's *The Sixth Extinction: An Unnatural History*, the story of this prehistorical mass-extinction is often coupled with the extinction of the Neanderthals. Taken together we get the impression of mankind as a species that spread far and wide, overcoming the barriers of ecological niche, precisely because of the lack of instinctual determinations. The Neanderthal, our close cousins, left no cave paintings, no culture, no artifice, and thus our eradication of the Neanderthal can be traced to our ability to create culture, to invent tools, and ways of managing the world.[2] By this logic, not only is the Anthropocene a product of human nature, stemming directly from our capacities as animals defined as either 'speaking' or 'tool-making', but also an effect of our nature. We are the species that lacks instinctual determination, open instead to the influence of culture and history, and thus we are the species that lacks any particular ecological niche. Focus on the lack of instinctual determination and ecological niche, the spread of homo sapiens across nearly every continent and across multiple ecosystems, does not just offer an explanation of the great extinctions of the mammoth and Neanderthal, it also explains the gradual transformations brought about by human migration and communication, both intentional, the transportation of crops from the old world to the new and vice versa, and unintentional, the introduction of the Norway rat to islands and continents.[3] Humanity since its emergence as a species has transformed nature. The Anthropocene is in some sense naturalised, we humans are not unlike a

1   Kolbert 2015, p. 44.
2   Scranton 2015, p. 31.
3   Kolbert 2014, p. 105.

meteor or a volcano, or, in the words of Agent Smith from *The Matrix*' 'a virus' infecting the planet.

From this periodisation, definitions of the Anthropocene end up duplicating definitions of the human, of the anthropos from philosophical anthropology. Two ideas are most relevant. First, humanity as a species is defined by lack of instinctual determination. This idea was developed most strongly by Arnold Gehlen, for whom humanity's openness, its capacity to develop language and culture, is primarily defined as a lack, as a lack of instinctual determination and organ specialisation. 'In terms of morphology, man, in contrast to all other higher mammals, is primarily characterised by deficiencies, which, in an exact, biological sense, qualify as lack of adaptation, lack of specialisation, primitive states, and failure to develop, and which are essentially negative features'.[4] Second, there is the idea developed by Andre Leroi-Gourhan that the defining feature of humanity is the externalisation of memory, habits, and knowledge in the form of tools, signs, and images.[5] This artificial memory supplants the missing instincts, tools replacing biological specialisation making possible the adaption to any ecosystem. This is the 'anthropos' remaining off-scene in most definitions of the Anthropocene, humanity as the undetermined and thus unlimited maker of tools and environments and transgressor of limits and transformer of nature.[6]

However, if we start with a later date, placing the Anthropocene with the industrial revolution and the world-transforming effects of the exploitation of fossil fuels, placing it not with the specific ecological effects of mankind's spread across the globe, and interspecies competition with other hominids, but within the effects of capitalism and industrialisation, the very nature of the anthropos in question changes as well. Such a periodisation is less about the essence of man, about mankind as a species, than the particular institutions of capitalism, industrial production, and fossil fuel use. The turn to fossil fuels unleashed potentials for work and movement unimaginable in agricultural society.[7] At the same time, the turn towards carbon in the ground as a source of fuel and energy deepens the 'metabolic rift', as carbon, nitrogen, and methane are unleashed from the ground but never returned.[8] The merits of such an explanation, tying the Anthropocene to capitalism and the rise of technology, is that it is less about a species than it is about particular economic

---

4   Gehlen 1980, p. 26.
5   Leroi-Gourhan 1993, p. 188.
6   Scranton 2015 p. 94.
7   Scranton 2015, p. 57.
8   Wark 2015, p. xiv.

and social structures, history rather than nature. Whereas the first periodisation suffers from an almost neo-Malthusian account of natural competition between species, the second renders the Anthropocene itself contingent, even historical. There is little that can be done to address the fundamental expansive and underdetermined nature of *Homo Sapiens* as a species, except perhaps to genetically modify it, or repress its necessarily rapacious nature, but capitalism as an institution can be replaced or at least transformed. It is not only less concerned with human nature; it places humanity outside of nature, as a destructive force.[9]

There are of course other dates, other periodisations: the Neolithic revolution, the birth of agriculture, etc., but the two selected above are remarkable in that they run the gambit of the nature/social divide. In the first the Anthropocene is a product of human nature, of our paradoxical status as a species that has no defined place or determined behavior; whereas, in the second, it is entirely the product of culture, of politics, of our existence as something outside of nature. These periodisations mirror the natural/social doublet, what Jason Moore calls 'Cartesian Dualism'. In the first, humanity and the Anthropocene are entirely a part of nature. Humanity becomes one more natural calamity affecting the surface of the earth, like an ice age or the eruption of a giant volcano. In the second, the Anthropocene is entirely artificial, social; it is a product of technology, capitalism, and industrialisation. Thus, what is played out in the different periodisations of the Anthropocene is nothing other than the entirely ambiguous status of humanity as a species at once internal and external to nature.[10] Moore argues that such a simple inclusion or opposition fails to grasp the actual relation between human society and nature. Moore replaces the simple inclusion or opposition of humanity and nature with what he refers to as the history of the double inclusion of humanity and nature.

> 'History', in this sense, is the history of a 'double internality': humanity-in-nature/nature in humanity. (And yes, there is a longer history of earth and all the rest that precedes humans.) In this double internality, everything that humans do is already joined with extra-human nature and the web of life: nature as a whole that includes humans.[11]

There is no nature as such, just different historically produced natures, but these natures are not produced by some society, industry, or capital, something

---

9   Moore 2015, p. 175.
10   Viveiros de Castro 2014, p. 44.
11   Moore 2015, p. 5.

outside of nature, but by a species (us) that is always simultaneously producing and produced by nature. Everything that we produce is nothing other than a reorganisation of existing natural properties, biological, chemical, and physical, and as such every social institution, every economy, must contend with the limits of these properties, including the limits of human nature itself. Humanity is not simply a part of nature or apart from it, but is produced and productive of nature.

Historicising this double inclusion means understanding the relationship between capitalism and nature; such an understanding demands moving beyond such concepts as commodification or exploitation. Capital must be understood as not just a mode of production, but as a way of organising nature, as process of both exploiting labour power and appropriating nature. 'The first is premised on exploitation: abstract social labor/capital and wage labor. The second is premised on appropriation: abstract social nature/capital and unpaid work/energy'.[12] In positing such a double relation, Moore takes his initial bearings from feminist critiques of Marx. As Silvia Federici, Mariarosa Dalla Costa, and others argued, the exploitation of waged labour power does not constitute the entirety of capitalism as social relation.[13] Such exploitation is only possible, only profitable, if it is founded on the appropriation of the unpaid work of reproduction, housework, care work, and the reproduction of children. It is this work that keeps labour power functioning, and functioning cheaply, reducing the cost of necessary labour and thus increasing surplus labour. Contrary to the tendency towards full commodification, the more labour power can be replaced cheaply, by unwaged work and noncommodified nature, the more it is profitable for capital. Moore extends this principle to argue that the capitalist exploitation of labour is dependent on cheap nature, cheap labour power (made cheap by unpaid housework), cheap food (made cheap by agricultural revolutions), and cheap fuel (made cheap by failures to pay for its larger costs). It is not just reproductive work, the work of housework, that keeps labour costs low, it is also cheap food and energy. Of course the 'cheapness' of these various commodities is not fixed, and the changing costs of nature explain capital's transformation from agricultural production to industrial production, as well as the shift from coal to oil, and so on. Capital must find new cheap natures to reproduce the ones that are exhausted or used up. In order to understand this, it is necessary to understand what drives the cost of nature, at what point it ceases to be cheap.

---

12   Moore 2015, p. 214.
13   Dalla Costa and James 1972, p. 27.

The cheapness of various natures is often the cumulative effect of millennia of biological and physical processes. The vast nitrogen stores that have made possible the various 'breadbaskets' of civilisation, and the buried carbon of the various fossil fuels, cannot be reproduced in human history. Their appropriation constitutes a kind of ecological primitive accumulation, an initial exploitation that makes capitalisation possible. As with the reproduction of labour power in the home, what makes these natural processes cheap is simply that they are not paid for, or, put differently, there is no attention paid to their reproduction and to the negative effects of their appropriation. These factors lead to increasing costs of production: nature gets less cheap.[14] This rising cost is in part due to the way that nature is appropriated; cheapness comes at a cost of not including negative effects or long-term costs of reproduction, but it also comes from capital's own tendencies toward commodification and subsumption. As much as capital relies on the uncommodified labour of reproduction and the uncommodified nature that constitutes the basis for cheap nature, it also tends towards the capitalisation of reproduction, commodifying the uncommodified world of nature. Capital is divided between its tendency to rely on cheap nature, on an outside of wage labour and commodities that it ceaselessly appropriates, and its tendency to subsume more and more of life, commodifying needs and transforming the social relations that exist outside of it into jobs.[15] The first keeps labour costs low, but the second provides the conditions for realising the value that is produced. Capital destroys the very uncommodified ground it stands on, constantly seeking new territories, new cheap natures.

Moore's account of capitalism, of its history and dynamic, is in part one of competing and conflicting tendencies, commodification and appropriation, the exploitation of labour power against the appropriation of energy. In that sense, it is a capital doomed by its own contradictions. At the same time, however, this contradiction between tendencies, between cheap nature and commodification, is itself the effect of another contradiction, a contradiction between the nature that is internal to its historical production, and the nature that is in excess of it. It is a contradiction between the nature that is produced, and the natural limit of that production. As Moore writes, 'At some level, all life rebels against the value/monoculture nexus of modernity, from farm to factory. No one, no being, wants to do the same thing, all day, every day. Hence, the struggle over the relation between humans and the rest of nature is necessarily

---

14   Moore 2015, p. 120.
15   Moore 2015, p. 238.

a class struggle'.[16] Capital comes up against the limits of not only its own conflicting tendencies, but against the limits of nature itself; or, more to the point,
these limits are themselves intertwined. Nature is always more than the nature
that is historically produced, hence the double internality: nature is inside of
history, constituting different 'natures' in terms of agriculture, fossil fuel extraction, genetic manipulation, etc., but history is also inside of nature, inside of
processes that exceed it. As much as capital can be identified with the process
of creating abstract social nature, a nature which can be mapped, quantified
in units, and thus extracted, nature exceeds this. There are always externalities
that are not included in this abstraction, qualities not quantified and costs not
included in the price.

Moore's formulation here is provocative to say the least, on two counts. First
it posits a 'life' that is something other than the abstract nature required by capital, but this life is not conceived of in primarily vitalist terms, but as itself an
instance of class struggle. One could argue that Moore's thesis returns us to the
earliest readings of Marx, to alienation, to the idea of something in humanity
that resists its transformation into labour power, only now alienation is expanded to include the natural and animal worlds as well. It is not just human life
that resists being made into a means of mere life, of abstract labour power, but
all of life that resists being transformed into calories and kilowatts, energy and
fuel. It is a non-humanist concept of alienation in that it extends the very problem of alienation beyond the human.[17] However, Moore insists that this resistance must be thought of as not just the intractable excess of life over its measure and utility, but as class struggle. Which is to say as something organised, as
something other than the natural limits of life. Moore's critique of 'Cartesian
dualism' means that neither 'nature' or 'society' can be used as an explanatory
principle, either of the Anthropocene or of the limits to capitalism. The Anthropocene is neither an effect of a rapacious and unlimited species, humanity, nor
is it the effect of an unnatural technology upon nature, but the intersection of
both. Or put differently, the limit of capital is nature, but not nature as such
but nature's inability to completely coincide with cheap nature, living labour
with abstract labour. These limits, like capital itself, must be thought of as both
natural and social. As Timothy Mitchell argues, the shift from coal to oil as an
energy source is driven as much by the political struggle over conditions of

---

16   Moore 2015, p. 205.
17   In a similar manner Barbara Noske has referred to the conditions of animals in factory
      farming and industrial activity as an 'alienation from species life,' as a loss of such species
      specific characteristics as communication, hierarchy, and social existence (Noske 1997,
      20).

extraction as by the natural limits of particular fossil fuels. Coal requires a mass of workers, and the means of extraction make strikes incredibly disruptive. Oil, by contrast, requires fewer workers, and can be shipped and stockpiled easily, thus implying a necessarily diffuse form of struggle.[18]

2   Natural/Historical

What I referred to above as the anthropology underlying the Anthropocene was, by and large, implicit and unstated. Writers and thinkers on the Anthropocene are primarily concerned with theorising the environmental, ecological, and even geological effects of mankind's activity on earth, not with understanding what this implies for a definition of humanity. However, as we have seen with Moore, accounts of the Anthropocene reproduce the 'natural/social' divide, placing man on one side or the other, either as part of nature or outside of it. Despite Moore's critical points, he does not develop specifically what the Anthropocene means for human nature. It would seem then that the Anthropocene also demands a new understanding of anthropos, of humanity as something irreducible to nature, a dominant species or natural calamity, or society, an artificial order imposed on nature from the outside. Paolo Virno has taken up this problem from a different angle, one not associated with capital's exploitation of nature, but its relationship with human nature. Despite these differences it has strong points of intersection with Moore's notion of double internality.

For Virno humanity is defined by particular attributes that can best be defined as Natural-Historical. The capacity for language, for developing new customs, habits, and fashions, all have at their basis particular natural or species-specific qualities. Language is dependent upon the mental and physical characteristics of human beings, the formation of the tongue and lips as well as speech centres in the brain, while habits and clothing too have a natural basis in the lack of instinctual determination of behavior or need for shelter and protection from the elements. Despite the natural basis of these activities, or faculties, their actualisation is not determined by nature itself. Nothing in nature dictates a particular language, a particular set of customs, or that a particular fashion should come to pass; such things are part of the contingency and conflict of history. History is not just the actualisation of these potentials, the resolution of possibility into fact, but carries with it the generic capacity. The

---

18   Mitchell 2011, p. 21.

capacity for speech is in every utterance, the capacity to form habits in every sedimented behaviour. As Virno writes with respect to language,

> The difference between the faculty of language and historically determined languages confers an institutional tonality upon the natural life of our species; this difference, far from healing itself, persists even into adulthood, making itself evident every time someone produces an utterance. It is exactly this difference that implies an extremely strong connection between biology and politics, between *zoon logon ekon* and *zoon politikon*.[19]

Moreover, these faculties are not attributes of the individual human animal, nor could they be. Language, habits, customs, fashion, only exist in relation with others, they are necessarily transindividual. These attributes are not faculties of the individual mind, but potential of humanity as a species, part of species being, to use Marx's term. The individual's utterance, gesture, and action is situated between a preindividual condition, the capacity for speech, habits, and custom, and its transindividual articulation.

Virno's philosophical anthropology could then be considered part of a general revival of the anthropological question, a revival that includes Étienne Balibar and Bernard Stiegler. This revival is best considered 'post-anthropological', in that humanity, the essence of humanity, is defined in such a way that it exists only in its specific historical articulations. Such an anthropology can be considered a variant of the sixth of Marx's *Theses on Feuerbach*, which defines the human essence as existing only in and through the ensemble of social relations.[20] The essence of humanity is less something outside of history, than something that can be thought only in its singularity, relationality, and historicity. The very things that define humanity, constituting its particular anthropogenesis, the capacity for language, habits, and culture, exist only in and through the historical ensemble of social relations. Virno maintains the general idea of humanity as undetermined and open to cultural reinvention, a defining characteristic of the history of philosophical anthropology. Where Virno differs from this field is in his insistence that this nature must be thought in its specific historical articulation. Human nature is its history.

It is possible to consider Virno's philosophical anthropology as a kind of anthropology for the Anthropocene. It runs the gambit between the generic

---

19   Virno 2008, p. 47.
20   Balibar 2017b, p. 130.

species definition of man, man as the creature unmoored from any instinctual determination and thus an environment, a creature that constitutes its own habits, signs, and references, and the specific organisation of those capacities that constitute the institutions of capitalism. In this way Virno's 'historico-natural' has strong parallels with Moore's concept of the double internality of nature in history and history in nature. It could even be considered the anthropological corollary of the latter. They are both, in a certain sense, variants of a kind of natural history in which nature exists and only exists in its historical articulation. As Virno writes, 'Natural history inventories the way in which human beings experience human nature'.[21] In each case, nature exists only as it is both articulated in, and the limit of, a specific historical manifestation. Nature is nothing other than its unfolding in history, and history is nothing other than particular articulations of nature.

However, as much as those parallels exist, there are important differences as well, differences that stem from two added dimensions of Virno's analysis. First, as much as Virno asserts the 'historico-natural' as a general anthropological principle, as the intersection between nature and history, biology and culture, he argues that the intersection of the historical and natural takes on a particular valence in capitalism. This valence takes two forms, or two articulations; the first is part of the general definition of capitalism, its formal conditions of selling labour power, while the second is with its contemporary exploitation of communication and services. With respect to the former, what capital buys is not individuals, or even the capacity to perform a delimited task, but labour power, the capacity to do work. With capitalism the discrepancy between potential and act, generic capacity and its specific manifestation, 'becomes a historical fact'.[22] This is true of capital from its inception. Real subsumption, or contemporary capitalism, only intensifies this relation. Contemporary capitalism no longer exploits labour power as the physical capacity to do work, or to engage in a definite and repeated task, contemporary labour exploits the very capacity to learn new habits, develop new thoughts and ideas. It does not exploit existing habits, utterances, and statements so much as it exploits the very capacity to create and learn new ones. As Virno writes,

> What matters is not what is progressively learned (roles, techniques, etc.) but the display of the pure power to learn, which always exceeds its par-

---

21   Virno 2009, p. 135.
22   Virno 2015a, p. 160.

ticular enactments. What's more, it is entirely evident that the permanent precarity of jobs, and even more the instability experienced by contemporary migrants, mirror in historically determinate ways the congenital lack of a uniform and predictable habitat. Precarity and nomadism lay bare at the social level the ceaseless and omnilateral pressure of a world that is never an environment.[23]

This is Virno's particular take on the concept of the 'general intellect'; for Virno the general intellect is less a particular subset of knowledge put to work in the production of knowledge, images, and social relations, as it is 'the intellect in general', the general capacity to learn and communicate.[24] This not only liberates the general intellect from any attachment to specific labours, or any specific vanguard, but it brings this contemporary concept back to the very basis of history. Contemporary capitalism, the capitalism of services, precarity and mobility, is not just one historical articulation of the actualisation of these natural capacities, but is, in some sense, the exploitation of these very capacities.

> Human nature returns to the centre of attention not because we are finally dealing with biology rather than history, but because the biological prerogatives of the human animal have acquired undeniable historical relevance in the current productive process.[25]

Previous societies, even earlier stages of capital, were grounded upon the production and reproduction of a particular set of habits, concepts, and comportments, but with capitalism, all that is solid melts into air, and what comes to light is not this or that habit, but the very capacity of gaining (and losing) them. Virno's argument is a variant of the precapitalist/capitalist divide found in Marx and Engels's *Manifesto*, in which capitalism is identified with abstraction and indifference that causes all that is solid to melt into air. The important difference is that for Virno this difference between capitalism and precapitalism takes on an anthropological, or even biological significance; capitalism is the direct exploitation of anthropogenesis. It puts to work the very capacity to learn new habits, to adopt new characteristics, which is the paradoxical artifice that is human nature.

---

23   Virno 2009, p. 143.
24   Virno 2004, p. 66.
25   Virno 2009, p. 142.

It is at this point that Virno's argument comes very close to asserting, in its own strange way, that capitalism is human nature. Or that, in capitalism, all the various codes, or norms of society, are stripped bare, and humanity is left face to face with the natural fact of anthropogenesis, with its own potential. However, as much as Virno asserts a significant mutation in the intersection between nature and history at the heart of capitalism, this is not an identity. Human capacities, the capacity for speech, custom, and habit, precisely as capacities, can never be actualised, can never be realised as such. There must be an irreducible difference between mankind's capacities and their actualisation in any historical formation. 'Potential does not, as such, fall in time'.[26] The capacity for speech, labour power, and the intellect in general can become more manifest, clearer in their indeterminacy and creative dimension, but can never become directly present in history. Even as one sells one's potential to learn new habits, new languages, and ways of thinking, one can never actually put to work potential as such. As much as one sells labour power, one is engaged in effective labour: as much as one puts to work the general intellect, it is actualised in specific forms of labour. Knowledge as such can never be a productive force, just as abstract labour must always be concretised. For Virno the very exploitation of the generic capacity in the present social relations leads to a kind of confusion; the present moment is taken not as an instantiation of the generic faculty, one other historical articulation of its condition, but of the manifestation of the generic faculty itself. Virno compares this historical confusion with the temporal confusion of déjà vu. Virno argues that the experience of déjà vu is best understood from the perspective of Henri Bergson, from the memory that is internal to the experience of the present. Memory, the very possibility of temporal experience, is integral to every actual temporal experience.[27] Déjà vu confuses this memory that makes the present possible with a memory of the present. Rather than memory being a condition of the present, it seems as if the present itself is being remembered. The faculty is manifest not as a potential, but is confused with a fact. This psychological confusion explains, or is analogous to, our historical confusion in which the current historical organisation of language, thought, and habit, appears as the manifestation of the very capacity for thought, language and habit. Déjà vu and our historical condition are both defined by the apparent presence of what is a potential. The condition of memory appears as a memory, the condition of history appears in history. The end of history is analogous to a cultural déjà vu. As Virno writes,

---

26   Virno 2015a, p. 68.
27   Virno 2015a, p. 17.

To put it another way: the spectacle is the form that the déjà vu takes, as soon as this becomes an exterior, public form beyond one's own person. The society of the spectacle offers people the 'world's fair' of their own capacity to do, to speak, and to be – but reduced to already-performed actions, already-spoken phrases and already-complete events.[28]

Or, put differently, everything appears to be already done, to be said, or thought. Capital appears to offer everything, or at least the possibility of offering everything. The immense accumulation of commodities is but an immense accumulation of experiences and capacities.

To risk an immediate connection to the Anthropocene, it is possible to see this historical déjà vu, this misrecognition of the current social relation, as nothing other than the full realisation of humanity, to explain one of the difficulties in coming to grips with the Anthropocene. Roy Scranton has argued that we will never deal with the Anthropocene unless we as a society learn how to die, how to accept that this way of life, carbon-fuelled and based on high levels of consumption, cannot go on.[29] Virno's concept of déjà vu helps us understand why this is so difficult. If the current historical condition appears to us as the very realisation of humanity as such, of our potential, desires, and activities, then any transformation of it would necessarily seem like a destruction of human nature. We can only imagine getting out of the Anthropocene by some repression of our needs, desires, and potential. We have made this particular organisation of nature our environment, and are unable to imagine a life or a humanity outside of it. To cite the often repeated phrase from Fredric Jameson, it is easier to imagine the end of the world than the end of capitalism because the end of the latter seems like the end of the former to us. If nature, including human nature, only appears in particular historical moments, then those moments, the particular organisation of nature, can always appear as nature itself.

3 Politics of Renaturalisation/Historicisation

What then does Virno's concept of anthropogenesis offer the idea of the Anthropocene? I imagine that many would argue that it is beside the point. That the Anthropocene is not really a matter of 'anthropos', of man, but what is

---

28   Virno 2015a, p. 55.
29   Scranton 2015, p. 207.

at stake in the concept of the Anthropocene is precisely what is happening to the natural world, the nonhuman. As we have seen, however, every concept of the Anthropocene hinges on a concept of man, of humanity, that is often wise enough to remain out of sight, whether this concept is in some sense about *Homo Sapiens* as a fundamentally rapacious species, or about man as the species that breaks with nature, creating an industrial revolution that is unnatural. Against this dualism of nature and history what is needed is an understanding of how the Anthropocene is both nature (including human nature) and history, including natural history. This explains both its contingency and stability: it is a historically specific, and thus non-necessary, organisation of human society, but as such it produces not only its own culture, its justification, but also its own nature, including human nature.

Moore argues that the limit that capital comes up against is the limit of cheap nature, this limit is not just the limit of fuels and calories, but the cheap labour of reproducible laboru power. This is the corollary of the statement that the resistance of nature to capital is a kind of class struggle. It is possible to consider the struggle over labour power as itself a struggle over nature, over the attempt to make human nature repeatable, flexible, and abstract; or, alternately, it is just as possible to consider the limitation of different strategies of the appropriation of nature as class struggle, to see conflict in the appropriation of the earth. We are part of nature, and nature is part of history. Moore's analysis, or, more to the point, his terminological linking of class struggle and alienation across the natural and human divide, makes possible a new way of conceptualising the struggle against capital. Workers' struggle and the ecological struggle would not be two separate struggles with their own different logics and underlying ontologies. They are linked through the similar themes of exhaustion, the limits of reproduction, and the demand for life beyond abstract nature.

As much as Moore pushes class struggle and alienation beyond the nature/society divide, seeing both in nature, we might ask what remains of fetishism and ideology, those concepts that Marxist thought has used to explain the barriers to revolution, to seeing beyond the nature/society divide. As Moore argues, human thought is embodied in the web of life, and this must include its mystifications as well as its realisations.[30] Virno offers another way of thinking this connection, of arguing why we cannot imagine a possible solution to our ecological peril, and seem so oddly content to continue living out each day until the seas rise, the oceans die, and the soil blows away. We have confused this particular organisation of our capacities with their very existence. Capital

---

30   Moore 2015, p. 195.

does not just appear as one historical organisation of our desires, but as their very condition. The current historical conditions appear as the conditions of any history whatsoever. Of course one could argue that this has always been the case, that every historical formation has imagined its conditions to be the eternal conditions of any social formation. However, where capital differs from this general foreclosure of the historical imagination is that the confusion here has to do with capital's proximity to the generic conditions of existence, that it does not elicit specific beliefs or practices but exploits the very capacity or potential to act, speak, and create habits. It is capital's abstraction from the specificity of belief and norms, its ability to act on the potential for norms and belief, that make it so pervasive. That with capital 'all that is holy is profaned, and all that is solid melts into air' is an observation as old as the *Communist Manifesto*, but one in need of revisiting. Whereas Marx understood capitalism's destruction of beliefs, prejudices, and hallowed ideals to be part of its eventual demise, exploitation become manifest, it is necessary to understand how capital sustains itself precisely through its abstraction from specific beliefs and norms. Virno's philosophical anthropology in many ways addresses this question, arguing that the capitalist mode of production appears to be identical with human nature. Capital is human nature, but not in the sense that it realises some naturally existing drive towards competition, but because it appropriates and exploits the very thing that defines our status as human, putting our anthropogenesis to work.

What connects these two is the recognition that we, our thoughts, are part of nature too. If we are natural and historical then our actions, including our reflections, fears and actions are not something outside of the economy, or the existing historical articulation of nature, but part of its organisation. Moore offers a way to reorganise our hopes and desires. Moore's explanatory analysis of the intersection of capital and nature, the worker who can barely make it through another day, the parent exhausted by the demands of caring for children, and the ocean on the point of crisis, can be seen as the struggle of different 'cheap natures' against their appropriation and exploitation. Moore's theoretical articulation of the intersection of capital and nature can thus become a basis for redrawing lines of struggle. What Virno reminds us, however, is that our thoughts and ideas are already part of nature, part of the mode of production. Capitalism captures not just a specific set of habits, puts to work not just a specific set of words and beliefs, but the very capacity to form habits and interact through language. It exploits our very potential as potential. It appears to us as the only possible way to live, as the fullest realisation of our potential. If capitalism organises nature, then we have to take seriously its ability to organise human nature as well, ultimately appearing as the fullest realisation of human capacities. We are internal to the system in both our resistance and subjection; this fact constitutes both the limit of transformation and its necessity. If the Anthropocene can in part be understood as a kind of multiplication of natural limits, as oceans, the atmosphere, and various ecosystems reveal their irreducibility to abstract nature, to nature for capital, than anthropogenesis can in part explain why resistance to capital is found more on the side of nature than culture. Nature is surprisingly resistant, and we ourselves are incredibly inert. Humanity has demonstrated an amazing ability to not only adapt to the existing demands of capitalist exploitation, but see that adaptation as activity, as new possibilities for activity and entrepreneurism, to borrow two words. As Jonathan Crary writes,

> Now there are numerous pressures for individuals to reimagine and refigure themselves as being of the same consistency and values as the dematerialized commodities and social connections in which they are immersed so extensively. Reification has proceeded to the point where the individual has to invent a self-understanding that optimizes or facilitates their participation in digital milieus and speeds.[31]

This adaptation is partial to say the least, affecting only those in the countries and cities most subject to the neoliberal transformations, and it might even be temporary – perhaps the atmosphere of acquiescence and complacency can change with the change of the Earth's atmosphere. Perhaps we too will show our resistance to be transformed into abstract nature. Until that moment, however, thinking anthropogenesis in the Anthropocene is a matter of thinking that we, abstract labour, are less resistant than the appropriation of nature.

Moore offers a powerful way of linking together resistance of the capitalist exploitation of work with the capitalist appropriation of nature, recognising that both are struggles of a nature irreducible to its abstraction and appropriation.[32] Virno reminds us that we, humanity, are the weak link in this chain of struggles; our nature is malleable, not only less resistant to its abstraction but an active agent. If this seems too pessimistic, it is important to remember that the flipside of this reorganisation of our nature is the increase in its communicative potential, of the general intellect. The points of resistance might be scattered, but they now have an increased capacity for communication.

---

31   Crary 2013, p. 100.
32   Along these lines, Yves Citton has offered an interesting and provocative way of thinking together the 'unsustainable' nature of economic, ecological, and media practices (Citton 2012, p. 13).

Bibliography

Adorno, Theodor 1974, *Minima Moralia: Reflections from Damaged Life*. Translated by Edmund Jephcott, New York: Verso.

Adorno, Theodor 1972, *Negative Dialectics*. Translated by E.B. Ashton. New York: Continuum.

Adorno, Theodor 2000, *Introduction to Sociology*. Translated by Christoph Gödde and Edmund Jephcott. Stanford: Stanford University.

Albiac, G. 1996. Spinoza/Marx: le sujet construit. In *Architectures de la raison: mélanges offerts à Alexandre Matheron*, 11–17. Edited by A. Matheron and P.F. Moreau. Saint Cloud: ENS Editions Fontenay.

Alliez, Eric and Michel Feher 1987, *The Luster of Capital*. Translated by Alyson Waters. *Zone* 1/2.

Alliez, Éric and Maurizio Lazzarato 2016, *Guerres et Capital*. Paris: Éditions Amsterdam.

Althusser, Louis 1969, *For Marx*. Translated by Ben Brewster. London: New Left.

Althusser, Louis 1970, 'The Object of *Capital*'. Translated by Ben Brewster, in Louis Althusser and Etienne Balibar, *Reading Capital*. London: New Left.

Althusser, Louis 1971, *Lenin and Philosophy, and Other Essays*. Translated by Ben Brewster. New York, Monthly Review.

Althusser, Louis 1972, *Montesquieu, Rousseau, Marx: Politics and History*. Translated by Ben Brewster. New York: Verso.

Althusser, Louis 1976, *Essays in Self-criticism*. Translated by G. Lock. London: New Left Books.

Althusser, Louis 1979, *The Crisis of Marxism*. In *Power and Opposition in Post Revolutionary Societies*, 325–38. Translated by G. Locke. London: Ink Links.

Althusser, Louis 1990a, 'Marxism Today'. In *Philosophy and the Spontaneous Philosophy of the Scientists*. Translated by James Kavanagh. New York: Verso.

Althusser, Louis 1990b, 'Philosophy and the Spontaneous Philosophy of the Scientists'. Translated by Warren Montag. In *Philosophy and the Spontaneous Philosophy of the Scientists*. New York: Verso.

Althusser, Louis 1990c, 'Is it Simple to be a Marxist in Philosophy?' In *Philosophy and the Spontaneous Philosophy of the Scientists and Other Essays*, 203–40. Translated by Graham Locke. Edited by Gregory Elliot. New York: Verso.

Althusser, Louis 1990d, 'The Transformation of Philosophy'. In *Philosophy and the Spontaneous Philosophy of the Scientists*. Translated by G. Locke. New York: Verso.

Althusser, Louis 1994a, 'Le courant souterrain du matérialisme de la rencontre'. In *Écrits philosophiques et politiques*, vol. 1, 539–579. Paris: Stock/IMEC.

Althusser, Louis 1994b. 'Marx dans ses limites'. In *Écrits philosophiques et politiques*, vol. 1, 349–530. Paris: Stock/IMEC.

Althusser, Louis 1994c, *Sur la philosophie*. Paris: Gallimard.

Althusser, Louis 1995, *Sur la reproduction*. Paris: PUF.

Althusser, Louis 1995a, Du côté de la philosophie (cinquième Course de philosophie pour scientifiques), in *Écrits philosophiques et politiques*, vol. 2. Paris: Stock/IMEC, 1995.

Althusser, Louis 1995b, 'Notes sur la philosophie (1967–8)', in *Écrits philosophiques et politiques*, vol. 2. Paris: Stock/IMEC, 1995.

Althusser, Louis 1997, 'The Only Materialist Tradition, Part I: Spinoza'. Translated by T. Stolze. In *The New Spinoza*, edited by T. Stolze and W. Montag. Minneapolis: University of Minnesota.

Althusser, Louis 1999, *Machiavelli and Us*. Translated by G. Elliot. New York: Verso.

Althusser, Louis 2003, *The Humanist Controversy and Other Writings*. Translated by G.M. Goshgarian, edited by François Matheron. New York: Verso.

Althusser, Louis 2006a. *Politics et Histoire de Machiavel à Marx: Cours à l'École Normale Supérieure, 1955–1972*. Paris: Seuil.

Althusser, Louis 2006b, 'The Underground Current of the Materialism of the Encounter'. In *The Philosophy of the Enounter: Later Writings, 1978–1987*. Translated by G.M. Goshgarian. New York: Verso. Originally published as 'Le courant souterrain du matérialisme de la rencontre'. In *Écrits philosophiques et politiques*, vol. 1. Paris: Stock/IMEC, 1994.

Althusser, Louis 2014a, *Initiation à la Philosophie Pour Les Non-Philosophes*. Paris: Presse Universitaires de France.

Althusser, Louis 2014b, *On the Reproduction of Capitalism: Ideology and Ideological State Apparatuses*. Translated by G.M. Goshgarian. New York: Verso.

Althusser, Louis and Étienne Balibar 1965, *Lire le Capital*. Paris: Editions Découverte,

Althusser, Louis and Étienne Balibar 1970, *Reading Capital*. Translated by B. Brewster. London: New Left Books

Anderson, Perry 1974, *Lineages of the Absolutist State*. New York: Verso.

Badiou, Alain 1993, 'Qu'est-ce que Louis Althusser entend par "philosophie"?' In *Politique et philosophie dans l'oeuvre de Louis Althusser*. Edited by Sylvan Lazarus. Paris: Press Universitaires de France.

Badiou, Alain 1999, *Manifesto for Philosophy*. Translated by Normal Madarasz. Albany: State University of New York.

Badiou, Alain 2005, *Metapolitics*. Translated by J. Barker. New York, Verso.

Balibar, Étienne 1985, 'Intellectuels, idéologues, idéologie: quelques reflexions'. *Raison Presente*, 73.

Balibar, Étienne 1991, 'Class Racism'. Translated by Chris Turner. In Étienne Balibar and Immanuel Wallerstein, *Race, Nation, Class: Ambiguous Identities*. London: Verso.

Balibar, Étienne 1994a. *Althusser's object*. Translated M. Cohen and B. Robbins. *Social Text*. 3, 157–8 (Summer) 39.

Balibar, Étienne 1994b, 'Rights of Man and Rights of the Citizen: The Modern Dialectic of Equality and Freedom'. In *Masses, Classes, Ideas: Studies on Politics and Philosophy before and after Marx*. Translated by James Swenson. New York: Routledge.

Balibar, Étienne 1994c, 'The Vacillation of Ideology in Marxism'. In *Masses, Classes, Ideas: Studies on Politics and Philosophy before and after Marx*. Translated by James Swenson. New York: Routledge, 1994c.

Balibar, Étienne 1995. 'The infinite contradiction'. Translated by J.M. Poisson with J. Lezra. In 'Depositions: Althusser, Balibar, Macherey, and the labor of reading', *Yale French Studies*, 142–65, 88.

Balibar, Étienne 1996, 'Structural causality, overdetermination, and antagonism'. In *Postmodern Materialism and the Future of Marxist Theory*. Edited by A. Callari and D. Ruccio, 109–120. Hanover: Wesleyan.

Balibar, Étienne 1997a, 'Jus, Pactum, Lex: On the Constitution of the Subject in the *Theologico-Political Treatise*'. Translated by Ted Stolze. In *The New Spinoza*. Minneapolis: Minnesota.

Balibar, Étienne 1997b, *Spinoza: From Individuality to Transindividuality*. Rijnsburg: Eburon.

Balibar, Étienne 1998. *Spinoza and politics*. Translated by J. Swenson. New York: Verso.

Balibar, Étienne 2002a, '"Possessive Individualism" Reversed: From Locke to Derrida'. *Constellations*. Volume 9, Number 3.

Balibar, Étienne 2002b, 'Violence, Ideality, and Cruelty'. Translated by James Swenson. In *Politics and the Other Scene*, New York: Verso.

Balibar, Étienne 2002c, 'Three Concepts of Politics: Emancipation, Transformation, Civility'. Translated by C. Turner. In *Politics and the Other Scene*. London: Verso.

Balibar, Étienne 2004, *We, the People of Europe? Reflections on Transnational Citizenship*. Translated by James Swenson. Princeton: Princeton University.

Balibar, Étienne 2014, *Equaliberty: Political Essays*. Translated by James Ingram Durham, NC: Duke University Press.

Balibar, Étienne 2015, *Violence and Civility: On the Limits of Political Philosophy*. Translated by G.M. Goshgarian, New York: Columbia.

Balibar, Étienne 2017a, *Citizen Subject: Foundations for Philosophical Anthropology*. Translated by Stephen Miller. New York: Fordham.

Balibar, Étienne 2017b, *The Philosophy of Marx*. Translated by Chris Turner and Gregory Elliot. New York: Verso.

Balibar, Étienne 2020a, *Passions du Concept: Épistémologie, théologie et politique: Écrits II*. Paris: La Découverte.

Balibar, Étienne 2020b, *On Universals: Constructing and Deconstructing Community*, Translated by Joshua David Jordan. New York: Fordham.

Benjamin, Walter 1978, 'Critique of Violence'. Translated by Edmund Jephcott. In *Reflec-*

tions: Essays, Aphorisms, Autobiographical Writings. Edited by Peter Demetz. New York: Schocken.

Berardi, Franco 'Bifo' 2009, *The Soul at Work: From Alienation to Autonomy.* Translated by Francesca Cadd and Giuseppina Mecchia. New York: Semiotext(e).

Berlant, Lauren 2001, *Cruel Optimism.* Durham, NC: Duke University Press.

Bove, Laurent 1996. *La stratégie du conatus: affirmation et résistance chez Spinoza.* Paris: Vrin.

Brown, Wendy 2005. 'Neoliberalism and the End of Liberal Democracy'. In *Edgework: Critical Essays on Knowledge and Politics.* Princeton, NJ: Princeton University.

Brown, Wendy 2006, 'American Nightmare: Neoliberalism, Neoconservatism, and De-Democratization'. *Political Theory*, 34/6.

Callari, A. and Ruccio, D.F. 1996. *Postmodern Materialism and the Future of Marxist Theory: Essays in the Althusserian Tradition.* Hanover: Wesleyan University Press.

Carré, L. 2014, 'Violence, institutions, "politique de la civilité": Étienne Balibar et les enjeux d'une "anthropologie politique"'. In *Pourquoi Balibar, Raison Publique*, 19 (Fall).

Chabot, Pascal 2013, *The Philosophy of Simondon: Between Technology and Individuation.* Translated by Graeme Kirkpatrick and Aliza Krefetz. London: Bloomington.

Citton, Yves 2006, *L'Envers de la liberté: L'invention d'un imaginaire spinoziste dans la France des Lumières.* Paris: Éditions Amsterdam.

Citton, Yves 2010, *Mythocratie: Storytelling et Imaginaire de Gauche.* Paris: Éditions Amsterdam.

Citton, Yves 2012a, *Gestes D'Humanités: Anthropologie sauvage de nos experiences esthetiques.* Paris: Armand Colin.

Citton, Yves 2012b, *Renverser L'insoutenable.* Paris: Seuil.

Citton, Yves and Frédéric Lordon 2008, *Spinoza et les sciences sociales: De la puissance de la multitude á l'économie des affects.* Paris: Éditions Amsterdam.

Combes, Muriel 2013, *Gilbert Simondon and the Philosophy of the Transindividual.* Translated by Thomas LaMarre. Cambridge: MIT.

Crary, Jonathan 2013, *24/7: Late Capitalism and the Ends of Sleep.* New York: Verso.

Dalla Costa, Mariorosa and Selma James 1972, *The Power of Women and the Subversion of the Community.* Bristol, England: Falling Wall.

Dardot, Pierre and Christian Laval 2013, *The New Way of the World: On Neoliberal Society.* Translated by Gregory Elliot. New York: Verso.

De Brunhoff, S. 1976 [1973], *Marx on Money.* Translated by M. Goldbloom. New York: Urizen.

De Angelis, Massimo 2007. *The Beginning of History: Value Struggles and Global Capital.* London: Pluto.

Deleuze, Gilles 1988a, *Foucault.* Translated by Sean Hand, Minneapolis: University of Minnesota Press.

Deleuze, Gilles 1988b [1970], *Spinoza: Practical Philosophy*. Translated by R. Hurley. San Francisco: City Lights.

Deleuze, Gilles 1990 [1969], *The Logic of Sense*. Translated by M. Lester and C. Stivale. New York: Columbia.

Deleuze, Gilles 1994 [1968]. *Difference and Repetition*. Translated by P. Patton. New York: Columbia.

Deleuze, Gilles 1995, 'Postscript on Control Societies'. Translated by M. Joughin in *Negotiations: 1972–1990*. New York: Columbia.

Deleuze, Gilles 1997, 'The Actual and the Virtual'. Translated by E.R. Albert. In *Dialogues II* by Gilles Deleuze and Claire Parnet. New York: Columbia.

Deleuze, Gilles 1997b, 'Spinoza's and the Three *Ethics*'. In *Essays Critical and Clinical*. Translated by D.W. Smith and M. Greco, Minneapolis: University of Minnesota.

Deleuze, Gilles 2004, *Desert Islands and Other Texts: 1953–1974*. Translated by M. Taormina. New York: Semiotexte.

Deleuze, G. and Foucault, M. 2004b. 'Intellectuals and Power'. Translated by Michael Taormina. In *Desert Islands and Other Texts (1953–1974)*. New York: Semiotext(e).

Deleuze, G. and Guattari, F. 1983, *Anti-Oedipus: Capitalism and Schizophrenia*. Translated by R. Hurley et al. Minneapolis: University of Minnesota.

Deleuze, G. and Guattari, F. 1987, *A Thousand Plateaus: Capitalism and Schizophrenia*. Translated by B. Massumi. Minneapolis: University of Minnesota.

Derrida, J. 1999, 'Marx & Sons'. Translated by G. Goushgarian. In *Ghostly Demarcations: A Symposium on Jacques Derrida's Specters of Marx*. Edited by Michael Sprinker. New York: Verso.

Descartes, R. 1985a. Objections and replies. In *The philosophical writings of Descartes*. Volume 2. Translated by J. Cottingham et al. Cambridge: Cambridge University Press.

Descartes, R. 1985b. 'Rules for the direction of the mind'. In *The philosophical writings of Descartes*. Volume 1. Translated by J. Cottingham et al. Cambridge: Cambridge University Press.

Federici, Silvia 2012, *Revolution at Point Zero: Housework, Reproduction, and Feminist Struggle*. Oakland: PM Press.

Fischbach, Franck 2002, *L'Être et l'acte: Enquête sur les fondements de l'ontologie modern de l'agir*. Paris: Vrin, 2002.

Fischbach, Franck 2005, *La production des hommes: Marx avec Spinoza*. Paris: PUF.

Fisher, Mark 2009, *Capitalist Realism: Is There No Alternative?* London: Zero Books.

Foucault, M. 1977, *Discipline and Punish: The Birth of the Prison*. Translated by A. Sheridan. New York: Vintage.

Foucault, M. 1978, *The History of Sexuality: Volume 1: An Introduction*. Translated by Robert Hurley. New York: Vintage.

Foucault, M. 1982, 'The Subject and Power'. Afterward to *Michel Foucault: Beyond Struc-*

turalism and Hermeneutics. By Hubert L. Dreyfus and Paul Rabinow. Chicago, IL: University of Chicago Press.

Foucault, M. 1994, 'Les mailles du pouvoir'. In *Dits et Ecrits Tome IV: 1980–1988*. Edited by D. Defert and F. Ewald, 182–201. Paris: Editions Gallimard.

Foucault, M. 1997. *'Il Faut Défendre la Société' Cours au Collège de France 1976*. Paris: Editions Gallimard,

Foucault, M. 2000, *Truth and juridical forms*. Translated by R. Hurley. In *The essential works of Michel Foucault, 1954–1984*. Volume 3. Edited by P. Rabinow. 1–90. New York: New Press.

Foucault, M. 2008. *The Birth of Biopolitics: Lectures at the Collège de France, 1978–1979*. Translated by Graham Burchell. New York: Palgrave Macmillan, 2008.

Gehlen, Arnold 1980, *Man in the Age of Technology*. Translated by Patricia Lipscomb, New York: Columbia.

Goldstein, P. 2004. 'Between Althusserian science and Foucauldian materialism: The later work of Pierre Macherey'. *Rethinking Marxism* 16, 3: 327/37.

Gramsci, Antonio 1957, *The Modern Prince and Other Writings*. Translated by Louis Marks. New York: International.

Gramsci, Antonio 1971, *Selections from the Prison Notebooks*. Translated by Q. Hoare. New York: International.

Guéry, François and Didier Deleule 2014, *The Productive Body*. Translated and introduced by Philip Barnard and Stephen Shapiro, London: Zero.

Hardt, Michael and Antonio Negri 2000, *Empire*. Cambridge, USA: Harvard.

Hardt, Michael and Antonio Negri 2004, *Multitude: War and Democracy in the Age of Empire*. New York: Penguin.

Hardt, M. 1991, 'Translator's Foreword'. In *The Savage Anomaly: The Power of Spinoza's Metaphysics and Politics*. Minneapolis: University of Minnesota.

Hardt, M. 1993. *Gilles Deleuze: An Apprenticeship in Philosophy*. Minneapolis: University of Minnesota.

Harvey, David 2007. *A Brief History of Neoliberalism*. Oxford: Oxford University Press.

Haver, W. 1997, 'Queer Research; or, How to Practice Invention to the Brink of Intelligibility'. In *The Eight Technologies of Otherness*. Edited by S. Golding. New York: Routledge.

Hegel, G.W.F. 1977. *The Phenomenology of Spirit*. Translated by A.V. Miller, Oxford: Oxford.

Hegel, G.W.F. 1991a, *Elements of the Philosophy of Right*. Translated by H.B. Nisbet. Cambridge: Cambridge University.

Hegel, G.W.F. 1991b, *The Encyclopedia Logic*. Translated by T.F. Geraets et al. Indianapolis: Hackett.

Heller, Agnes 1984, *Everyday Life*. Translated by G.L. Campbell, New York: Routledge.

Henry, Michel 1982, *Marx: A Philosophy of Human Reality*. Translated by Kathleen McLaughlin. Bloomington, Indiana University Press.

Hindess, B. and Hirst, P. 1975, *Pre-capitalist modes of production*. New York: Routledge.

Holland, Eugene 1999, *Deleuze and Guattari's* Anti-Oedipus: *Introduction to Schizoanalysis*. New York: Routledge.

Horkheimer, Max and Theodor Adorno 1987, *Dialectic of Enlightenment*. Translated by John Cumming. New York: Continuum.

Jameson, Fredric 1980, *The Political Unconscious: Narrative as a socially symbolic Act*. Ithaca: Cornell.

Jameson, Fredric 1988, 'Marxism and Historicism'. In *The Ideologies of Theory: Essays 1971–1986, Volume 2: The Syntax of History*. Minneapolis: University of Minnesota.

Jameson, Fredric 1990, *Late Marxism: Adorno, or the Persistence of the Dialectic*. New York: Verso.

Jameson, Fredric 1991, *Postmodernism; Or, the Cultural Logic of Late Capitalism*. Durham, NC: Duke University Press.

Jameson, Fredric 1997, 'Marxism and Dualism in Deleuze'. *The South Atlantic Quarterly* 96: 3.

Jameson, Fredric 2010, *The Hegel Variations: On the Phenomenology of Spirit*. New York: Verso.

Keenan, Thomas 1997, *Fables of Responsibility: Aberrations and Predicaments in Ethics and Politics*. Stanford: Stanford University.

Kolbert, Elizabeth 2014, *The Sixth Extinction: An Unnatural History*. New York: Picador.

Laclau, Ernesto and Chantel Mouffe 1985, *Hegemony and Socialist Strategy*. London: Verso.

Laclau, Ernesto, Judith Butler and Slavoj Zizek 1985, *Contingency, Hegemony, Universality: Contemporary Dialogues on the Left*. London: Verso.

Laval, Christian 2007, *L'homme économique: Essai sur les racines du néolibéralisme*. Paris: Gallimard.

Lazarus, S. 1996, *Anthropologie du nom*. Paris: Seuil.

Lazzarato, Maurizio 2002, *Puissance de l'invention: La psychologie économique de Gabriel Tarde contre L'économique politique*. Paris: Les Empêcheurs de Penser en Rond.

Lazzarato, Maurizio 2004, *Les Révolutions du Capitalisme*. Paris: Les Empêcheurs de Penser en Rond.

Lazzarato, Maurizio 2009, *Expérimentations Politiques*. Paris: Éditions Amsterdam.

Lazzarato, Maurizio 2012, *The Making of Indebted Man: An Essay on the Neoliberal Condition*. Translated by Joshua David Jordan. New York: Semiotexte.

Lazzarato, Maurizio 2014, *Signs and Machines: Capitalism and the production of subjectivity*. Translated by Joshua David Jordan. New York: Semiotexte.

Lecercle, J. 2005, 'Deleuze, Guattari, and Marxism'. *Historical Materialism* 13:3.

Lecourt, D. 2001, *The mediocracy: French philosophy since the mid-1970s*. Translated by G. Elliot. New York: Verso.

Lefort, C. 1992, *The Political Forms of Modern Society: Bureaucracy, Democracy, Totalitarianism*. Translated by J.B. Thompson, Cambridge: MIT Press.

Lemke, Thomas 2002, 'Foucault, Governmentality, and Critique'. *Rethinking Marxism*, 14, 3.

Lordon, Frédéric 2002, *La Politique du Capitale*. Paris: Odile Jacob.

Lordon, Frédéric 2003, 'Revenir à Spinoza dans la conjoncturee intellectuelle présente', *L'Année de la regulation* 7, 149–68.

Lordon, Frédéric 2006, *L'intérêt souverain: Essai d'anthropologie économique spinoziste*. Paris: Editions La Découverte.

Lordon, Frédéric 2012, 'Derrière l'idéologie de la légitimité, la puissance de la multitude: Le *Traite Politique* comme théorie générale des institutiions sociales'. In *La Multitude Libre: Nouvelles lectures du Traite Politique*. Paris: Éditions Amsterdam.

Lordon, Frédéric 2013, *La Société des affects: pour un structuralism des passions*. Paris: Éditions du Seuil.

Lordon, Frédéric 2014, *Willing Slaves of Capital: Spinoza and Marx on Desire*. Translated by Gabriel Ash. New York: Verso. Originally published as Frédéric Lordon *Capitalisme, désir et servitude: Marx et Spinoza*, Paris: La fabrique éditions, 2010.

Lordon, Frédéric and André Orlean 2008, 'Genèse de l'État et Genèse de la monnaie: le modele de la potential multitudios'. In Yves Citton and Frédéric Lordon, *Spinoza et les sciences sociales: De la puissance de a multitude à l'économie des affects*. Paris: Éditions Amsterdam.

Lukács, G. 1971, *History and class consciousness: Studies in Marxist dialectics*. Translated by R. Livingstone. Cambridge: MIT.

Macherey, Pierre 1979, *Hegel ou Spinoza*. Paris: F. Maspéro.

Macherey, Pierre 1992, *Avec Spinoza: études sur la doctrine et l'histoire du spinozism* Paris: Presses universitaires de France.

Macherey, Pierre 1995, *Introduction à l'Éthique de Spinoza: La troisème partie, la vie affective*. Paris: Presses universitaires de France.

Macherey, Pierre 1997a, *Introduction à l'Éthique de Spinoza: La quatrième partie, la condition humaine*. Paris: Presses universitaires de France.

Macherey, Pierre 1997b, *Introduction à l'Éthique de Spinoza: La second partie la réalité mentale*. Paris: Presses universitaires de France.

Macherey, Pierre 1998a, *Introduction à l'Éthique de Spinoza: la première partie la nature des choses*. Paris: Presses universitaires de France.

Macherey, Pierre 1996, 'The Encounter with Spinoza'. Translated by M. Joughin. In *Deleuze: A Critical Reader*. Translated by P. Patton. Oxford: Blackwell Publishers, 139–61.

Macherey, Pierre 1998, *In a Materialist Way*. Translated by Ted Stolze, edited by Warren Montag. New York: Verso.

Macherey, Pierre 1999, *Histoires de dinosaure: faire de la philosophie 1965–1997*. Paris: Presses universitaires de France.

Macherey, Pierre 2009, 'Althusser and the Concept of the Spontaneous Philosophy of Scientists'. Translated by Robin Mackay. In *Parrhesia*, 6: 14–27.

Macherey, Pierre 2014, *Les Sujet des Normes*. Paris: Éditions Amsterdam.

Macherey, Pierre 2015, 'The Productive Subject'. Translated by Tijana Okić, Patrick King, and Cory Knudson. *Viewpoint Magazine* Online.

Machiavelli, N. 1994. *The Prince*. Translated by D. Wootton. Indianapolis: Hackett.

Marx, Karl 1861, 'The New-York Daily Tribune', https://www.marxists.org/archive/marx/works/1861/10/21.htm. Accessed 2 July 20222.

Marx, Karl 1963a, *The Eighteenth Brumaire of Louis Bonaparte*. New York: International.

Marx, Karl 1963b, *The Poverty of Philosophy*. Translated by unknown. New York: International.

Marx, Karl 1964, *The economic and philosophic manuscripts of 1844*. Translated by D. Struik. New York: International.

Marx, Karl 1970a. *Critique of Hegel's 'Philosophy of right'*. Translated by A. Jolin and J. O'Malley. Cambridge: Cambridge University Press.

Marx, Karl 1970b. *Theses on Feuerbach*. In *The German Ideology*. Translated and edited by C.J. Arthur. New York: International Publishers.

Marx, Karl 1973, *Grundrisse: Foundations of the critique of political economy*. Translated by M. Nicolaus. New York: Penguin.

Marx, Karl 1977, *Capital: A critique of political economy, Volume I*. Translated by B. Fowkes. New York: Penguin.

Marx, Karl 1978a [1843], 'On the Jewish Question'. In the *Marx/Engels Reader*. Edited by Robert Tucker. New York: Norton.

Marx, Karl 1981, *Capital: A critique of political economy, Volume III*. Translated by D. Fernbach. New York: Penguin.

Marx, Karl 1988, *Das Kapital. Werke Band 23*. Berlin: Dietz Verlag.

Marx, K. and Engels, F. 1955, *Selected Correspondence*. Edited by S.W. Ryanzkaya and translated by I. Lasker. Moscow: Progress Publishers.

Marx, K. and Engels, F. 1970. *The German Ideology*. Translated by C.J. Arthur. New York: International.

Marx, K. and Engels, F. 1978, *The Communist Manifesto. The Marx-Engels Reader*. Edited by R. Tucker. New York: Norton.

Massumi, Brian 1992. *A User's Guide to Capitalism and Schizophrenia: Deviations from Deleuze and Guattari*. Cambridge: MIT Press.

Massumi, Brian 2002, *Parables for the Virtual: Movement, Affect, Sensation*. Durham: Duke.

Matheron, Alexandre 1969, *Individu et Communauté chez Spinoza*. Paris: Les Editions de Minuit.

Matheron, Alexandre 1971, 'Le Traité Theologico-Politique vu par le jeune Marx'. *Cahier Spinoza*, 1: 159/212.

Mezzadra, Sandro 2018, *In the Marxian Workshop: Producing Subjects*. London: Rowman & Littlefield.

Mirowski, Philip 2013, *Never Let a Serious Crisis Go to Waste: How Neoliberalism Survived the Financial Meltdown*. New York: Verso.

Montag, Warren 1995, '"The soul is the prison of the body": Althusser and Foucault 1970/75'. Depositions: Althusser, Balibar, Macherey, and the labor of reading. *Yale French Studies*, 88: 53/78.

Montag, Warren 1996, 'Beyond force and consent: Althusser, Spinoza, Hobbes'. In *Postmodern Materialism and the Future of Marxist Theory*. Edited by A. Callari and D. Ruccio, 91–109. Hanover: Wesleyan.

Montag, Warren 1998, 'Althusser's nominalism: structure and singularity (1962–6)'. In *Rethinking Marxism*, 64–73. Volume 10, Number 3.

Montag, Warren 1999. *Bodies, masses, power: Spinoza and his contemporaries*. New York: Verso.

Montag, Warren 2003, *Louis Althusser*. London and New York: Palgrave-Macmillan.

Moore, Jason 2015, *Capitalism in the Web of Life: Ecology and the Accumulation of Capital*. New York: Verso.

Nealon, Jeffrey 2008, *Foucault Beyond Foucault: Power and its Intensification Since 1984*. Stanford, CA: Stanford University Press.

Negri, A. 1989, *The Politics of Subversion: A Manifesto for the Twenty-First Century*. Translated by J. Newell. Oxford: Polity.

Negri, Antonio 1991, *Marx beyond Marx: Lessons on the Grundrisse*. Translated by Harry Cleaver et al. New York: Autonomedia.

Negri, Antonio 1991a, *Marx Beyond Marx: Lessons on the Grundrisse*. Translated by H. Cleaver et al. New York: Autonomedia.

Negri, Antonio 1991b, *The Savage Anomaly: The Power of Spinoza's Metaphysics and Politics*. Translated by M. Hardt. Minneapolis: University of Minnesota.

Negri, Antonio 1995, 'On Gilles Deleuze and Félix Guattari, A Thousand Plateaus'. Translated by C. Wolfe. *Graduate Faculty Philosophy Journal*, 18:1.

Negri, Antonio 1996a, 'Notes on the evolution of the thought of the later Althusser'. Translated by Olga Vasile. In *Postmodern Materialism and the Future of Marxist Theory*. Edited by A. Callari and D. Ruccio, 51–69. Hanover: Wesleyan,

Negri, Antonio 1996b, 'Twenty theses on Marx: interpretation of the class situation today'. Translated by M. Hardt. In *Marxism Beyond Marxism*. Edited by S. Makdisi, C. Casarino, and R. Karl, 149–81. New York: Routledge.

Negri, Antonio 1997. 'Reliqua Desiderantur: A Conjecture for a Definition of the Concept of Democracy in the Final Spinoza'. Translated by T. Stolze. In *The New Spinoza*. Edited by T. Stolze and W. Montag. Minneapolis: University of Minnesota.

Negri, Antonio 1999a. *Insurgencies: Constituent Power and the Modern State*. Translated by M. Boscagli. Minneapolis: University of Minnesota.

Negri, Antonio 1999b. 'The Specter's Smile'. Translated by P. Dailey and C. Costantini. In *Ghostly Demarcations: A Symposium on Jacques Derrida's Specters of Marx*. Edited by M. Sprinker. New York: Verso.

Negri, Antonio 2003, 'Kairos, Alma Venus, Multitudo'. In *Time for Revolution*. Translated by M. Mandarini. New York: Continuum.

Negri, Antonio 2004. *Subversive Spinoza: (Un)contemporary Variations*. Translated by T. Murphy. Manchester: Manchester University.

Nietzsche, F. 1969, *Thus Spoke Zarathustra*. Translated by R.J. Hollingdale. New York: Penguin Books.

Noske, Barbara. 1997. *Beyond Boundaries: Humans and Animals*. Montreal: Black Rose Books.

Patton, P. 2000. *Deleuze and the Political*. New York: Routledge.

Pasquinelli, Matteo 2008, *Animal Spirits: A Bestiary of the Commons*. Rotterdam: NAi Publishers.

Perelman, M. 2000, *The Invention of Capitalism: Classical political economy and the secret history of primitive accumulation*. Durham: Duke.

Postone, Moishe 1996, *Time, Labour, and Social Domination: A Reinterpretation of Marx's Critical Theory*. Cambridge: Cambridge University.

Read, Jason 2003, *The Micro-politics of Capital: Marx and the Prehistory of the Present*. New York: SUNY Press.

Read, Jason 2016, *The Politics of Transindividuality*. Chicago: Haymarket, 2016

Ree, Jonathan 1978, 'Philosophy and the History of Philosophy' in *Philosophy and its Past*. Edited by J. Ree et al. New Jersey: Humanities.

Resnick, S. and R. Wolff 1987, *Knowledge and Class: A Marxian Critique of Political Economy*. Chicago: University of Chicago.

Rousseau, J.J. 1992, *Discourse on the Origin of Inequality*. Translated by D. Cress. Indianapolis: Hackett.

Scranton, Roy 2015, *Learning to Die in the Anthropocene: Reflections on the End of a Civilization*. San Francisco: City Lights.

Seltzer, Mark 1993, 'Serial Killers (1)'. In *Differences: A Journal of Feminist CulturalStudies*, 5, 1.

Sévérac, Pascal 2005, *Le devenir actif chez Spinoza*. Paris: Honoré Champion.

Sharp, Hasana 2011, *Spinoza and the Politics of Renaturalization*. Chicago: University of Chicago.

Sibertin-Blanc, Guillaume 2016, *State and Politics: Deleuze and Guattari on Marx*. Translated by Ames Hodges. New York: Semiotexte.

Silva, Jennifer M. 2013, *Coming Up Short: Working Class Adulthood in an Age of Uncertainty*. New York: Oxford.

Simondon, Gilbert 1958, *Du mode d'existence des objets techniques*. Paris: Aubier.

Simondon, Gilbert 1989, *L'individuation psychique et Collective*. Paris: Aubier.

Simondon, Gilbert 2005, *L'individuation à la lumière des notions de forme et d'informa-tion*. Grenobe: Jerome Million.

Simondon, Gilbert 2009, 'Technical Mentality'. Translated by Arne de Boever. *Parrhesia* 717–27.

Sloterdijk, Peter 1988, *Critique of Cynical Reason*. Translated by M. Eldred. Minneapolis: University of Minnesota.

Sohn-Rethel, Alfred 1978, *Intellectual and Manual Labor: A Critique of Epistemology*. Atlantic Highlands: Humanities Press.

Southwood, Ivor 2010, *Non-Stop Inertia*. Winchester, UK: Zero Books.

Spinoza, Baruch 1985. *Treatise on the Emendation of the Entellect*. In *The Collected Work of Spinoza: Volume One*. Translated and edited by E. Curley. Princeton, N.J.: Princeton University Press.

Spinoza, Baruch 1994, *The Ethics*. In *The Collected Works of Spinoza*. Translated and edited by Edwin Curley. Princeton: Princeton University.

Spinoza, Baruch 2001, *Theological political treatise*. Translated by S. Shirley. Indiana-polis: Hackett.

Spivak, Gayatri 1988. *In Other Worlds: Essays in Cultural Politics*. Routledge: New York.

Spivak, Gayatri 1999, *A Critique of Postcolonial Reason: Toward a History of the Vanishing Present*. Cambridge: Harvard University Press.

Sprinker, M. 1987. *Imaginary Relations: Aesthetics and ideology in the theory of Historical materialism*. New York: Verso.

Stiegler, Bernard 2008, *La télécratie contre la démocratie*. Paris: Flammarion.

Stiegler, Bernard 2009, *Acting Out*. Translated by David Barison, Daniel Ross, and Patrick Crogan. Stanford: Stanford University.

Stiegler, Bernard 2010, *For a New Critique of Political Economy*. Translated by Daniel Ross. London: Polity.

Stiegler, Bernard 2017, *Automatic Society. Volume One: The Future of Work*. Translated by Daniel Ross. London: Polity.

Tosel, André 1997, *Superstition and Reading*. Translated by T. Stolze. In *The New Spinoza*. Edited by W. Montag and T. Stolze. Minneapolis: University of Minnesota Press.

Tronti, Mario 1979, *Working Class Autonomy and the Crisis*. London: Red Notes.

Virno, Paolo 1996a, 'The Ambivalence of Disenchantment'. Translated by Michael Tur-its. In *Radical Thought in Italy: A Potential Politics*. Edited by M. Hardt and P. Virno. Minneapolis: University of Minnesota.

Virno, Paolo 1996b, 'Notes on the General Intellect'. Translated by Cesare Casarino. *Marxism Beyond Marxism*. Edited by S. Makdisi et al. New York: Routledge.

Virno, Paolo 2003, 'The Multitude and the Principle of Individuation'. *Graduate Faculty Philosophy Journal*, 24, 2.

Virno, Paolo 2004, *A Grammar of the Multitude*. Translated by I. Bertoletti, J. Cascaito, and A. Casson. New York: Semiotexte.

Virno, Paolo 2006, 'Reading Gilbert Simondon: Transindividuality, Technical Activity, and Reification'. *Radical Philosophy*, 136 (March/April), 34–43.

Virno, Paolo 2008, *Multitude: Between Innovation and Negation*. Translated by Isabella Bertoletti, James Cascaito, and Andrea Casson. New York, Semiotexte.

Virno, Paolo 2009, 'Natural-Historical Diagrams: The "New Global" Movement and the Biological Invariant'. Translated by Alberto Toscano. In *The Italian Difference: Between Nihilism and Biopolitics*. Edited by Lorenzo Chiesa and Alberto Toscano. Melbourne: re.press.

Virno, Paolo 2015a, *Déjà vu and the End of History*. Translated by David Broder. New York, Verso.

Virno, Paolo 2015b, *When the Word Becomes Flesh: Language and Human Nature*. Translated by Giuseppina Mecchia. New York: Semiotexte.

Virno, Paolo 2016, *L'Usage de la Vie: et autres sujets d'inquiétude*. Translated by Lise Belperron et al. Paris: Éditions de l'Éclat.

Viveiros de Castro, Eduardo 2014, *Cannibal Metaphysics: For a Post-Structural Anthropology*. Translated by Peter Skafish, Minneapolis: Univocal.

Wallerstein. I. 1991, 'The Ideological Tensions of Capitalism: Universalism versus Racism and Sexism'. *Race, Nation, Class: Ambiguous Identities*. New York: Verso.

Wark, McKenzie 2015, *Molecular Red: Theory for the Anthropocene*. New York: Verso.

Weeks, Kathi 2012, *The Problem With Work: Feminism, Marxism, Antiwork Politics, and Postwork Imaginaries*. Durham, NC: Duke University Press.

Williams, Robert 2000, *Hegel's Ethics of Recognition*, Berkeley, CA: University of California.

Wittfogel, K. 1957, *Oriental Despotism: A Comparative Study of Total Power*. New Haven: Yale University Press.

Zizek, S. 1989, *The Sublime Object of Ideology*. New York: Verso.

Index